RAGGED LONDON

THE LIFE OF LONDON'S POOR

MICHAEL FITZGERALD

First published 2011

The History Press
The Mill, Brimscombe Port
Stroud, Gloucestershire, GL5 2QG
www.thehistorypress.co.uk

British Library Cataloguing in Publication Data.
A catalogue record for this book is available from the British Library.

ISBN 978 0 7524 6005 5

Typesetting and origination by The History Press
Printed in Great Britain
Manufacturing managed by Jellyfish Print Solutions Ltd

CONTENTS

Children playing in the street. Family and community spirit were key in impoverished London.

INTRODUCTION

Ragged London deals with an area of British social history that has always been neglected. It studies the life and hard times of the London 'submerged' during the period when Britain experienced the greatest contrast between wealth and poverty it has ever known. In spite of that the 'submerged' people had a tremendous sense of community which Londoners have rarely experienced. Their world was bounded by three or four streets, yet within their narrow universe, they not only survived but even managed to be happy.

The 'submerged' people of London lived in areas that became known as 'rookeries'. For three hundred years these districts were a byword for poverty, crime, squalor and disease. The conditions under which people eked out a precarious existence seem barely credible now. The people of the rookeries nor only endured but managed to make a better life for themselves.

The entrepreneurial spirit of the area was unrivalled. The submerged people turned the most desperate conditions to their own advantage. They engaged in some of the most unpleasant, dangerous and poorly paid occupations of the time and still managed to earn a living for themselves and their families.

Most of the building work in London was carried out by the submerged, as well as the majority of railway building and track-laying. Long before middle-class females began to talk about having careers, the women of the rookeries worked themselves to the point of exhaustion. In their case it was not from choice but necessity, since it was almost impossible to support a family on the man's wage alone. Even the children of the submerged worked, scavenged, begged and stole to make ends meet.

Crammed one hundred or so to a house, often forty to a room, and with only the most limited of facilities for washing or cooking, they struggled, endured and triumphed. The difficulties under which they laboured would have defeated the great captains of industry in Victorian times, yet they not only survived but even prospered to an extent. The average earning of a submerged family in the rookeries often compared favourably with those of other working-class families. Through their ingenuity and sheer dogged determination they epitomised the famous 'bulldog' spirit of the British people. They defeated Napoleon as their descendants were later to overcome Hitler.

In 1831 nearly a million people lived in the rookeries of London. They were both feared and despised by the authorities and only a few brave souls dared to champion their cause. By the beginning of the twentieth century, the majority of their homes had been destroyed, and with them a way of life that had lasted three hundred years. This book tells their story.

1

THE ORIGINS OF THE ROOKERIES

The problem of the urban poor in London became an urgent political concern from the 1830s onwards. The main focus of the attack on poverty became concentrated on those areas known as 'rookeries'. The term 'rookery' was first used to describe the dwellings of the London poor in the latter part of the eighteenth century. The earliest example of its use in print was by the poet George Galloway in 1792.

What was a rookery, and how did it differ from a simple slum? The *Oxford English Dictionary* defines rookeries as follows: 'a cluster of mean tenements densely inhabited by persons of the lowest class.' It was primarily overcrowding that distinguished a rookery from a slum. The fact that every part of the building from attic to cellar was inhabited earned its nickname – these dwellings were so called because of their imagined resemblance to the nests of rooks. Rooks live high up in the trees and gather together in vast numbers. In the same way, the human 'rooks' were crammed in to narrow spaces from basement to garret.

Experiments with a variety of plans designed to reduce poverty in London were carried out during the eighteenth century, and the proposal that found most favour with Victorian legislators was the workhouse system. This originated in the rookery of St Giles and tried to lead boys away from a life of crime and into productive employment. The problem of poverty became acute during the 1830s, and the generally adopted practice of 'outdoor relief' placed a serious financial strain upon the ratepayers of the poorer parishes, where the burden of poor rate expenditure was concentrated. The response of the government was to introduce a revised 'Poor Law' in 1834.

Under the new system, 'outdoor relief', while not formally abolished, was seriously curtailed. It was also hedged around with so many new restrictions and qualifications that the now mandatory 'workhouse test' drastically reduced the numbers applying to the parish for assistance. The architects of the new system declared proudly that this demonstrated that the majority of claimants under the old Poor Law were simply idle and impecunious and had no genuine basis for seeking assistance. Opponents of the workhouse challenged this argument fiercely. They pointed out that the conditions in them were so harsh and the process of applying to them for relief so degrading that many people preferred to seek help elsewhere. Family and friends, private charity, and of course criminal acts were preferred to 'troubling the parish'.

Conditions in the workhouse were certainly made as inhospitable as possible. In an ironic editorial, *The Times* suggested sending applicants for poor relief to prison and placing criminals in the workhouse, remarking that it might be hard on the felons, but that at least they deserved punishment, whereas the people in the workhouse were guilty of no crime other than poverty.

The reasons for the rise in poverty between 1830 and 1900 are complex. One of the principal factors was the decline of traditional London industries, most notably the clothing and shoe trades. A further contributory factor was the rapid rise in rents following the collapse of the building trade after 1825. Coupled with the reluctance of landlords in a shrinking market to repair and renovate their properties, these led to a serious deterioration in the physical condition of homes. The result was that the middle classes began to move out of central London into the suburban areas. This in turn left a stock of formerly 'genteel' housing unoccupied. Landlords responded by letting out the vacant properties to lodgers. Soon multi-occupancy of buildings became the norm in inner London.

The new tenants were largely casual workers, for whom periodic and seasonal unemployment was an everyday reality. When around forty of them were crammed into a single room, it was inevitable both that their health suffered from the extreme living conditions and that the physical environment of their home deteriorated further.

The increasing overpopulation of the rookeries considerably disturbed the more thoughtful middle-class Londoners. Reformers called on Parliament to legislate against the overcrowding and squalid conditions but could not agree a satisfactory remedy for the problem. Some, notably Lord Shaftesbury, called for programmes of renovation. Others, again including Shaftesbury, favoured building 'model dwellings' for the poor. Some called for the restoration of outdoor relief, others for the outlawing of 'middlemen', and some for the total demolition of slum properties.

Those who opposed reform generally argued that Parliament had no business seeking to interfere with the rights of property, that the workhouse constituted adequate provision for the truly destitute, and that those who chose to live in the rookeries did so from a conscious preference for overcrowded and squalid conditions.

London had a history of slums dating back to the Middle Ages, but the metropolis then was a compact city with a small and stable population. Its geographical extent was confined to the City of London, the City of

Westminster and Bankside in Southwark. There were small suburbs to the east and west of the City and Westminster.

The old slum areas in the City of London and its environs started to become overcrowded following the Dissolution of the Monasteries in 1539. The monks had provided education, care for the sick and maintained the poor from their charitable endowments and other income. The seizure of their assets by Henry VIII created severe problems for the London poor. People flooded into the city from the countryside looking for work. An agricultural depression and war with Scotland, with its accompaniments of men called up to fight and farms burned by raiding parties, added to the economic problems faced by rural workers. An influx of immigrants, particularly from Holland and France, added to the pressure on space, even though they settled, not in the City of London, but in the nearby suburbs. French hat makers moved into Southwark, Dutch, French and Belgian weavers to Spitalfields and Shoreditch, Dutch printers into Clerkenwell and Westminster, while the Belgians in Southwark introduced the brewing of beer with hops. This created a drink that was much stronger than the traditional 'ale' and which rapidly became very popular.

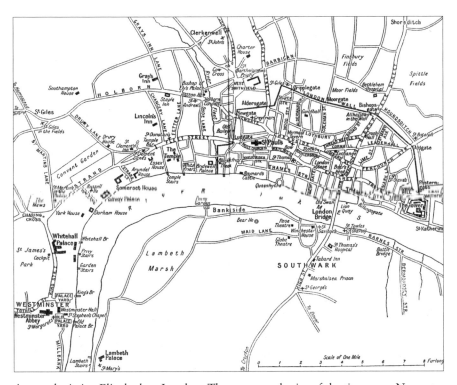

A map depicting Elizabethan London. The worst rookeries of the time were Newgate, Bridewell, East and West Smithfield, St Katherine's by the Tower, Bankside, Clerkenwell and Cripplegate. As most of the land south of the river was owned by the Bishop of Southwark, development there was deliberately discouraged.

The increase in population also led to overcrowding, the rapid expansion of slum areas and multi-occupancy of dwellings. The foundations of the rookeries were laid, but it was nearly another hundred years before true rookeries arose in London.

The continuing expansion of London concerned the authorities to such an extent that in 1580 Queen Elizabeth I issued a proclamation forbidding any new building in the metropolis. The result was to increase overcrowding within the areas already heavily populated. It also led to a considerable expansion of the suburban areas immediately outside the city.

Far from improving the situation, this led to a considerable deterioration in housing conditions. The extreme overcrowding, made much worse as a result of the royal proclamation, was at least a contributory factor to the high death rate in London. During the Great Plague of 1665, over 100,000 Londoners died, 15,000 of them within the walls of the City of London.[1]

It was not until the Great Fire of London in 1666 that the old slum areas of London were finally swept away. Though most of the City was rebuilt over the next few years, the government took care to prevent the creation of any new slums in the area. They also tried to remove as many of the existing ones as possible.

The entire population of London was evacuated during the fire, and found shelter in the surrounding areas – Moorfields (now Moorgate), Lincoln's Inn, Gray's Inn, Hatton Garden, Covent Garden and St Giles. Soon all these places were full of people and the homeless Londoners moved further afield, as far as Highgate and Islington. Tents were set up on open ground and refugees from the fire camped out for miles around. The fire made almost 80,000 Londoners homeless. Many of them had relied upon the income from letting out their homes to tenants and were now forced to appeal for public charity. The strain on charitable resources was enormous.

The owners of those buildings in the City that had survived the fire seized the opportunity to raise rents. According to one contemporary estimate, rents increased by 90 per cent; according to the more reliable evidence of Pepys, a civil servant, the rise was around 40 per cent. Many of the poor managed to return to their former homes in the City, but the majority were forced to move out. Clerkenwell, Holborn, St Giles, Shadwell, Stepney, Whitechapel and Wapping became full of refugees from London. The result was that the neighbourhoods turned into new slums and, within a short time, new rookeries.

It is difficult to overestimate the effect of the fire on the growth of London. In time the city would have expanded naturally, but the fire accelerated the process. When most of the City of London lay in ruins, finding a home in other areas became a necessity. Even when it had eventually been rebuilt, most of those who had moved out remained where they were. They had found new dwelling places, new sources of employment, new and better roads than the narrow and congested streets of the City. In addition, the new homes that were built in the City of London were far more expensive than the old ones had been. They were also, even if more fire-resistant, still liable to sudden and unexpected collapse. As the wealthy for the most part had also decided to migrate en masse to the West End, a whole new area of employment opportunities opened up.

Eighteenth-century builders.

Tradesmen, formerly shackled by the tight regulations of the guilds and livery companies, found that they could operate on a more straightforwardly commercial basis. Instead of being the throbbing and vibrant heart of England, as it once was, the City of London became a ghost town. It remained the financial capital of the country, but as an area in which to live, it was no longer viable. Even before the fire, Clerkenwell, Holborn, Hatton Garden and Spitalfields had begun to take away the traditional City trades of goldsmiths and silversmiths, jewellers, woodworkers, and even tailoring. Cripplegate remained the strongest area for gold and silverwork, but it too was technically outside the control of the City of London.

With the sudden opportunities for new building, property speculators sprang up. Perhaps the most flamboyant of them was Nicholas Barbon, whose extraordinary life and behaviour surprised even his contemporaries. Barbon bought up land after the fire and covered every available space with housing. The quality of his workmanship was poor, even by the standards of his day, and his methods of operation defied belief. If the owners of existing properties refused to sell their homes to him, he simply got his workmen to pull down their houses. For almost thirty years he was constantly involved in lawsuits, but was so adept at finding loopholes, at delaying proceedings, at appealing and counter-appealing, that he was rarely called to account for any of his actions. Instead of taking out loans to finance his development, he relied entirely upon non-payment of bills. His creditors spent years in costly litigation. He was no better at paying the rents on land that he had leased, being perpetually in arrears and refusing to honour his debts.

Not surprisingly, the quality of his homes was substandard. Unlike most builders in London, he ignored the new regulations, except as regards building in brick rather than wood. Some of his more successful undertakings, like Essex Street, Buckingham Street, Lincoln's Inn, New Square and Bedford Row, still survive. Most, though, collapsed completely only a few years after they were built. He died in 1698, regretted by none. The contemporary observer Narcissus Luttrell gave an amusing account of a skirmish between the lawyers of Gray's Inn and some of Barbon's workmen:

Dr Barbon, the great builder, having some time since bought the Red Lion fields near Gray's Inn walks to build on, and having for that purpose employed several workmen to go on with the same, the gentlemen of Gray's Inn took notice of it and, thinking it an injury to them, went with a considerable body of a hundred persons upon which the workmen assaulted the gentlemen and threw bricks at them, and the gentlemen at them again. So a sharp engagement ensued, but the gentlemen routed them at last and brought away one or tow [sic] of the workmen in Gray's Inn. In this skirmish one or tow [sic] of the gentlemen and servants of the house were hurt, and several of the workmen.[2]

Two years after Barbon's death, the once compact City of London had swallowed up Holborn, Clerkenwell, the Strand, Whitehall and Shoreditch. Further east, Stepney, Whitechapel, Wapping and Limehouse were also becoming densely populated suburbs. Bankside to the south of the river expanded rapidly. The City of London was still full of empty houses and even the business districts had not yet recovered from the fire. Elsewhere in London, by contrast, the constant expansion westwards and eastwards continued relentlessly.

The writer John Evelyn cried out in astonishment:

> To such a mad intemperance was the age come of building in the city, by far too disproportionate already to the nation: I having in my time seen it almost as large again as it was within my memory.[3]

The frenzy of speculative building by Barbon and others of his kind finally persuaded Parliament that uncontrolled development in London could not continue. In spite of the new regulations that had been introduced after the fire, not only were the new homes collapsing with alarming frequency but smaller fires continued to break out in them.

The beginning of the eighteenth century saw further Acts of Parliament introduced to improve the standards of new buildings. Although they still permitted numerous unsafe structures to be constructed, they at least drastically reduced the risks from fire. The most important features of the new building regulations were to prohibit the then fashionable wooden eaves that jutted out from so many buildings in London. These were now hidden behind a parapet and covered up with brick or stone. It was also illegal to have wooden frames flush with the outer walls. These now had to be set back further, into the brickwork itself, with one side of the corner bricks now exposed.

The economy of London was buoyant between 1700 and 1750. This was a magnet for migrants from other parts of Britain and Europe, attracted by labour shortages and the opportunity to earn better money than was possible at home. Available property for rent was difficult to find, so landlords crammed houses from top to bottom with lodgers. The living conditions were overcrowded, but there was no shortage of people renting space in a rookery house. No public housing provision existed, and the cheapness of the lodgings meant that those living on subsistence wages could always find a bed for the night.

The lack of transport made it essential for people to live within walking distance of their jobs. Those who lived in St Giles were near the West End and its great houses, with its consequent opportunities for employment in domestic service. They were also near the Covent Garden market, where many of them became stallholders. The people in the East End were near the jetties where ships and boats loaded and unloaded their cargoes. They were also near the City of London, where they carried out a variety of jobs from clerical to manual. London south of the river was largely confined to the Bankside area of Southwark, primarily noted for its pubs, prostitutes and bear-baiting. West London was hardly developed at all, remaining a primarily rural region.

Until about 1815 the living conditions in the rookeries remained fairly constant. At the end of the Napoleonic Wars a building boom followed. The result was not only the rapid expansion of London but also the creation of entirely new rookeries. The first of these was Agar Town on the site now occupied by St Pancras station. North London soon saw two more rookeries arise, one the Battlebridge area around King's Cross and the other the new estate of Somers Town. South London saw the areas of Nine Elms and Lambeth arise from what, only ten years previously, had been sleepy Surrey villages. West London spawned two entirely new rookeries, Notting Dale and the Potteries of North Kensington. In the East End, the existing rookeries expanded and grew with the rise of the new docks, while the eastern districts of London also began to encroach upon the villages and suburbs of Essex. Soon places like Canning Town turned into new rookeries.

During the seventeenth and eighteenth centuries, the poor managed to eke out a subsistence level at worst. They could still eat, drink and dress well during the early nineteenth century. They might not have lived on the same level as the wealthy or even the middle classes, but they lived well enough. The years between 1830 and 1880 were perhaps the harshest time for the poor in the entire history of London. From the 1830s onwards, with the new and more repressive attitude towards those who were casually employed, poverty became an abiding reality for the dwellers in the rookeries. It was under the Victorians that Londoners starved.

Victorian entrepreneurs and legislators alike saw the inhabitants of the rookeries as simply a danger and a problem to be eradicated. The general perception of them by the authorities was that they were drunken, lazy, criminal and sexually promiscuous. The people who lived in the rookeries came to be described as 'the great unwashed', or, by more sympathetic commentators, 'the submerged'. Marx and Engels, living in London themselves, referred to them as the 'lumpen proletariat'.

The founders of Marxism saw no alternative to violent revolution, though both believed that the 'underclass' was utterly incapable of revolt. The philanthropists believed that new housing and better living conditions would transform the people and make them able to hold their own with the other sections of society.

Factors adding to the overcrowding in rookery neighbourhoods were the transformation of the City of London from a residential area to a primarily commercial district and also, crucially, the arrival of the railways in London. The effects of both these changes are studied in detail in later chapters of this book.

The people of the rookeries laboured under intense disadvantages yet showed no desire to move away. There were three principal reasons why they chose to remain in the slums. The first was simply familiarity, the sense of community within the rookeries being intense and compounded by the fact that many families had lived there for hundreds of years. Secondly, there was the need to live close to their sources of employment, a factor that affected casual workers even more than those in regular occupations. Finally, there was no realistic means of escape for them. They could afford neither the rents in the new suburbs nor the transport costs to move out there and travel in to their places of work, so were forced to remain where they were.

Having sketched the origins of the rookeries, we shall now turn our attention to studying the way of life of the people who lived in them, as well as examining the worst examples in greater detail. The primary focus will be upon St Giles-in-the-Fields, most notorious of all the rookery areas, so much so that it was often referred to simply as '*the*' rookery. Other areas are studied in less detail, most attention being devoted to Saffron Hill, the second worst rookery. Briefer descriptions are also given of other rookeries in London.

Notes

1 C.C. Knowles & P.H. Fitt, *The History of Building Regulations in London*, Architectural Press, 1972.
2 Narcissus Luttrell, *A Brief Historical Relation Of State Affairs*, 1857. Luttrell's observations relate to an incident on 10 June 1684.
3 John Evelyn, *Diary*.

2

HOME LIFE IN THE
ROOKERIES

London in about 1600 was not only the largest but also one of the most vibrant and exciting cities in the world. Its poets and playwrights were globally renowned. Men like Drake and Raleigh were not only discovering new countries but also laying the foundations of the British Empire. Elizabethan London was a place of ceaseless activity; the sailors who fought the Spanish brought home vast treasures to the capital, the merchants on the exchange dealt in the new goods and new industries and new commercial opportunities grew rapidly.

The streets swarmed with the constant press of people. New and exotic products were landed in the docks and began to appear in the shops and on the tables of the citizens. Even the people themselves were caught up in the excitement and the sense that the Elizabethan age represented a new era for England, the beginnings of greatness for the country.

It was in this climate of optimism and prosperity that St Giles turned from a village into a suburb of London. The rookery might have been a slum but it felt like a New Town and not a Third World shanty town. There were no shacks built of tin or wood, no open campsites in the fields. Even the poor in London still lived in houses. There was a small number of people who slept rough, in brick-kilns, shop fronts and similar structures. Even so, the proportion of rough sleepers and vagrants actually declined dramatically between 1640 and 1800.[1] It was not until the Victorian period that homelessness once more became a problem on the streets of London, but even the poor in St Giles were not as poor as their counterparts in foreign cities. The conditions in which they lived might have been unpleasant, but they compared very favourably with those of Paris, Berlin, Vienna or Moscow at that time.

St Giles-in-the-Fields.

Apart from the constant noise and bustle, one of the first things that a visitor to St Giles (or indeed almost any part of London) would have noticed was the quite extraordinary smell pervading the air. Almost every visitor to the city remarked upon the stench of the streets. It was a heady brew of leather from the tanning factories, brick dust from the kilns, rotting vegetation, rain upon the stones, beer being brewed and bread baked, tallow fat being burnt to produce candles, to say nothing of 'greasy cooks at sweating work' and 'stinking breaths and uncleanly carcasses'.[2] In addition, there were the unwholesome exhalations from graveyards, the presence everywhere of manure and faeces and, above all, the pervasive smell of smoke. Not only did the almost incessant burning of coal poison the atmosphere of London but it also covered the city in a semi-permanent pall of fog. Meteorologists of the time began to refer to the phenomenon of 'great stinking fog'.[3]

Although the living conditions were squalid and dangerous, the actual environment in which the dwelling places were set was one of the most magnificent in London, if not the world. Not far away, Hyde Park and other open spaces gave the growing city 'lungs'. These were open to the public and many of the St Giles folk enjoyed promenading in them. Inigo Jones' stunning

Piazza in Covent Garden was one of the wonders of the world, admired by generations of Londoners. That too was open for anyone who chose to walk within it.

Under James I, the restrictions on renovation and new building in the city were relaxed slightly. Expansion was still forbidden, but green fields and large houses within London slowly began to vanish. They were replaced by smaller and cheaper brick-gabled houses. In the suburbs of St Giles, still outside the area of London altogether, new homes for the poor were built. As late as 1595 St Giles was still largely a sleepy village. The next twenty years saw an explosion of building.

The contrast is clearly shown on an examination of the Assessment Books of St Giles in 1623. This document lists no fewer than 897 houses in the area. It also breaks down the pattern of development to an extent, stating that there were:

> 47 houses, exclusively of six courts or alleys branching from them into Aldewych West, all of which ground was until nearly that time unbuilt on. And at Town's End, which lay to the west of the church, there are enumerated thirty-eight housekeepers, besides those in Rose and Crown Yard, on the same site, which amounted to eleven more.[4]

The same source also gives the names of the courts and alleys, together with the number of housekeepers:

HOUSEKEEPERS[5]

Paviours Alley	35
Black Beare Yard	29
Greyhounde Alley	10
Swanne Alley	35
Canter's Alley	22
Town's End, and Rose and courtyard as before	
Middle Row	26

Twenty courtyards and alleys were built in the area between 1595 and 1622. No fewer than 100 houses were built on the north side of St Giles High Street alone.[6] The homes were certainly not on the same level of quality as the houses being built for the rich, but on the other hand they were nowhere near as bad as some of the slums in the City of London that were left over from the Middle Ages. All in all they represented a reasonable standard of accommodation for the new influx of poor people coming to London.

The city was going through one of its periodic property booms. Land and houses had become such valuable commodities that ditches were filled in and built upon. Roads were turned into dwelling-places and alleys constructed in the narrow areas where there was no space to build any more ambitious homes. Even when there was no possibility of building outwards any more, extra upper storeys were added, 'oversailing' (to use a contemporary term) the alleys and passages.

London before 1615 had been built by generations of workers in the craft guilds of masons and carpenters. The role of an architect was essentially to follow tradition rather than to create a new vision. Then, in 1615, James I appointed Inigo Jones as Royal Surveyor. At first Jones simply worked on public commissions, but in 1630 the Earl of Bedford wanted to build upon the land behind his house on The Strand. For the first time a major private development in London became subject to planning controls.[7]

The result of Jones' work on the earl's estate was the new Covent Garden. The sheer impressiveness of its revolutionary construction and the new opportunities for employment that it suddenly afforded led to yet more people flocking to the nearby village of St Giles. During the 1630s the population of the area doubled, from 10,000 to 20,000 inhabitants. In the mid-sixteenth century, the population of the entire West End had only been about 1,500. By 1600 it had reached 3,000, and by 1640, had climbed as high as 18,500. Adding in the inhabitants of St Giles, we see a phenomenal surge in population for the area.[8]

The restoration of the monarchy in 1660 led to a gradual relaxation of planning controls. By the early 1660s Bloomsbury was already starting to become a suburb of London. St Giles, though still a slum, benefited from the return of Royalist nobles from exile. Many of them chose to settle and build new homes in the area. In the 1664 poll tax register, for example, less than 20 per cent of the population was too poor to pay. The district of St Margaret's, Westminster, by contrast, produced a figure of 47.4 per cent of the population exempted from the tax.[9] There was also some evidence of the area actually becoming more prosperous after the Restoration. The number of pensioners in the area was comparatively high, almost double the proportion in St James Clerkenwell, for example.[10]

The effect of the Great Fire of London in 1666 was to destroy the old slum areas of the City. Naturally this also offered openings for casual labourers, since there was now a sudden and urgent demand for building workers. After the fire the entirely new development of Seven Dials was built. This linked St Giles to St Martin-in-the-Fields and laid the foundations of what was to become in time one continuous stretch of rookery. The nobility, sensing new opportunities to make money, began to remove their palaces from The Strand and replace them with terraced houses for the poorer citizens.

The principal effect of this was to allow the rise of the property developer. These people, especially in the period from 1670 to 1720, were largely opportunists whose sole concern was to make money quickly. Since safety and quality cost money, they did not figure on the agenda of these speculators. Vast fortunes were made by men whose character was often not simply dubious, but positively criminal.

In St Giles and areas like it, shoddy tenements were jerry-built as quickly as possible and packed full of residents. Every available space from cellar to attic was taken up with tenants: whole families lived and worked in these dark, damp and airless dwellings. Gardens vanished as they were built over and turned into squalid 'courts'. Even if (as happened frequently) poor workmanship led to the injury or even death of the occupants, the landlords were not responsible and no compensation was paid. Flooded cellars were a particularly frequent cause of death, since so many people in St Giles lived in basements. These were generally entered through trap-doors set in the pavement. A 'St Giles cellar' became an expression for the worst possible kind of living accommodation. During the Middle Ages they had been used as storage areas, shops or even burial vaults; now they became people's homes.

The houses were constructed with one room at the front and one at the back, a passage and staircase on one side of the rooms. Each floor would have the same arrangement of rooms, however high the dwelling. Until the new building regulations of 1707 it was normal for wooden eaves-cornices to be a prominent feature of houses. Then they were made illegal and parapet walls introduced to hide them.[11]

It was also not at all uncommon for bad roofing to lead to the death of passers-by from falling slates or masonry. At about the same time as the outlawing of the wooden cornices, the fashion in windows changed from casements to sash windows.

The rapid development of St Giles can be seen by comparing the figures from the 1623 assessments with later statistics. By 1685, there were 2,000 houses in the area; by 1710 the number was 3,000; by 1801, the date of the first census, 3,861; in 1811, the census records 4,828 houses. This represents an increase of almost 1,000 houses over a ten-year period.[12]

In some ways the Great Fire of London actually improved the quality of life for people in St Giles and other rookeries. Before 1666 the new houses for the poor were extremely badly built. They not only lacked the most basic facilities but were also positively dangerous. In the event of fire they were death-traps, but the structure of the buildings was so bad that they were hazardous to live in at all.

After the fire, new building regulations were drawn up. Under the new laws all houses had to be built of brick and stone. Four classes of accommodation were drawn up, ranging from houses for nobility to homes for the poor. They also had to have windows and proper roofs and even walls of reasonable thickness. The degree of thickness depended on the class of the property.[13]

The new homes, though built of solid brick and with walls far thicker than their predecessors, were dark and airless. The large numbers of people who lived in them also made them dirty, squalid and unhealthy before long. The new houses might have had windows but the glass inside them did not last long. It was very early in their existence that the windows were broken and left open to the elements. The landlords made no attempt to repair or replace them, so the tenants and lodgers would simply hang up rags at the windows as the best way to keep out the cold and the rain.

Doors too soon decayed and eventually disappeared altogether, either through lack of maintenance or else because they were deliberately destroyed for firewood. Since the people in the lodgings had nothing to steal, locked or closed doors were hardly necessary. In spite of these and many other hazards, people continued to flood into St Giles and the other rookeries.

Landlords, aristocratic and otherwise, profited immensely from the continual influx of people into the areas. A speculator would buy up a whole street and then sublet each house in turn to landlords, or, as they were known in the language of the time, 'housekeepers'. These housekeepers in turn would let off individual rooms within each house and the tenant of the room in his or her turn would sublet areas of the room to other occupants. The result, unsurprisingly, was overcrowding on a scale never seen previously. As there was constant influx of new people into the city, the demand for even the most insalubrious accommodation meant that anyone who had a room could make good money. Anyone with a house could become positively rich.

During this period, a housekeeper would pay a sum of between £3 and £25 per year for each house he leased, depending on the area. He would then sublet the house to lodgers who would pay between 6*d* and 10*s* 6*d* per week. In St Giles at this time a rented room would cost around a shilling a week, or £2 a year. Poor tenants would maximise their own income and reduce their costs by subletting their own room in turn to other lodgers. Single women or widows were particularly prone to sharing their room with other females. As can be seen from the above sums, a housekeeper who paid £3 a year for a house in, say, St Giles could expect to do pretty well out of it. Even in a three-roomed house he would clear double his initial investment. Most homes in St Giles were larger than that, so the return on his outlay was very good indeed.[14]

On the other hand there was no 'rack-renting'. Tenants could rent a space for as little as 1*d* a day in some quarters. The average amount of money spent in rent in proportion to wages was about a tenth of the tenant's income. Since rents were low it was possible for poor people to live reasonably well in the rookeries at that time.[15]

The living conditions might have been unpleasant but nobody went without food or clothing. Life in the rookery was tough, but it was certainly not as bad as it became later. Wages were comparatively high, rents low, and food was plentiful and cheap. Compared with either the Elizabethan or Victorian periods, this was, relatively speaking, a 'golden age' for the poor.

The lack of space and massive overcrowding in almost every house in the St Giles area made cooking meals extremely difficult. The result was an explosion of restaurants, public houses and other eating-places. Among one of its more unacknowledged claims to fame, St Giles can fairly be said to have invented the takeaway!

Another problem within the homes was washing. Water came from a single pump and was stored in jugs and bowls for use later. There would only be one tap within the house and access to it among such overcrowding was difficult. The result was that most people, especially in St Giles, used the public baths.

More of a problem than cooking and bathing was the constant difficulty and danger created by an absence of decent sanitation. There simply was no proper way of disposing of waste material, whether it was simple rubbish or the even worse – excrement. The streets of London became covered with the waste products of dogs, horses and humans, as well as littered with every conceivable type of garbage. All chamber pots were either emptied into a cesspit, onto a compost heap, or simply directly on to the street or river. Even the cesspits, the most relatively hygienic means of disposal, were only emptied occasionally.

One of the main reasons for the high mortality rate in London compared with the rest of the country was the appalling sanitary conditions. Not only did the homes where the people lived swarm with fleas, lice, rats and other vermin, but the quality of the drinking water was so poor as to constitute in itself a serious health hazard. In addition the existence of open sewers and the overwhelming tendency to use the streets and rivers as dumping grounds for waste created a plague scenario waiting to happen. The real surprise is that public health was not even worse. As it was, outbreaks of cholera and typhoid were frequent and devastating. They were perhaps the two most common causes of death in the rookeries at that time.

A typical vagrant.

It was not until the eighteenth century that any serious attempts were made to address the problems of sanitation. There was a sewer at The Strand, but it was not even connected with the Earl of Bedford's estates until the end of the seventeenth century, still less with St Giles. The poor simply continued using the streets and rivers as their sewers.

In 1671, the Sewage and Paving Act of 1671 ordered that a road had to be cambered into a side drain, rather than diverting water into a stream down the centre of the road, as previously. Its effects were probably marginal but at least it was a step in the right direction.[16]

In the meantime the 'gong-farmers' drove their carts around London and emptied the cesspits, making a fair if unpleasant living by selling their contents as manure to farmers. Inefficient and unpleasant as this system of waste disposal was, it represented the only available means of getting rid of sewage.

The people of the rookeries lived on limited incomes, in overcrowded and insanitary conditions, and faced the constant threat of disease and crime. The curious thing, though, is that so few of them wanted to leave. Even when the opportunity of better living conditions in the expanding suburbs began to beckon, very few of the rookery-dwellers showed any inclination to move from the area. They liked living close to their work, and the strong sense of community within the neighbourhood also made conditions more bearable.

One of the most distinctive aspects of St Giles was that, at least between the sixteenth and eighteenth centuries, most of its residents were immigrants. Some came from Scotland, Ireland and Wales, or even from European countries. Most, however, were folk from the English countryside, looking for work. They gazed in awe and wonder at the veritable palaces that surrounded them. Even their own environment was possibly the most beautiful in the entire city.

Perhaps because of the predominance of newcomers from rural areas, the people of St Giles formed a very close-knit community. They lived within a world whose boundaries were formed by a few small streets and alleys. Within this area they recreated almost a village atmosphere to the rookery. Anything less like the anonymous and indifferent modern city it is hard to imagine. Not surprisingly, in such a closed community, gossip was a major source of diversion for the inhabitants. It was almost impossible for the residents to achieve *any* sort of privacy. People peered out through windows, listened at doors and overheard snatches of conversation in pubs and shops. Men and women would exchange anecdotes and gossip about their neighbours, employers, and newcomers to the district. Market traders and publicans were particularly well-informed about all the local goings-on. The high proportion of women from St Giles who worked in domestic service meant that even the 'doings' of the wealthy and aristocracy soon became known among the people of the area.

It was not just a matter of curiosity and simple 'nosiness', however. The people of St Giles saw to it that certain aspects of behaviour were firmly regarded as being unacceptable. Drunkenness, for instance, was tolerated, but if it led a man to beat his wife as a result, the neighbours would soon intervene on her behalf. It might have been an area where the police force of the day (such as it was) ventured only very reluctantly and occasionally, but the neighbourhood itself policed its own people.

One of the more curious aspects of the 'code' of St Giles was the attitude towards honesty. Even though there were numerous thieves in the area, a dishonest trader would be quickly driven out of business. He would be socially shunned and his livelihood would collapse as a result of the public disapproval of his neighbours.

It was extremely common for defendants in courts of law to summon character witnesses to testify on their behalf. In 1745, for instance, Sarah Davis of St Giles, on being accused of theft, summoned character witnesses from as far away as Rotherhithe to declare their belief in her honesty.[17]

As well as restraining unacceptable behaviour within the rookery, the people of St Giles also formed a network of mutual support. Clothes, food and even money were freely lent from one person to another, and the absolute necessity for trust in such a closed society meant that such loans would almost invariably be returned.[18]

During the eighteenth century the area began to deteriorate rapidly. In part this was because of a rapid influx of newcomers, but primarily it was because of a change in the habits of the local population. It was at this time, between the 1720s and 1750s, that St Giles really did become seedy, squalid and dangerous.[19] The root cause of this drastic decline in living conditions and behaviour was, of course, the discovery by the inhabitants of a new drink, gin. Not only was this much stronger than their normal drink, beer, but it was also cheaper. The effects of the 'gin craze' will be described in the chapter on food and drink in the rookeries. Its most notable long-term effect was to inspire the great painter William Hogarth to produce his series of pictures known as 'Gin Lane'.[20] Hogarth was not the only creative artist to frequent and find inspiration in the St Giles neighbourhood. In 1728 the popular poet John Gay wrote his classic work *The Beggar's Opera*. This was a satirical musical, or perhaps more accurately an operetta, which attacked corrupt politicians and the grinding poverty in which so many people of the day lived. Its vision of the London of the time, in spite of Gay's lightness of touch and easy humour, still has the power to shock. Perhaps most horrific of all is that he does not in any way exaggerate the conditions of the period.

In Gay's London, highwaymen dominated the suburbs. The streets of London swarmed with beggars, pickpockets, muggers and prostitutes. People literally starved to death without being noticed. Public hangings, floggings and the pillory were all part of the habitual entertainment of the day. Drink and sex were the only escapes from a life of grinding, monotonous misery. There was no honour among thieves, nor indeed anybody else. London as a city was seen as essentially a place of darkness, corruption and desolation. Gay's tragic dark vision is perhaps even more powerful because of the beauty of the music and lightness of tone of the libretto he wrote for it. Rarely has such a profound sense of compassion run through an essentially humorous piece. It was a slice of London life and spirit, a perfect example of the Cockney 'gallows humour'. Naturally, this most Londonesque of works was set in St Giles.

By 1816 the social conditions and high crime rate of the area had become so notorious that Parliament commissioned an official enquiry into the district. They found that 10,000 Irish people lived there, as well as many more English poor.

The end of the Napoleonic Wars in 1815 led to a temporary boom in house building. This relieved the pressures of overcrowding slightly but was short-lived. By 1825 the building boom had collapsed entirely. The result was that many more people had to be crammed into the same amount of available accommodation. It also led to higher rents as speculators tried to recoup their losses in the only way they knew – by squeezing the tenants.

In Victorian times, a new callousness on the part of the authorities, based on the absurd assumption that there were 'deserving' and 'undeserving' poor, led to a worsening of conditions as a direct result of government policies. Just as Elizabeth I had created the rookeries by her disastrous legislation of the 1580s, so too Parliament made the situation a thousand times worse by the passage of the new Poor Law in 1834. One of the most badly thought-out and disastrous Acts of Parliament ever to get on the statute book, this had a terrible effect on the people who lived in the rookeries. It is difficult to think of a more misconceived and positively harmful law passed by any Parliament under the Victorians. Slums were of course a problem, and the burden of poor relief had been increasing. The new Poor Law, however, made the situation infinitely worse.

Under the new Poor Law, the payment of benefits directly to the claimant was virtually abolished. Instead, applicants for parish relief had to go to the workhouse, where they were required to perform such pointless and degrading tasks as turning cranks, walking on treadmills and other equally useless forms of 'work', simply in order to be given food. Workhouses were not invented by the Victorians, but the nature of the institution changed radically under their preconceptions. They were convinced that poverty and unemployment were entirely the result of idleness and drunkenness on the part of the poor. This belief made them think that forcing them to work under conditions of virtual slavery would make them change their ways and lead them to become honest, hard-working citizens.

Families were broken up as a result of the Poor Law, and many of the beadles who operated the new policy were hopelessly corrupt and inefficient as well as lacking any compassion for the unfortunate inmates. For the most part, they had committed no crime other than that of simply being poor. The result of their harsh treatment was that people preferred to sleep on the streets or even starve rather than go into the workhouse. While there have always been tiny numbers of homeless people in London, the Victorians resurrected the long-forgotten scourge of the Elizabethan beggar. For an age that liked to consider itself progressive, it was an astonishingly reactionary policy, and with results that made a difficult situation altogether intolerable. Homelessness was virtually created by the Victorians.

This Act made the already intolerable conditions in St Giles and other rookeries worse. The local authorities, who had to build new workhouses and pay for their staffing and upkeep, were under severe pressure to cut costs. Their only solution to the problem of financing these wretched institutions besides that of scrimping on the facilities offered within them, was to raise rates. The landlords responded in kind by raising rents for their tenants.

An economic recession also led to falling wages and worse conditions of work, as well as higher levels of unemployment. Perhaps understandably in the circumstances, the middle classes now abandoned the area altogether as a result. Even in the worst times beforehand, there had always been small pockets of gentility in most of the rookeries, particularly St Giles. They had, somehow, continued to exist in the midst of all its tribulations. Now, abruptly, under this new combination of higher costs and lower income, they simply abandoned the area altogether. Their now forlorn and desolate buildings lost their old splendour, becoming instead new tenement dwellings, let out, in the familiar multi-room occupancy pattern, to the hordes of desperately poor people.

The combination of rising rents, higher unemployment, an agricultural depression and exploitative labour practices meant that the poor of the rookeries were virtually forced into criminality in order to survive. Instead of there being a few pockets of crime, whole neighbourhoods became 'no-go' areas. St Giles, for instance, soon became so dangerous that even police officers refused to enter it except in groups of at least two, and preferably three. Another wholly unnecessary problem was created as a direct result of incompetent and wrongheaded government intervention.

In addition, the new policy of slum clearances also compounded the problem. Landlords were compensated when their properties were demolished, but tenants were simply expected to disperse – absolutely *no* provision was made for their rehousing. It was as if the authorities simply expected the poor to vanish into thin air. The government made pretty speeches about the new opportunities now opening up for the people. They suggested that they could all move into the expanding suburbs and finding work there, or at least become commuters, working in the West End and the City of London but not living there. Even they must have known that these suggestions were both absurd and insensitive.

Charles Dickens, who began his writing career as a journalist, visited the London slums and rookeries frequently. He was so appalled by what he found there that it furnished ideas for many of his books. In his first publication, *Sketches by Boz,* he gave a devastating but wholly accurate account of life in St Giles. His third book, *Oliver Twist,* is usually regarded as having been based upon St Giles. It has, however, also been suggested that it was inspired by either Saffron Hill in Clerkenwell or Jacob's Island in Bermondsey, two rookeries of the time that were almost as notorious as St Giles. Probably it was a composite of all three.

A survey of occupiers of houses in the St Giles district on 6 November 1834 reveals many being in arrears. Against a whole series of names, the word 'excused' is written with regard to the outstanding amount. A study of the rates for the area from midsummer 1835, only a year after the passage of the new Poor Law, is even more instructive. In Castle Street, for instance, containing only fourteen buildings, nine of the householders were in arrears. Only four householders and one shopkeeper paid their rates in full. In Angel Court, Gill Luke, the owner of five houses in the street, was seriously in arrears.[21]

In 1837 and 1838 further government surveys found that the rate of mortality was frighteningly high in the rookeries compared with other areas of London. By 1842 the problem had attracted the attention of Edwin Chadwick, a top civil servant of the day. His job was to survey the sanitary conditions of London, and the result of his enquiries horrified him. The conclusion of his survey was that the health and living conditions of the people in St Giles and other rookeries were simply too intolerable to be allowed to continue. As a solution to the problem, he proposed a massive programme of slum clearance. He also commissioned the engineer Joseph Bazalgette to create the first modern sewage system in Britain since Roman times.[22] Chadwick was thus responsible for three of the most radical innovations in government policy: the creation of workhouses, slum clearance, and modern sewage. Only in respect to the third should he be honoured.

Under the Victorians, conditions in the rookeries deteriorated so much that the areas actually became a sort of macabre tourist attraction. Travellers from all over the world came to observe the appalling living conditions of the inhabitants. In spite of all the new difficulties they faced, the people of the rookeries continued to soldier on. They worked and lived and struggled and endured. Most of them even managed to avoid the workhouse. Their tenacity and ingenuity continued to serve them well, enabling them to overcome the new difficulties put in their way by government. Once again the spirit of the rookeries shone through and triumphed over the most tremendous odds.

The population also continued to rise no matter how bad the living conditions within it were. As late as 1550 only 300 people lived in St Giles. In 1574 the parish of St Martin-in-the-Fields, one of the principal churches in the area, had only 164 ratepayers, who raised £36 for poor relief.[23] By 1600 the population figures for St Giles had reached the thousands. By the time of the 1623 assessments they had reached several thousand. By the nineteenth century, the population pressures had become intense.

Taking St Giles as the most representative rookery and using figures from the various census records, we see that in 1801 it consisted of 3,861 houses and a recorded population of 36,502 inhabitants. Only ten years later this had risen to 4,871 houses with a recorded population of 48,536 inhabitants. By the time of the 1821 census, 4,911 houses were listed with a recorded population of 51,793 people. When one considers that the transient nature of many residents of St Giles made the very collection of such data extremely difficult, the figures above, grim reading though they make, are almost certainly an *underestimate*.[24]

The 1829 assessments for the area also make interesting reading:[25]

Number of Houses	Rental	£20 or under	£30	£50	£100	£150	£150 +
2,980		781	673	827	443	75	63

It is clear that the majority of homes in the area were occupied by the poor. No amount of persuasion, cajoling or evictions seemed to be able to shift them. They lived, for the most part, either by casual employment or trading.

The first house built on St Giles High Street at the west end was owned by Henry le Calicer, who also owned the property to the east. His neighbour was Robert le Crucer, then Robert le Rous de Gervimine, beyond the house and shop of Gervase de Lyngedrap (a linen draper). Stephen Hereward's house and land came next. There was also a tenement belonging to William de Tottenhall, together with some land he had been granted by William Seman Russell. Although this was inhabited by relatively poor people, it was certainly nothing like a rookery.[26]

Throughout the seventeenth century St Giles was noted for the extreme contrasts of wealth and poverty. Not only middle- but even upper-class inhabitants shared the area with the poor. A parchment roll of 1639, for instance, detailing the rents payable on some of the properties in the area, makes very interesting reading indeed. The streets covered include Kynaston Alley and Court, St Martin's Lane, Hop Garden, Goodwin's Court, Duke's Court, Hemmings Row, Castle Street, White Hart Court, Hunts Court, Bear Street, Cranbourne Street and Passage, Bedfordbury, New Street, Chandos Street, Round Court, Charing Cross, Hedge Lane, Suffolk Street and Market and Panton Streets.[27] Curiously, since the alleys, courts and passages were generally favoured by the poorer inhabitants, Kynaston Alley (with rents ranging from £4 to £10 a year) boasted a famous inhabitant, the sculptor

Shoe Lane, 1834.

William Wright, who also kept a yard at Charing Cross. Wright paid £10 a year for his dwelling place. Even more remarkably, St Martin's Lane showed an extreme variation both in rent paid and in the class of occupant. The Countess of Salisbury paid £150 a year in rent, Sir Charles Cotterel £100, while a certain Robert Laskley paid only £5 a year for his home. Such a wide variation in rent and the nature of occupancy is very unusual.

The rents in Hop Gardens ranged from £6 to £25 a year. In St Martin's Court, they began at £6 and reached a top figure of £8 a year. The more expensive houses were built of brick, while the half-timbered houses were those rented out to the poor.[28]

By 1725 the expansion of building in the area attracted the attention of a contemporary writer. He commented that it presented 'an amazing scene of new foundations, not of houses only, but as I might say of new cities, new towns, new squares and fine buildings, the like of which no city, no town, nay, no place in the world can show.'[29]

By 1734 there were 2,000 houses in the St Martin's area alone and by 1800 this had risen to 4,344. This doubling of the housing stock involved at least a quadrupling of the population who lived there.[30]

Dyott Street became known as one of the worst of all the St Giles rookeries. Its reputation had become so fearsome by the eighteenth century that it inspired a popular song of the day:

> St Giles was all consternation
> The street they call Dyott
> Portended a riot,
> Belligerents all botheration.[31]

In Dyott Street there was a building known as Rat's Castle, described by an observer as 'a shattered house then standing on the east side, and so called from the rat-catchers and canine snackers who inhabited it, and where they cleaned the skins of those unfortunate stray dogs who had supped death the preceding night.'[32] To the east of Dyott Street, two other streets were almost as notorious; Bainbridge Street and Buckbridge Street. Both roads were built on property acquired by a speculator during the time of Charles II. By 1762 they had become densely populated and infamous throughout London. John Strype records in 1723 that Bainbridge Street 'which falleth into St Giles's near the Pound, hath a small place called Maynard Lane which falleth into Lawrence Lane.'[33] These two lanes are mentioned only by Strype and presumably were alleys so small that they soon became swallowed up in the vast redevelopment of the area. Strype also says 'Buckridge Street, situate on the west of Dyott Street, is another narrow and ordinary place, which falls into St Giles's, by the Pound also, and is over against Hog Lane.'[34] Parton comments (1822) that both streets 'are, as is the whole neighbourhood, inhabited by the lowest order of people.'[35]

By the time of Parton, the area had reached nearly rock-bottom. In spite of the conditions, however, people continued to flood into St Giles. Nor, indeed, was the area yet to witness the absolute abject poverty into which it was driven under the Victorians, particularly as the result of the Poor Law and 'slum clearances'.

In Victorian times, the already wretched living conditions passed from the squalid to the barely credible. Witness after witness described in total disbelief the conditions under which life was passed in the area. Dickens, Mayhew and numerous other observers went to the district and found scenes that outraged them. It was their protests and the support from influential people they were able to mobilise that began to change public opinion.

In spite of all the squalor and the danger, however, the inhabitants not only showed extreme reluctance to move, but the population of the area continued to increase. The area, known for over a hundred years previously as having a high concentration of Irish, became flooded with them after the 1845 famine. Before long, St Giles was nicknamed 'Little Ireland'. The Irish of St Giles engaged in every conceivable occupation, but, even by the already low standards of the area, the houses they lived in were noted for their exceptional squalor, filthiness, disease and state of disrepair. As a result of their transient working patterns, their propensity for large families, their tendency to keep not only dogs but even pigs and other animals in the living quarters, their homes became notorious even for St Giles. It was also remarked upon with wonderment by other dwellers of the rookery that they managed to exist while eating almost nothing. The Jews, who were accused by all other inhabitants of undercutting everyone else, complained in their turn that even they could not sell cheaper than the Irish.

In spite of the ethnically diverse nature of St Giles, and the appalling living conditions within it, the area had an exceptionally strong sense of community. People did move within it, but generally only from one house in a street to another, or at most another street in the same neighbourhood. Even the slum clearances only shifted the population into more overcrowded accommodation in properties that had not yet been destroyed. The people clung on to their foothold in the area in spite of every attempt that was made to dislodge them. It was not until the end of the nineteenth century that St Giles finally began to turn from a primarily residential to a largely commercial district. As late as the 1930s, it was still described as 'not a very savoury area'.[36]

Between about 1600 and 1910, St Giles remained the outstanding example of a rookery. It displayed to the full all the faults and virtues of its kind. Some of the houses so wantonly destroyed were among the finest examples of British domestic architecture. The people, who had built the homes, roads and railways, traded as effectively as any great industrial entrepreneur, and provided soldiers and sailors for the victories of Nelson and Wellington, were finally expelled from the area they had made their own. It was an operation on a par with the Highland Clearances. The same fate was meted out to Saffron Hill, Clare Market and the rest of the rookeries. In spite of the beauty of the buildings and the bravery and endurance of the people, they could not defeat the dead hand of bureaucracy and the grasping embrace of the developers.

Fetter Lane, 1900.

Notes

1   For the figures, see R.A.P. Finlay, *Population and Metropolis: The Demography of London, 1580–1650*, Cambridge, 1981; Peter Earle, *A City Full of People: Men and Women of London 1650–1750*, Methuen, 1994; A.L. Beier, *Masterless Men: The Vagrancy Problem in England 1560–1640*, Methuen, 1985; A.L. Beier & R.A.P. Finlay, *The Making of the Metropolis: London, 1500–1700*, Longmans, 1986; E.R. Dewsnup, *The Housing Problem in England: Its statistics, Legislation and Policy*, Manchester, 1907; D.J. Olsen, *The Growth of Victorian London*, Penguin, 1979.

2   Quoted by Peter Ackroyd, *London: The Biography*, Doubleday, 2000.

3   Ackroyd, op. cit.

4   *Assessment Book*, St Giles, 1623.

5   Ibid.

6   John Parton, *Some account of the Hospital and Parish of St Giles-in-the-Fields*, Luke Hansard, 1822.

7   Rowland Dobie, *History of the United Parishes of St Giles-in-the-Fields and St George, Bloomsbury*, published by the author, 1829.

8   Ibid.

9   Ibid.

10 Ibid.

11 C.C. Knowles and P.H. Fitt, *The History of Building Regulations in London*, Architectural Press, 1972.

12 Dobie, op. cit.

13 Knowles and P.H. Fitt, op. cit.

14 Ibid.

15 Thomas Beames, *The Rookeries of London*, 1850.

16 Ibid.

17 Knowles and Fitt, op. cit.

18 Peter Earle, *A City Full of People: Men and Women of London 1650–1750*, Methuen, 1994.

19 Liza Picard, *Dr Johnson's London: Life in London 1740–1770*, Weidenfeld, 2000.

20 Ibid.

21 *Occupiers of Houses*, St Giles District, 6 November 1835.

22 Edwin Chadwick, Report on the Sanitary Condition of the Labouring Population of Great Britain, Parliamentary Paper 1842, XXVII.

23 Katherine A. Esdaile, *St Martin in the Fields, New and Old*, Society for the Propagation of Christian Knowledge, 1944.

24 Census figures.

25 Assessment of Rates, St Giles, 1829.

26 Stow, *Survey of London*, 1598.

27 Parchment roll detailing occupiers of homes and rents paid in St Giles, 1639.

28 Ibid.

29 *Applebee's Journal*, 1725.

30 Rectors of St Giles and Luke Hansard, statement to Messres Easterby, Tuely and Taylor, 10 July 1827.

31 'The Sons of Carew', a popular song of the time

32 J.T. Smith, *The Cries of London*, 1839

33 John Strype, *A Survey of the Cities of London and Westminster*, Churchill, 1720

34 Ibid.

35 Parton, op. cit.

36 E.V. Lucas, *A Wanderer in London*, Methuen, 1936.

3

WORK & EMPLOYMENT

One of the distinguishing features of employment in St Giles and the other rookeries was the overwhelming reliance upon casual labour or trading goods and services. Workers in the building trade met in pubs to be hired. Porters, often female, did casual work lifting almost superhuman weights. The workers on the docks and the railways kept the city moving. The market traders, slop-sellers, mudlarks, sellers of matches, crossing sweepers – all these and more were the stock-in-trade of employment in St Giles. No matter how tiring, dangerous, difficult or degrading the job, somewhere in the area could be found hands willing to perform it.

In medieval times, when the area was a small village, St Giles was not noted for its abundance of casual, unskilled labour. Local craftspeople worked on projects, mainly for the Church or rich merchants. They often belonged to the London guilds.[1] Entry into these powerful, prestigious and wealthy organisations took place through the apprenticeship system.

A street porter.

St Giles continued to provide 'masters' with apprentices well into the late eighteenth century, when the guild system had almost died out everywhere else in London.[2] This was partly because of its location in the rapidly expanding West End of the city; however, it was also due to the curious fact that the population lived principally by casual labour and street trading. They also chose to reside in an insalubrious and overcrowded area because it was convenient for their work. As such they were less hostile than other sections of the working class to the effects of two Acts of Parliament which incensed more settled workers.

These two Acts were the Statute of Apprentices, which laid down a requirement that a seven-year apprenticeship must be served in certain trades, and the Law of Settlement, which attempted to prevent mobility of labour.[3] The Statute of Apprentices was an amendment to an existing law, the Statute of Artificers, passed under Elizabeth I in 1563. The Tudor Act had laid down strict regulations that, in theory at least, seemed intolerably harsh. Under its terms it was possible for a child to be 'bound apprentice' as early as eleven years old, and forced to continue in that status until the age of twenty-four. In practice, however, most children only served a period of seven years, almost invariably starting between the ages of twelve and sixteen. Nor were its provisions, as has often been falsely claimed, simply an attempt to extort cheap labour out of the English poor. A clearly astonished Italian visitor to London remarked in 1498, 'No one can be mayor or alderman of London, who has not been an apprentice in his youth; that is, who has not passed the seven or nine years in that hard service described before'.[4] Even the highest officials in London had to serve their apprenticeship before entering into their guilds and becoming eligible for civic office. The apprenticeship system, whatever its faults, was genuinely intended to be the first step on the ladder of a trade and a position in the livery companies. Of course some masters abused the system, but they were a minority, and strongly disapproved of by their fellow guildsmen.

In spite of the poverty of the area, there was no shortage of apprentices from the neighbourhood of St Giles. Considering that the cost of 'placing' an apprentice with an employer was frequently as high as £100 and could run as high as £1,000, their ability to find such large sums of money is remarkable.

All the same, though the eventual rewards were good, the life of an apprentice was a hard one. A source of 1667 describes the obligations of a master towards his apprentice. These were essentially to feed, clothe and instruct him, 'with a due manner of chastisement.'[5] Curiously, the mistress of the house was forbidden to beat her husband's apprentice. If she did so, he was entitled to break his contract at once![6]

Girls could be apprenticed as well as boys. In 1667, for instance, a female was bound apprentice to a 'waterman'.[7] Other examples of female apprentices also survive, though the 1667 case is probably one of the most unusual career choices for a seventeenth-century girl. Presumably the mistress rather than the master of the house would 'instruct' and 'chastise' female apprentices?

Although these theoretically harsh Elizabethan regulations remained on the statute books for over two hundred years, by the late seventeenth century they were becoming a dead letter. Defoe, writing in the early eighteenth century, complained bitterly that things had changed for the worse since the times when 'the Apprentices of the Shopkeepers and Ware-house-keepers submitted to the most servile employments of the families in which they served such as cleaning their Masters' shoes, bringing Water into the Houses from the Conduits in the Street, also waiting at table'.[8]

In spite of the criticisms subsequently made of the amended Statute of Apprentices, it afforded security and stability and the chance to earn a steady if not always wealthy living. The people of St Giles vastly preferred a settled residence and security of employment when they could obtain it. They did not mind remaining where they were and serving the same master for seven years. The prospect of eventual financial prosperity made them prepared to accept the long hours and hard work that the apprenticeship system required. They continued to enter their sons and daughters as apprentices long after the system had died out in the rest of London.

As well as the enthusiastic volunteers from the citizens of St Giles there were also a whole crop of orphans disposed of by the parish through a corrupt abuse of the apprenticeship system. Rather than maintain them, as was their statutory duty, they simply 'apprenticed' them to masters and mistresses for £5 a time. Their employers were happy, as they had a plentiful supply of cheap labour about whose welfare no one was concerned. The parish was happy, as it was cheaper to pay £5 to be rid of the cost of maintenance than to support the children until they became adults. This was a practice that largely created the trade in boy chimney sweeps. The other principal customers for these 'apprentices' were the watermen.

Girls were generally sent into domestic service, or retail work if they were luckier. The type of master or mistress who would buy a child for £5 rather than the going rate was hardly likely to invest any time or trouble in training them. They were 'maids of all work' in most cases, doing all the heavy and unpleasant work that the mistress of the house or the other servants did not want to carry out. In effect, the parish sold the boys and girls into slavery, since, unlike a proper apprenticeship, which was at least tightly regulated and enforceable by law, these 'indentures' had no time limit and were effectively for life.

The passage of a regulation in 1691 which made a period of forty days spent as an apprentice sufficient to qualify the boy or girl for a 'settlement', or more accurately the right of residence, made the lot of the parish apprentice even worse. Parishes competed desperately to 'farm out' poor children on to neighbouring authorities. No matter how obviously unsuitable the 'employer', the parish was delighted to be rid of the burden on the poor rates. The chimney sweeps, always anxious for a fresh supply of 'climbing boys', benefited most from this new laxity on the part of the Poor Law authorities. Boys as young as four years old climbed sooty chimneys to save the parish money. St Giles and the neighbouring rookeries became full of 'climbing boys' carrying out this dangerous work.

Sir William Blackstone, representative of all that was least enlightened about eighteenth-century thought, actually admitted that the system was a form of slavery, which he also defended on the spurious grounds that it was 'the same state of subjection for life, which every apprentice submits to for the space of seven years, and sometimes for a longer time.'[9]

Complaints by genuine apprentices against their masters and mistresses were also not uncommon, and were taken seriously by the courts. In 1695, for instance, John Knight, apprentice to James Cuffe, a clockmaker, asked to be freed from his service, 'alleging that the said Cuffe resides in Salisbury Court, near Whitefriars, for fear of being arrested for debt; that he has no work in the said trade to employ an apprentice and did not supply him with necessary food and drink.'[10]

Perhaps the most common complaints by boy apprentices concerned excessive beatings by their masters, inadequate food and failure to provide clothing. The girls tended to complain about excessive beatings and sexual abuse. If the court believed their stories, they would be freed from their apprenticeships.

The life of an apprentice was supposed to be lived by strict rules, but the youngsters found them hard to follow, and many made no attempt. In theory, they were forbidden to drink, yet tales of drunken behaviour from their numbers are legion, frequently attracting the attention of the courts. They were also forbidden to associate with 'lewd women', another prohibition conspicuously ignored by the young boys. From time to time they let out their frustrations by rioting. They were also fond of raiding brothels, allegedly with the intention of 'protecting the virtue of the citizens'. It is doubtful whether even their contemporaries believed that particular excuse.

John Stow, writing in 1598, at a time when St Giles was beginning to change from a small village in Middlesex into a part of the expanding West End, divided the citizens of London into three main classes. He wrote:

> They consist of these three parts, – merchants, handicraftsmen, and labourers. Merchandise is also divided into these three sorts, – navigation, by the which merchandizes are brought, and carried in and out over the seas; invection, by the which commodities are gathered into the city, and dispersed from thence into the country by hand and negotiation, which I may call the keeping of a retailing or standing shop. In common speech, they of the first sort be called merchants,

and both the other retailers. Handicraftsmen be those which do exercise such arts as require both labour and cunning, as goldsmiths, tailors, and haberdashers, skinners, etc. Labourers and hirelings I call those *quorum operæ non artes emuntur,* as Tullie saith; of which sort be porters, carmen, watermen, etc. Again, these three sorts may be considered, either in respect of their wealth or number: in wealth, merchants and some of the chief retailers have the first place; the most part of retailers and all artificers the second or mean place; and hirelings the lowest room: but in number they of the middle place be first, and do far exceed both the rest; hirelings be next, and merchants be the last. [11]

It is curious that in 1598, in spite of the vast expansion of population in London, Stow still claims that the majority of the people were what would nowadays be called middle class. It is perhaps a sign of how different attitudes to social status were in Elizabethan times that tailors and even skinners – a dirty and unpleasant job if ever there was one – could be considered as belonging to the 'second or mean place'.

The first 'shop' in St Giles of which we have record was a blacksmith's, first mentioned in 1225. It survived the Dissolution of the Monasteries and continued to trade for centuries. [12]

As late as 1688, Gregory King, in one of the earliest attempts to provide a statistical analysis of the people of Britain in terms of occupations, lumped what he called 'labourers' in a grouping he referred to as the 'agricultural classes'. This was made up of 'freeholders, farmers, labourers, outservants, cottagers and paupers', a suspiciously miscellaneous collection of people with almost nothing in common in terms of either their mode of work or the income they derived from their employment. He regarded this group as forming 4,265,000 people, the remainder being engaged in what he called 'manufacture', to which he assigned the figure of 240,000 workers, and 'commerce', which he estimated as employing 246,000 people. [13]

King's economic analysis is deeply flawed as a result of his failure to break down 'the agricultural classes' into a more accurately subdivided group. Farmers, for instance, could be wealthy, while paupers by definition could only ever be poor. Indeed, the general definition of a pauper in late Stuart times would be someone who either never worked at all or at best engaged in casual labour at below subsistence level. Equally, his somewhat rigid definition of 'manufacture' leads him to grossly underestimate the amount of small manufacturing that went on throughout London and the country as a whole. His population estimates, however, were astonishingly accurate. Although King did not break down his figures regionally, an examination of other sources from the period shows that St Giles contained an amazing variety of occupations. There were market gardeners, who grew fruit, vegetables and flowers for resale in such outlets as the Covent Garden market; there were manufacturers of almost every item that *could* be produced domestically; and there were traders, retailers, street-sellers and wholesalers. In addition to these groups, there was also a large pool of casual labour.[14]

A contemporary of King's, Richard Baxter, gives an interesting account of life for the artisan at this time. He claims that they were better off than the farmers:

> It is much easyer with the handicrafte labourer that hath a good trade. A joyner or a turner can worke in the dry house with tolerable and pleasant worke and knoweth his price and wages. A weaver, a shoemaker or a taylor can worke without the wetting or the tiring of his body and can thinke and talke of the concernes of his soule without impediment to his labour.[15]

By 1700 a breakdown of the occupations of Londoners showed that 20 per cent worked in the textile or clothing trade. London was also the manufacturing capital of the country. Long Acre in the heart of St Giles was pre-eminent in the field of coachbuilding, while printing, stationery and cabinet-making were also large local employers.

The influx of Huguenot refugees following the 1685 persecution in France led to a mass emigration, many of them settling in St Giles. A contemporary account specially mentions the Sieurs Dupré and Moise du Boust, 'now living in the parish of Saint Giles-in-the-Fields, persecuted in their persons and their estates, their houses demolished before they fled into this country.'[16] The Huguenots brought the art of making crystal and jewellery other than gold and silver to the St Giles area.[17]

The employment opportunities available to women were more limited than those open to males. In spite of the fact that female apprentices did exist, they formed a very small proportion of the 'indentured' workforce. Domestic service accounted for 20 per cent of female employment in London generally. The figure in St Giles was far higher, with the proximity of so many wealthy houses in constant need of servants and the ready availability of young girls to perform the duties. Most girls only went into 'service' as a precursor to marriage. Two-thirds of female servants were aged twenty-five or under and almost no women remained in domestic service later than the age of forty-five.

A servant's lot could also be a hard one, though generally it was the middle and working classes who treated their 'domestics' harshly rather than the nobility. Beatings were administered at the slightest excuse and girls were also frequently exposed to sexual abuse and even rape at the hands of their employers. Again, the law of the land was harsh, laying down a legal requirement that 'all single men between twelve years old and sixty, and married ones under thirty, and all single women between twelve and forty, not having any visible livelihood, are compellable to go out to service, for the promotion of honest industry.'[18]

In the case of the aristocracy, this law simply meant that they might become 'ladies in waiting' to the royal court or other noble families. For women from the middle classes, of whom St Giles had a large number until Victorian times, it generally meant becoming a 'waiting woman', not at all an enviable situation. It was comparable with the position of a governess, but with a much lower status and a wider range of responsibilities. She would act as a secretary, chaperone, companion and slightly higher status maid. The woman would also be required to sing and play some kind of musical instrument. She would, at least in theory, eat at the same table as her master or mistress, and was considered in law to be of the same social status. Although she was unlikely to have been beaten or raped, it was not at all uncommon for her 'master' to attempt to seduce her and more common still for him to display 'undue familiarity'. Generally a waiting woman would seek to take advantage of her employers' circle of friends to find a husband and escape her situation.[19]

Unappealing as the lot of a waiting woman was, the life of an ordinary servant was far worse. Girls frequently tried to escape, often stealing from their employers when they fled. Even the harsh punishments for such offences, ranging from public whippings to hanging, did not deter the poorest and most exploited females. Capture and conviction was anything but certain in those days. Juries were often inclined, especially when a capital sentence was involved, to deliberately undervalue the goods stolen so that the girl's life would be spared from the gallows. Newspapers regularly ran advertisements seeking the return of property stolen by servants and even offering rewards for information leading to their capture.[20]

In theory servants enjoyed rights under the law protecting them from dismissal 'unless upon reasonable cause, to be allowed by a Justice of the Peace'. In practice this law was flouted constantly. Instant dismissal for no reason at all was a common occurrence. The need for references led to a growing trade, particularly in St Giles, for forged testimonials and spurious 'referees' who would give dismissed servants the 'character' that enabled them to find fresh employment in the same field.

Servants in middle-class or working-class households, where they might well be carrying out all the domestic chores unaided, had to work very long hours. Laundry work meant that the girl had to get up at 1.00 a.m. in order to finish the washing in time for supper.[21] She would also not be able to go to bed until her master and mistress came home at night. Then the lady of the house would expect the girl to undress her. It was not at all uncommon for a servant girl, particularly in a middle-class family, to have to work eighteen hours a day.[22]

Servants were of course entitled to food, lodging and clothes from their employers, although the quality of all three varied considerably depending on the economic position of their master and mistress. Those employed by the nobility could expect rich food, good tips from guests and a plentiful supply of high-quality 'cast-offs' in the way of clothes. Middle-class families would spend less money, be less generous with the food, and provide the girls with cheap outfits. Working-class families, where the employer was often not much better off than the servant they employed, tended to be generous with the food but pay low wages and give the girl only the most basic of clothes for her work. The pay of servants also varied dramatically. Those who worked for the aristocracy commanded the highest wages and had the best living conditions. Those employed by the working classes would receive around £3 a year. The middle classes paid their servants around £7 of £8 a year. Sir William Blackstone praised the system on the grounds that 'by service all servants except apprentices became entitled to wages.'[23]

There was also a surprising variety of what would nowadays be referred to as 'non-traditional' occupations performed by women. Females laboured in the market gardens, the pottery kilns, on the river-boats, as porters, even coal-heavers and 'gong farmers', disposing of the refuse of the city. Even during the medieval period, women were frequently recorded as performing the heaviest of manual labouring tasks.[24] By far the most common means of employment for both sexes in St Giles, however, was some form of 'selling'. This could take the form of an actual retail shop, a public house, a stall on a street market, or simply 'hawking'. Keeping a pub was a particularly popular occupation for women in the area. It not only gave them a good income but also brought in social life, entertainment, and additional opportunities for making money besides their principal source of remuneration. As well as keeping a public house another popular activity in the area was brewing. Perhaps surprisingly this was often carried out by women. During the Middle Ages the proportion of females who brewed beer was a staggering 80 per cent.[25] In addition to the lady brewers a number of women bought beer and resold it, often in combination with criminal activities like prostitution and disposing of stolen goods.[26]

Because of the often transient nature of work in St Giles, the area soon saw pubs functioning as 'employment exchanges'. Those in need of jobs and those who wanted to hire workers both congregated in the local pub and deals were struck over a friendly pint or two. The first proper 'employment agency' was started in St Giles in 1656, while Oliver Cromwell was still ruling the country.[27] It was originally designed to recruit clerical workers but the idea caught on and was democratised by the working classes. Before long the local pub became a normal venue for hiring staff.

Charladies, laundresses, seamstresses and other variations on cleaning and clothing made up the bulk of the remaining female employment opportunities. A good laundress could command a high price for her services and was also considered a very desirable wife![28]

A laundress and an orange seller, just two of the occupations used by women to make money.

There were a number of markets within easy reach of St Giles, all founded in the seventeenth century. The largest and most prestigious was Covent Garden. Newport Market was more patronised by 'locals' than visitors and Clare Market had a very undesirable reputation. Later, Monmouth Street also spawned its own market, frequently selling stolen goods. Other markets in the area were Pall Mall Fields, Haymarket and Bloomsbury, though none of the latter three survived much beyond the eighteenth century. Seven Dials also hosted a 'Bird Fair', at which birds were bought and sold, rather like the old animal market at Club Row in the East End.[29] Most of the regular stall-holders at these markets were men, though women were certainly represented to a large extent. In terms of 'street selling', women predominated over men, though generally within a more confined radius. A man might walk miles to sell his goods, whereas a female would stick to a local 'pitch' and cry her wares there.

The 'cries of London' were heard perhaps more often in St Giles than any other part of the city, even the Square Mile itself. St Giles women soon acquired a reputation for loud voices, a cheeky repartee and great ingenuity in sales patter. They were regarded as capable of being outshouted only by the fishwives of Billingsgate! Even the men of the area were frequently on the receiving end of their sharp tongues. Many contemporaries were fascinated by the various cries of the street sellers of the area, so much so that they were even turned into a

A lemonade vendor.

series of paintings and then etchings. It was not unknown for visitors to come to St Giles simply to hear the sellers hawking their wares. In its own way, perhaps the area can lay claim to the first attempts to preserve English folk culture and song.[30]

St Giles can also claim to have been a pioneer in using the visual appeal of a shop to entice customers to purchase. The more traditional retailers in the City of London simply piled their wares high and made no attempt to attract the eye. The folk of St Giles used colourful shop signs, displays in windows and outside the front of the shop, as well as hiring 'hawkers' to cry their wares to the public as they passed by. Not surprisingly, this new method of trade, which was among the earliest examples of retail advertising, soon generated such large profits that the traditional shopkeepers in the City, to the disgust of Daniel Defoe, were forced to follow the example of their competitors in St Giles if they wished to survive.[31]

Another prominent local occupation in the rookeries was tailoring. During the Middle Ages, curiously, this had been an occupation largely controlled by wealthy London women, at least in so far as they dominated the silk trade.[32] In the late seventeenth century, St Giles became the seat of the London trade in clothes-making. Obviously the wealthy wore the most fashionable and expensive clothes but they developed a bad habit of not paying their tailors! A master tailor might make a good living from his art but more common was the journeyman tailor. They struggled to turn much of a profit, and the unskilled tailors lived on a subsistence level at best. There arose a saying, 'cucumbers for a penny, tailors twice as many'.[33] It was said that an unskilled tailor could be trained up enough to produce saleable garments in as little as two weeks. The extreme difficulty of making a living led them to adopt a practice known as 'cabbaging', which involved substituting inferior (and therefore cheaper) material for better quality cloth, while charging for the clothes at the higher rate. Although illegal, cabbaging was essential for the lowest grade of tailors, who were literally starving outside the good summer months. The tailors of St Giles, with the area's long tradition of expertise in deception, were the most skilful 'cabbagers' in London.

During the eighteenth century the already large Irish population of St Giles was swelled by groups of labourers for seasonal work in the hayfields. Many of the men stayed on and became involved in the building and brewing industries. By 1780 there were 20,000 Irish living in London, the overwhelming majority of them in St Giles. The

Lavender sellers.

nineteenth century saw an even bigger influx of Irish, particularly after the previously mentioned Irish Potato Famine of 1845. They were also attracted by the relatively generous Poor Law provisions in London compared with the relief available in Ireland. Irish workers from St Giles largely built London's canals, as well as the majority of those in the country as a whole. Later, they proved equally adept as railway workers. Running pubs was another area in which they displayed exceptional ability.

Clerical work in St Giles was in considerable demand during the seventeenth and eighteenth centuries but declined sharply between 1840 and 1880. Most people in the area could read and write but there was very little in the way of office work available. The majority of office work opportunities were for the banks, lawyers and insurance services, most of them located in more 'upmarket' parts of London.

With the deterioration of the area from the 1830s onwards and the exodus of 'genteel' residents, the demand for 'white collar workers' collapsed almost to zero. It was not until the clearances of St Giles in the 1880s and the consequent building of new retail and commercial premises that clerical work in the area began to revive.[34] Another more 'professional' sphere of employment was teaching. Schools in the rookeries, particularly in St Giles, were of a surprisingly high standard. Most residents had elementary education until around the age of twelve. Men and women taught in roughly equal numbers and the variety of subjects that even a poor child learned at school was quite remarkable. Salaries for teachers in the area were not high but there seemed to be no shortage of people willing to take on the burden of educating the local children. It was also possible for poor children to become the eighteenth- and nineteenth-century equivalent of 'classroom assistants' and hopefully go on to become teachers in their turn.[35]

Another job opportunity open to the inhabitants of the rookeries was the trade of an apothecary, which would nowadays be known as a pharmacist or chemist. There was a scheme operated by the Pharmaceutical Society under which 'scholarships' were offered to poor people to enable them to train as apothecaries. Apothecaries always dressed in black and their shops always contained a skull, no doubt to emphasise the perils of not buying their concoctions. They offered a wide range of remedies, though how effective most of them were is open to question. Among their most popular ranges were 'love philtres'. Most of their medicines were herbal concoctions made from the most bizarre variety of ingredients. They included such unlikely substances as moss, henbane, 'may dew', smoked horses' testicles, spiders wrapped in their own silk, nutmeg, 'Turkey rhubarb' and sulphuric acid. Tobias Smollett gives a vivid account of an apothecary's shop in the mid-eighteenth century. He writes:

> Oyster-shells he could convert into crab's eyes; common oil into oil of sweet almonds, Thames water into aqua cinnamoni; when any common thing was ordered for a patient, he always took care to disguise it in colour or taste, or both, in such a manner as that it could not possibly be known.[36]

For the truly destitute, there were the unappetising choices of scavenging, begging or applying to the workhouse. A sad story of a 'seller' on the very margins of society comes from St Giles. Of a woman named Elizabeth Price, it was remarked: 'For these several years past, she had followed sometimes the business of picking up rags and cinders, and at other times that of selling fruit and oysters, crying hot-puddings gray-pease in the streets'.[37]

The first workhouse appears to have been set up in the City of London during the 1670s by Thomas Firmin.[38] In 1699 the Bishopsgate workhouse opened, which became a 'model' for those who saw the opportunity to rid themselves of the curse of 'pauperism' through forcing poor people to enter workhouses and become a source of cheap or even, at times, virtually slave labour. Regulations were drawn up around this time requiring the recipients of poor relief to wear a badge announcing their status to the world, in what was obviously simply an attempt to humiliate them. One victim of this was the unfortunate Joanna Garwood from St Giles who 'wore a badge as one of the poor of the parish of St Andrew Holborn'.[39]

When the parish apprenticeship system was finally abolished in 1844 the Poor Law Guardians, who had used, indeed abused it, to such advantage for 200 years soon found a means of circumventing the new law. Instead of apprenticing women and children to employers they organised convoys of people from St Giles and the other rookeries in London to be transported to the mill-towns in the north of England. Employers from the industrial north also tried to recruit voluntary workers from London but their efforts met with little enthusiasm. People in St Giles and the other rookery areas preferred to remain where they were if they had any choice in the matter. There was a small amount of relocation to Lancashire and Yorkshire but on such a tiny scale that the results of the voluntary scheme were disappointing even to its advocates.

Since there was little enthusiasm among those who had a choice for moving to the mill-towns and working in the textile factories, the Poor Law Guardians did as they had been doing for centuries and compelled children or those who applied to them for relief to take 'positions' in the north. Some came back at the earliest opportunity but most remained. Though the work was hard, it was steady, much better paid than anything they could find in London, and the living conditions were immeasurably better. Throughout the nineteenth century, wages in the north of England continually outperformed those anywhere else in the country. Outside the aristocracy and the bankers, most rich people in Britain during that period came from the north. Even the poor were better off in Yorkshire and Lancashire than they were in London. Paid holidays, cleaner air, new homes with better facilities, higher wages and a better quality of life in general meant that most of the deported Londoners remained where they were sent.[40]

From 1835 onwards it was primarily through casual labour and variations on selling that the inhabitants of St Giles earned their living. It was a hard life for them but they struggled and persevered and managed somehow to cling on to a precarious subsistence living. Until Victorian times, though life in the rookeries was hard, it was not impossible for people to become prosperous as a result of their own honest labours. The Victorians took away even that last vestige of self-respect from them.

The 1834 Poor Law also dramatically and disproportionately affected the people of what was then the poorest parish in Britain. It removed at a stroke their ability to receive 'outdoor relief' which they had previously relied on to see them through hard times. Now there was the absurd assumption by the authorities that if they did not work they must be idle and dishonest. Only if they agreed to enter the dismal prison of the workhouse could they hope to receive any support from the parish.[41]

The St Giles workhouse had a particularly unpleasant reputation, no doubt as a result of the prejudices of the overseers against the population of the area. Under the workhouse system husbands and wives were separated from one another. Women were often parted from their children as well. Since no actual work could be offered to them, a substitute was found in the form of pointless and punishing tasks, in the belief that only those who worked deserved the not-very-appetising food on offer at the workhouse.

The illusion that genuine, purposeful work was carried out at these institutions was part of a propaganda offensive by the Whig and Liberal governments to disguise the reality of their complete inability to either diagnose or treat the real problem of poverty. It never fooled enlightened Tories like Richard Oastler and Michael Sadler, who became so radicalised by the scandal of the workhouse system that they were led to advocate universal suffrage and an almost welfare state policy as the only remedy for the sufferings of the poor. It never fooled reforming Conservatives like the Earl of Derby, the Earl of Shaftesbury and Benjamin Disraeli, although they were often perplexed as to what to replace it with. They knew the system was rotten, inhumane and economically inefficient, yet lacked the vision to abolish it and introduce a proper network of social services, as Bismarck did in Germany. Instead they introduced reforms, tried to check the worst excesses of the system, and hoped for better times to come along.

When tomorrow continually failed to arrive and the increasing poverty of the area led to a rising tide of criticism, the only long-term answer by the authorities was to demolish the homes in the area and hope that the people would relocate to the new suburbs that were growing up all over London. It was a hope as foolish as it was forlorn, since the displaced population could not afford the fares to travel in to their places of work and most of the new suburban areas offered few employment opportunities locally. All that happened was a cynical process of demolition, leaving a trail of thousands of homeless people in its wake.

Not until the Liberals shed their Gladstonian prejudices in favour of *laisser-faire* when the Earl of Rosebery took over the leadership was any real attempt made to actually find a solution rather than simply transferring the problem elsewhere. Under Rosebery's guidance the Liberal Party suddenly became radical and what might nowadays be called 'welfare stateist' or 'social democrat.' It was Rosebery and his Liberal Party that began building the first council houses in Britain, an idea that Gladstone would never have countenanced. Whether the path that the earl chose to solve the problem was the right one is open to question in hindsight, but it was at least a decision taken out of simple humanity. Few other decisions affecting St Giles and the other rookery dwellers were taken by any motivation other than cost-cutting and prejudice against the inhabitants.

Notes

1   Ian Anders Gadd and Patrick Wallis (eds), *Guilds, Society and Economy in London 1450–1800,* Centre for Metropolitan History, 2002.

2   Peter Earle, *A City Full of People: Men and Women of London 1650–1750,* Methuen, 1994.

3   Adam Smith, *The Wealth of Nations* (first edition, 1776), denounces both these measures as holding back British economic progress. Since the laws were a dead letter in many parts of the country, and were positively welcomed by the workers of St Giles, the poorest part of London, it is difficult to see how Smith's criticisms can be considered justified. They were even more extraordinary in the light of the growing prosperity of Britain throughout the eighteenth century. As late as the 1930s, lightermen on the London docks still had to serve a seven-year apprenticeship. Even during the 1960s a modified form of the apprenticeship system continued to survive. Smith's strictures from a twenty-first-century perspective seem positively irrational as well as unjustified.

4   Andrea Trevisan, *Relation or rather a True Account of the Island of England,* 1847, (first edition 1498).

5   Rose's *Almanac,* 1667.

6   Sir William Blackstone, *Commentaries on the Laws of England,* (4 vols), London, 1765–9.

7   Fly's *Almanac,* 1667.

8   Daniel Defoe, quoted in Alice Clark, *Working Life of Women in the Seventeenth Century,* London, 1919.

9   Blackstone, op. cit.

10   GLRO/Middlesex County Records/Session Book 525, October 1695, p. 41.

11   John Stow, *Survey of London,* first edition, 1598. The quotation comes from Cicero, often called Tully by Elizabethans. It means 'whose work is not skilful'.

12   Edward C.W. Gray, *St Giles of the Lepers.*

13   Gregory King, 'estimate of the population and incomes of various classes, "calculated for the year 1688"', 1696. King's analysis is given in full in Peter Laslett, *The World We Have Lost Further Explored,* Methuen, 1983.

14   Gray, op. cit.

15   Richard Baxter, *The Poor Husbandman's Advocate to Rich, Racking Landlords.* (*c.* 1690).

16   Cited in Edward Akber (ed.), *The Torments of Protestant Slaves,* London, 1908.

17   Gray, op. cit.

18   Blackstone, op. cit.

19   A fascinating example of the trials of being a 'waiting woman' is given by Pepys. See *Samuel Pepys, Diary,* Bell, 1979–83.

20   The *Mercurius Publicus* was perhaps the best-known vehicle for these advertisements.

21   Pepys, op. cit. Mercifully, the general frequency of laundering was around every 2–4 weeks. The Restoration also saw a huge increase in the numbers of what would nowadays be called 'launderettes', especially in St Giles. The profession of the 'laundry woman' became another expanding career opportunity for local females.

22   Ibid.

23   Blackstone, op. cit.

24   See, for example: R.A. Brown, H.M. Colvin and A.J. Taylor (eds), *The History of the King's Works, vol. 1, The Middle Ages,* London, 1963. As well as unskilled labouring, other surprising career choices for women in this period included foundry work and the manufacturing of chain mail and even plate armour. See: Heather C. Swanson, *Medieval Artisans, an Urban Class in Late Medieval England,* Oxford, 1989.

25   J.M. Bennett, 'Women and men in the Brewers' gild of London c. 1420', in: E.B. DeWindt (ed.), *The Salt of Common Life,* Kalamazoo, 1995.

26   Swanson, op. cit.

27   Gray, op. cit.

28   A number of books have studied the nature of women's employment, coming to surprisingly different conclusions. The following works are particularly useful:
Sally Alexander, *Women's Work in Nineteenth Century London: A Study of the Years 1820–1850*, Journeyman, 1983.
Andrew August, *Poor Women's Lives: Gender, Work and Poverty in Late Victorian London*, Associated University Presses, 1999.
L. Charles and L. Duffin (eds), *Women and Work in Pre-Industrial England*, Croom Helm, 1985.
Alice Clark, *Working Life of Women in the Seventeenth Century*, Routledge, 1919.
Michael Hiley, *Victorian Working Women: Portraits from Life*, Gordon Fraser, 1979.
Ivy Pinchbeck, *Women Workers of the Industrial Revolution 1750–1850*, Frank Cass, 1969.

29   Calendar of State Papers Domestic.

30   A collection of these cries, and an account of the lives of the people who made their living shouting or singing their merchandise on the street, is given in Sean Shesgreen (ed.), *The Cries and Hawkers of London*, Stanford University, 1990.

31   Daniel Defoe, *A Tour through the Whole Island of Great Britain*, Penguin, 1971 (first edition, 1709).

32   M.K. Dale, 'The London silkwomen of the fifteenth century', *Economic History Review*, 4 (1933), pp. 324–35.

33   Quoted in Peter Earle, *A City Full of People: Men and Women of London 1650–1750*, Methuen, 1994.

34   Thomas Beames, *The Rookeries of London*, Frank Cass, 1970 (first edition 1850).

35   Ibid.

36   Tobias Smollett, *Roderick Random*, 1748.

37   Regrettably, the sad woman's destitute condition did not prevent her from being hanged for theft.

38   Thomas Firmin, *Some Proposals for the Imploying of the Poor, especially in and about the City of London*, 1678.

39   GLRO/Depositions, DL/C/246.

40   For the statistics, see:
A.L. Bowley, *Wages in the United Kingdom in the 19th Century*, Augustus M. Kelley, 1972.
J. Shield, *The Effects of Machinery on Wages*, Swann Sonnenschein, 1893.

41   It is only fair to say that the 1834 Poor Law did *not*, as has often been falsely claimed, *abolish* the payment of 'outdoor relief'. It did however make it so difficult to obtain, and its granting was hedged round with so many conditions, that for all practical purposes, outdoor relief constituted a small percentage of the money paid out by the Poor Law Boards. Most of the fortunate recipients of it were widows and even then strenuous attempts were made to discover family members who might be able to support her. It is also fair to add that the boards always tended to err on the side of non-payment rather than disbursement of funds when doubtful cases arose. Dickens' caricature of the beadle in *Oliver Twist* was, sadly, all too often a sober reality. What is more, it was based on the assumption that the poor were idle and chose to live their lives holding out the begging bowl. It stands in stark contrast to the previous Poor Law statutes of 1572, 1597, 1603 and 1662, all of which explicitly admitted that the poor had *not* chosen their poverty and that only a minority of them were idlers. The previous Acts laid down a clear duty on local parishes to provide relief for the poor who lived there out of the rates levied on citizens. In 1650, the remarkable sum of £250,000 had been raised in poor rates; by 1700, this had risen to £700,000. See G. Taylor, *Problems of Poverty 1660–1834*, Longmans, 1969.

4

LOVE & MARRIAGE

Much has been written about the situation of marriage among the wealthy and to what extent emotional factors entered into the choice of partners. Comparatively little work has been done on the love lives of the urban poor and not much more on the rural situation. The picture that emerges from a close study of the evidence is a complex and somewhat contradictory one.

Several clear facts arise from the statistics of births and marriages during the period between 1660 and 1900. Londoners consistently reported a higher level of illegitimate births than dwellers in the countryside. They also got married at a much later age than farm labourers. Rural couples tended to marry early, in their late teens or early twenties, whereas Londoners married in their middle or even late twenties. The pattern of late marriage and childbirth among dwellers in London is not the recent phenomenon that some commentators believe but a consistent trend from the Middle Ages onwards.[1]

Another trend common in Londoners but rare among country people was the relative ease with which they separated when relationships broke down. In rural areas the strange custom of 'wife-selling' was a form of divorce that, though not recognised by the law, was locally accepted as valid. Among Londoners, while not unknown during the Middle Ages, this barbaric custom fell out of favour. 'Merry meet, merry part' best describes the attitude of the London poor towards a failed relationship. On the other hand the evidence suggests that marriages among the poor were primarily based upon genuine affection, which should surprise no one. Even among the upper and upper middle classes the extent to which love was involved in their relationships has been consistently underrated. The aristocracy and upper middle classes enjoyed reading the romances of Madeleine de Scudéry, and even the subversive though strangely romantic feminist Aphra Behn. Later they were enthusiastic readers of the romantic fiction of Samuel Richardson. The working classes may not have been exposed to works of that type but they loved their chapbooks and ballads with their tales of star-crossed lovers or love winning through in spite of all obstacles.

Furthermore, since almost everyone who lived in the rookeries was on the same economic footing, there was no question of marrying for money. Unlike the vast fortunes that could be involved when nobility or even merchants chose to wed, the London poor looked above all else for companionship. The majority of them had no illusions that they would ever rise above their state of poverty and simply chose to marry for companionship and indeed love. In so far as one can quantify such a thing it seems certain that love played the dominant part in their relationships. That was far less the case with the aristocracy and middle classes, whose first instinct was always to protect their money and assets and economic considerations were paramount.

The law regarding marriage was very different until the Victorian era. It was possible for a girl to become engaged at the age of seven and to marry at twelve. It was possible for her to be married even younger – the earliest example I have come across so far is a ten-year-old – although the law allowed her to 'dissent till she be fourteen'.[2] Curiously, this provision does *not* seem to have resulted in a large number of older men marrying girls under the age of puberty. In every case I have come across, from the Middle Ages to the early nineteenth century, it appears to have been two young people of around the same ages. In fact, the percentage of young girls marrying older men seems to have been *lower* than in other European countries and lower even than in the English countryside. Such at least is the evidence of the parish registers.

That this continued to be the trend in Britain at least as late as 1851 is shown by some very curious statistics published by a French researcher in 1859.[3] His evidence is given in the form of two tables, as follows:

Marriages with Women of Fifty Years and upwards
(In a million marriages)

IN FRANCE		IN ENGLAND	
Age (of bachelors)	Number of marriages	Age (of bachelors)	Number of Marriages
18–20	64	16–20	0
20–25	109	20–25	5
25–30	151	25–30	12
30–35	188	30–35	22
35–40	257	35–40	40

Marriages with Men of Sixty Years and upwards

IN FRANCE		IN ENGLAND	
Age of Girls	Number of Marriages	Age of Girls	Number of Marriages
15–20	94	15–20	2
20–25	139	20–25	15
25–30	176	25–30	32
30–35	242	30–35	49

What conclusions can be drawn from such strange statistics is not clear. It could be argued that the tables prove that the English were more romantic than the French; that French men were more willing to marry women much older than themselves for money than their English counterparts; or that French girls were more in need of a father figure than British women. None of these seem probable.

The lot of a wife in those days was not an enviable one. During the seventeenth century, 25 per cent of women remained unmarried, whether by choice or not is unclear. Under the civil law that applied until the 1850s, her legal status on marriage changed from what was known as a *feme sole* to a *feme covert* and her husband was known as a *baron* or *barone*.[4] The result was that 'by marriage the husband and wife are one person in law, that is, the very being or legal existence of the wife is suspended during the marriage, or at least is incorporated and consolidated into that of the husband.'[5]

The husband also had the right to 'lawful and reasonable correction. How far that extendeth I cannot tell to the woman beaten by her husband, that retaliation [is] left to her to beat him again [back], if she dare.'[6] The earlier *Laws Resolution of Women's Rights* sums up the economic position succinctly: 'That which the husband has is his own; that which the wife has is the husband's.'[7]

Women were also forbidden to make contracts or even draw up a will without the consent of their husbands. Even Blackstone, in a rare moment of what may have been guilt or perhaps a heavy-handed attempt at humour, remarked, 'A married woman perhaps may doubt whether she be either none or no more than half a person. But let her be of good cheer; in criminal and other special cases our law argues them several persons.'[8] In other words, a woman could be condemned for a crime of which she was found guilty but she was not legally entitled to leave her money to her children, nor even to have any redress against her husband. Blackstone's remarks on the status of widowhood are altogether more appropriate. He said:

Why mourn you so, you that be widdows? Consider how long you have been in subjection under the predominance of parents, of your husbands, now you be free in liberty. Maidens and wives vows were all disavowable by their parents or husbands but the vow of a widow no man hath power to disallow of.[9]

What is known today as a 'common law' marriage is of ancient origin, being recognised as valid from medieval times. All that was needed was a declaration by both parties that they chose to consider themselves as married. As *Laws Resolution* explains: 'There needs no stipulation or curious form of contract in wedlock making. It may be made by letters.'[10]

Since no legal costs were involved, such as payments to the clergy, recording the marriage and other expenses, 'marriage by declaration' was a popular choice among the poor. In 1661, following a lawsuit, a judge declared that such marriages were equally as valid as the official church ceremony.[11] In addition there were clandestine marriages. There were a number of places in London where these could be performed, principally St Pancras, St James's in Duke Street and most notoriously, the Fleet prison. There were two different types of clandestine wedding, one where the bride was willing and one where she was not. In the first case, as long as she was at least twelve years old and had given her express consent, the marriage was legal, although the clergyman, bride and groom could be fined if the agreement of the parents had not been secured.[12] In the second, it was not, but such instances were comparatively rare, and almost always involved an heiress carried away by a man in search of her money. It was not unknown under such circumstances for the woman to simply make the best of things and settle down to her

A scene from a typical Fleet marriage.

new life as a wife. If she chose to disavow her forced marriage the penalties were severe. As the law stood, 'all ravishments and wilful taking away and marrying of any maid, widow or damsel against her will or without the assent or agreement of her parents' carried the death penalty.[13] On the other hand, the heiress would be 'ruined' and might well feel unwilling to pass the rest of her life as a social outcast.

Ironically, the poor clandestine marriages, unlike the normal variety, were generally motivated by financial reasons. Widows who did not wish it to be known that they had remarried; servant girls who wanted to keep their married status secret from their employers; apprentices who married in spite of the prohibition on their doing so; pregnant girls marrying anyone simply to give their child a 'name' – these were the type of poor people who married in secret. It was not until 1751 that these marriages were finally declared illegal. The result was the rise of Gretna Green as an option.

Bigamy, of course, was not uncommon, though the penalty for committing it was severe. Punishments up to and including death could be imposed on a bigamist. All the same, particularly in the case of marriages by declaration or clandestine weddings, it was probably more common than it is today. The difficulties of keeping, much less checking records, were far greater than in modern times.

Divorce, of course, was impossible to obtain. The only legal means of becoming divorced was to apply for an Act of Parliament to dissolve the union. Such an action was, of course, entirely out of the question for the poor. The result was that unhappy couples separated, or one partner deserted the other. In some cases new and technically bigamous unions were entered into.

It is difficult to assess the extent of adultery within marriage, but scandals among the aristocracy would occasionally surface. The eighteenth and early nineteenth centuries saw the rampant promiscuity of the Restoration years replaced by a growing tendency to frequent prostitutes or take a single mistress rather than maintain a whole stable of concubines. Among the poor it is much harder to form an assessment. Certainly there were cases where adultery led directly to crime, generally assault or murder, and thereby came to the notice of the court. The 'hidden' level of adultery within the rookery population remains unknown.

The London poor had the same feelings as anyone else. They were equally capable of love, of jealousy and infidelity. The bearing of illegitimate children was more common in London than other parts of the country but there were fewer stigmas attached to illegitimacy than in the countryside. To judge from the statistics the overwhelming majority of children, even among the London poor, were born to wedded parents. Where adultery occurred it seems generally to have been either as the result of a drunken 'fling' or else to have arisen out of genuine love for another man or woman.

Prostitution, of course, flourished in the rookery areas. Although it had been known in London throughout medieval times, the beginnings of what is now referred to as 'the sex industry' date from the 1660s. By 1709 there were enough brothels in London for Ned Ward to compile a guide to them.[14] Some of the best-known women became rich and famous, or at least notorious. Brothel-keeping was a very profitable occupation and one of the few ways in which a woman could make a great deal of money in those days. On the other hand, the penalties were severe. With fines generally not sufficient to deter the habitual madam, the pillory became increasingly used as a punishment for this type of offence. At least one woman who kept a brothel died as a result of her punishment.

Homosexuality was, of course, illegal in those days, and in theory, a crime punishable by death, although the capital sentence was rarely carried out for the offence. A more common punishment was the pillory, although this too, given the unpopularity of homosexuality among the London working classes at that time, was sometimes a death sentence or at least the certainty of permanent injury. One man was whipped by an angry coachman even before he arrived at the pillory to endure further suffering. In spite of the penalties, gay brothels flourished. The most notorious was run by Margaret Clap, who was sentenced to the pillory for allowing her premises to be used for that purpose.[15] Brothels of all kinds, gay and straight, were one of the easiest ways to earn large amounts of money in eighteenth- and nineteenth-century London, and no matter what the penalties, people seemed willing to take the risk.

Prostitution, of course, was an occupation almost entirely motivated by economic factors. Whenever they could make a living without resorting to it, women in the seventeenth, eighteenth and nineteenth centuries invariably chose not to follow that profession. The majority of prostitutes did not become wealthy out of their activities and the dangers of unwanted pregnancies and, still worse, sexually transmitted diseases, were a constant occupational hazard. The first widespread use of contraception began at this period. Boswell described in his diary how he 'enjoyed' a girl 'in armour' and how reluctant he was to have unprotected sex with prostitutes.[16]

During the Victorian era, conditions worsened for prostitutes, as they did for almost everyone on subsistence incomes. The transactions were between men with money and desperate women, ready even to sell their daughters to a stranger in order to live. Dostoyevsky, who visited London in the early 1860s, was appalled, particularly by the horrific level of child prostitution.[17]

Mercifully, the majority of women who lived in the rookeries did not resort to prostitution to support themselves. Prostitution was always the last resort for poor females and every other type of legitimate and criminal enterprise would be tried before the road of 'walking the streets' was embarked upon. Almost everyone who commented on the Victorian prostitutes from the rookeries noticed how thin, starved, miserable and desperate they appeared.

In the eighteenth century such remarks were only made occasionally. Under the Victorians they were almost invariable.

The status of women, in spite of the laws, was relatively higher in the seventeenth and eighteenth centuries. Women's technical inferiority was not generally reflected in the real world. Scandals among the aristocracy, including a notorious trial for bigamy, may have fascinated the London poor in the same way that people read accounts of the lifestyle of celebrities but had no impact on their own behaviour. In the lives of ordinary people, female labour was necessary. For the numerous small business people and even street sellers, the wife's contribution was often not simply crucial but even more important than the husband's. Even the wealthy had a more relaxed attitude to infidelity. Both men and women who strayed were generally forgiven by their partners.

With the growth of hypocrisy in the 1830s, perhaps largely as a reaction against the supposedly licentious period that preceded it, the values of the middle class began to predominate. It would probably be more accurate to say a section of the middle classes, because there were always men and women from that social group who not only rejected the cant that passed for morality among the Victorians but also actively challenged it. Florence Nightingale, for example, not only improved the standard of nursing for soldiers at war, but was a remarkably radical, if cautious, feminist. Family life among the middle classes was portrayed as a domestic idyll, with a non-working wife waiting eagerly for her husband to return.

Family life was of course quite different for the dwellers in the rookeries. The Victorian fantasy of 'the Angel in the House' would have made them laugh out loud. Men, women and children knew that they had to work as hard as possible, for as many hours as possible, and as young as possible. Until the Victorians widened the class system, they had an outside chance of escape and discovering a comfortable life. Once the Whigs had imposed their vision of Britain upon the people, there was not the slightest chance of ever escaping the poverty in which they lived.

Most families in the rookeries lived together, usually in one room or even part of a room. The husband, wife and children would all be expected to contribute their labour and share their money in a common 'kitty'. There was, in general, affection between husband and wife and the other family members, even though their first priority was survival. During the seventeenth, eighteenth and early nineteenth centuries, rookery dwellers loved to dress in the height of fashion and copy the styles of the wealthy, often wearing 'cast-offs' bought from street traders or servant girls. Under the Victorians this too came to an end. A large market for second-hand clothes continued but they were certainly not of sufficient quality to enable the wearer to strut around like lords or ladies.

Drinking became a serious problem under the Victorians for the first time since the 'gin craze'. Observers noticed, with some surprise, that women drank more than the menfolk. This certainly did not help to make family life pleasant or easy, but then the lives of the men and women themselves were a constant struggle for survival through drudgery.

Perhaps the most unfair piece of legislation affecting women was the 1857 Matrimonial Causes Act, which for the first time made it possible for divorces to be granted without the passing of a special Act of Parliament. Under the 1857 Act, a husband could divorce his wife on the grounds of her adultery, but she was not permitted to divorce him on the same grounds. A wife wishing to divorce her husband had to show, not only that he was guilty of adultery, but that he had also treated her cruelly. Apart from the stigma of publicly raising such matters, they were also difficult to prove.

Even in the event of a successful divorce, a wife, even if she had been able to show that her husband was cruel and unfaithful, would usually have to give up the custody of any children of the marriage to her husband. She did not even enjoy any rights of access to them, it being entirely at her ex-husband's discretion where, when, how often and even *if* she could ever see them at all. However, with all its faults, and it was undoubtedly unfair to women, it did at least, for the first time in English legal history, make it *possible* for women to be awarded the custody of their children.

The status of women incensed Florence Nightingale so much that she remarked acidly, in a work that she was unfortunately persuaded not to publish during her lifetime:

Women are never supposed to have any occupation of sufficient importance not to be interrupted, except 'suckling their fools'; and women themselves have accepted this, have written books to support it, and have trained themselves so as to consider whatever they do as not of such value to the world as others, but that they can throw it up at the first 'claim of social life'. They have accustomed themselves to consider intellectual occupation as a merely selfish amusement, which it is their 'duty' to give up for every trifler more selfish than themselves.

Women never have an half-hour in all their lives (except before and after anybody is up in the house) that they can call their own, without fear of offending or of hurting someone. Why do people sit up late, or, more rarely, get up so early? Not because the day is not long enough, but because they have 'no time in the day to themselves'. The family? It is too narrow a field for the development of an immortal spirit, be that spirit male or female. The family uses people, not for what they are, not for what they are intended to be, but for what it wants for – its own uses. It thinks of them not as what God has made them, but as the something which it has arranged that they shall be. This system dooms some minds to incurable infancy, others to silent misery.[18]

Admittedly, Nightingale was a middle-class woman, chafing at the restraints imposed upon her by the society in which she moved, but she was keenly aware of the poverty of working-class women, and campaigned vigorously for the unpopular cause of alleviating their condition throughout her life. It is not generally realised quite how radical Nightingale's views actually were, not least because she was cautious about expressing them. She supported the campaign for women's suffrage, for instance, but refused to 'go public' with her views or to make speeches or to write on behalf of a cause with which she was in total agreement.

One example of the different way in which even enlightened middle-class women like Nightingale and the women of the rookeries viewed marriage is given in the account by Emmeline Pethick-Lawrence of her activities as a social worker in the East End during the 1890s:

> Drunkenness was extremely common . . . It seemed for many the only refuge from depression and misery. The effect of drunkenness upon the ordinary relationship of husband and wife, parents and children, was disastrous.
>
> There was a woman whose husband used to knock her about badly when in drink. But he went to the Mission Hall in the district, was converted and signed the pledge. All went well for some time until she again turned up with several bruises.
>
> 'Oh, Mrs. Smith, has your husband taken to drink again?' She replied: 'Oh, no, that was another lady what done that! Since my husband went to the Mission Hall, he ain't like a husband at all – he is more like a friend!'
>
> There was a particular point of view with regard to wife-beating. A friend of mine was once walking along the street and she passed a woman with a black eye. At the same time two other women passed, and one of them remarked: 'Well, all I can say is, she is a lucky woman to have a husband to take that trouble with her.' Another woman who had gone through a similar experience remarked: 'Well, it ain't pleasant to be knocked about, but the making-up is lovely.'[19]

Although this attitude, together with a certain amount of 'well, she probably deserved it', has always existed among women, it was under the Victorians that it became almost a dogma. An important study of the situation of women who were victims of domestic violence or desertion by their husbands has shown beyond any reasonable doubt that English society before the early nineteenth century was far more inclined to be sympathetic towards women than has often falsely been claimed. In a massive and scholarly work, Joanne Bailey has studied court records, newspaper accounts and other primary sources to show that in reality, the lot of women was far less harsh than it became later.[20] Alice Clark and Margaret Hunt also reach strikingly different conclusions in their respective analyses of domestic violence in the eighteenth and nineteenth centuries.[21]

The high point of the absurd ideas concerning the place of women in the family was between about 1835 and 1870. From that point onwards, reformers began to make inroads. An important landmark was the passing of the Married Women's Property Acts, the first of which became law in 1870. It was followed by further Acts in 1874 and 1882, the last of which at last gave married women reasonable control over their own property and assets.

The question of property and assets, of course, made little or no difference to the females who toiled and struggled in the London rookeries. To them, whatever their own political views, life itself was the best they could hope for. If they made it through to another day, and preferably with enough to eat and drink, that was enough for them. The struggles of these proto-feminist campaigners were curiously remote from their own lives. They hoped their husband would find work, bring in enough money to maintain them, and of course knew that they too had to juggle the business of earning a living with rearing children. Long before the middle-class females decided that they wanted to 'have it all,' working-class women in the rookeries of London would have given almost anything *not* to be forced into employment that bordered on slavery. The idea that a woman could live on her husband's wage alone would have seemed like a fantasy to them.

Family life for the London poor deteriorated rapidly after 1834. With the drastic curtailment of 'outdoor relief', women could no longer rely on the parish to support themselves and their children if times were hard. The authorities offered them a choice of four brutal options – work at whatever wages they could get; the slavery of the workhouse; prostitution; or crime. Begging on the streets reached levels not seen since the 1540s. The only response of the authorities was to punish those found 'guilty' of the crime. If a woman chose the workhouse option, the institution set out, almost certainly deliberately, to destroy her family. She was forbidden to live with her husband, her children were often taken away from her, and her life of drudgery became even worse as she was forced into pointless work to satisfy the absurd dogmas of *laisser-faire*. Throughout the century the workhouse was *always*, and quite understandably, the *last* resort of any rookery dweller. Even a prison sentence was not served under such harsh conditions.

The effect of poverty on the break-up of the family in Victorian times can hardly be overstated. Levels of separation remained low compared with those in Europe, France seeing a particularly dramatic rise in marital breakdowns over the twenty years from 1850 to 1870. Even so, the figures still rose inexorably.

Knowing from bitter experience that there was security in numbers, the families who lived in the rookeries tried to stay together under the most trying of circumstances. To live as a member of a family which was struggling was still preferable to trying to 'make it' as a single woman. In the eighteenth century, Blackstone had commented that a widow's lot was a fortunate one. That comment, however ill-informed and smug, could certainly not have been made under the Victorians. Widowhood in Victorian times meant abject poverty and the loss of all kinds of informal support systems from the family and the extended social groupings that characterised the dwellers in the rookeries. The family structure, and the motivations of its members, changed radically under the Victorians. The old gaiety was gone and a grim determination to survive at all costs replaced it. A sense of injustice at their treatment also arose and the class divisions became more marked. The dwellers in the rookeries were becoming ripe for revolution. But for the First World War they might well have revolted. Even the reforms of the Asquith government which laid the foundations of the welfare state were not enough to keep their anger at bay. By 1914, even though most of the rookery dwellers had been dispersed to the London suburbs, their fury had erupted into sustained political action. Their resentment helped to build a new vision of society in Britain. The despised and downtrodden rookery residents were the 'shock troops' of the new political radicalism in Britain. Had it not been for the assassination of Franz Ferdinand in Sarajevo in 1914, they would have led a British revolution.

Notes

1   A study of parish registers from about 1400 onwards points clearly to the prevalence of all these factors.
2   Anonymous, *The Laws Resolution of Women's Rights*, 1632.
3   Adolphe Bertillon, 'Mariage', in *Dictionnaire encyclopédique des sciences médicales*, 1859.
4   Blackstone, *Commentaries*, 1776.
5   Ibid.
6   Ibid.
7   *Laws Resolution of Women's Rights*.
8   Blackstone, op. cit.
9   Ibid.
10   *Laws Resolution of Women's Rights*
11   Fox, George, *Journal*.
12   *Calendar of State Papers Domestic*, 1668.
13   Ibid., 1661.
14   Ned Ward, *The London Spy*, 1709.
15   *Old Bailey*, 11 July 1726, Reference t17260711-54.
16   Boswell, *London Journal*.
17   Fyodor Dostoyevsky, *Winter Notes on Summer Impressions*, 1862.
18   Florence Nightingale, *Cassandra*, 1852.
19   Emmeline Pethick-Lawrence, *My Part in a Changing World*, Hyperion, 1976.
20   Joanne Bailey, *Unquiet Lives: Marriage and Marriage Breakdown in England, 1660–1800*, CUP, 2003.
21   Alice Clark, 'Humanity or justice? Wifebeating and the law in the eighteenth and nineteenth centuries', in C. Smart (ed.), *Regulating womanhood: historical essays on marriage, motherhood and sexuality*, 1992.
     Margaret Hunt, 'Wife-beating, domesticity and women's independence in eighteenth-century London', *Gender and History*, 4, 1992.

5

ENTERTAINMENT

The life of dwellers in the rookeries was not all work and struggle. They loved to relax when they could and sport was one of their favourite activities. Both as players and spectators they enjoyed a variety of games, and most are still popular today. One of the most favoured sports was cricket. The precise origins of the game remain uncertain but some form of it was certainly played at least as far back as the thirteenth century, in its earliest form being known as 'creag'. It was generally played against a tree with an improvised wooden bat which could be either similar to the modern bat but without the bevelling, or with an instrument more akin to the type of bat used in rounders, softball or baseball.

The earliest recorded match took place in 1550, by which time creag had developed into a game essentially similar to the modern sport. It was known as cricket, creckett or crickett and was primarily popular in London, Middlesex, Surrey, Kent and Hampshire. By the eighteenth century it had become popular throughout the south and had also spread to Nottinghamshire, Yorkshire and Lancashire.

Matches attracted huge crowds of spectators and there was heavy drinking, gambling and often rowdiness among the spectators. Even at the most prestigious games crowd disorder was extremely common. This often resulted in such violence that the militia had to be called in to disperse the unruly spectators. On one occasion the Prince Regent had to flee for his life from a hostile and drunken crowd in London.

Women as well as men played the game. During the eighteenth century it was very common for the winning team to be paid in ale or lace gloves rather than money. Crowds of over 2,000 spectators eagerly watched and betted on the results of the games. Pitch invasions were anything but rare, especially in the more working-class areas.

A popular attraction was what might be called 'novelty' matches, where teams of players with one arm took on teams with one-legged players, men played women, married women contested with single females, or left-handers battled right-handers. In London the game was particularly popular in the East End and the Southwark area. One of the most entertaining, and certainly most financially remunerative cricket matches played during the early nineteenth century, took place in Dalston in 1811. It was the first official women's county cricket match and Surrey and Hampshire were the teams taking part. Two noblemen put up a prize of 1,000 guineas and the players' ages ranged from girls of fourteen to women in their sixties. The prize money must have allowed them all to live in comfort for the rest of their lives. Women players were highly regarded and judged on ability rather than their sex. It was in fact a female cricketer, Christina Willes, who pioneered a fundamental change in the game, from underarm to overarm bowling, in the 1830s. Her brother copied her action and it was eventually to become the normal form of bowling in the game.

Allen Guttmann, in *Sports Spectators*, notes that there were frequent disorders at eighteenth-century matches,[1] while John Ford goes somewhat further in arguing that 'when there was not some sort of commotion it seemed to be thought unusual.'[2]

During the eighteenth century, cricket matches were among the largest and most popular of all sporting events. The opportunities for gambling led to heated passions, particularly in 'local derby' games. It was not at all uncommon for matches to be fixed and players to take bribes to 'throw' a match. A match between the parish of Slindon in Surrey and a London XI played in 1742 was publicised in the press as 'the greatest match at cricket that has been played for many years' and a call for spectators to remain calm and orderly was made. Apparently there was heavy betting on a particular Sussex player to score exactly 40 runs.[3]

Cricket matches were so popular that crowds of several thousand turned up to watch. In 1751 a game at London's Artillery Ground attracted no fewer than 10,000 spectators. Brookes estimates that this constituted around 1 in 50 of the entire population of London at the time.[4]

In 1693 Thomas Reynolds, Henry Gunter and a woman known as Elenor Lansford were fined for their part in riot and battery. The three convicted felons sent a petition to the queen seeking remission from their fines on the basis that, they were 'only spectators at a game of crickett'. The clear implication of this appeal was that it was unfair to impose a fine upon them because disorderly behaviour at cricket matches was normal behaviour. It is also interesting in displaying that Lansford, a female, was as active and violent in terms of what would now be termed as hooligan behaviour as her male colleagues. It is curious that this type of hooliganism at sporting events only tended to involve women when a game of cricket was being played. Females did not seem to behave in such an unruly way at football or even boxing matches, for example, where crowd disorder and violent behaviour were almost exclusively confined to the male spectators.[5]

Violence at cricket games, particularly at London's Artillery Ground, continued to cause concern to the authorities throughout the eighteenth century. In 1744, a match between Kent and England at the Artillery Ground nearly had to be abandoned as a result of crowd trouble. In 1747 a match between Charlton and Westdean and Chilgrove was attended by so much rowdiness that it became impossible for the players to continue. In 1750 the Prince of Wales gave a woman whose leg was broken in a crush the sum of 10 guineas as compensation. 1796 even saw a match at Montpelier Gardens between two teams of pensioners deteriorate into an all-out fight with two people being arrested.

Another hazard of cricket matches, an inevitable accompaniment of any event in which large crowds gathered together, was the prevalence of pickpockets and muggers. The practice continued until about the 1820s in spite of numerous arrests and the harsh penalties imposed by the law for the crime.[6]

From the 1740s onwards the authorities became so concerned about the high level of crowd disorder and general criminal activity at cricket matches that they began taking steps to improve the situation. The first step was to hire what would now be called security guards. The earliest example of their employment seems to have been in 1744, when George Smith was hired to control the crowds at the notoriously turbulent Artillery Ground. The same year saw a certain 'Captain Vinegar', accompanied by what are described as bruisers and bulldogs, policing a match at Walworth.

In 1748 the prices at the Artillery Ground were increased to try to keep out the rookery dwellers. They loved their cricket and no doubt also the mayhem that seemed to be a normal accompaniment of their day's entertainment. They continued coming in large numbers in spite of the price increases and their behaviour continued to be as rowdy as ever. If anything, the price rises actually led to an increase in the 'patronage' of the sport by pickpockets.

In 1764 the magistrates of Westminster seriously considered banning cricket altogether, at least from the London area, so frequent had violence and disorder among the crowds become. They decided against it, probably wisely, since such a ban would only have led to more rioting among the London poor. 1777 saw yet another price rise at the notorious Artillery Fields ground 'to prevent the players being interrupted'. In spite of this further increase, the crowds continued to pour into the ground and the measure also had absolutely no effect on the level or frequency of disorder, violence and crime at cricket matches.

1826, for instance, saw Cooper 'and two principal officers of Queen-square' hired to preserve order at the match between the Westminster Town Boys and Westminster King's Scholars. As late as 1864, the level of crowd trouble at cricket matches was sufficiently high for the MCC to hire off-duty police officers to maintain order. A match at Lord's in 1866 led to such a furious uproar over a disputed boundary that play had to be abandoned for the day and the Prince of Wales, who had been watching the game, was forced to flee for his own safety.

The latter part of the nineteenth century saw the gradual decline of cricket hooliganism. In part this was a direct result of the process of the destruction of the rookeries and the dispersion of their inhabitants to other parts of London, in part to the rising popularity of organised football and thirdly in part simply to a change in attitudes among the working classes. Most of all, however, it was the introduction of formal boundaries between players and spectators that caused the decline of pitch invasions and other rowdy behaviour. A purely technical development in the game led to the end of what had been 150 years of rowdiness and criminal behaviour at cricket matches, particularly in London, where the rookery dwellers became involved in crowd trouble on the slightest pretext.

An early attempt at creating some kind of boundary between the players and spectators was tried in 1744 by Captain Vinegar. His 'bruisers and dogs' were employed to 'make the ring', a phrase borrowed from prizefighting, with the intention of separating the players and spectators and thereby reducing the incidence of crowd trouble.[7] The innovation does not seem to have been generally imitated. Cricket remained the most popular sport in London until about the late 1890s, when it was overtaken by football. Its association with rowdiness and hooliganism died out comparatively recently, during the late nineteenth century.

Another sport which often attracted large crowds was boxing. Prizefighting, and indeed *any* form of fighting, seemed to be tremendously popular, not simply with the rookery dwellers but with the British in general. In 1602 Clerkenwell entertained the crowds with wrestling matches, female fencers and acrobats. In 1697, a French visitor by the name of Mission declared that 'anything that looks like fighting is delicious to an Englishman.' A German visitor to London in 1710, Zacharias von Uffenbach, made the same observation, adding that the watching crowd encouraged the mayhem by throwing money at the fighters.

James Figg was not only one of the leading prizefighters of his day but also the principal promoter of the sport. He presented fights on a regular basis, involving women as well as men, though predominantly male fighters. Prizefights were one of the most popular sporting events of the day. As with cricket, heavy betting took place on the results. Naturally bouts were not

Jem Mace, champion prizefighter.

always entirely 'straight', bribes to the various fighters to 'throw' the match being frequently offered. 1722 saw one of the most notorious fights of the eighteenth century, during which a woman from Clerkenwell named Elizabeth Wilkinson challenged another female, Hannah Hyfield from Newgate Market, to fight her in public for a prize of 3 guineas. Each woman had to punch the other in the face while holding half a crown in each fist. The first woman to drop a coin would be adjudged the loser of the fight. John Trenchard's *London Journal* claims that Wilkinson and Hyfield 'maintained the Battle with great Valour for a long Time, to the no small Satisfaction of the Spectators.' Apparently this was a 'grudge match' between the women, although how much of this claim was simply hype by the promoter is uncertain.

In August 1725 the first recorded instance of a 'mixed' match took place, which involved Figg and a woman called Long Meg of Westminster fighting Ned Sutton and an unknown woman. The prize was £40 and Figg and Long Meg emerged victorious. In the same year Figg also put on a fencing match between an English and Irish woman at Marylebone Gardens, which resulted in an English victory.

In 1768, two women prizefighters contested at the London Spa, Clerkenwell, for a dress with the value of half a crown. On the same bill two women fought against two men for a guinea each. The next notable contest between two women took place in 1822 when Martha Flaherty fought Peg Carey for a purse of £18. The fight was staged at 5.30 a.m., and Flaherty won, in spite of her unorthodox training methods, which by all accounts consisted largely of drinking a pint of gin before the bout. The prize money was generous, being over a year's wages at the time.

The rules of prizefighting by this time were still not fully fixed, especially where contests between women were involved. Jackets, petticoats and 'Holland drawers' were the normal attire for female fighters, and wrestling, kneeing and kicking were allowed as well as punching.

James Figg himself became the first man to be recognised as heavyweight champion of the world in 1719. He continued to dominate the sport until 1734. The next major force in the sport was James Broughton, the leading prizefighter of his generation, who was so concerned at the frequent injuries and even occasional deaths caused by the sport that in 1743 he drew up the first set of laws, known as the London Prize Ring Rules, to govern 'pugilism', as it became known.

Broughton's rules governed boxing for the next hundred years, and represented a genuine and successful attempt to make the sport safer. The most important aspects of them were outlawing hitting an opponent when he was 'down', making the use of wrestling holds or clinching the opponent illegal, declaring pulling the opponent's hair a foul move, and restricting the areas of the body that could be regarded as legitimate targets of punches. The unpleasant practice known as 'fish-hooking', which involved deliberately inserting the fingers into the opponent's mouth and pulling, was also outlawed. From 1743 onwards, the majority of prizefights were conducted under Broughton's new rules, although matches that were far less well regulated continued and attracted large crowds. Fairground fights were still operating under pre-Broughton conditions until the early part of the nineteenth century.

Although each round still ended with a knockdown, a fighter would be given thirty seconds to 'come up to scratch', a line scratched in the sand or dirt which was the equivalent of the modern 'corner' in boxing. It was also no longer required for a fight to go to a 'finish', and a fight could be stopped if one opponent was taking too much punishment or was simply unable

Two pugilists in typical eighteenth-century garb.

to continue. The London Prize Rules allowed a fighter to drop on one knee and take a mandatory 30-second count whenever he wished. In a modern boxing match, such an action would lead to immediate disqualification.

Broughton also invented boxing gloves, which he called 'mufflers', and gave exhibition fights using the new implements, which he clearly felt represented the future of the game. His rules undoubtedly humanised prizefighting, and laid the foundations of the modern sport of boxing. The Queensberry Rules that govern the sport now are, in essence, simply an improved version of those devised by Broughton in 1743.

As with cricket, the frequency of betting on boxing matches led to bribery of boxers and promoters and frequent claims that fights were 'fixed' to protect the financial interests of wealthy backers or those who had made large bets. There is little doubt that abuses of this kind went on. However, the top prizefighters of the time, like Figg, Broughton and the nineteenth-century bare-knuckle boxers Jem Mace (who gave his name to the Cockney rhyming slang for 'face') and Tom Cribb seem on the whole to have been genuinely the best boxers of their generation.

Another popular sport in the eighteenth century was stickfighting. This sport was either a variant of fencing using wooden staves, when it was known as singlestick, or a descendant of the medieval quarterstaff play. This involved two men, or more rarely women, setting about each other with sticks and trying to beat the other into submission. The crowd became particularly enthusiastic whenever a blow from a stick drew blood. Although popular, it never achieved the same degree of crowd enthusiasm as cricket or boxing. It died out towards the end of the eighteenth century as a popular amusement, although the 'singlestick' form of the sport was taken up by the middle classes in the Victorian period as an amusement and physical exercise.

Bloodsports were extremely popular with the people of the rookeries, especially bear-baiting, humans fighting animals (generally dogs or bears) and cock-fighting. These 'sports' continued well into the nineteenth century, though bear-baiting was in decline during the later part of the eighteenth century. Once again heavy betting took place and frequent disorder resulted. Most of the matches involving humans fighting animals were generally rigged, although accidents did happen in which the humans were savaged, especially when bears were involved. It was also not unknown for bears to escape from their posts and attack passers-by.

Cock-fighting was a particular favourite of the Prince Regent, who came to the rookery areas frequently to watch two 'contestants' try to kill each other. Again, it was claimed that many matches were rigged, although it is more difficult to see how the result of a contest between two birds could be staged than it is to see how humans could be persuaded to cheat. As public sentiment began to change, these sports fell out of fashion and eventually both were declared illegal.

Entertainment on a lighter note was provided by the numerous 'fairs' in London. The City of London began holding a fair every September, the official title of which was Our Lady Fair. Unofficially, it became known as the Southwark Fair, since it was located in the notorious rookery of Southwark. Entertainment on offer at the fair included plays, acrobatic performances, prizefighting and 'freak shows', where dwarves, giants (including, it is alleged, women over 8ft tall), three-breasted women and other oddities of nature were displayed for the amusement of the crowd. However, in 1763, the level of drunkenness, prostitution, crime and violence at the Southwark Fair finally became unacceptable to the authorities and the fair was closed down. An engraving of it by William Hogarth in 1733 still survives.

Other important fairs in the rookeries were Bartholomew Fair and the May Fair. May fairs were notorious for drunkenness and sexual promiscuity but were also venues that provided a variety of entertainment. Freak shows such as 'bearded ladies' and 'seven-legged horses' were particularly popular. Singing, dancing, acrobatic acts, prizefighting displays and theatrical performances, generally on a much less sophisticated level than those in the West End, were also provided, although performances of Shakespeare's plays were not uncommon. Perhaps the most unusual example of theatrical entertainments provided at fairs was the use of horses to re-enact battles or even scenes and incidents of rural life.

It was the coming of the railways that destroyed the English fairs. Once it became possible for people to travel, they lost interest in their own local amusements and festivals, preferring to go further afield in search of entertainment. The railways played a leading role in the demolition of the rookeries throughout the nineteenth century and their part in the destruction of popular culture is another example of how technological progress does not always improve every aspect of life.

Theatre in the eighteenth and early nineteenth century was a very different experience from that of modern audiences. Apart from the fact that the London poor were habitual playgoers, especially at the Drury Lane Theatre, where the audience would often largely consist of residents of the St Giles and Clare Market rookeries, a whole range of popular entertainment took place on the London streets. Particularly popular with the crowds were Punch and Judy shows, pantomimes, mime shows, acrobatics, singers, ballad mongers and clowns. Acts involving animals that could perform tricks were also much in demand. Astley's Amphitheatre gave displays of horsemanship and other animal acts which laid the foundations of both modern show-jumping and of the circus.

In 1710, the enterprising Irish puppeteer Martin Powell set up the first puppet theatre in St Martin's Lane, the heart of the central London rookery.

His show proved so popular that other entrepreneurs soon followed his example. Powell's theatre, even though the 'actors' were only puppets, included proper scenery, footlights and backcloths. His acts also performed in a Covent Garden tavern and eventually all over the country. Powell's marionettes satirised the politicians and 'celebrities' of the day, as well as making fun of popular fashions, in particular Italian opera, which had been introduced to Britain at about that time. The two other principal puppet theatres in London were Punch's Theatre in James Street and the Patagonian Theatre in Exeter Change. Powell and his imitators dominated the London puppet scene until 1770. Then a troupe of *fantoccini*, or Italian marionettes, brought a new style of puppet theatre to London. The Italians added to the stock marionette tradition by extensive use of special effects. They also presented shows in the style of the Italian *Commedia dell'Arte*. Those featuring Harlequin and Columbine became particular favourites, while imitations of Italian comic operas were also popular with the crowds. There is no doubt that these shows were much more sophisticated than those put on by Powell and his imitators, and by 1777 there were four puppet companies in the West End, as well as yet another innovation in the art, an oriental-style shadow theatre show known as *Ombres Chinoises* or Chinese Shadows.

Philip Astley was the founder of the famous and influential Amphitheatre, and he managed a 'shadow play' show, as they were also known, for a while. He put on a display of shadow theatre in a show at Piccadilly. Before long rival theatres and showmen were producing increasingly elaborate and spectacular events.

By the end of the eighteenth century the cost of putting on a puppet show was too expensive for the majority of operators. Puppet shows began to scale down the extent and sophistication of their productions, a trend first begun at the large London fairs. Mr Punch, one of the most

Horseback acrobatics
– a scene often
encountered in Astley's
Amphitheatre.

A female knife-juggler, just one of the entertainers on show.

popular of all the 'marionette' characters, became a simple gloved puppet rather than the full-blown theatrical version he had been previously.

Philip Astley was a cavalry Sergeant-Major in the 15th Light Dragoons. On leaving the army he began his career as an equestrian showman, performing various tricks with horses at the pleasure gardens in London, particularly Vauxhall and Ranelagh. Deciding that he preferred to start his own show rather than work for other people, in 1768 he set up his own riding school at Lambeth near Westminster Bridge. In the morning he taught his pupils the art of horsemanship; in the afternoon and evenings, he displayed his repertoire of equestrian tricks in a 'ring'. He chose the ring shape because riding in tight circles aided the creation of centrifugal forces that made it easier to perform his tricks with the horses, particularly those in which he stood on the animal's back. His first ring was 64ft in diameter but he reduced its size to 42ft, still the standard dimensions for circus rings.

Although Astley's displays of horsemanship were popular, they did not bring in the large crowds he had hoped for. He began to add other acts to his show, beginning with a clown (known as Mr Merryman), jugglers, acrobats and the highly popular tightrope walkers. Astley enclosed his ring, adding seating and a roof, which became the ancestor of the modern circus 'Big Top'. He soon realised the importance of advertising and publicised his 'Amphitheatre Riding Ring' with great success. He took his show to Paris in 1772 and made a number of subsequent visits to Europe, establishing the circus as a truly world phenomenon. It was Astley who, almost by accident, invented the circus in the London rookeries.[8]

Another aspect of London life at this time which was enormously popular with all classes of society was the pleasure gardens. They were open to the public at very reasonable admission charges. The two main pleasure gardens in London were at Vauxhall and Ranelagh. In the gardens, illuminated fountains cascaded, orchestras played a variety of music as entertainment, the avenues in the gardens were decorated with lights of various colours, and firework displays entertained the crowds. Among the most popular musical contributions were songs and concertos from Haydn and Handel. The gardens were also venues for drinking the fashionable beverage of tea and generally provided an attractive social ambiance.

Tea gardens were less ostentatious versions of a similar model. They offered tea either in a 'tearoom' or in the gardens outside. These gardens were more popular with the middle classes than the larger venues of Vauxhall and Ranelagh and Sunday was the normal time to visit the tea gardens. In spite of these promising beginnings, the pleasure gardens soon became venues that attracted prostitutes and other criminal elements, particularly pickpockets. Vauxhall and Ranelagh quickly became dangerous and fell out of favour, closing altogether after a comparatively short period as popular entertainment venues. During the late eighteenth and early nineteenth century, Vauxhall Gardens became a popular venue for watching balloon ascents. Thousands of spectators gathered to watch 'aeronauts' flying high above them in hot-air balloons. An account from 1831 gives a flavour of the proceedings:

There was a numerous assemblage of company on Monday night, to view the novelties and splendours announced in honour of the birthday of the Queen. Particular interest appeared to attend the ascent of Messrs. Green in the same balloon in which he made his aerial excursion on the occasion of the opening of London Bridge. The ascent, which took place a little before ten, was extremely well managed; the balloon appeared to great advantage, and rose magnificently, the aeronaut taking with him a strong light, by means of which his course was perceived not only from the Gardens, but from all parts of the town, for more than half an hour. After extinguishing the light, Mr. Green threw out at intervals several red lights, the descent of which had a novel and very pleasing effect. In the illuminations no expense was spared; the devices in honour of the occasion were tasteful and splendid. The fireworks and the illuminated representation of London Bridge, excited general admiration; indeed, nothing could be more perfect than the general entertainment. The aeronauts after being in the air an hour and a half, and having twice crossed the Thames, descended about half-past 11 o'clock, in a field belonging to a lady named Fitch, at Parson's Green, Fulham, where they received every necessary assistance, and at half-past two in the morning they arrived at Vauxhall gardens, and were warmly cheered by the company.[9]

Balloon exhibitions were one of the most spectacular amusements available to the people of the rookeries. They loved watching the balloon ascending and hovering above them and recognised the bravery of the people inside them. A Mrs Graham acquired instant celebrity status by becoming the first woman to ascend in a balloon, choosing Vauxhall Gardens as the venue for her display.

Ranelagh Gardens north of the Thames were equally famous and popular. They were created in the large grounds of a house belonging to Lord Ranelagh. Standing on the east side of Chelsea Hospital, they were more popular than Vauxhall with the fashionable of London. On the other hand, their position also meant that they were frequented by the inhabitants of some of the worst rookeries of London – Clare Market, St Giles, Pye Street and St Margaret's. One advantage that Ranelagh had over Vauxhall was that its activities were not disrupted by poor weather. Perhaps its most striking feature was a large Rotunda, which enabled spectators to shelter from the rain and continue to enjoy whatever entertainment was provided irrespective of the cold or wet weather. The Rotunda was much admired, being not only extremely large but also possessing boxes in which the fashionable 'set' could enjoy tea and supper parties. Above the boxes was placed a gallery. In the centre, a raised orchestra extended up to the arched roof, so that the crowds could see and hear all the entertainment. In winter, heating was provided, and a series of brackets, chandeliers and sconces provided lighting for the hours of darkness. The standard of music on offer was excellent, and the popular pastime known as 'masquerades' was one of the principal attractions of Ranelagh Gardens. This involved the wearing of masks and the donning of costumes different from those normally worn by the 'masqueraders', such as noble ladies dressing as milkmaids, men wearing women's clothes and females in male garb, noble lords dressing as their footmen, and similarly untypical behaviour by the wealthy of London.[10]

The fashion for masquerades also appealed to the poor, who always tried to copy the latest fashion in aristocratic society. Even in the rookeries, it was very common indeed for men to wear discarded wigs, which could be bought surprisingly cheaply from street traders. In the same way the men and women of the rookeries liked to dress up in either 'cast-offs' from the wealthy or at least the closest possible approximation to their costume that they could acquire.

Another historian has traced the close and distinct overlapping between the fashion for masquerades and contemporary prostitution in London. Carter drew attention to a large number of prints sold throughout London in the eighteenth century which clearly equate or at least closely relate masquerades to prostitution. One of the most common comparisons made at that time was to suggest both that prostitutes themselves were essentially masquerading and that female masqueraders were at least playing at being prostitutes. The equation of the masquerade with deceit, sexual deviancy and outright prostitution was a very common criticism of it at the time.[11]

Firework displays were also popular attractions at both gardens. Ranelagh was often open until 3 o'clock in the morning, later even than the opening hours of its fierce rival Vauxhall. However, it fell out of favour much sooner than its South London counterpart, being entirely abandoned by the wealthy after 1804. No doubt its proximity to four of the worst rookeries in London was a principal factor in this sudden desertion of what was one of the wonders of the city. The Rotunda, sadly, no longer exists, and one of the great architectural and landscaping features of London fell victim to the vandalism of later ages.

As well as Ranelagh, Chelsea offered three other venues for popular entertainment, Don Saltero's[12], the Old Chelsea Bun House and Cremorne. Cremorne was particularly noted for its firework displays, and indeed its most impressive show was a portrayal of the bombardment of Gibraltar including the firing of rockets on to the gardens from steamboats located on the Thames to simulate gunfire and cannon.

Another popular form of street entertainment was singing, particularly of ballads. These works, some of the earliest surviving examples of folk music, were hugely popular. As well as listening to their hawkers performing the songs, the books in which the words and music were written also sold in huge numbers. The myth of illiteracy is flatly contradicted by a whole range of evidence, not least the vast sales of chapbooks and ballad-sheets. They sold, not to the wealthy, but to ordinary men and women in London, for the most part poor, and living in the rookeries.[13]

Dancing in a variety of forms was also popular with the people. They loved to dance themselves and enjoyed displays of dancing by professionals in a variety of styles. During the eighteenth century, choreographers came to prominence and began using dance to tell a kind of story. As early as 1717 John Weaver, an English ballet master, staged a show known as *The Loves of Mars and Venus* at the Drury Lane Theatre. Weaver was a strikingly innovative choreographer and it would not be too much to claim him as the true founder of ballet. Before his time dance shows were always accompanied by speech to tell the story. Weaver instead used a mixture of mime and dancing to progress the narrative and tried to involve the audience emotionally in the progress of the ballet.

The spectators thrilled to the dazzling displays of dance, particularly a father and son act, Gaeton and Auguste Vestris. Most ballerinas wore high-heeled shoes and long skirts, which restricted their movements. Men wore an early ancestor of the tutu, known as a tonnelet. Costumes for both sexes were much larger than in modern ballet. The result was that male and female dancers had to perform alongside each other rather than facing. The greater freedom of movement afforded by their costumes meant that men tended to perform the more spectacular moves in ballet and the audiences came to watch the male stars rather than the ballerinas. In spite of this, two female dancers, Hester Booth and Nancy Dawson, were great favourites with theatregoers.[14]

Nancy was a Clare Market girl herself and one of the most remarkable 'characters' produced by the rookeries. She was born and raised in the poverty of a cellar dwelling in Drury Lane. At the age of sixteen she joined Griffin's troupe and danced at Sadler's Wells. Before long she was a great favourite with the crowds, although it was surprisingly late in her career that she found fame. In 1759, in a production of Gay's *Beggar's Opera*, the man who danced the hornpipe became ill, and Nancy was put on instead. She not only became the most popular dancer in town but even had a nursery rhyme written about her, 'Here We Go Round the Mulberry Bush', as well as a song, enormously successful in its time, called 'The Ballad of Nancy Dawson', written in 1759 by George Stevens. The first two verses are as follows:

> Of all the girls in our town
> The black, the fair, the red, the brown,
> That dance and prance it up and down
> There's none like Nancy Dawson.
>
> Her easy mien, her shape so neat,
> She foots, she trips, she looks so sweet,
> Her ev'ry motion's so complete,
> I'll die for Nancy Dawson.[15]

Even street children put on their own theatrical productions, known as 'penny gaffs', 'low theatres' and 'toy theatres'. Toy theatres were the most sophisticated of these forms of entertainment, involving characters who were cut out and pasted on cardboard, then being moved about the stage. These too drew crowds and enabled the children of the rookeries to earn a little extra money to keep themselves alive.

Another popular diversion was playing the lottery. This was introduced to England in 1567 by Queen Elizabeth I, when 'a very rich lottery general of

The children of the poor made their own entertainment in the rookeries.

money, plate, and certain sorts of merchandise' was declared. The jackpot prize was valued at £5,000, £3,000 of which was paid in cash, £700 in plate, and the remainder in 'good tapestry meet for hangings, and other covertures, and certain sorts of good linen cloth.' All the prizes were to be seen at the house of Mr Dericke, the queen's goldsmith, in Cheapside. A wood cut was appended to the original proclamation in which a tempting display of gold and silver plate is profusely delineated. There were 400,000 'lots' available for purchase and the first draw took place in January 1568. The final drawing of lots was not completed until May of the following year. The draw took place in a specially constructed building in the vicinity of St Paul's Cathedral. Each lot cost 10s and it was expressly laid down that they could be subdivided for the 'convenience of the poorer classes'. The original Elizabethan lottery was not as successful in raising revenue as the queen had hoped but by the late seventeenth century it had become, especially in London, an enormously popular activity. In 1714, excitement reached a new level as record numbers of 'punters' purchased tickets.

Even this was eclipsed by the 1718 lottery, when the sum of £1,500,000 was expended in buying tickets. By this time the draw usually took place in Mercer's Hall, Ironmonger Lane, Cheapside. Tickets were drawn by Bluecoat boys. There were two wheels, one for blanks and the other for winning tickets. Fortune tellers made money by advising customers about which numbers were 'lucky'. Doctors were always present in large numbers at the draw in case of adverse reactions to the news of their good or bad fortune.

In 1736, the need for a second bridge in London led to the passing of an Act of Parliament to build a bridge at Westminster through the sale of lottery tickets, 125,000 in total at a purchase price of £5. The lottery was so successful that Parliament quickly sanctioned other lotteries and the entire bridge was built out of the proceeds of lottery tickets. The lottery office 'keepers' also engaged in extensive advertising to publicise the draw. From about 1815 they began distributing handbills using poetry to woo the public into parting with their money. By 1820 they were using wood engravers to make their adverts more visually appealing as well.

Distributing handbills to promote the lottery in the nineteenth century.

The following is a specimen sent out by a large contractor named Sivewright:

> When possess'd of sufficient
> We sit at our ease;
> Can go where we like,
> And enjoy what we please.
> But when pockets are empty,
> If forced to apply
> To some friend for assistance,
> They're apt to deny.
> Not so with friends Sivewright,
> They never say nay,
> But lead us to Fortune
> The readiest way.
> They gallop on gaily;
> The fault is your own
> If you don't get a good share
> Before they're all gone

Another example is one depicting a fisherwoman, who claims proudly:

> Though a dab, I'm not scaly I like a good plaice,
> And I hope that good-luck will soon smile in my face;
> On the 14th of June, when Prizes in shoals,
> Will cheer up the cockles of all sorts of soals.

There had always been opposition to the lottery from its inauguration, and the British government eventually succumbed to a vigorous campaign by middle-class Evangelicals who considered it immoral for national revenues to be obtained through the proceeds of gambling. The last Act of Parliament for creating a national lottery was passed on 9 July 1823.

On 18 October 1826, the last 'State Lottery' before its recreation under John Major in the 1990s was drawn in England. The venue chosen was Cooper's Hall, Basinghall Street. Vast crowds thronged the building, to such an extent that it was difficult for the proceedings to be conducted at all. The abolition of lotteries led to the loss of government revenue in the region of £250,000 or £300,000 a year (1826 figures!). It also led to the abrupt departure of the lottery office keepers, who were not only very numerous but also rented property across the country to act as offices.[10]

The popularity of the lottery was enormous. Throughout the eighteenth and early nineteenth century, it represented one of the few legitimate methods for working-class people to escape from their lives of grinding poverty into a comfortable existence. Its abolition and the consequent fall in government revenues led directly to an increase in crime, the introduction of the workhouse system on a compulsory basis, and the decline of the rookery areas of London into the worst slums in the world.

Notes

1   Allen Guttmann, *Sports Spectators*, Columbia University Press, 1986.

2   John Ford, *Cricket: A Social History, 1700–1835,* David & Charles, 1972.

3   J. Marshall, *Sussex Cricket: A History*, 1959.

4   C. Brookes, *English Cricket: The Game and its Players through the Ages*, Weidenfeld & Nicolson, 1978.

5   M. Smith, *Violence and Sport,* Butterworth's, 1981.

6   See, for example, *The Times*, 10 August 1796.

7   K. Sheard, *Boxing in the Civilizing Process*, Unpublished Ph.D. thesis, Anglia Polytechnic, Cambridge, 1992.
    R. Holt (ed.), *Sport and the Working Class in Modern Britain,* Manchester University Press, 1990.
    W. Vamplew, 'Sport Crowd Disorder in Britain, 1870–1914: Causes and Controls', *Journal of Sport History*, 7 (1980), pp. 5–20.

8   An account of Astley's circus by Dickens, following his visit, gives a flavour of the entertainment on offer there.

9   *Bell's Weekly Messenger,* No. 1846, 21 August 1831.

10 Terry J. Castle, *Masquerade and Civilization, The Carnivalesque in Eighteenth-Century Culture and Fiction,* Stanford, 1986, is the leading work on the subject of masquerades, although some of his conclusions are controversial.

11 S. Carter, '"This female proteus": representing prostitution and masquerade in eighteenth-century English popular print culture', *Oxford Art Journal*, Volume 22, No. 1, pp. 55–79, 1999.

12 A fascinating account of Don Saltero's coffee house is given by Richard Steele in the *Tatler*, 1709. Items in the coffee house included 'a nun's penitential whip, four evangelists' heads carved on a cherry stone, the Pope's infallible candle, a starved cat found many years earlier between the walls of Westminster Abbey, William the Conqueror's flaming sword, Queen Elizabeth's strawberry dish, a cockatrice, petrified rain, barnacles, a rose from Jericho, a necklace made of Job's tears, a whale's pizzle, a wooden clock, with a man mowing the grass from the top, manna from Canaan, a petrified oyster, a pair of garter snakes from South Carolina, an Indian ladies' back scratcher, a 15-inch long frog, and the horns of a shamway.' Richard D. Altick, *The Shows of London*, 1978.

13 The myth of widespread illiteracy in the eighteenth and nineteenth centuries has long since been demolished. Statistics from the 1851 census, for instance, show that over 2,500,000 children were educated on a daily basis. Even more bizarrely, *less* money was spent on education in 1901, when it was compulsory, than in 1833, when it was entirely voluntary. Most ironically of all, a study of children in the Edwardian era demonstrates an actual *decline* in the level of literacy compared with the era before compulsory education. Among the most important books dealing with the subject are:
    Richard D. Altick, *The English Common Reader: A social history of the mass reading public, 1800–1900*, Cambridge University Press, 1957.
    E.G. West, *Education and the Industrial Revolution*, Batsford, 1975.
    Mark Blaug, 'The Economics of Education in English Classical Political Economy: A Re-examination', in: Skinner, A. and Wilson, T. (eds), *Essays on Adam Smith,* Clarendon Press, 1975.

14 Nancy Dawson, *Authentic memoirs of the celebrated Miss Nancy Dawson*, 1762.

15 George Alexander Stevens, 'Ballad of Nancy Dawson', 1759. Nancy Dawson's portrait also hangs in the Garrick Club in London.

16 William Hone, *Every Day Book*, vol. ii, 1826.

6

FOOD & DRINK

The residents of the rookeries made a number of surprising innovations in the field of food and drink, many of which are still with us today. Perhaps their most remarkable and longest-lasting contribution was to invent the take-away. In general, a study of their diet, particularly during the eighteenth century, reveals some surprising conclusions. The amount of meat eaten by even the poorest residents in eighteenth century England astonished foreign visitors. Servants in particular ate very well, being able to share in the richer food that their wealthy employers could afford, such as venison, turkey, partridge and other luxury items. Evening meals often contained a plate of cold meat, and even the wealthy often ate cold meat except when entertaining.[1]

Because of the popularity of meat, it became necessary for it to be transported from the farms to the urban areas. In the absence of modern refrigeration methods, the quality of meat that arrived was not always good.[2] This did not stop it from being sold and consumed eagerly by the rookery dwellers, who were much less fastidious than the wealthy about the quality of the food they ate. A doctor in 1788 wrote a book called *The Honours of the Table* in which he claimed that meat smelled so much that it should be held as far away as possible from one's nose while eating.[3]

Soups were also popular, particularly pease soup. This was generally served during the winter months. It contained dried peas simmered in stock or water with onion, celery and seasoning.[4] Peas, which could be dried and therefore stored for long periods of time, were a staple part of the diet of ordinary people at this time. Also popular, particularly as an evening meal in winter, was gruel, a dish made up of boiled oatmeal and butter. It was often fortified with alcohol (wine, beer or brandy being the usual accompaniments), and warmed people up in the colder months of the year.[5]

Fruit and vegetables were also eaten, though of course only in season. The ironic fact is that fruit was viewed with deep suspicion by the middle classes, who believed that uncooked fruit would give them indigestion or even the plague. The wealthy, by contrast, had no such inhibitions, while the rookery dwellers would eat almost anything. They consumed fruit in large quantities, particularly oranges and apples, which may explain the remarkable absence of scurvy among them compared with the sailors of the time.[6] Blackberries, as well as being eaten, were also used as a dye for clothing.[7] Vegetables were normally prepared for cooking in a mixture of butter and flour.[8] In fact, one of the many ironies of the rookeries was that because the middle classes despised vegetables as 'food for the poor', the rookery dwellers had a healthier diet than their supposed social superiors.[9]

Another popular food was cheese. During the eighteenth century, over forty different types of cheese have been identified. Many of them, such as Cheddar, Cheshire and Wensleydale, are still with us.[10] A curious recipe for making Cheddar cheese, dated 1700, survives. It recommends taking the milk of twelve cows in the morning and the cream of twelve in the evening, adding three spoons of rennet, breaking the curd, then the whey, and working 3lb of butter into the curd, after which it should be put in a cheese press, turned for an hour, and then allowed to lie in the press for 30 or 40 hours before washing it in whey, laying it in a dry cloth, and then placing it upon the shelf, and turning it.[11]

It was the invention of the muslin cloth for steaming food that led to the craze for puddings in England. Puddings were stuffed with all kinds of fillings: meat, poultry, even custard. This characteristically British dessert was popular with all classes of the population. Among their ingredients were flour, eggs, milk, butter, suet, raisins, sugar and even marrow. They were generally cooked either in a cauldron or a metal pot over an open fire. In those days they were usually cooked together with meat.[12] Even foreign visitors appreciated the 'English pudding', and it remains the case that no one can cook puddings quite like the English, continental desserts being entirely different in their constituents and method of preparation and cooking.

Sugar was enormously popular with all classes of society, and in the 1790s, a study showed that 4kg of sugar per person were consumed each year. Bread, of course, was one of the staple items of diet, and alum was employed to bleach the bread and make the loaf appear bigger than it really was.[13] Milk was widely distrusted, and levels of consumption were unsurprisingly far higher in the country than in the city.[14]

Tea, so often considered the national drink of England, was beyond the pocket of the rookery dwellers. On the other hand, servants of the wealthy made a good living by reselling the used tea leaves to the ordinary people.

Although illegal, the practice was so widespread that enforcing the law was impossible. As a result, tea became the most popular non-alcoholic drink among the working classes.[15] There was considerable opposition to tea-drinking throughout the eighteenth century as there had been in the seventeenth. Jonas Hanway, best known for his charitable work among chimney sweeps, thundered against tea as a drink that had destroyed the beauty of 'the fair sex'. He wrote, with his accustomed hyperbole, 'Your very chambermaids have lost their bloom by sipping tea.'[16] He also claimed that its use was known to 'hurt the nerves (Bohea especially) and cause various distempers; as tremors, palsies, vapours, fits, etc.'[17] In spite of these claims, drinking tea spread steadily throughout the population to the point where a visiting Frenchman could exclaim in astonishment, 'the drinking of tea is general. You have it twice a day and, though its expense is considerable, the humblest peasant has [it] twice a day just like the rich man.'[18]

Arthur Young, the English farmer and writer best known for his *Travels in France,* complained that the drinking of tea by the 'lower classes' was 'an abomination' which was directly responsible for their poverty.[19]

Coffee, like tea, was a drink for the wealthy, and there is little evidence of its popularity among the working classes until the end of the nineteenth century, when it became more affordable and the rising artisan class began to indulge in habits formerly restricted to the middle and upper classes. Syllabub was an enormously popular drink throughout the eighteenth century. Its ingredients were either cider or wine, sweetened with milk, nutmeg and cream, and flavoured with rosemary, lemon or spices. In the large country houses, the long-suffering milkmaid was expected to spurt the milk from the cow directly on to the broth to make an exceptionally frothy head. In London and other towns, this method was of course not practical.[20]

'Saloop' was a popular drink among the London poor that has long since vanished. It was hot and sweet, made out of sassafras wood and flavoured with milk and sugar. During the summer months, it was sold from street stalls; during the winter, the vendors sheltered under makeshift tents. It was alleged to be a cure for a hangover, and certainly thousands of rookery dwellers were willing to try any drink that held out that promise! Chimney sweeps were particularly fond of it.[21]

The eighteenth century saw a number of technological innovations, including those in the food industry. The use of iron led to improvements in kitchen utensils and even the types of cooking ranges. Cattle no longer had to be killed at the beginning of winter and salted to keep them fresh during those months. The new processes meant that fresh meat was available all the year round. New types of fruit and vegetables were imported, and fish could be brought to the cities still fresh from the sea. Roast and boiled meat was consumed in large quantities by every section of society. The rookery dwellers ate far more bread than the rich, but also, curiously, more cake. Perhaps Marie Antoinette was *not* being simply insensitive about the French poor?[22]

Many foods were made with dangerous ingredients. Copper and lead were used to add colour to sweets, to give cheese a red rind, and to give pickles their green colouring. Pepper, an expensive spice, was mixed with floor sweepings to make it last longer. Even the copper and brass pans used for cooking contained dangers. If acidic food was cooked in them, the result was a layer of poisonous verdigris.[23]

What would now be called 'fast-food' outlets or 'takeaways' proliferated throughout London, especially in the rookery areas. To begin with, there was a lack of cooking facilities in the home, especially those given up to multi-occupancy. Secondly, life was lived outside the home as much as possible, and cooking meant preparation, cleaning, spending money on fuel and a range of other incidental tasks and expenses. François Maximilien Misson, a French writer, was so impressed by them in the 1690s that he gave a detailed description, and the establishments did not change significantly in the following 150 years or so:

> There are cookshops enow in all parts of the town, where it is very common to go and chuse upon the spit the part you like, and to eat it there. Generally four spits, one over another, carry round each five or six pieces of Butcher's meat (never anything else); if you would have a fowl or a pidgeon, you must bespeak it; Beef, Mutton or Veal, Pork and Lamb; you have what quantity you please cut off, fat, lean, much or little done; with this, a little salt; and mustard upon the side of a plate; a Bottle of beer; and a roll.[24]

Boswell reported on another such establishment in 1762, stating that the meal cost a shilling.[25]

Fish, except freshwater varieties, was cheap and widely eaten, and once again, the rookery dwellers pioneered the fish and chip shop. Crayfish was abundant at the time and large quantities of it were eaten, the Billingsgate fish market selling it to the traders who dispersed it to the rookery dwellers. Shellfish was even more plentiful, so much so that oysters were despised as food of the poor. Cockles and crab were also popular and street-sellers sold large quantities of them.

The history of alcoholic consumption in the rookeries during the eighteenth century falls naturally into three distinct periods. The first is what might be called the beer and brandy phase; the second the domination of gin; and the third the triumph of porter. At the beginning of the eighteenth century, beer was the normal drink of choice for the poor and the working classes, brandy being drunk if a stronger effect was desired.[26] Then, during one of the interminable wars with France, the government of King William III, partly guided by economic self-interest, since the Dutch were the leading producers of gin, unwisely decided to promote what was known variously as 'Dutch courage' and 'Hollands gin' rather than French brandy. They were aware that the production of spirits would enable them to solve the problem of a surplus of corn. The result was the production of gin on a huge scale, and it was sold at remarkably low prices. This led to the phase in the history of London known as the 'gin craze'.[27]

It was at this time that Hogarth painted his famous portrayal of 'Gin Lane', clearly based on St Giles. By 1740, there were 9,000 gin shops in London alone, of which the majority were based in St Giles. The consumption of spirits in London reached 14 gallons per head. Beer and ale also continued to be popular, with 90 gallons of beer per head being consumed.[28]

During the 'gin craze', one in every four shops in St Giles sold gin, and it was not simply off-licenses and pubs that traded in the spirit. Landlords of rented homes and street-sellers pushing barrels through the street also sold vast quantities of the cheap 'Geneva' or 'Jeniver', as gin was known then.[29]

The government was so alarmed by the massive rise in crime fuelled by the insatiable desire for cheap gin, particularly after the public outcry that followed the tragic case of Judith Defour's murder of her own daughter, that it was forced to raise the duty to a level that made it too expensive for most

Drinking was very popular in the rookeries.

working-class people to buy. They generally returned either to their more traditional drink, beer, which had far less harmful effects than gin, or to the newly fashionable porter, a kind of stout first mentioned in 1721, and probably invented by accident a few years earlier.[30]

Porter was a dark-coloured form of beer, developed by using dried brown malt and brewed with soft rather than hard water. It became particularly popular with the street and river porters of London, who carried heavy goods on and off the Thames and drank it to refresh themselves after their exhausting work humping about loads that would test the strength and stamina of a modern bodybuilder.[31] Porter was the first beer capable of being mass-produced, and the London brewers of the drink, most notably Truman, Whitbread and Thrale, became wealthy as a result of manufacturing and supplying the drink. Until 1860, it was the most popular beverage among the London working classes.[32]

Beer, generally in the form of ale, remained the most popular drink in London, as the statistics show. In 1786, for example, in London alone (and London was, though a large city, a fraction of its present size and a minute fraction of its present population), no fewer than 1,178,856 barrels of 'strong beer' were produced. This did not count less potent versions of the beverage. It was made in a very large variety of flavours, colours and strengths. Hogarth

Maidenhead Tavern, Dyott Street.

championed the drinking of beer as a symbol of Englishness rather than the foreign spirit, gin. He was also well aware that it was much weaker and did not have the same detrimental effects upon health. Porter, however, at least when it first became available in the early eighteenth century, remained stronger than even the strongest ale. In spite of this, Hogarth approved of porter as well, considering it a manly drink, suitable for the strong men who drank it.[33]

Police monitor the market.

Pubs in London were far more than simply places to drink. They were the centres of local community life, the employment exchanges of their day, the usual means by which news was transmitted among the population, places of exchange for stolen goods, places of assignation for prostitutes and their clients, and also places where a variety of entertainments were provided to amuse and divert the people.[34]

The eighteenth century, on the whole, was (relatively speaking) a 'golden age' for the poor. Though their lives may have been hard, their life expectancy short, their wages low and their work hard, hardly anyone in the rookeries starved, and there was a natural, spontaneous gaiety about them that visitors from the country or abroad found both surprising and refreshing. All this changed with the coming of the Victorians. Drinking was frowned upon by the middle classes, and made a convenient scapegoat for the poverty of the dwellers in the rookeries. Food became more expensive, as did most staple necessities of life, and the welfare system was abruptly curtailed, the harsh 'workhouse test' being used to force the poor to take any kind of employment at starvation wages rather than enter its oppressive doors. Multi-occupancy of dwellings expanded to such a point that hardly any homes in the rookeries had any kind of cooking facilities, though landladies did offer meals for a price.

Street markets continued to flourish, and Covent Garden, Billingsgate and Smithfield still served the traders of the city. They bought their meat, fish and vegetables, and sold them on to street traders who hawked their wares around the rookeries in handcarts, at roadside stalls, or makeshift cafés. The full bellies were gone, and the gaiety replaced by a grim earnestness as survival became everyday life.

In the eighteenth century, stealing food was almost unknown, except among poachers, whose activities were largely confined to the countryside, and tended to involve killing deer or rabbit, both luxury items on the table. The Victorian age saw the poor resorting to scavenging through dustbins and other leftovers, as well as the blatant theft of items of food. The penalties were severe, though mercifully not as extreme as they would have been before the 1820s, but the desperation of the starving people led them to consider a prison sentence a preferable alternative to death by hunger.

Soup-kitchens for the poor began to appear as charitable people, appalled at the spectacle of starvation in their own city, the wealthiest in the world, tried to help the hungry in the most basic of all ways.[35] Their attitude continued to be unpopular, and it was not until the Boer War in 1899, and the discovery that thousands of men who had volunteered to fight out of economic necessity were not remotely physically fit, that led finally to a long overdue change in attitudes.

The prejudice against the poor still continued, but the Victorian complacency had been badly shaken. It was the beginning of a new way of looking at the world, and recognising that perhaps the problems of poverty had structural causes

A dinner at a cheap lodging-house.

rather than simple laziness on the part of the poor themselves. This realisation came too late to save the dwellers in the rookeries, since by 1899 around 95 per cent of their homes had already been destroyed and the inhabitants scattered to the poorer London suburbs. First Rosebery, then Campbell-Bannerman, Asquith, Churchill and Lloyd George not only challenged *laisser-faire* beliefs but also introduced practical measures to alleviate the worst excesses of Victorian poverty. The economist Alfred Marshall had been urging this since the 1870s; Shaftesbury, Oastler, Sadler and Carlyle since the 1830s. After the long sleep, awakening came at last.

Notes

1   Colin Clair, *Kitchen and Table*, Abelard-Schuman, 1965.
2   Arnold Palmer, *Movable Feasts*, OUP, 1953.
3   Clair, op. cit.
4   Maggie Lane, *Jane Austen and Food*, Hambledon, 1995.
5   Ibid.
6   Reay Tannahill, *Food in History*, Crown Publishers, 1989.
7   Dorothy Hartley, *Food in England*, Macdonald, 1962.
8   Palmer, op. cit.
9   See, for example, John Parkinson, *Paradisi in Sole*, 1656.
    Richard Bradley, *The Country Housewife and Lady's Director*, 1719.
    G. Dodd, *The Food of London*, Longmans, 1856.
10 Hartley, op. cit. See also: Hannah Glasse, *The Art of Cookery made Plain and Easy*, 1747.
11 Hartley, op. cit.

12   Clair, op. cit.
13   Anonymous, *Poison Detected, or Frightful Truths,* 1756.
14   Clair, op. cit.
15. Lane, op. cit.
16   Jonas Hanway, *An Essay on Tea,* 1757.
17   Ibid.
18   François de la Rochefoucauld, *A Frenchman in England,* 1784.
19   Arthur Young, *Annals of Agriculture,* 1784–1809.
20   Lane, op. cit.
21   Charles Lamb, *Essays of Elia.*
22   Hartley, op. cit.
23   Ibid.
24   F.M. Misson, *Memoirs and Observations on his Travels over England in 1696,* 1719.
25   James Boswell, *Boswell's London Journal 1762–1763,* Heinemann, 1951.
26   Ralph French, *Nineteen Centuries of Drink in England,* Longmans, 1884.
27   Norman Longmate, *The Waterdrinkers,* Hamish Hamilton, 1968.
28   Ibid.
29   Patrick Dillon, *The Much-Lamented Death of Madam Geneva: The Eighteenth-century Gin Craze,* Review, 2002.
30   Ian S. Hornsey, *A History of Beer and Brewing,* Royal Society of Chemistry, 2004.
31   Ibid.
32   Peter Mathias, *The Brewing Industry in England 1700–1830,* CUP, 1959.
33   John P. Arnold, *Origin and History of Beer and Brewing,* Beer Books.com, 2005.
34   Maurice Gorham, *Inside the Pub,* Architectural Press, 1950.
35   Soup kitchens will be dealt with in the chapter on philanthropy and reform.

7

CRIME & PUNISHMENT

St Giles was close enough to the City of London during the Middle Ages to make it a place where criminals often chose to make their escape. As the area expanded, with the growth of population associated with that process, so too the level of crime within St Giles itself rose dramatically. By 1600 it had already changed from a sleepy village into what resembled a 'New Town'. By 1640 it had become a part of London in which the majority of the inhabitants were poor and at least disposed to take short cuts rather than always follow the letter of the law.

The penal code of the time was harsh, not only in terms of the brutal nature of the punishments available to judges but even in terms of the offences themselves. Many acts that would not be considered crimes at all today were punished severely. Many more that would now be regarded as minor offences were treated as serious felonies, attracting altogether disproportionate sentences. The death penalty was freely applied to an astonishingly wide variety of crimes. Even the kind of death that a prisoner might be sentenced to could be made more or less barbaric. The most common method of execution was, of course, hanging. This took place in public, and Tyburn, until executions there were moved to a less turbulent part of London, provided the usual venue for the inhabitants of St Giles to witness the law at work. All too often it was the local people themselves who would be swinging at the end of a rope there. Even when the custom of hanging prisoners at Tyburn was abolished this was largely on the grounds of the riots among the crowd that frequently accompanied the executions. Public hanging continued in London until it was finally abolished in 1868.

Women were less fortunate than men if found guilty of a capital crime. On the sophistical grounds of 'preserving the decency of their sex',[1] they alone could be subjected to the barbarity of being burned alive. Murder of a husband by his wife was also regarded as 'petty treason' and thus punished more severely than when a wife was murdered by her husband. Burning the woman alive was the usual penalty.[2]

Even children were not immune from the savagery of the law. Boys and girls as young as five were publicly executed for such trivial offences as the theft of food or handkerchiefs.

Treason, except where the offender was of aristocratic birth, was still punished by the barbarous 'hanging, drawing and quartering' of the unfortunate criminal. A noble lord who was found guilty of this offence would be beheaded, an unpleasant enough death but vastly less painful than the alternative.

A whole range of 'sexual offences' were also punishable by death, though in general less severe penalties were imposed. Bigamy was in theory a capital crime and sometimes in practice too. On 10 May 1676, an unnamed woman was 'indicted for having two husbands at once alive, which being fully proved she was found Guilty, and her sex not being capable of the benefit of the Clergy', was likewise condemned to die.[3]

Rape, homosexuality, lesbianism, paedophilia and bestiality were also capital crimes, though the ultimate penalty was not always enforced for these offences. Again, in general women found guilty of 'sexual offences' were punished more harshly than men convicted of the same crimes. For example, two contrasting rape cases from St Giles show how harshly the law was applied. In the first instance, that of Alice Gray, the woman was clearly guilty of assisting in the commission of a rape on a child; but in the case of Sarah Blandford, it was equally clearly a gross miscarriage of justice. Both women were executed.

Alice Gray's case was reported as such:

John, alias Thomas Smith, in the committing of a Rape on the body of Catherine Masters, of the Age of 10 years and upward, on the 28th of February last. The first Evidence was the Girl her self, who Deposed, that the Prisoner and her self lodged together, that the Night when this thing happen'd, she went to Bed at eight a Clock, and about 11 the Prisoner came with a Man to her Lodging, that being sleepy, she did not perceive when the Prisoner came to Bed; but awaking about 2 a Clock in Morning, found a Man in Bed with them, that as she was endeavouring to get away, the Prisoner pull'd her back again, and held her down in the Bed, and stopt her Mouth (that she could not cry out) while the Man gain'd the perfect knowledge of her Body. Others Deposed, that the Girl the next Morning acquainted them how she had been abused, and Inspecting her Body, found that a Man had been with her, and had given her the Pox. The Evidence being very plain against the Prisoner, and she saying little for her self, the Jury found her guilty of the indictment.[4]

Appalling though Gray's crime was, it would not be considered a capital offence in most countries that still retain the death penalty. In 1707, the climate of opinion was different, and she was executed.

Sarah Blandford's conviction and execution was beyond doubt one of the grossest miscarriages of justice during the eighteenth century. Like Gray, she was accused of abetting a rape, this time alleged to have been committed by Hugh Leeson with the active assistance of Blandford. Essentially, the supposed victim, Mary May, had a husband who owed money to Blandford's husband, a man simply referred to as Exton. Leeson was a lodger in the same house as Blandford, and May claimed that he locked her in a room and raped her, Blandford then opening the door and laughing. Leeson denied that he had ever met May, and several witnesses testified that she had been propositioning him for sex.

Two midwives also swore that there was no sign of assault or any other kind of damage on May's body, as did a surgeon who examined her. The surgeon also confirmed that May had gonorrhoea, while Leeson had no sign of any sexually transmitted disease. Other witnesses testified that she was not far short of being a prostitute, while Leeson and Blandford brought in witnesses who testified to their own good character. In spite of the overwhelming volume of evidence that both Leeson and Blandford were innocent of the crime of rape, and that May had obviously concocted the whole story out of revenge against Blandford's husband Exton, the jury, for what reason we are not told, found them both guilty and they were sentenced to death. [5]

Another crime for which women could be sentenced to burning alive was what was known as 'coining' or 'clipping the currency'. This particular offence was so widespread that coiners, more often than not, got away with it. One criminal who was not so fortunate was a resident of the St Giles area:

Mistris Ann Petty, Widdow, a person of above sixty years of age; she lived lately near Holborn Conduit, but formerly in the Green-yard in Leaden-Hall, her Husband some Years since, in a very melancholy Discontented humour upon I know not what provocations went and hang'd himself, since whose decease this woman hath followed several indirect courses, but more especially for Clipping of money, for which purpose she held a Correspoddence with some wild Apprentices, Servants, or Casheirs to eminent Citizens, who (it is said) brought her sums of large lawful money which she clipt and returned, allowing them five pound in the Hundred more or less, and yet got considerably her self for her own pains, as she then apprehended, though now she is like to pay dear enough for it: for she was here indicted, and Evidence came in that saw her at the Clipping trade, and others that had bought divers quantities of silver melted down of her, besides the violent suspicion for that some of her tools were taken in the house, together with Fileings and Clippings to a good considerable value; upon which she was brought in guilty of high Treason, and sentenced to be Drawn on an

Hurdle or Sled to Smithfield (the usual place for such Executions) and there to be burned to Death: A Youth her Son was also indicted, but not being proved to be in any way concerned in his Mothers ill practises was acquitted.[6]

To a modern mind, almost as appalling as the cruelty of the sentence is the casual, almost light-hearted way in which the trial records proclaim the elderly woman's doom. The late seventeenth century, except for a very few enlightened souls, was anything but an age of humanitarian sentiments.

Most forms of theft were also generally punished by execution as well, though a lot depended on the value of the goods and the degree of humanity of the jury. Since in theory stealing goods of lesser value than a shilling was *not* a capital offence, jurors frequently undervalued stolen property to save the thief from the gallows. As the eighteenth century began to see the growth of a more humane attitude towards criminals, this practice became so widespread that judges were often enraged into imprisoning jurors until they delivered the 'correct' verdict. To their credit, most jurymen refused to bow to this illegal pressure, summoning writs of *Habeas Corpus* to free them from their unlawful imprisonment.

For non-capital crimes, the usual punishments were whipping, branding, other forms of mutilation, transportation (before 1776 to America, then to Australia) and, for a few fortunate people, fines. Prisons were still primarily regarded as places to hold the inmates securely before their sentence rather than punishments in themselves, though some felons were sentenced to terms in prison. On the whole, though, imprisonment was not generally imposed as a punishment.

Most of the long-term inmates in gaol were debtors, whose conditions in the prisons of the time were a disgrace. They were not in any position to pay for their keep, yet it was laid down as a legal obligation that they had to pay their gaolers for food, water and clothes. Most were reduced to begging passers-by in the street for assistance. The law with regard to debtors truly was, in the words of Dickens, an ass, since it was an axiom of the courts that anyone who owed money should be sent to prison until they paid it off. Quite how they were expected to repay the debt from inside a gaol was never explained.

Crimes against property were, in general, treated more harshly than 'crimes against the person'. Though in theory rape, violent assault and murder were supposed to attract the death penalty, lesser sentences were frequently imposed. In cases of theft and burglary, such commutations were much rarer.

The law of the land was in the hands of a class of property owners. In their eyes, only the severest penalties would serve to deter the poor from stealing what did not belong to them. As well as shaping the law to act as an instrument of protection for themselves against the people of Britain, they also added hypocrisy and stupidity to their self-interest. One of the clearest examples of this is shown in their stubborn and irrational belief that the ease with which a

A corner in Nine Elms.

crime could be committed meant that it deserved a severer punishment than a more 'difficult' offence. Burglars, through this twisted logic, *might* be able to avoid the death penalty but an unfortunate child who picked a pocket or stole clothes from a washing line was almost certain to be hung for the offence.[7]

Other nations in Europe had repressive, unjust and barbaric laws, but none of them had so many offences against property on their statute books, over 200 by the end of the eighteenth century. Nor did any other country besides Britain have such a savage penal code to protect the 'rights of property', including hanging children for stealing a handkerchief.

The much-misunderstood and misrepresented Adam Smith, one of the most enlightened thinkers of the century, saw clearly the extent to which the obsession with protecting private property was distorting the legal system of Britain and preventing justice from being dispensed fairly and equally. Contrary to the myths that have been put out about him by his alleged

Arguing with the police.

disciples and avowed opponents, he was actually a humanitarian, a radical, and anything but an advocate of *laisser-faire*.[8] He even commented, with the dry Scottish wit that so often pervaded his writing, that a slave was more likely to enjoy the protection of the law under 'an arbitrary government' than he was in a 'state governed by a legislature', where, as Smith pointed out, he would be accused of interfering with 'property rights'.[9]

A particularly absurd, not to say obscene, example of the tangles that the law became enmeshed in over the issue of 'property rights' arose in 1729. After some particularly notorious examples of abuse of their positions by gaolers in the Fleet and Marshalsea prisons, the two leading gaols for debtors in London, Parliament was moved to investigate. It found clear evidence of brutality towards prisoners, theft of what little property they had by warders and fraudulent conversion of bequests from charities to aid prisoners into the pockets of the prison staff.

Appalled by the abuses, Parliament attempted to act, but soon found itself faced with a quite impossible hurdle to overcome. The people who ran the prisons had purchased their offices as gaolers, which were therefore their private property. As such, it was impossible for Parliament to take any action against them, since that would have meant confiscating the gaolers' freehold property. The consequence was that the abuses continued and reform of the prison system had to be postponed until the nineteenth century.

The ironic fact was that, in spite of the ferocity of the penal code, the number of actual felonies declined during the seventeenth and eighteenth centuries. The contemporary claims that a 'crime wave' was sweeping the country were partly the result of simple paranoia and also propagandist excuses put out to justify the harshness and injustice of the laws.[10] In spite of the fact that crime was falling, legislators *increased* the number of capital offences. Yet fewer people were actually put to death when found guilty, a curious fact that cannot be entirely explained by the reluctance of juries to convict for what they clearly felt were excessive penalties for a crime. As Sharpe points out, 'despite the increase of capital statutes from the late seventeenth century onwards executions fell'.[11]

One of the most common crimes was pickpocketing, which was extremely easy to carry out in the crowded London streets. Another prevalent crime was the theft of clothes and other goods by servants and apprentices. Highway robbery was a crime carried out on the outskirts of London rather than in St Giles, even though a number of famous highwaymen were based in the area.

As one of the poorest parts of London, St Giles contributed more than its fair share of criminals to the legal process. Every conceivable offence was represented by one inhabitant or another at some point during its long history of criminal behaviour. A disproportionate number of residents feature in the *Chronicles of Newgate*, not least with regard to those who were executed.[12]

Treason, the crime that attracted the most barbaric of all punishments, the guilty party being sentenced to 'hanging, drawing and quartering', was defined far more widely during the seventeenth and eighteenth centuries than would be the case now. Forging money or 'clipping' coins, for instance, was regarded as being treasonable, even though in practice the lesser verdict, of theft, was more commonly returned. Even to suggest that a new issue of coins or banknotes might make the currency less valuable was a statement that, according to the strict interpretation of the law, could be regarded as treason. In general, however, very few of the citizens of St Giles were arraigned for treasonable acts, except in cases concerning forgery or clipping the coinage.[13]

Witchcraft remained a capital crime until 1736, though cases of 'witches' being brought to trial were rare in London after 1640. The sentence was generally death by hanging, though imprisonment was becoming a more common sentence as judges and juries began to display signs of rationality in sifting the 'evidence' offered at those few trials that continued to take place. It was very common for accused women to be acquitted altogether; it was extremely rare for them to be put to death even if found guilty. In St Giles, the attitude towards such 'offences' was one of a mixture of guarded superstition and open contempt.[14]

There were three courses open to a prisoner charged with a capital crime. He or should could plead guilty, in which case the court would pronounce sentence; not guilty, when the prisoner would be sent for trial by jury; or they could refuse to enter a plea, and:

> reply that he wished for the judgement of God, in which case the trial is finished, for, guilty or not, he is irrevocably doomed to death; yet this does not render the family infamous, as he has not been declared guilty; and on that account the customary public method of punishment is not made use of with him, nor are his effects confiscated, but descent to his natural heir.[15]

The contemporary who made this observation then described the barbaric consequences of such an action:

Arguments in the rookeries were often public affairs.

He is then stretched upon the ground on his back, having a stone underneath him, which raises his loins upwards, and is covered with a table loaded with heavy stones, which are not all laid upon him together to crush him at once, but one after another, so as to prolong his death to a great length of time.[16]

This barbaric practice, known as *peine forte et dure,* was not common practice in Britain after the Civil War, though it was occasionally carried out when a defendant who wanted to be able to leave his estate to his family but knew that he had little or no chance of being acquitted chose this course to protect his fortune. As such, it was one of the few punishments more commonly applied to the rich than to the poor.[17]

If the prisoner chose trial by jury, he or she faced a number of obstacles in their path. It was not permitted for a defendant to hire a lawyer, even if (as would not have been the case for the majority of citizens of the rookeries) they could have afforded one. They could not subpoena witnesses to attend court on their behalf, nor was it even necessary for the prosecution witnesses to be in court themselves, statements by them read out to the court being accepted as sufficient evidence. Of course this took away the opportunity of cross-examining them and possibly exposing inconsistencies or other errors in their testimony. If the jury sympathised with the prisoner, they might be declared innocent in spite of these hurdles, but more common among jurors was an attitude best expressed in the words of the great eighteenth-century poet and humanitarian, Pope: 'and wretches hang that jurymen may dine.'[18] An even more scathing comment on jurors was made in the late seventeenth century by Samuel Butler, who remarked:

> Do not your juries give their verdict
> As if they felt the cause, not heard it?
> And as they please, make matter of fact.
> Run all on one side, as they're pack'd[19]

Perhaps the final word on the competence and integrity of the average juror may be left to Shakespeare, who makes one of his characters remark:

> The jury, passing on the prisoner's life,
> May, in the sworn twelve, have a thief or two,
> Guiltier than him they try.[20]

The eighteenth century saw the beginning of a more humane approach towards crime and punishment. Juries, however anxious they may have been to dine, began to bring in not guilty verdicts in defiance of the evidence if they felt the law was unjust. Even the law itself began to be challenged by reformers. The poet Charles Johnson wrote:

The rulers of the world,
Unmercifully just, who punish all
To the severest rigour of the laws
Are most unjust themselves, and violate
The laws they seem to guard; there is a justice
Due to humanity.[21]

The last woman to be executed in London for a crime other than murder was Ann Mary Chapman, hanged at Newgate on 22 July 1829 for attempted murder, while the last to be hanged for robbery was Amelia Roberts, executed at Newgate on 2 January 1827.

The last to be executed for swearing a false oath to obtain property was Mary Barrington, also known as Margaret Crimes (a perhaps appropriate alias), who was hanged on 22 February 1809 at Newgate. Four years earlier, on 13 November 1805, Mary Parnell became the last woman to be hanged at Newgate for forgery. On 20 January 1823, Giles East became the last person to be hanged for rape.

Attitudes began to change during the 1820s, and the number of offences under the law for which the death penalty could be imposed was cut dramatically. By 1838 only six people were executed, five for murder and one for attempted murder, a marked contrast to earlier times. In 1820, for example, of 103 executions, only 9 were for the crime of murder.[22]

Perhaps the most notorious criminals to come out of the rookeries were Mary Read the pirate and Jack Sheppard the house-breaker and escapologist. Even his enemies never had a bad word to say about Sheppard, and seemed almost to admire him. The people of the rookeries certainly loved him. Mary Read, a more complex character, still emerges as a fundamentally likeable person. Sheppard was a St Giles boy and could not only read and write competently but was remarkably good at arithmetic. He had begun as an apprentice to a carpenter, but at a pub in Drury Lane known as the Black Lion, he met the woman who was to be his constant companion throughout his brief life, Elizabeth Lyon, known as 'Edgeworth Bess'. He also met a man named Hind, who taught him that robbery was a quicker and easier way to riches than carpentry.

At first he continued to work as an apprentice by day and carry out his robberies under cover of night. When his master became suspicious, he broke his indentureship and moved in with Edgeworth Bess. Once there, he joined forces with a thief known by the nickname of 'Blueskin', one of the notorious Jonathan Wild's men, as well as his own brother Thomas. Edgeworth Bess was soon arrested, being caught with a large amount of stolen plate. She was placed in St Giles's Roundhouse, where Jack Sheppard came to visit her. The gaoler refusing him admittance, Sheppard knocked him down and carried

Bess away. This exploit 'acquired him a high degree of credit with the women of abandoned character.'[23]

Unfortunately, a month later, Jack's brother Thomas was arrested and turned King's Evidence against his brother to save his own life. In spite of this Jack was able to hide out in the rookeries for quite some time before he was unwise enough to venture out to play skittles in a Seven Dials tavern. The invitation was a trap and he found himself under arrest. Sheppard was imprisoned in St Giles's Roundhouse in his turn. Amazingly he managed to escape by loosening the tiles on the roof, jumping down onto the street and crying out 'there he goes!' as he pretended to be pursuing himself. The next day, however, he was rearrested while picking pockets in Leicester Fields and imprisoned in St Ann's Roundhouse. When Edgeworth Bess came to visit him she too was arrested. The couple were lodged together in the strongest ward of New Prison.

Even Sheppard found this a difficult escape to manage. Bess's capacious petticoats proved a considerable obstacle. It was only after he had cut two bars from his cell window and made a ladder from his blankets to enable them to reach the courtyard below that he told Bess to strip naked and make her perilous descent down the makeshift ladder. He then managed to get them both over the high wall that surrounded the prison. Once again, Jack Sheppard and Edgeworth Bess were free.

Sheppard's next brush with trouble came after he fell out with Jonathan Wild, the self-styled 'thief-taker'. In reality, Wild colluded with criminals,

Jack Sheppard.

fenced stolen property for them, but often turned them in to the authorities as well for the reward. Wild framed Jack Sheppard for perhaps the only crime of which he was not guilty. The result was that in August 1724 Sheppard found himself once again in prison. He was placed in the 'condemned hole', which inspired a contemporary rhyme, as follows:

> All ye that in the condemned hole do lie,
> Prepare you, for tomorrow you shall die.
> Watch all and pray, the hour is drawing near,
> That you before the Almighty shall appear.
> Examine well yourselves, in time repent,
> That you may not to eternal flames be sent;
> And when St Pulcher's bell tomorrow tolls,
> The Lord above have mercy on your souls.
> Past twelve o'clock.[24]

On 30 August, leaning against the wall, Jack Sheppard plotted his latest escape. Edgeworth Bess had visited him in prison and brought a number of female friends with her. After they had got the guards drunk, Sheppard was able to remove the iron bar from his cell and was once more a free man. Quickly he was dressed in petticoats, a shawl and bonnet. The company, pretending to be in mourning for the condemned prisoner, filed out past by the drunken gaolers.

For a while he lay low in Northamptonshire, but the locals were afraid of a man with his reputation. Sheppard began to worry that he might be betrayed and therefore returned to London. On the day after his return he smashed the window of a jeweller's shop and stole three watches. After this he took refuge briefly in Finchley, then a tiny village on the perimeter of London, but was betrayed by Edgeworth Bess out of jealousy after he took a local girl as his new mistress.

This time, the authorities were taking no chances. He was handcuffed, chained to the floor, his legs chained together and he was padlocked in at night. The warders searched him thoroughly, taking away all his tools and watched him day and night. They also made money out of exhibiting him to passers-by. Sheppard bided his time, read the Bible and pretended to be disconsolate, while in reality he was already planning his next escape. Somehow he managed to slip his hands out of his cuffs at will and was fortunate enough to find a loose nail in the floor of his cell. He used this to pick the lock of the padlock chaining him to the floor, slipping out of his cuffs at the same time and then snapping the chain binding his legs. He used the broken link of his chain to dig out an iron bar that prevented him accessing the chimney and then climbed up into a room above.

In seven minutes he picked the lock of the door, which brought him to a passage leading to the chapel. He then had to make a hole in the wall and draw the bolt that locked the door. Then he broke off an iron spike, opened the door on the far side of the chapel and found two more doors in front of him. It took him half an hour to pick the lock of the first door but the second was even more difficult, being locked, barred and bolted. When he eventually managed, working in the darkness, to unlock it, he found himself facing yet another door, which, to his relief, was bolted on his own side. Opening it he climbed out on to the roof of the prison.

Sheppard was too exhausted to make the large drop from where he stood to the ground below. Instead, he went back through the doors and chimneys, making his way to his own cell and lowered himself down with his blankets. Then he returned to the roof, where he lowered himself down to the roof of the house next door and managed to enter. He snatched a few hours of sleep, waking about midnight. He then slipped quietly out on to the street outside the prison. Sheppard found a blacksmith, persuaded him to remove the chains on his legs and laid low for two days in a cow house.

For two months he managed to evade the authorities, continuing his career of burglary from his haunts in the St Giles regions. Eventually, on 31 October, drunk, he was arrested by a police officer and secured in Newgate. This time, Sheppard was unable to find any means of escape from his position. After a tearful farewell with Edgeworth Bess, he was led out to Tyburn and hanged. Jack Sheppard, scourge of prisons, was only twenty-two years old at the time of his death. He had killed no one, nor had he ever used violence in the course of his robberies. His body was laid to rest in the church of St Martin-in-the-Fields.[25]

Mary Read, the 'female pirate', was not quite the rarity she has been made out to be. Women pirates were not unknown in her period, or even earlier, but she was perhaps the most attractive character of them all. Born illegitimate, to an unknown father, even the date and place of her birth is doubtful, although the most probable location is Wapping, the dock area of London, and the most plausible candidate for her father is another sailor.

Mary's mother was married to a sailor and was pregnant when he sailed away and was never seen again. She gave birth to a son and then, a year or so later, 'being young and airy, met with an accident which has often happened to women who are young and do not take a great deal of care.'[26] This 'accident' was a daughter who became Mary Read. The mother went off to Islington, then a sleepy country village on the outskirts of London, with her two children. Soon after her arrival, the boy died. Mary's mother worked as a domestic servant, as a seamstress and at selling haberdashery for four years before times grew hard. Mary, who was a strong and healthy child, then became the pawn in a desperate attempt by her mother to improve her own situation. Her thoughts turned to her mother-in-law, they returned home to Wapping and made plans.

Her husband's mother was 'in some circumstances', as Mary put it and it was to her that Mary's mother and daughter applied for assistance. Her own mother dressed Mary up in boy's clothing and her natural strength and independence of nature enabled her to carry off the deception. The mother and mother-in-law came to an agreement whereby Mary continued to live with her mother but her grandmother paid a crown a week for her maintenance.

Mary, according to her own account, enjoyed being a boy and soon came to prefer it to her old status as a female child. Then the grandmother died and Mary, aged thirteen, tall and strong, went out to work. She could have returned to her life as a woman but nine years as a boy had led her to develop quite different interests and ways of behaviour. Instead, she began her working life as a footman. It was not long before Mary decided that the life of domestic service, even as a footman, was not for her. Instead she 'entered herself aboard a man-of-war'. She worked hard and gave a good account of herself on board ship but soon grew tired of that life too, no doubt chafing at the harsh discipline of the Navy in the eighteenth century. Instead, she signed up as a cadet for an infantry regiment and saw action in Flanders. While she showed herself a good soldier, noted for her bravery under fire, it was in Flanders that the feminine side of her nature reasserted itself for the first time. She fell in love with a handsome Flemish trooper. Wherever the object of her affection went, she followed, until at last he asked why she exposed herself to such needless danger. It was then that she told him that she was a woman and in love with him. The Flemish soldier, having recovered from his initial shock, proposed that she should become his mistress. However, there was always a curious vein of respectability in Mary's nature and she insisted indignantly that it was marriage or nothing.

At the end of the campaign, they married, leaving the army and keeping a pub in Breda, Holland, known as the Three Horseshoes. Unfortunately, her husband died and once more she joined the army. The coming of peace left her idling and restless, so she took sail with a ship for the West Indies.

The ship on which she sailed was captured by pirates and Mary, once more disguised as a man, decided that a life of piracy was an attractive option. She joined up with the buccaneers herself and before long was a member of a privateer's fleet. When the crew mutinied, they turned to piracy instead. Mary was a willing and enthusiastic member of the ship's company.

Before long she teamed up with John Rackham, better known by his nickname of 'Calico Jack' from his fondness for having his clothes made out of calico. Also on the ship was another female pirate, the notorious Anne Bonny, who seems to have been a much less likeable person than Mary Read. Ann was already married but chose Calico Jack as her lover. When her husband threatened her with a public flogging for her adultery, she responded by stealing a ship and joining Calico Jack and his crew, swearing that she would kill her husband with her own hands.

On board ship, Ann Bonny was attracted by Mary, still dressed as and posing as a young man. Rackham became jealous and threatened to cut her throat. It was only when Mary revealed her true identity that domestic harmony returned. Mary went on a number of voyages with Rackham, capturing treasure of varying degrees of worth. It was the final trip that was to prove their undoing. Mary had already fallen in love once again with a fellow pirate and began by winning his friendship while still posing as a man. Only when she felt confident that he was fond of her did she reveal the truth about herself 'by carelessly showing her breasts, which were very white.'[27]

When her new lover was challenged to a duel by one of his fellow pirates, Mary picked a quarrel with the man herself and killed him 'with sword and pistol'. In her statement about the matter following her arrest, Mary said that she did not want him to withdraw from the quarrel for fear of being considered a coward but could not entertain the idea of his being killed, so chose instead to kill his opponent herself. This kind of curious mixture of gallantry, self-deception and genuine affection is quite typical of the warm-heartedness that made her so popular with the other pirates.

In 1720, Rackham and his crew were finally caught by the governor of Port Royal. According to the accounts of both sides only Ann Bonny, Mary Read and one man – unnamed, but almost certainly Mary's sweetheart – fought with courage. They shouted insults at the men, including Calico Jack, who lay hidden in the ship's hold, refusing to come out and fight. An incensed Mary not only taunted them with words but fired shots at her own crew, killing one and wounding several.

All this display of courage proved ineffectual, as the ship was eventually captured and the crew taken as prisoners to Port Royal. Both Ann Bonny and Mary Read were pregnant at the time, which enabled Ann to escape the gallows altogether and Mary to be 'respited' until the birth of her child. Rackham and most of his crew were hanged. Mary, though languishing in prison, hoped, not without good grounds, for a pardon. Instead she caught typhus and died at Port Royal. She remains one of the most colourful characters ever to emerge from the London rookeries. Mary's age at her death is a matter of some dispute, estimates ranging from as low as twenty years old to as high as thirty-two. The most commonly accepted estimate is that she was twenty-four years old at the time of her death. Her passing coincided, appropriately but fortuitously, with the dying days of the age of piracy.

Notes

1   Sir William Blackstone, *Commentaries on the Laws of England*.

2   Ibid.

3   Proceedings of the Old Bailey, 10 May 1676, Ref: 116760510-2.

4   Old Bailey, 23 April 1707, Ref: t17070423-26.

5   Old Bailey, 27 April 1715, Ref: t17150427-43.

6   Old Bailey, 12 December 1674, Ref: 116741212-2.

7   William Paley, *Principles of Morals and Political Philosophy*, 1785. This extraordinary work is one of the most ingenious attempts to defend the indefensible ever produced. Even in his own time, some of Paley's arguments were challenged by more enlightened contemporaries. Paley is probably best remembered today for his description of God as 'a watchmaker'. If Blackstone is perhaps the supreme example of hypocrisy among eighteenth-century thinkers, Paley is surely the arch-exponent of 'cant'.

8   Smith originated neither the phrase *laisser-faire* nor the philosophy behind it. The expression itself was used a hundred years earlier by a French merchant arguing with the then Prime Minister Colbert, who demanded from the government 'laisser-faire, laisser passer, laisser allez'. Colbert, to his credit, indignantly refused to agree to such a suggestion. The 'philosophy' of *laisser-faire* was proposed and practised by a group of eighteenth-century French economists known as the Physiocrats, whose most prominent exponents were Turgot and Quesnay. Their economic policies brought France to the brink of ruin and helped create the conditions for the French Revolution. Smith, by contrast, always urged the necessity for the government to be prepared to intervene in the interests of the people.

9   Adam Smith, *The Wealth of Nations*, 1776.

10   William Cobbett, Parliamentary History, VIII, 26 February 1729.

11   J. Sharpe, 'Domestic homicide in early modern England', *Historical Journal*, xxiv, 1981. As well as murder, Sharpe's analysis shows that crimes against property were also decreasing. The popular perception of Britain, and especially London, as 'lawless' clearly needs serious revision. The truth appears to be quite the opposite, that the population, apart from a small minority who were either professional criminals or else so destitute that they had nothing to lose, was becoming more, not less, law-abiding.

12   J. Sharpe, *Crime in Early Modern England, 1556–1750*, Longmans, 1984. The actual figures are dramatic, showing a fall of 90 per cent in the number of executions during the late seventeenth and early eighteenth centuries from the total in the Tudor and early Stuart period.

13   A. Griffiths (ed.), *Chronicles of Newgate*, 1987.

14   Christina Hole, *Witchcraft in England*, Fitzhouse, 1990. The last trial for witchcraft in London seems to have taken place in 1702, concerning a woman from Southwark. I have not yet been able to determine the last person from St Giles to be tried for that particular 'offence'.

15   Count Lorenzo Magalotti, *Travels of Cosmo the Third Duke of Tuscany Through England During the Reign of King Charles II 1669*, 1821.

16   Ibid.

17   Ibid.

18   Alexander Pope, *The Rape of the Lock*, 1712.

19   Samuel Butler, *Hudibras*, 1680.

20   William Shakespeare, *Measure for Measure*, 1608.

21   Charles Johnson. I found this piece of verse in Henry G. Bohn, *A Dictionary of Quotations from the English Poets*, Bell, 1908. Bohn does not give the source. I am not sure who Charles Johnson was but suspect that he was the same as the man who published an 'exposé' of the Hell-Fire Club during the 1760s and perhaps also the man who wrote an account of famous pirates.

22   Proceedings of the Old Bailey.

23   The Ordinary of Newgate, His Account of the Behaviour, Confession and Last Dying Speeches of the Condemned Criminals . . . Executed at Tyburn.

24 Rhyme quoted in: T.V. Buley, 'The Houdini of Newgate', from: *Fifty Greatest Rogues, Tyrants and Criminals*, Odhams, c. 1935.
25 Buley, op. cit.
26 Charles Johnson, *General History of the Robberies and Murders of the Most Notorious Pyrates*, 1734.
27 Ibid.

8

THE STORY OF
ST GILES-IN-THE-FIELDS

'On Newgate steps Jack Chance was found,
And bred up near St. Giles's Pound.' (Old Song)

It is perhaps appropriate that the worst slum in the history of the world should have begun life as a colony for lepers. For most of its history St Giles was a place where the outcasts gathered together to live. Even today it attracts beggars and the homeless of the city. Queen Matilda founded a hospital for lepers in the area as long ago as 1101.[1] It encompassed modern-day Charing Cross Road, Shaftesbury Avenue, New Oxford Street and St Giles High Street. It was situated by the junction of Aldwych and Drury Lane.

The land on which the hospital stood was marshy, almost providing a kind of natural barrier to keep the lepers apart from the rest of the dwellers in London and its environs. There was an existing church in the vicinity and had been one since Saxon times. Before long it became the site of a monastic institution. With the foundation of the monastery, the hospital became loosely attached to it. Soon it was serving the needs of the small community of the local village as well as ministering to the leper colony. Even at this early stage the outcasts of London and ordinary people mingled together in the same area.

London during the Middle Ages was still not much larger than it had been during Roman times. Most of the population lived within the old walls of the City of London. Work was primarily conducted within the City itself or the immediate environs. The role of the state, both at local and national level, was largely confined to the defence of the realm from external enemies and the protection of the citizens within it from crime. Education, medical care and even social security were the responsibility of the Church. Monasteries in particular looked after the people of London and indeed the whole of England. In spite of the charity the monasteries dispensed, by the sixteenth century London had spawned a whole crop of areas that were largely inhabited by the poor. The most notorious and densely populated were East Smithfield and St Katherine's by the Tower in the City of London, together with the Mint in Southwark. They might have been poor and overcrowded but they had not yet grown into fully-fledged rookeries. At least the existence of the monasteries and the encouragement by the Church of private charity offered a measure of relief for the desperately poor. Beggars went to their gates and received food as the servants of the wealthy gathered up the scraps after a feast and distributed them to the people waiting outside.

Both the monastic institution and the hospital lasted until 1539. They then became casualties of Henry VIII's policy of dissolving the monasteries. Not only did the charity that the monks had once doled out to the people come to an abrupt end but even provision for the sick was entirely abandoned. The hospital was closed down and the lepers and local people left to fend for themselves.

Even though the population of St Giles itself was still only around 1,000 people, the effect of the sudden removal of all health care and 'social security' provisions was devastating. Suddenly the area changed from a sleepy but reasonably comfortable village in Middlesex into a district where only poor people lived. Not only were the lepers abandoned to their fate but begging by the newly poor created a new problem for the area and indeed for London as a whole. Areas outside the City of London such as St Giles were decisively affected by the Dissolution of the Monasteries.[2]

Begging was rife in St Giles and the other rookeries.

By 1545 the problem had become so serious that the king decreed the harshest punishments for anyone found begging in the capital. The law, of course, was completely impossible to enforce. More and more beggars sprang up until by 1569 it became necessary for the government to imprison thousands of 'maisterless men'. By 1600, no less than 12,000 beggars were permanently resident in London.[3]

Under the wholesale redistribution of monastic property that took place during the reign of Henry VIII, the land and buildings of St Giles's monastery and hospital were given to the Duke of Northumberland. They then passed into the hands of his son, Elizabeth I's favourite, the Earl of Leicester. He turned the old manor house of St Giles into Dudley House. This lay on what is now the Charing Cross Road. The old hospital chapel was turned into a parish church in 1547. This was demolished in 1624 and a replacement built in 1630. This too was pulled down in 1730 and a new church established in 1734, the present church of St Giles.

Covent Garden, which included St Giles, passed out of the hands of the Abbot of Westminster into those of the Earl of Somerset. In turn they passed to the Earl of Bedford. His redevelopment of the area a hundred years later was permanently to change the face of London.[4]

Elizabethan London was still a small city, only a fraction of the area it now occupies. It consisted only of the City of London itself, Westminster, Southwark, East and West Smithfield, St Katherine's by the Tower, Barbican, Clerkenwell, Grays and Lincoln's Inn, and the Temple. St Giles at this time was simply the nearest village to Westminster. It was not in London at all but at best a suburb to the west of Drury Lane and north of Covent Garden.

From the 1560s onwards thousands of immigrants began pouring into London. There were two main groups that came to the city, Protestant refugees from Catholic persecution in Europe and farm labourers who came looking for work. English agriculture was in one of its many periods of depression and people simply abandoned the countryside, flooding into London. In spite of its small size the population of London more than doubled during the fifty years of Elizabeth I's reign. In 1563 it contained 93,000 people; by 1605 this had grown to at least 200,000. Some estimates put it at 250,000.[5]

The result of such a vast and sudden increase of population was to turn London from a city that was compact and reasonably stable into a nightmare of bustling streets. It changed from an essentially medieval place into a Wild West frontier town. London became a city without a centre or any local government beyond the tiny parish councils. Life became cheap and death frequent, especially for the young. From early times it had attracted immigrants; now the majority of its inhabitants came from other regions of the country or even abroad.

Contemporaries began to describe London as a 'noisome' city. Worse than the noise and overcrowding was the unbearable stench that came with the new immigrants. The rivers and streets of London turned into one open sewer. Epidemics of typhoid, cholera and smallpox ravaged the city. The already overcrowded conditions created a perfect breeding-ground for the spread of disease. Eventually they were to culminate in the Great Plague of 1665.

Rightly or wrongly the immigrants were blamed for bringing these epidemics into the city. They were also resented for taking jobs and homes from ordinary Londoners, being willing to work for lower wages than the citizens.

As the contrasts between rich and poor became extreme, crime soared. Prostitution increased as young girls from the country found that it was often the only way they could earn money. Pickpockets also flourished and the new crime of mugging made the streets of London more dangerous than they had ever been. By the 1580s the problem had become so serious that the government decided to take action. Unfortunately the policy that they adopted was disastrous. Instead of easing the overcrowding of London it turned most of the city into a vast slum. In 1580 Elizabeth I issued a decree forbidding the building of *any* new homes in London. The inevitable result was greater overcrowding in the areas that were already occupied. Far from improving the state of London, it made things worse. Crime, disease and the 'noisomenness' of London increased dramatically. An almost equally bad decision followed this disastrous one by the queen in 1580. In 1585 she simply expelled all foreigners from the City of London.

There were three main reasons why she took this course of action. In the first place many of the foreigners were Spanish, French and Italian merchants – Catholics were automatically suspected of plotting against the queen. The second consideration was the protection of native merchants finding the competition from German and Dutch traders hard to overcome. The Continental merchants, often heavily subsidised by their governments, were able to undercut English traders. This threatened the position of the City of London. Finally most of the Protestant refugees were extremely poor. Not only were they becoming a drain on the parish poor relief funds but they were also resorting to crime to support themselves.

Elizabeth I's expulsion of the foreigners from the City of London in 1585 led to a significant increase in the population of London outside the walls. The thousands of displaced foreigners had to find somewhere else to live. Most of them moved to St Giles. In the same way the queen's refusal to allow the further expansion of London meant that the continued increases in population led to dramatic overcrowding within existing areas of settlement. The overspill from Westminster in particular found St Giles to be a satisfactory location. It was convenient for the merchants who wanted to carry on business with the City of London. The poor foreigners were also close enough to the West End for them to be plenty of job opportunities for them.

The earliest rookeries began in the mid-1580s as a direct result of the new policies introduced by the queen. As early as the time of John Stow's great *Survey of London* in 1598 the eastern districts of the City of London were already becoming more squalid, overcrowded and generally poorer than the western areas.[6]

The same pressures of population that hit the City so badly also spread to St Giles. Before long it had become so unpleasant to live in that the wealthy began to move out. Their place was taken by a continuous influx of poor people. St Giles-in-the-Fields was soon to become the first and worst of all the rookeries. By 1607 it had already become notorious. Though the word itself was not used until the 1790s it was during the 1630s that St Giles first turned into a rookery.

The marriage of Charles I to the French princess Henrietta Maria created additional problems. As the new queen was a Roman Catholic, and Catholicism was illegal in Britain at that time, she was given special dispensation to worship in two chapels of her own. One was at Somerset House and the other at St James's Palace. Many ordinary Catholics took advantage of this loophole in the law to worship in the queen's own chapels.

Because of the unfortunate fact that Ireland was going through one of its periodic 'times of trouble', leading to conflicts that eventually resulted in open rebellion in 1641, many Irish began to flock to the area. Some had already been coming over anyway, ever since the 'flight of the earls' in 1607, when the majority of the Irish Catholic aristocracy fled abroad. This left the native Catholics without the powerful protectors who had previously helped them. The result was a steady trickle of Irish emigrants to London from 1608 onwards. The fact that from 1629 onwards they could also worship openly in the queen's chapels led to the trickle becoming a flood. By 1637 the majority of the population of St Giles was Irish.[7]

Because of the unprecedented demand for accommodation in the area houses were soon being let out room by room. Even cellars were highly sought after. Literally hundreds of families were soon living in each available house. The profits from rents made local publicans and shopkeepers very wealthy indeed. Many young Irishmen came over and worked in London, generally as casual labourers. They sent money to their families back home. Their inability to afford the rent of a whole room themselves made them sublet parts of the room to other tenants. This process of subletting went on to the point where a small corner of a room was rented from someone renting two corners. They in turn rented from someone owning three corners. The process went on back to the tenants, the middleman or landlord's agent and ultimately the landlord.

The restoration of the monarchy in 1660 led to a gradual relaxation of the planning controls that had been fairly rigidly enforced under Cromwell's rule. The Great Fire of London also destroyed the old slum areas of the City. Naturally this also offered openings for casual labourers. There was now a sudden and urgent demand for building workers. This had two principal effects. One was to disperse some sections of the Irish community of London into the City and particularly the East End – this laid the foundations of new slums and rookeries. The second consequence, as discussed earlier, was the rise of the property developer. These people, especially in the period from 1670 to 1720, were largely opportunists whose sole concern was to make money quickly. Since safety and quality cost money, they were not high on their list of priorities. In St Giles and areas like it tenements were built as quickly as possible and filled up with tenants.

Even if poor workmanship led to the injury or death of the occupants the landlords were not responsible and no compensation was paid. The presence of thousands of poor people in desperately overcrowded conditions also led to disease. Even the outbreak of the Great Plague in 1665 has been shown to originate in St Giles. Smallpox, cholera and typhoid were also major killers, though more so in the rookeries. The death rate in St Giles was truly horrific – far higher than the national average.[8]

The transformation of St Giles from a small village into a densely populated slum changed the nature of the population. It became not only disease-ridden but also highly dangerous. Crime soon became one of the principal sources of income for the inhabitants. It would, however, be wrong to suggest that most of the people of St Giles were living on the proceeds of crime. On the whole, they worked hard, at honest jobs, and struggled to feed and clothe their families without resorting to theft. They even tried to dress in the height of fashion to the best of their limited means.

In spite of the extreme conditions they faced, one thing that struck many people who mixed with the folk of St Giles in the seventeenth century was their cheerfulness in the face of adversity. There was almost a touch of admiration mixed in with the pity and fear they felt for the people of the rookery. In spite of the appalling conditions in which they lived, everyone noticed their unquenchable spirit. In a later chapter we shall look at the homes they lived in. We shall see how their ingenuity and determination turned even the worst living conditions that Londoners have ever endured into a kind of triumph.

An attempt by Parliament in 1733 to remove the legal disabilities of Jews resulted in riots in the streets. St Giles took the lead in this rioting. By contrast the anti-Catholic mobs who terrorised London in 1780 attacked St Giles with its higher than average Catholic population. Poor Protestants from other parts of London denounced St Giles as the centre of 'popery'.

Throughout the French Revolutionary and Napoleonic Wars the British government was terrified that St Giles and the other rookeries would erupt into revolution themselves. In fact the dwellers of St Giles and the like served

Seven Dials Market, 1860.

in the Army and Navy with distinction. What rioting and civil unrest there was in Britain at that time took place outside London. Even the 1798 and 1803 rebellions in Ireland had no impact on the Irish of St Giles.

By 1816 the social conditions and high crime rate of the area had become so notorious that Parliament commissioned an official enquiry into the area. They found that 10,000 Irish people lived there, as well as many more English poor.

The end of the Napoleonic Wars led to a temporary boom in housebuilding. This relieved the pressures of overcrowding slightly but was short-lived. By 1825 the building boom had collapsed entirely. Matters were soon made even worse by the passage of the new Poor Law in 1834. This Act also made the already intolerable conditions in St Giles and other rookeries worse. The local authorities now had not only to build new workhouses but also to pay for their staffing and upkeep. Their only solution to the problem of financing these wretched institutions was to raise rates. The landlords responded in kind by raising rents for their tenants. An economic recession also led to falling wages and worse conditions of work as well as higher levels of unemployment. Perhaps understandably in the circumstances, the middle classes now abandoned the area altogether as a result.[9]

Even in the worst times previously, there had always been small pockets of gentility in St Giles. They had somehow continued to exist in the midst of all its tribulations. Now abruptly, under this new combination of higher costs and lower income, they simply abandoned the area altogether. Their now forlorn and desolate buildings lost their old splendour and became instead new tenement dwellings. They were let out in the familiar multi-room occupancy pattern to the hordes of desperately poor people.

In 1837 and 1838 further government surveys found that the rate of mortality was frighteningly high in the rookeries compared with other areas of London. By 1842 the problem had attracted the attention of Edwin Chadwick, a top civil servant of the day. His job was to survey the sanitary conditions of London. The result of his enquiries horrified him. The conclusion of his survey was that the health and living conditions of the people in St Giles and other rookeries were simply too intolerable to be allowed to continue. As a solution to the problem he proposed a massive programme of slum clearance.[10]

During the 1840s the Statistical Society of London produced a series of surveys showing how most working-class Londoners lived in one room with multi-occupancy.[11] These figures at last shocked the middle classes out of their complacency. Although they finally became less reluctant to pay taxes for the purpose of slum clearance, and even resigned themselves to the necessity of it, they still saw no reason why anyone should be compensated for the destruction of their property other than the landlords. Consequently what little incentive there had been for owners to maintain the ramshackle abodes disappeared altogether. They simply allowed the conditions to deteriorate to the point where their buildings were condemned and pocketed a tidy sum from the taxpayer on top of their rents. The tenants were simply turned out on to the streets and left to fend for themselves. Now that the landlords had a financial incentive to allow their buildings to be pulled down, the days of the rookeries were finally numbered. It was to be a sad end to a story that is, in essence, one of triumph over the most daunting odds.

In spite of all the hardships that the area forced them to endure, the majority of the population of St Giles chose to remain there. They might have to move to another house, even another street, but very few chose to leave the area altogether. For all its privations the close-knit world of St Giles ran on a basis of friends, family and contacts. Even the most abjectly poor tried to help each other as best they could. One feels compelled to compare 'The Spirit of St Giles' with 'The Spirit of Dunkirk' or 'The Spirit of the Blitz'. These brave people struggled daily against poverty, squalor, filth, hunger, disease, unemployment and exploitation. Their very survival in the face of such things was itself a veritable triumph of the human spirit.

Notes

1   John Parton, *Some account of the Hospital and Parish of St Giles-in-the-Fields*, Luke Hansard, 1822.

2   John Stow, *Survey of London*, 1598.

3   A.L. Beier, *Masterless men: the vagrancy problem in England 1560–1640*, Methuen, 1985.

4   Rowland Dobie, *History of the United Parishes of St Giles-in-the-Fields and St George*, Bloomsbury, published by the author, 1829.

5   Estimating the population of London at this time is difficult given the lack of anything approaching proper census data. However, the probability is that the true figure is closer to 205,000 than to 250,000.

6   Stow, *Survey*. The late Elizabethan period certainly saw an exaggeration and steep rise in this trend, but even during medieval times, the east and south were always the poorer regions of London.

7   Vestry Minutes of St Giles, 1637.

8   John Graunt, *Natural and Political Observations upon the Bills of Mortality*, J. Martyn, 1676.

9   Occupiers of Houses, St Giles District, 6 November 1835.

10 Edwin Chadwick, Report on the Sanitary Condition of the Labouring Population of Great Britain, Parliamentary Paper 1842, XVVI.

11 Statistical Society of London, *The State of the Inhabitants and their Dwellings in Church Lane*, St Giles, Vol. XI, 1848.

Saffron Hill & other London Rookeries

Throughout the Victorian age two districts of London were repeatedly singled out as displaying the worst examples of the problems occurring in the rookeries. The most frequently cited was St Giles-in-the-Fields, but Saffron Hill, a suburb on the outskirts of the City of London and extending into Holborn, was invariably given second place.

Victorian legislators and reformers argued repeatedly over the reason for the district's insalubrious character. It was pointed out frequently that the area contained a disproportionate number of thieves and prostitutes. Those who saw the inhabitants of the rookeries as largely criminal were at pains to stress these factors and argue that they were the predetermining causes in the squalid conditions of the area. Those who wished to reform the conditions there argued that the physical state of the houses themselves and the overcrowding into which the inhabitants were forced by poverty were the causes.

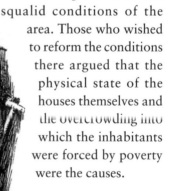

Gossip in a barber's shop.

Saffron Hill was one of many rookeries visited by Dickens. He described it as follows:

> Near to the spot on which Snow Hill and Holborn Hill meet, there opens, upon the right hand as you come out of the City, a narrow and dismal alley leading to Saffron Hill. In its filthy shops are exposed for sale huge bunches of second-hand silk handkerchiefs, of all sizes and patterns; for here reside the traders who purchase them from pickpockets. Confined as the limits of Field Lane are, it has its barber, its coffee-shop, its beer-shop, and its fried-fish warehouse. Here, stores of old iron and bones, and heaps of mildewy fragments of woollen-stuff and linen, rust and rot in the grimy cellars.[1]

Another writer in 1850 called it 'a squalid neighbourhood between HOLBORN and CLERKENWELL, densely inhabited by poor people and thieves. It runs from Field-Lane into Vine-Street. The clergymen of St Andrews, Holborn, have been obliged, when visiting it, to be accompanied by policemen in plain clothes.'[2]

Saffron Hill lay between Field Lane and Holborn Bridge. It included Cross Street, Kirkby Street, Field Lane, Chick Lane (renamed West Street), Saffron Hill itself, Vine Street and Hatton Wall. Its western boundary was Ely

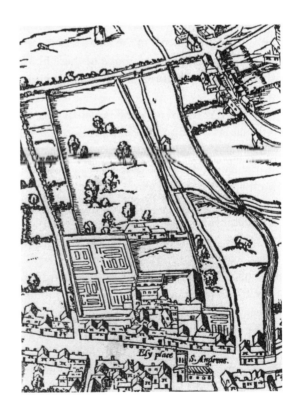

Ely Place, Saffron Hill.

Place; Clerkenwell and St Saviour's forming its eastern extent, its southern boundary being Holborn Hill and its northern extent reaching to Brook Street, generally nicknamed Mutton Hill. On the eastern side of Saffron Hill lay the Fleet Ditch, the largest open sewer in London. Once this had been the Fleet River and had seen thousands of ships navigating their way into London bringing goods from all over the world. The river was eventually enclosed but its foetid exhalations continued to pervade the atmosphere. The Fleet Ditch was described in 1850 as 'a most unsavoury black stream, that did not so much flow as rush impetuously between the walls of the houses on each side. It carries along with its current all sorts of refuse floating on the water. It is difficult, even in cold weather, to stand a few minutes in the room when the windows looking down upon it are opened. In summer, the stench is intolerable.' It was also described as 'a wide deep open sewer . . . running just under the kitchens of the houses.'[3]

The building of a series of so-called 'thieves' houses' in 1683 turned Saffron Hill from a squalid and dangerous slum into a full-blown rookery. The person responsible for these dwellings was a man known as McWaullen or McWelland, allegedly the chief of a tribe of gypsies. These 'thieves' houses' were not only a meeting place for criminals but also a place where stolen property could be deposited. Among their most notorious inhabitants were Jack Sheppard, Jonathan Wild and Dick Turpin. These 'thieves' houses' remained in existence until the 1840s when they were demolished as part of the road improvements in the area.

We have a description of one of these houses from an informant in 1844, who witnessed it before it had been pulled down. He describes it as follows:

> The most extraordinary and ingenious part of the premises, I consider to be the means of escape. If a prisoner once got within their walls, it was almost impossible to capture him, there were so many outlets and communications. The most active officer had scarcely a chance of taking the thief, if the latter only got a few minutes start of him.[4]

Apparently a rotating staircase was employed to enable the thief to make his escape and ensure that the pursuing law officer became hopelessly lost. There were also trapdoors, holes in the walls and concealed cellars through any one of which a criminal could flee before the police could track him down.

Saffron Hill was largely made up of lodging houses. Hardly any of the homes in the area were inhabited by ordinary family units. At the bottom of the house was a cellar where it was customary to dispose of the entire household rubbish and waste. Above that, covered only by the thinnest of boards, was the sitting room for the lodgers to meet. The floorboards were usually so rotten that the fumes from the cellar below wafted upwards into the sitting room. Above the sitting room were the sleeping quarters, to which the lodgers gained access by climbing a ladder. These consisted of a few small rooms, with the beds packed so closely together that it was difficult even to walk between them. It was very common indeed for two or more people to sleep in these beds, as many as four or five if young children were involved. Bed linen was also of the most basic kind, where it existed at all. The provision of water for these dwellings was also inadequate. Three times a week the supply was turned on and tenants literally fought one another to get the tiny quantities released during this brief 'wet' period.

The exteriors of the buildings were no better. Apart from the decaying bricks and fallen tiles, long-broken windows were stuffed with rags in place of the glass that had once filled them. The streets themselves were covered with mounds of ash, left behind by the dustmen after their visits. The inhabitants eagerly sifted through even these middens in search of anything usable or saleable. The ingenuity of the people knew no bounds when it came to turning the filthiest rags into merchandisable goods.

Access to many of the rookery courts was obtained by going through a low archway, formed out of boards and planks. They were uneven squares, sloping, often steeply, down the hill on which they had been built. Enclosed on three sides, their narrowness was oppressive and somehow threatening in itself. Against the wall, heaps of rubbish and filth lay abandoned, waiting for scavengers or dustmen to remove them at some indeterminate time in the future. As well as the hazards of disease from the inadequate diet and the insanitary conditions of the buildings, there were other sources of danger to health. Keepers of lodging houses habitually bought furniture, crockery, beds and other items from houses or even hospitals where the previous occupants or users had died from smallpox, cholera, tuberculosis and other infectious diseases.

Field Lane, Saffron Hill.

Field Lane,
Saffron Hill.

The standard price for these 'goods' was *9d* an item, so it was extremely cheap and easy to furnish a rookery home from items that no one else would have bought even in extreme desperation.

The impoverishment of Saffron Hill was so great that in 1801 the parish council, meeting to decide on a Poor Rate, seriously considered whether or not it would be possible or even desirable to levy rates upon the inhabitants at all. The parish clerk gave notice of the meeting as follows:

> The inhabitants of the Liberty of Saffron Hill Hatton Garden and Ely Rents in this Parish are desired to meet at the workhouse upon Little Saffron Hill on Thursday next at Three o'Clock in the Afternoon precisely to make a rate for relief of the poor of the said liberty.
>
> The above notice was published in the Parish Church of Saint Andrew Holborn on Sunday the 20th day of December 1801 immediately after divine Service in the Morning by me.
> Rd Perry. Par. Clk.[5]

The authorities decided to levy a Poor Rate on the inhabitants but it proved anything but easy to collect it from them. In 1829 a severe notice was issued by the chairman of the Saffron Hill Ely Place Committee, in which the following instructions were given:

> The Ely Place Committee deem it very Essential that you direct your Collectors <u>IMMEDIATELY</u> to demand the 2 rates assessed on the inhabitants of Ely Place, and beg to inform you it is necessary that such demand be made before Michaelmas Day next, and that you allow him to leave printed notices at each house, stating the said demand.

I am, Gentlemen, On behalf of the said Committee,

Your very obedt Servant

B I Armstrong

Chairman

Workhouse, Saffron Hill, 24th Sept 1829[6]

The area was noted for its high concentration of thieves, prostitutes and fences. The majority of the fences were generally described by outside observers as Jewish. Many scholars believe that Fagin was based on a Jewish fence in Saffron Hill, whom Dickens had encountered and turned into a character in *Oliver Twist*. Certainly the den of thieves into which Oliver first enters is set in Saffron Hill.

One of the great misconceptions people have about the dwellers in the rookeries is that they were more or less entirely occupied by the criminal classes. Most men were not thieves and most women were not prostitutes. They struggled to make an honest living under trying circumstances. Saffron Hill was also known for its printers, street singers, crossing sweepers, muffin sellers, match sellers, sellers of dog and cat food, cabmen, dustmen and sellers of watercress and fruit.

Another aspect of the area is that it contained the centre of the trade in diamonds, other precious stones and jewellery within its precincts. Hatton Garden was perhaps the only part of Saffron Hill where the inhabitants were prosperous. There is no doubt that many of the dealers in the area dealt with fences and were not always particular about the source of the gems that they were offered from time to time. On the other hand it was probably a necessity of life for them to handle and recut stolen jewellery (known colloquially as 'tomfoolery') rather than risk being robbed by criminals themselves. By providing a means of 'laundering' stolen gems, the diamond and gold dealers ensured their own continuing prosperity.

During the 1840s a large influx of Italian immigrants to the area changed its character slightly, mainly for the better. It became the centre of the ice cream trade in London as well as many entertainers. Acts ranging from clowns, opera singers, Punch and Judy shows, barrel organists with monkeys in tow, Italian folk singers and women dancers in bright Italian costume were among the most popular 'draws'.

The Italian community in Saffron Hill liked to live and work out in the open air as much as possible. Their colourful clothes, theatrical manner and community spirit made the living conditions within the rookery easier to tolerate. Even so, unlike the native inhabitants, the Italians in Saffron Hill moved out as soon as the chance of better accommodation came their way. Italian immigration continued throughout the Victorian age and it was not until the Second World War that this part of London ceased to be the 'Italian Quarter'.

A muffin seller.   A pedlar.

As late as 1881 tables compiled by the great social scientist Charles Booth showed clearly that Holborn, the district that included Saffron Hill and a number of other lesser rookeries, was the poorest district in London.[7]

Table of Poverty: London, 1881

DISTRICT	PERCENTAGE OF POVERTY
Holborn (including Saffron Hill)	48.9
St George in the East	48.9
Bethnal Green (including the jago)	44.6
St Saviour's Southwark	43.4
St Olave's Southwark	42.2
Shoreditch	40.2
Whitechapel	39.2
Stepney	38.0
Greenwich	36.9
Poplar	36.5
Westminster	33.0
City of London	31.5
Islington	31.2

DISTRICT	PERCENTAGE OF POVERTY
St Pancras	30.4
Camberwell	28.6
Wandsworth	27.4
Marylebone	27.4
St Giles-in-the-Fields	26.7
Mile End	26.1
Lambeth	26.1
Woolwich	24.7
Fulham	24.7
Kensington	24.7
Chelsea	24.5
Strand	23.9
Hackney	23.1
Paddington	21.7
St George's Hanover Square	21.6
Lewisham	18.1
Hampstead	13.3
Whole of Metropolitan London	31.0

The curious aspect of these statistics is that the official poverty figures for the district bore no relation to those who applied to the Charity Organisation Society for relief. Holborn, including Saffron Hill, was not even close to being the largest claimant area. The following table shows this clearly.[8]

Table of Applicants for Relief from the C.O.S., 1881

Battersea	429
Camberwell	401
St George in the East	357
St James's Soho	346
Mile End	336
Greenwich	210
Lambeth	209
South St Pancras	205
North St Pancras	201
Southwark	200
Holborn (including Saffron Hill)	126
Hackney	126
Brixton	85
Wandsworth	60
Sydenham	53

It would be possible to argue from the previous statistics that poverty was greater in South London than in any other part of the metropolis. Besant certainly thought so but it is perhaps more likely that either the C.O.S. was more active south of the river or that people in that area were more willing to make a claim or perhaps had a greater expectation that they might be successful in obtaining relief if they claimed.

Nor was the problem of overcrowding in the area made any easier by the sporadic and unsystematic attempts at slum clearance made from the 1830s onwards. As late as 1893, Booth showed on the basis of the 1891 census that overcrowding in the rookery areas had steadily increased as a result of the clearances.

Table of Overcrowding by District[9]

DISTRICT	PERCENTAGE OF OVERCROWDING
St George in the East	59.5
Holborn (including Saffron Hill)	56.5
Whitechapel	55.5
Shoreditch	50.5
Bethnal Green	49.5
St Giles-in-the-Fields	47.0
St Saviour's Southwark	44.0
St Pancras	42.5
Marylebone	41.5
Westminster	40.5
Strand	38.0
St Olave's Southwark	36.5
St George's Hanover Square	29.5

The overcrowding figures, already shocking many Victorians in the early 1840s, became worse as the programme of slum clearance began. Over a period of forty years Saffron Hill lost a high proportion of its housing stock. As happened in other rookery areas, the majority of the population remained in the district where they lived. They did not move out to the expanding suburbs.

The extent to which the slum clearance programmes actually *increased* multi-occupation are clearly seen by comparing the figures for overcrowded districts with those for areas of London that experienced substantial loss of housing stock.

Table of Districts where Housing Stock Declined, 1841–81[10]

DISTRICT	HOUSES PER ACRE	
	1841	1881
Central (including City of London)		
Whitecross Street	48.39	25.15
Cripplegate	34.91	12.27
St James's	30.88	26.44
St Botolph	30.02	15.20
St Clement Danes	28.59	13.15
Saffron Hill	24.23	12.20
St Giles South	24.22	18.61
Castle Baynard	23.95	5.87
Christchurch	23.89	6.02
St Sepulchre's	23.54	10.15
St Bride's	22.63	10.70
St Giles North	22.61	15.63
Queenhithe	20.80	7.02
Finsbury	20.71	10.34
All Hallows	19.74	9.04
Broad Street	19.21	10.62

The above table is a sample of some of the worst rookeries and demonstrates clearly how the process of demolishing slum housing made overcrowding and the living conditions of the inhabitants deteriorate further. Far from improving their circumstances, the clearances made every aspect of their lives worse than before.

Employment statistics for the area also reveal some surprising results. Based on a comparison of occupational figures from the 1861 and 1891 censuses, a number of conclusions that might be described as counter-intuitive clearly emerge. In the following tables, the Central district included St Giles, Strand, Holborn, Saffron Hill, Clerkenwell, St Luke's, the City of London and its immediate suburbs; East London included St George in the East, Shoreditch, Bethnal Green, Whitechapel, Stepney and Mile End; North London included Marylebone, St Pancras, Islington, Hackney, and Hampstead; South London included St Saviour's and St Olave's (both in Southwark), Lambeth, Bermondsey, Rotherhithe, Camberwell, Newington, St George's South, Wandsworth, Lewisham and Greenwich; while West London contained Westminster, St James', St George's Hanover Square, Chelsea and Kensington.

Table of Male Occupations by District, 1861 Census[11]

Occupation	Central %	East %	North %	South %	West %
Retail	12.91	10.80	11.65	10.50	9.86
Transport	12.50	18.47	11.71	15.03	12.86
Construction	7.57	7.82	12.11	9.97	12.50
Wood Trade	6.23	8.47	5.93	4.47	3.56
Engineering	6.16	6.21	3.62	6.70	3.16
Service	5.63	2.60	4.88	3.50	10.24
Clothing	5.55	3.27	3.62	2.63	4.72
Printing	5.47	1.80	2.52	2.00	1.02
Shoe Trade	4.74	5.11	3.80	3.29	3.27
Professional	4.69	1.84	7.09	3.75	7.40
Labouring	4.67	8.01	5.49	8.43	6.62
Precision Industry	4.27	1.49	3.49	0.80	1.37
Clerical	2.97	1.91	5.19	3.02	2.33
Finance	2.84	1.58	4.33	2.60	2.91
Administrative	0.58	0.52	2.00	3.07	2.19
Food & Drink	1.77	3.22	1.06	1.62	1.02
Leather Trade	1.65	0.87	0.87	2.43	0.72
Manufacturing	1.46	1.61	1.29	1.88	1.03
Chemical Trade	1.29	1.65	0.90	1.48	0.77
Textiles	1.22	4.50	0.96	1.09	0.44
Entertainment	0.70	0.39	0.69	0.41	0.61
Defence	0.64	0.56	1.21	3.64	3.67
Shipbuilding	0.08	3.51	0.08	1.70	0.10
Agriculture	0.58	0.52	2.00	3.07	2.19
Other Trades	2.58	2.16	3.30	3.80	4.43

Table of Female Occupations by district, 1861 Census[12]

Occupation	Central %	East %	North %	South %	West %
Service	21.58	11.95	26.18	20.00	33.80
Clothing	11.54	13.54	8.97	8.55	7.70
Printing	1.45	0.41	0.21	0.38	1.09
Professional	1.36	1.27	2.78	2.28	2.86
Wood Trade	1.30	0.76	0.74	0.46	0.34
Shoe Trade	0.96	1.76	0.49	0.81	0.26
Manufacturing	0.55	0.53	0.32	0.30	0.18
Finance	0.37	0.21	0.14	0.08	0.19

Leather Trade	0.32	0.17	0.06	0.25	0.03
Food & Drink	0.31	0.21	0.17	0.17	0.15
Entertainment	0.28	0.14	0.30	0.19	0.23
Engineering	0.21	0.11	0.07	0.07	0.02
Precision Industry	0.18	0.04	0.08	0.03	0.03
Transport	0.14	0.06	0.05	0.06	0.04
Chemical Trade	0.11	0.11	0.05	0.07	0.01
Agriculture	0.05	0.05	0.04	0.17	0.18
Construction	0.04	0.02	0.03	0.01	0.02
Labouring	0.03	0.04	0.02	0.04	0.04
Administrative	0.02	0.03	0.04	0.05	0.08
Shipbuilding	0.00	0.00	0.00	0.01	0.00
Other Trades	55.74	62.86	57.37	63.95	52.51

Table of Male Occupations by District, 1891 Census[13]

Occupation	Central	East	North	South	West
	%	%	%	%	%
Transport	14.53	81.09	13.71	13.15	14.75
Retail	10.15	8.70	9.81	9.32	9.29
Service	8.66	3.15	4.26	3.34	9.08
Construction	5.00	5.20	8.19	8.13	9.58
Labouring	4.55	7.81	3.95	7.44	5.18
Engineering	4.46	4.53	3.41	5.09	2.69
Clerical	4.17	2.87	7.72	6.30	5.15
Professional	3.80	1.21	4.58	3.44	5.52
Precision Industry	3.15	0.95	3.40	1.17	1.42
Finance	2.91	1.16	4.15	3.41	3.12
Manufacturing	2.37	2.67	1.82	2.96	1.21
Administrative	2.13	1.03	1.87	1.84	2.30
Shoe Trade	1.53	4.36	2.04	1.29	1.45
Food & Drink	1.49	2.06	1.02	1.09	0.75
Printing	1.15	3.14	3.40	3.45	1.15
Leather Trade	1.02	0.97	0.80	1.38	0.51
Entertainment	0.84	0.28	0.68	0.57	0.82
Chemical Trade	0.74	1.09	0.78	1.21	0.57
Textiles	0.56	1.03	0.48	0.47	0.24
Defence	0.51	0.34	1.87	1.84	2.18
Shipbuilding	0.04	1.52	0.05	0.56	0.06
Others	13.92	15.50	15.50	17.34	16.92

Table of Female Occupations by District, 1891 Census

Occupations	Central	East	North	South	West
	%	%	%	%	%
Service	23.73	10.81	21.36	17.66	32.34
Clothing	7.54	10.48	8.03	5.94	6.98
Printing	4.40	2.49	0.82	1.21	0.12
Retail	3.05	2.53	2.06	1.90	1.60
Manufacturing	1.65	2.32	0.93	0.95	0.02
Wood Trade	1.57	1.30	0.80	0.34	0.25
Professional	1.42	1.05	2.72	2.47	2.62
Food & Drink	0.87	1.52	0.51	0.55	0.27
Textiles	0.87	1.42	0.60	0.42	0.23
Leather Trade	0.59	0.45	0.21	0.27	0.03
Entertainment	0.58	0.16	0.52	0.42	0.50
Clerical	0.51	0.17	0.54	0.38	0.40
Precision Industry	0.43	0.07	0.19	0.05	0.04
Transport	0.35	0.21	0.22	0.17	0.12
Engineering	0.32	0.12	0.10	0.10	0.03
Chemical Trade	0.26	0.40	0.16	0.09	0.02
Shoe Trade	0.25	1.63	0.41	0.14	0.11
Agriculture	0.16	0.04	0.08	0.07	0.09
Finance	0.15	0.06	0.10	0.08	0.08
Administrative	0.12	0.11	0.19	0.15	0.13
Construction	0.05	0.03	0.02	0.02	0.02
Labouring	0.03	0.03	0.01	0.03	0.02
Shipbuilding	0.00	0.01	0.00	0.00	0.00
Defence	0.00	0.00	0.00	0.00	0.00
Others	51.10	62.59	59.42	66.59	53.77

Perhaps the most immediately obvious conclusion that can be drawn from these statistics is the striking change in employment patterns in the East End. In 1861 only 14 per cent of men in East London worked in the field of transport, but by 1891 this accounted for almost 82 per cent of the male workforce. The principal area of employment for women remained domestic service but there was a sharp increase in women working in administrative and professional occupations, as well as a slight fall in the numbers of men performing those functions. The shoe trade and clothing trade were in decline by the early 1890s, which may perhaps account to some extent for the rise of the sweatshop in those areas of employment at this time.

The tables allow us to view a less dramatic but still significant shift in working patterns in Saffron Hill and its neighbouring areas. The change is much less pronounced in terms of female occupations but there are certainly clear signs of change in the female labour market, away from the traditional low-paid home industries and towards occupations with higher remuneration and more status. Saffron Hill was the worst rookery in the City of London. Other rookeries in the area will now be considered briefly. Some of them will be dealt with in the appendix as they fall slightly outside the time frame of this book.

BISHOPSGATE

The Bishopsgate area of London was one of the earliest parts of the City to turn into a rookery. Its western boundary was Gracechurch Street and Leadenhall Market; on the east, it extended as far as Houndsditch and its northern extent bordered on Spitalfields. The houses were built without proper foundations and the dirt and rubble excavated during their construction was simply left to rot on the road. Other rubbish was thrown into the ditch and the whole area became one of the most unpleasant in the entire City of London. It had an active life as a rookery until the 1860s, when it fell victim to the building of Liverpool Street station.

MOORGATE

This rookery arose after the Great Fire of London in 1666. It was destroyed by the City of London in 1830 when they embarked on an ambitious programme of new building and road widening. It was perhaps most noted as the site of Grub Street, described in 1754 by Samuel Johnson as 'a street near Moorfields, much inhabited by writers of small histories, dictionaries, and temporary poems, whence any mean production is called Grub Street.' However, it has a higher claim to literary fame than that – John Keats was born in Moorgate in 1795.

WHITECROSS STREET, FINSBURY

Perhaps the worst of all the City rookeries other than Saffron Hill was Whitecross Street, formerly known as Whitecross Place. Comments on it by observers included 'filthy lanes and death-breeding alleys' as well as the famous remark, 'It is said, God made everything. I don't believe it. He never made Whitecross Place.'

CRIPPLEGATE

The district of Cripplegate had long been notorious for its high proportion of beggars. Curiously, however, its name does not derive from 'cripple' in the sense of disabled but from the Anglo-Saxon 'crepel' which means, not the 'gate of cripples', but 'the narrow gate'. Its proximity to the rich merchants and traders of the City soon led to another overspill of immigrants settling in the area.

The main sources of employment in the Cripplegate area were spinning gold and silver, 'wire-drawing' and silk weaving. Women also worked in domestic service and as wet-nurses as well as the inevitable prostitution. As rookeries in the City went, Cripplegate was comparatively prosperous. Weaving was still done by hand, and it was possible for a weaver to amass quite a good living from the trade. The workers in precious metals had a ready market for their goods with so many goldsmiths and silversmiths living within the City. Even so, it was a squalid and dangerous area.

St Sepulchre

St Sepulchre in the Farringdon district was known for its blacksmiths, foundries, pewter manufacturing, brewers and watchmakers.

West Smithfield

West Smithfield was the main area for the sale of meat in London, and cattle were driven to the market and sold to butchers. It was common for bulls and pigs to attack and kill pedestrians. The stench of thousands of frightened animals being driven through the streets also added to the health hazards of the market. The Royal Hospital for the Sick, better known as St Bartholomew's Hospital, or 'Barts', was also situated there.

By the standards of the time the medical care provided there was very good indeed. Certainly the patients at the hospital ate well, as can be seen from the following menu for the week:

> ten ounces of bread a day, six ounces of boiled beef, two pints of beef broth, sixteen pints of beer, three pints of mutton broth, six ounces of beef, half a pound of boiled mutton, six ounces of cheese, two pints of milk pottage, three ounces of butter, one pint of rice milk, one pint of sugar 'soppes' and one pint of water gruel.

All this was free to the patients.

Clerkenwell

One of its most notorious areas was Turnmill Street (also known as Turnbull Street because of the large numbers of cattle driven across it on their way to Smithfield). Its proximity to the Fleet River, the dirtiest in London, added to the health hazards. The Fleet was little more than an open sewer into which all the waste matter of London was habitually and casually thrown. The area was notorious for prostitution, though it also became the centre of London's printing industry. The most graphic account of the rookeries of Clerkenwell was given in George Gissing's *The Nether World*, published in 1889.

Devil's Acre, Westminster.

St Bride's

The main industry in this area, like Clerkenwell, was printing. It also became noted for the number of journalists who lived and worked there. Even today, St Bride's is known as 'the printers' church' or 'the journalists' church'.

Pye Street, Westminster

This part of London was once an area of wide green fields, only a few small houses scattered among them. Westminster began to expand beyond the area of the abbey and Charing Cross and by the early seventeenth century aristocrats had built a number of homes in the area. Tothill Street and Tothill Fields also contained a hospital for poor women. By the mid-seventeenth century, Tufton, Marsham and St Peter's Streets were built.

Sir Robert Pye owned a house in the area during the Civil War. Following the Restoration, development of the district began. Pye Street, Duck Lane, Orchard Street, Palmer's Village and Stretton Grounds were built and a number of houses erected on the site. By 1720 a workhouse had been built in the area, on the site of Pye's former house. The 1720s saw the development of new streets and houses, most notably North Street and Smith Street. By

Old Pye Street and the Ragged School.

1741 the condition of the area had become so poor that it attracted the attention of Parliament.

The Pye Street rookery had the highest crime rate in the whole of London, higher even than St Giles or the East End, and Duck Lane was the most notorious street in the district. The rookery was demolished during the Victorian 'improvements'.

BERWICK STREET, SOHO

Development in the area began in about 1660. The district was marshy and in 1662 paving of the roads was introduced. In 1671 Colonel Thomas Panton built homes in Windmill Street. Sir Christopher Wren described the houses in the area as being, unlike the grand houses in St James's Fields, 'a receptacle for the poorer sort, and the offensive trades to the annoyance of the better inhabitants; the damage of the parishes already too much burdened with poor, the choking the air of His Majesty's Palace and park, and the houses of the nobility; the infecting of the waters – these habitations so complained of being continued and erected in Dog's Fields, Windmill Fields, and the fields adjoining Soho.'[14] In 1665 a 'pest house' was established here to receive victims of the Great Plague. In 1720 Strype described Berwick Street as 'waste and unbuilt ground; a street not over well inhabited.'[15] The writer Henry Fielding complained that the poor were moving into the area during the 1750s. To judge from Wren's comments, however, that can only have been a case of making a neighbourhood already largely inhabited by the poor totally so.[16]

Bad as the area was in those days, the nineteenth century saw Berwick Street sink from a decaying slum into one of the worst rookeries in London. In 1852 Beames described 'a mouldy, smoky, dilapidated air about the whole; some of the houses have sunk much; others are closed up with shutters, the windows, in many cases, broken or mended with paper.'[17] The inhabitants often kept cows, pigs and rabbits and the consequent smell upon their presence permeated the whole area. Beames declared that 'the houses are not so crowded as those in Church Lane or Saffron Hill,' though he added that 'the rooms are miserably small, mere closets.'[18] He added that 'some of the houses were occupied by chimney-sweepers, several by day labourers, some by men who got their living by selling baked potatoes. Under the houses are large cellars, which are piled with these vegetables, and from which the tin cans of the vendors are replenished. There are also several rag shops in this part of the parish, the cellars being filled to overflowing with rags.'[19]

The rents for these rooms were 3*d* a night, though no charge was made for lodging there on Sundays. In 1852, the year that Beames described their squalid conditions, a charitable society purchased the entire rookery, erecting 'model dwellings' in place of the homes that had previously stood there.[20]

AGAR TOWN

This rookery, in the St Pancras area, was built by William Agar, a lawyer, from 1815 onwards. He leased the land south of Agar Grove from the Church Commissioners and developed the streets around. His own house, Elm Lodge, was of good quality. The buildings in Agar Town, named after him, were well below the minimum that might have been expected, even by the standards of the time. By the 1830s it had become full of packed rows of densely populated cottages. The vast influx of labourers working on the new railways added to the already overcrowded and squalid conditions. By the 1840s it had grown to rival St Giles and Saffron Hill for the title of the worst rookery in London. Its appalling living conditions were, in some respects, even worse than those two most notorious districts.

During the enquiry by the Board of Health into the Sanitary Conditions of London during 1848–9, Agar Town was described as 'one of the most neglected parts of the metropolis'. The board criticised the state of the water supply, the conditions of the houses, the almost complete absence of sanitary provisions and the practice by all the inhabitants of 'scavenging'.[21]

In 1851 an account by the journalist W.M. Thomas in Dickens's magazine *Household Words* brought Agar Town firmly into the public eye. His description of how he had mistakenly come across the area and how appalled he had been by the living conditions of the people shocked his readers.[22] In 1861 John Hollingshead again slated the area in his book *Ragged London in 1861*. He pointed out that the houses had been built on a swamp and that they ran 'down to the canal in every stage of dirt and decay'.[23]

The area also contained the Fleet River, which had mercifully been covered over at the beginning of the nineteenth century. Even so, it briefly burst out of its underground prison in 1846, sweeping away three posthouses in a 'tidal wave of sewage' and even crushing a steamboat by Blackfriars Bridge. In addition the Regent Canal also ran through Agar Town. It became yet another open sewer for the inhabitants, at least for anything they did not scavenge. A local gasworks also added to the general stench and squalor of the whole area.

Eventually Agar's heirs sold his land to the Midland Railway in 1861–2. They promptly demolished the houses, paying nearly £20,000 compensation to the landlords. The tenants were simply evicted without any compensation at all. The social reformer Lord Shaftesbury managed to get an Act of Parliament passed that required the railway companies to state how many tenants would be displaced by their development, and to force the landlords to provide alternative accommodation. The railway companies, however, soon found a way round this provision. The leading philanthropist Octavia Hill described the way in which the evictions were carried out to avoid any need for making provision for the tenants. She described it as follows:

> Usually, the railway company communicate with the landlords, and tell them, 'We are going to take your property;' the landlord gives the ordinary weekly or monthly notice to the tenants, and long before the railway comes, the tenants have been got rid of, so that the landlord pockets the compensation. This is before the Act [of Parliament, licensing the particular railway development] is obtained. The companies, therefore, can go before Parliament, and say, 'We do not displace people;' there is nobody there.[24]

St Pancras station now occupies the site. It is, of course, an architectural masterpiece, but the human cost of its construction has never been taken into account. If a fraction of the money spent on the station had been given over instead to the provision of decent dwellings for the poor in Agar Town, their lives might have been transformed.

THE POTTERIES, NORTH KENSINGTON

One of the worst rookeries in West London was the Potteries in North Kensington. A report on the conditions there by Thomas Lovick, Assistant Surveyor for the Metropolitan Commission of Sewers, described it as follows:

> On the north, east and west sides this locality is skirted by open ditches, filled with the accumulations from the extensive piggeries attached to most of the houses. Intersecting in various parts, and discharging into the ditches on the

north and west, are many smaller but still more offensive open ditches, some skirting houses, the bedroom windows of which open over them; some running in the rear and fronts of houses, others at the sides and through the middle of the streets and alleys, loading the atmosphere throughout their course with their pestilential exhalations.

The streets are unpaved and full of ruts. The surface is strewn with refuse of almost every conceivable description. They are at times wholly impassable. At <u>all</u> seasons they are in a most offensive and disgusting condition, emitting effluvia of the most nauseous character.

The majority of the houses are of a most wretched class, many being mere hovels in a ruinous condition, are generally densely populated; they are filthy in the extreme, and contain vast accumulations of garbage and offal, the small gardens attached to some being purposely raised by this to a greater height.

Some are surrounded by banks formed of these accumulations. In the yards of some there are wells the water in which is so contaminated by the percolation of the foul drainage as to be wholly unfit for domestic use, the inhabitants being compelled to fetch water from a pump at some distance, belonging to Mr Bird, paying a yearly rent for the privilege.

That which has been described to me as 'the monster nuisance of the district' is a large stagnant piece of water called 'the ocean', occupying an area of between 50 and 60,000 square feet, or upwards of <u>one-fourth</u> the area of the Potteries.

Surrounding this locality are excavations much below the general level, formed by the abstraction of the earth for the manufacture of bricks; many of these have been abandoned, and are now filled with foul and foetid water.

A brick-field, now in use, belonging to Mr Bird, a large owner of property in this district, contains several pools of water, and is low and has a damp appearance.[25]

The Assistant Surveyor added a number of tables to support his claim that the entire area was unfit for human habitation. These are two of the statistics he gathered:

Tables of Sickness and Mortality in Kensington Potteries[26]

Districts	1846		1847		1848	
	Sickness	Mortality	Sickness	Mortality	Sickness	Mortality
Notting Hill, Norland, Pottery	360	(not stated)	550	(not stated)	602	(not stated)
Pottery, proportion of	67	27	133	15	180	37
Proportion in the Potteries to the Other Districts	⅓	–	¼	–	½	–

Proportion of Deaths at the Ages[27]

Districts	0–15	%	15–60	%	60+	%	Greatest Age at Death
Pottery	69	80	12	14	5	6	77
Notting Hill and Norland	34	43	26	33	19	24	80
Excess	**0-15**	**%**	**15-60**	**%**	**60+**	**%**	
In Potteries	35	37	–	–	–	–	–
In Norland and Notting Hill	–	–	14	19	14	18	–

LISSON GROVE

This district, around the Paddington and Edgware Road areas, was also one of the worst rookeries in London. As late as the 1890s it was a byword for drunkenness, violence and criminality. Police officers only patrolled it in pairs and the women of Lisson Grove were considered by them the most violent and foul-mouthed in London. The population were notoriously heavy drinkers, the police claiming that the women of the district were worse than the men.[28]

Suffolk Place, Lisson Grove.

JACOB'S ISLAND, BERMONDSEY

In spite of heavy competition, this was unquestionably the worst of all the rookeries in South London. It had some of the most beautiful dwellings of any of the London slums, which made contemporaries, struck by the contrast between its actual condition and how the surroundings suggested it ought to have been, refer to it as the 'Venice of Drains' or the 'Venice of Cholera'.[29]

The horrors of Jacob's Island, though certainly known to Dickens, who set the final scene involving Bill Sikes in the area when writing *Oliver Twist*, were perhaps most graphically brought to life by Henry Mayhew in a series of articles in *The Morning Chronicle* between 1849 and 1850.[30] These pieces launched Mayhew on his career as a journalist *par excellence* of the London underclass.

The area was known as 'Jacob's Island' as the result of a stagnant ditch, which cut off the district and turned it into an 'island'. Nearby stood a paper mill and 'the waters of the Thames were let into these tidal ditches three times a week.'[31] The floors of the houses were often below ground level and the bedrooms were normally approached via a ladder. The main road of the area was called London Street. Unlike most rookery dwellings, the houses were 'not inconveniently crowded'.[32]

Beames described Jacob's Island as follows:

> The houses are evidently old, the first stories slightly overhanging the ground floor. Still, the whole locality is curious because surrounded on four sides by stagnant water. The floors of the houses being below the level of the foot-path must be flooded in wet weather; the rooms are mouldy and ill-favoured; dark, small and confined, they could not be peopled as the alleys of St Giles, because their size would not admit of it. There is the usual amount of decaying vegetable matter, the uneven foot-path, the rotten doors, the broken windows patched with rags, ash heaps in front of the houses, dogs &c, housed there, ragged children, and other features well known to those conversant with such neighbourhoods.[33]

The whole district, surrounded as it was by a ditch filled with stagnant water, was the cholera capital of London. The only source of 'fresh' water was the ditch, which also functioned as 'the common sewer of the neighbourhood'.[34] The inhabitants drew water from the ditch, and let the liquid stand for a day or two before skimming the fluid and drinking it. Beames remarked: 'The most superficial observer will perceive an unnatural whiteness in the complexion, the scars of scrofula, and the sore eyes of the children.'[35]

RATCLIFF HIGHWAY

Once again, in spite of considerable competition, Ratcliff Highway was probably the worst of all the East End slums. It also had a few characteristics that made it not only unusual but in certain respects unique among the

London rookeries. It was one of the earliest of the 'new rookeries', dating back to at least 1600. As early as 1603 Stow remarked that there were 'many small tenements raised towards Radcliffe' [sic].[36]

The rookery stretched to the Thames to the south, the Commercial Road to the north, the basin of the Regent Canal to the east and the Minories to the west. It began as a district frequented principally by sailors. Many of the buildings in the area were wooden, since the Great Fire of London did not spread out as far as the East End. It was a district of long, narrow streets, courts and alleys, almost all of the alleys being culs-de-sac.

The whole economy of Ratcliff Highway was based around shipping, the docks and the presence of sailors on shore leave. The transitory nature of much of the population affected the behaviour of the permanent residents and also led to the area being one of the highest crime spots in the whole of London. In 1850 a survey of the area found that 25 per cent of the men in the area were sailors. Every nationality and language was represented in the rookery.

There were very few legitimate means of earning a living in Ratcliff Highway other than keeping a public house or renting out property. As might be expected in an area with a large number of sailors arriving and departing, prostitution was also a regular aspect of the area's life. Other retail outlets were shops selling slops and those catering for various aspects of the nautical trade. In the pubs, rooms were set aside for dancing while the walls were painted with nautical scenes ranging from shipwrecks to naval engagements. In the evenings musicians entertained the customers and dancing commenced. Acrobats and contortionists were also frequent entertainers in the pubs.

Crime was rampant in Ratcliff Highway, ranging from drunken brawls, muggings, assaults, robberies, selling stolen goods and a swindle that appears to have been unique to the area, known as 'crimping'. 'Crimps' were keepers of lodging houses for sailors. This was, however, largely a front for fleecing them out of their money. The crimps or 'crimpers' allowed the sailors to stay rent free, also providing food and drink, but all this was done as a 'loan' against payment from the sailor's wages. 25 per cent interest was charged on the loan and all kinds of false entries were often made on his account. Articles of clothing were also sold to them at inflated prices. Prostitutes worked with the crimps to relieve the sailors of their wages in more subtle ways. If the sailor refused to pay the debt, threats or violence were employed. Even murder of sailors was not unknown among the crimps. In addition to all this the lodging houses themselves were described as inclining 'considerably over the pavement with their ragged crumbling fronts' and as having 'crazy doors speaking of years of neglect.'[37]

Readers of Dickens may recall that Nancy was born and bred in Ratcliff Highway before she moved to the rookery of Field Lane, Saffron Hill. [38]

SPITALFIELDS

This began its life as a rookery in the early eighteenth century. Defoe commented:

> Within the memory of the writer hereof, all those numberless ranges of buildings called Spitalfields, reaching from Spital Yard at Norton Folgate and from Artillery Lane in Bishopsgate Street, with all the new streets beginning at Hoxton and the back of Shoreditch Church, north; and reaching to Brick Lane and to the end of Hare Street on the way to Bethnal Green, east; then sloping away quite to Whitechapel Road, south-east; containing, as some people say who pretend to know by good observation, above 120 acres of ground which are all now close built and well inhabited with an infinite number of people – I say, all of these have been built new from the ground since the year 1666. In a word, it is computed that above 200,000 inhabitants dwell now in that part of London, where within about fifty years past there was not a house standing.[39]

One could go on and on chronicling the depressing living conditions and poverty that the inhabitants suffered. I have identified eighty areas in London which were rookeries, eight in West London and Middlesex, six in North London, eighteen in South London, eighteen in East London, eighteen in the West End and twelve in the City of London. Out of the population of London as a whole, the proportion of rookery dwellers must have been in the region of 40 per cent at least. If you add to that figure those working-class people who lived on low incomes but in better living conditions, the overwhelming majority of Londoners during the Victorian age lived in poverty. It is a staggering indictment of what was at that time the most prosperous city in the world.

Notes

1   Charles Dickens, *Oliver Twist*, 1837.
2   Thomas Beames, *The Rookeries of London*, 1850.
3   Ibid.
4   Ibid.
5   Liberty of Saffron Hill, *Notice Book*, 1801–1817.
6   Liberty of Saffron Hill, Ely Place Committee, *Minute Book*, 1827–1837.
7   Charles Booth, 'First Results of an Enquiry based on the 1891 Census', *Journal of the Royal Statistical Society*, vol. LVI, December 1893. Also cross-referenced with Gareth Stedman-Jones, *Outcast London: A Study in the Relationship between Classes in Victorian Society*, London, 1976.
8   Charles Loch Mowat, *The Charity Organisation Society, 1869–1913, Its Ideas and Works*, Methuen, 1961.
9   Booth, art. cit.
10 Ibid.
11 Ibid.
12 Ibid.
13 Ibid.

14   Wren's comments are quoted in Beames, op. cit.
15   John Strype, *A Survey of the Cities of London and Westminster*, Churchill, 1720.
16   Henry Fielding, *An Enquiry into the cause of the late increase of robbery with some proposals for remedying this growing evil*, 1751.
17   Beames, op. cit., 1852 edition.
18   Ibid.
19   Ibid.
20   Ibid.
21   Board of Health, *Enquiry into the Sanitary Conditions of London, 1848–1849*.
22   W.M. Thomas, 'Agar Town', *Household Words*, 1851.
23   John Hollingshead, *Ragged London in 1861*, Smith, Elder, 1861.
24   Octavia Hill, quoted in: H.J. Dyos, 'Railways and Housing in Victorian London', *Journal of Transport History*, vol. 2, 1955.
25   Thomas Lovick, *Report on Drainage of Potteries Notting Dale*, Metropolitan Board of Sewers, 1851.
26   Ibid.
27   Ibid.
28   'Some Unfashionable Slums – Lisson Grove', *The Quiver*, 1894.
29   Henry Mayhew, 'A visit to the cholera districts of Bermondsey', *Morning Chronicle*, 24th September 1849.
30   Ibid.
31   Beames, op. cit.
32   Ibid.
33   Ibid.
34   Ibid.
35   Ibid.
36   John Stow, *Survey of London*, 1603 edition.
37   Beames, op. cit.
38   Dickens, *Oliver Twist*.
39   Daniel Defoe, *A Tour through the Whole Island of Great Britain*, 1726.

10

PHILANTHROPY
& REFORM

Throughout the Middle Ages a mixture of private, monastic and state charity played a part in alleviating the poverty that affected many ordinary Londoners. St Giles itself was founded as a charitable bequest by Queen Matilda. Although private charity continued after the decision to dissolve the monasteries, it was not on the same scale as before. One of the earliest examples of philanthropy following the dissolution was displayed by Avise Gibson, wife of a London grocer, who set up a free school at Ratcliffe 'for the instruction of sixty poor men's children, a schoolmaster and usher with fifty pounds; she also built alms houses for fourteen poor aged persons, each of them to receive quarterly six shillings and eight pence the piece for ever; the government of which free school and alms houses she left in confidence to the Coopers in London.'[1]

The collapse of most forms of aid after 1539 led to a growing crisis of poverty. Harsh sanctions against begging were the first remedy but it soon became apparent that they were both insufficient to deter the desperate and too blunt an instrument to be of much help to the genuinely poor.

Queen Elizabeth I introduced the first ever Poor Law. Under its provisions each parish was liable for the upkeep, maintenance and control of the poor within their boundaries. Before long, the burden on the rates led to a combination of brutal repression of people described as 'sturdy beggars' and a blatant attempt to export the problem of poverty to neighbouring parishes. A particularly cruel attempt to evade paying parish rates was the widespread practice of pushing women in labour or even after they had just given birth over the border so that they would not become a charge upon the neighbourhood. Although this was technically illegal it was an almost universally practised abuse.

After the Restoration private charity increased once more, no doubt aided by the considerable increase in the population of London and the consequent claims upon the Poor Law. One of the first attempts to break the cycle of poverty by educating the poor was made by William Shelton, whose charity school in St Giles was widely praised and imitated. Under the terms of his will in 1672, he created a trust to establish a charity school for the area. The document reads as follows:

Mr William Shelton, by his will dated the 5th of July 1672, devised all his messuages, lanes and tenements whatsoever, in Parker's-lane, in the county of Middlesex, to the minister and churchwardens of the parish of St Giles-in-the-Fields, in the said county, for the time being, and their successors, and to his (the testator's) heir at law for ever, upon trust, that out of the rents and profits they should lay out £15 yearly, for buying 20 gowns for 20 poor old men and women of the said parish; £7.10s for buying 10 gowns for 10 poor old men and women of the parish of St Martin-in-the-Fields; £31.15s for buying blue gowns for five poor old men and women of the parish of St Paul, Covent Garden; and also for every year thereafter hire and provide an able and fit schoolmaster, to teach school and instruct in learning, in the school room we had appointed, and for that purpose then used in Parker's-lane, 50 children of the poorest sort, 35 whereof to be of the said parish of St Giles, 10 of the said parish of St Martin, and five of the said parish of St Paul, Covent Garden, and to pay the said schoolmaster yearly £20, and to buy him a gown yearly of 20s value, and also a coat yearly for every one of the said 50 scholars, of the value of 6s, and to provide yearly two chaldron of coals, for a fire for the said scholars in winter. All the aforesaid coats and gowns to be of a green colour.[2]

On the death of Shelton's widow in 1681, the trustees discovered that the funds were insufficient to defray all the expenses laid down. The gowns were therefore discontinued after only two years. By 1763, on the death of the current schoolmaster, the trustees temporarily discontinued the school. It did not reopen until 1816, this time in a piece of ground adjoining St Giles Church. The cost was £964 12s 1d. Fifty children continued to be taken although this time from the united parishes of St Giles and St George, Bloomsbury.

According to the records of the school:

The ordinary expenditure on the school may be considered as consisting of the following items:

	£	s	d
Masters' salary (a guinea a week)	54	12	–
Masters' gratuity	10	10	–
Coat for the master	3	–	–
Clothing for the boys, about	59	–	–
Coals and candles for the school & master, about	25	–	–
Water rates £4, insurance £1. 2s. 6d	5	2	6
Stationery and books, about	10	–	–
Total	167	4	6

The trustees added that 'the estimate for clothing the boys, made when the school was re-established, was 30s a head but a saving in this article has been effected by having the clothes made in the workhouse, by which the charge has been reduced to the amount stated.'[3]

Another charity established in St Giles was the Parochial School of St Giles and St George, Bloomsbury. This was set up in 1705, one of its principal benefactors being Elizabeth Saywell, whose maiden name was Lloyd. She owned 'several messuages, houses or tenements . . . situated in a certain place, commonly called Lloyd's Court.'[4] The original location of the school was in King Street off Drury Lane. Saywell left a fourth part of her estate to the minister of St Giles and his successors 'towards the education and maintenance of the poor charity girls within the said parish of St Giles-in-the-Fields for ever.'[5] Her heir also left a further £10 a year 'to be applied by the said governor and trustees for the use and benefit of the said charity girls.'[6]

The next major charity to be established was an extremely important one. It was the result of years of campaigning by a sea captain named Thomas Coram, who was so affected by the condition of the street children that he spent years trying to improve their lot. The infant mortality rate in those days was horrific and Coram relentlessly compiled figures to show how the workhouses were actually making the situation worse. In the end, he stirred enough consciences and, crucially, managed to persuade enough wealthy individuals to contribute, to set up a home for them. It became known as the 'Foundling's Hospital'. Although it could take only a fraction of the poor children in London it did at least offer them care, a higher chance of surviving infancy and the opportunity to go into a trade.

Both boys and girls were admitted and this practical compassion by a rough sea captain whose heart had been touched by the sufferings of the rookery children was the first measure of help they had ever received. He enlisted influential friends like the painter Hogarth. Soon Coram's hospital was flourishing and saving lives. If Protestants had saints, Coram would certainly be among them.[7]

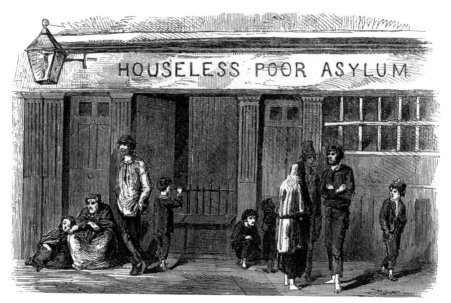

Asylum for the Houseless Poor, Cripplegate.

Another campaigner against abuses was the eccentric Jonas Hanway. Unlike Coram, about whom nobody had a bad word to say, Hanway was arrogant, vain and quarrelsome. His political views were also so bizarrely inconsistent that he managed to offend almost every section of opinion at one time or another during his long and ultimately successful campaign against a variety of social evils. Perhaps the most impressive of his campaigns was that against the employment of boy chimney sweeps, a widespread practice that was so dangerous to the life and health of the children working in the occupation that their life expectancy was dramatically below the national average.[8]

Following the end of the Napoleonic Wars, unemployment rose dramatically, partly with the return home of soldiers and sailors who had been fighting abroad for many years. The government's response was to introduce the Corn Laws, a measure that has often been criticised but was actually a well-intentioned attempt to reduce distress among the population. It was always the middle-class merchants who wanted it abolished, rather than the working classes and the utterly destitute. The existence of the Corn Laws made remarkably little difference to their lives, and, if anything, their lot became worse after their abolition than it had before.

Following the final return of peace to Britain in 1815 the House of Commons set up a committee to investigate possible reforms in the Poor Law. Some extremely interesting data was given by Sampson Stevenson. Stevenson reported that St Giles was plagued by organised gangs of beggars, who mainly collected shoes and clothing, making around 3–4s a day. There was apparently also an Irish doctor, described as having 'a beautiful hand' who wrote begging letters on behalf of the inhabitants, receiving 6d to 1s per letter. Stevenson went on to say: 'Are there many of the paupers lodging in this way parishioners of St Giles? No, that is an evil in St Giles's; there are so many low Irish, that of £30,000 a year collected by poor rates, £20,000 goes to the low Irish.'[9]

Stevenson, however, like his fellow commissioner Dobie, was quite clear about the difference between the beggars who frequented the area and those trapped in the cycle of casual employment and unable to maintain themselves because of temporary extremity. Like Dobie, he was anything but sympathetic to the workhouse and the notion of making it compulsory for the poor horrified him. The Commons heard his evidence and those of other Poor Law commissioners and decided to make no change in the existing system of outdoor relief.

Considering that the cost of the wars against France had nearly bankrupted the country and that the 1815 Parliament has often been described as the most callous and reactionary Commons ever elected, their decision to maintain Poor Law expenditure rather than going down the road of making the workhouse compulsory shows clearly that they were more sophisticated, enlightened and compassionate than historians have given them credit for previously. The persistent misreading of history through Whig eyes had led to an entirely distorted conception of the realities of the past in Britain.

The state of the prisons has already been mentioned. Two brave souls, one man and a woman, took it upon themselves to champion the unpopular cause of more humane treatment for prisoners. The first was John Howard during the 1770s. He had first-hand experience of what being a prisoner meant and determined to fight for better conditions for inmates. The second was the Quaker woman Elizabeth Fry, who campaigned in the early nineteenth century and shamed the authorities into action.

John Howard was born in Clapton, now a part of the expanding East End of London but in those days a sleepy Essex village on the borders of the city. He came from a wealthy family but his capture by a French ship and subsequent imprisonment in France led him to realise how poor the conditions in prisons were. On his return to Britain he began investigating the state of prisoners in his own country. He was particularly angered by the presence of people in gaol simply because they could not afford to pay the gaoler's 'fee'. In 1774 he made a report to Parliament which stirred the conscience of the legislators. 1777 saw the publication of his book, *The State of the Prisons*, which generated widespread support for his attempts to improve and humanise the conditions of prisoners.[10] On his death Howard became the first civilian to be honoured with a statue in St Paul's Cathedral.

Elizabeth Fry, born Gurney, was a radical. One of her friends championed universal suffrage and annual elections to Parliament. She was greatly influenced as a young woman by Mary Wollstonecraft, a classic feminist writer; William Godwin, the anarchist thinker, and Thomas Paine, champion of American independence and the French Revolution. In her youth, Fry wore a tricolour in her hat to symbolise her support for the ideas of republicanism and the Jacobin tradition.

After meeting a charismatic preacher called William Savery, Fry decided to dedicate her life to helping those less fortunate than herself. She visited the sick, collected clothes for the poor and taught local children to read. In 1799 she met a Quaker merchant called Joseph Fry, and she became his wife in August 1800, moving to his home in Plashet, East London. Within a period of twelve years she gave birth to eight children. It was the visit to Newgate by a family friend, Stephen Grellet, which turned her thoughts to prison reform. Grellet was horrified at the conditions he found but was told that the situation of the women prisoners was even worse. He paid a visit in spite of advice to the contrary and told the Frys about the suffering the women underwent in Newgate.

Fry characteristically decided to visit the prison herself. She observed 300 women and children crammed into two wards and two cells. Some of them were only remand prisoners. They slept on the floor without any form of beds or bedding or even proper clothing. They had to perform all their activities within the cell. After this experience Fry began to visit the women of Newgate regularly. She gave them clothes to wear, set up a school and even a place of worship. The women were taught to sew and also had Bible classes.[11]

In 1817 she formed the Association for the Improvement of the Female Prisoners in Newgate. Fry gave evidence to a House of Commons Committee on prisons in London. She described women sleeping thirty to a cell, each with barely sufficient space to move. Although some MPs were willing to listen to her ideas on prison reform, they certainly did not share her opposition to the death penalty, which she described as 'evil' and producing 'evil results'. In the same year Fry tried to save two women convicted of forgery from the gallows. The Home Secretary declared that Fry was a dangerous radical attempting to 'remove the dread of punishment in the criminal classes.' In 1822, however, Peel became Home Secretary and reformed some of the conditions in prison, as well as drastically reducing the number of capital offences on the statute book.

Fry continued to campaign for prison reform throughout her life, actively calling for the end of capital punishment, more humane conditions for prisoners, shorter sentences for minor offences and, above all, for imprisonment to be based on a philosophy of reformation rather than simply punishment. In her evidence to the House of Lords in 1835, she said:

I feel it to be the bounden duty of the Government and the country that those truths (in the Bible) should be administered in the manner most likely to conduce to the real reformation of the prisoners for though severe punishment may, in a measure, deter them and others from crime, it does not amend and change the heart.[12]

When Fry died in 1845 over 1,000 people went to her burial at Barking, standing in silence as a mark of respect. The London poor wept openly in the streets, especially those who had benefited from her campaigns against abuses in the prison system. It is a tribute to Fry that, in an inhumane age, she upheld humanitarian values.

The sanguinary penal code of the eighteenth and nineteenth century became much worse following the passing of the Black Act in 1722. At a time when rioting in London was commonplace and the fear of a Jacobite restoration still haunted the authorities, a new law was placed on the statute book. It was allegedly directed against poachers but in fact was used simply as an instrument of brutal repression. Under its auspices, over 200 crimes were now capital offences. It had no effect whatsoever on either the propensity of poor Londoners to riot or on the levels of crime, which were in any case declining at the time the Act was passed. It was one of the most misconceived and calamitous errors in the history of Parliamentary legislation.

We now turn to the ways in which governments began, ineffectively at first and against considerable opposition from manufacturers, to introduce various reforms to improve the working conditions and even the lives of ordinary people. Perhaps the first milestone was the Factory Act of 1802, steered through Parliament by Sir Robert Peel, father of the more famous Prime Minister of the same name. It had no 'teeth' and was evaded as far as possible by the employers but it did at least represent the first ever attempt by a British government to introduce legislation intended to improve the working conditions of the people.

The Act was passed by a Tory government, under the Premiership of Henry Addington, later Lord Sidmouth. Sidmouth was considered even by many in his own party as a right-wing extremist of the narrowest kind. There was considerable justification for this assessment of him. Nevertheless he allowed this extraordinary humanitarian measure to be passed at a time when the French Revolution had terrified the British establishment into frantic opposition to even the mildest proposals of reform. Peel's Factory Act, with all its faults, was a revolutionary measure. It put the interests of the workers in factories *above* the interests of the property owners who employed them.

This often derided and even more frequently forgotten piece of legislation represented the real start of what became known as 'Tory Reform'. As the opponents of the Act rightly claimed, once the sanctity of private property's supremacy over all other considerations had been challenged, the way lay open for other proposals, far more radical in their extent and intentions, to be carried into law.

Peel's son, like his father, was a reforming minister and eventually became a reforming Prime Minister. As Home Secretary he radically overhauled the prison system and the penal code. He insisted that women's prisons should be staffed and run by female warders and replaced the array of capital crimes under the Black Act with only three offences for which the death penalty could be imposed. These were treason, murder and attempted murder. Peel also improved the conditions of prisoners generally. He repealed the religious laws which made it illegal for anyone other than a member of the Church of England to become an MP and strongly supported the long campaigns by Lord Shaftesbury to curb the worst excesses of industrialism and make employers treat their workers more humanely. It was no accident that Peel, who in some ways might be considered the first 'spin doctor', changed the name of his party when he became leader. Giving up its old name of Tory, he campaigned instead under the banner of the Conservative Party.

What is more, Peel demonstrated throughout his leadership of the party a strong conviction that the ordinary people had rights. Even more radically, he believed that their interests were being overlooked and ignored by the greediness and selfishness of industrialists and others who saw no reason why they should pay the slightest attention to the welfare of their workers. When the Whigs introduced a Municipal Corporations Bill in 1835, Peel proposed an amendment to it which would have required the local authorities to provide open spaces for the use of the public. In Parliament, Peel spoke as follows: 'Most of the property of corporations was intended for the benefit of the community at large, and it would be desirable that the community should recover it as soon as possible.'[13] He added that it should be placed 'into the hands of the commonalty as speedily as possible consistent with justice to the rights of individuals.'[14]

Peel carried his measure through the Commons but the Lords removed the amendment from the Bill. Since the Whigs were struggling at the time to get their other policies through the Lords, they gave way on this point. The subject was raised again in 1837 when the Radical MP Hume proposed 'that in all Inclosing Bills provision be made for leaving an open space sufficient for the purpose of exercise and recreation of the neighbouring population.'[15] Peel threw his weight behind Hume's proposal and pointed out, perhaps the first time this claim was made in the House of Commons, that the people had 'a moral right' to enjoy the common land. This time the motion was passed.

Two years later another Radical MP, Harvey, put forward a resolution that 'provision be made for leaving an open space in the most appropriate situation sufficient for purposes of exercise and recreation of the neighbouring population.'[16] He also called for 'efficient fencing of the allotment'.[17] Once again Peel supported Harvey's motion and it was adopted by the Commons.

These two measures were the first examples of laws being passed which directly protected the environment, another first in British history.

Peel also attempted to extend public education, another striking example of how far ahead of his time he was on the majority of political issues that divided Britain. He was unsuccessful, but *no* satisfactory Education Bill was ever produced until 1918. All the previous attempts created different kinds of injustice.

In 1842 Peel decided to introduce a measure for popular education. It was attached to a Factory Bill and intended to be applied at first only to those children working in factories. However, its expressed intention was to extend the schools to serve the needs of all children living in factory areas. Religious intolerance, the factor that doomed every Education Bill throughout the nineteenth century to relative failure, led to its withdrawal. In 1846 Peel split the Conservative Party over the issue of the repeal of the Corn Laws. The faction that followed him became nicknamed 'Peelites', though they were surprisingly divergent in their political attitudes. Liberal Conservatives like Derby, centrist ones like Aberdeen and right-wing Whigs like Palmerston for a time all belonged to this rump of the Peelite tradition. It is difficult to find any ideological coherence in their political views. Possibly it was simply their respect for Peel as a man that led them to belong to his faction rather than the majority of the Conservative Party. The non-Peelite Conservatives provided a rather ineffective opposition who were woefully short of ideas until the Earl of Derby at last left the Peelites and became Conservative leader.

Derby has not been given anywhere near the respect he deserves as an exemplar of the tradition of 'Tory Reform'. He was the first leader of any party to campaign on behalf of the people of the rookeries, bitterly opposing in Parliament the programmes of slum clearance by which they were robbed of their homes and driven out into the street. Aided and abetted by Disraeli, the Conservatives under Derby's leadership became a reforming, even a radical party. Unlike Gladstone, who was obsessed with constitutional measures and free trade, Derby saw that the fundamental problem facing society was dealing with poverty.

Derby also recognised that it was time to extend the franchise. His first Bill for this purpose in 1859 was defeated but in 1867 he brought in the Second Reform Act, which, for the first time in British history, gave the vote to the majority of working-class people. He also consistently supported Shaftesbury's measures of reform and attempts to alleviate abuses in employment. His successor as leader, Disraeli, continued in the tradition of Derby and Peel. In fact, from 1822 to 1886, it would not be too much of an exaggeration to say that the Tory and Conservative parties represented the *progressive* wing of British politics and the Whigs and Liberals the *reactionary* elements. It was not until the disastrous split in the Liberal Party in 1886 and the consequent triumph of the right-wing within the Conservative Party that this situation changed.

After Gladstone's resignation as Prime Minister in 1894 he was succeeded by the Earl of Rosebery who represented the 'new Liberalism', the progressive wing of the party. Although he was himself a transitional figure, as was shown by his eventual departure from the party in 1909 when he found Lloyd George's radical proposals altogether too much for him to support, he was a true pioneer. He made a somewhat intemperate speech denouncing Lloyd George's policies which seems quite extraordinary nowadays. Nevertheless, particularly during his time in charge of the London County Council, Rosebery was a great reforming leader. Probably his most lasting legacy was building the first council houses in London (and indeed Britain). Whatever may be thought about the remoter consequences of these measures, Rosebery was at least addressing the central question of how to house the dwellers in the rookeries after their homes had been demolished. Like Derby, he has never received due credit for the part he played in improving the lives of the poor.

Of all the wealthy aristocrats who campaigned or passed laws to help the people of the rookeries, and indeed the poor generally, probably none has a more justified reputation than Shaftesbury. Anthony Ashley Cooper, Lord Ashley and later Lord Shaftesbury, the name by which he is best remembered, was one of the most complex and yet fundamentally attractive of all the philanthropists. Shaftesbury was fiercely religious, indeed intolerantly so. He hated Roman Catholics and Nonconformists and believed passionately that only members of the Church of England would be 'saved'. His arguments with the Anglo-Catholics in the Church became extraordinarily heated at times, as if a fiercer side to his nature came out there that he was unable to show in other aspects of his life. Nevertheless, it was his profoundly held Christian beliefs that first drove him to become involved in the welfare of the poor.

Shaftesbury campaigned particularly hard on the subject of children working in factories, but not, as is often wrongly supposed, simply the mills. It is one of the curious facts that historians of the period prefer to forget that London, *not* the North of England, was the manufacturing as well as the commercial capital of the world. The large industrial complexes in Yorkshire and Lancashire did indeed produce goods on a vast scale, but the thousands of light industrial units and workshops in London outdid them in their productivity. Unlike the large mills, where the inspectors were able to enforce successive Factory Acts, these 'sweated industries' enjoyed little or no protection under the law. Shaftesbury, well aware of the position, campaigned with zeal and energy to improve the conditions of the workers within them, particularly the children. He always advocated public education even though in general he distrusted spending State money unless absolutely necessary.[18] Shaftesbury became almost a one-man reform movement. He was always passionately concerned about the welfare of the dwellers in the rookeries, particularly in regard to their housing, clothing and food. He supported soup kitchens and free distribution of food and actively encouraged the building of 'model dwellings'. It was under the influence of Shaftesbury that Burdett-Coutts and Peabody began to build their own 'homes for the poor'.

Shaftesbury was also fiercely opposed to the misguided, destructive and generally hypocritical process of 'slum clearance' and Derby was almost the only leading politician who supported him in this objection. On his death, the poor wept in the streets and his funeral was almost a royal occasion. As one mourner put it: 'Our Lord's dead. How he loved us. We shan't see his like again.'

An organisation that has long been associated in the public mind with charity work is the Salvation Army. This institution, founded in the latter years of the nineteenth century by William Booth, managed to carry out an astonishing variety of practical help for the rookery dwellers from a very early stage of its existence.

The Middlesex Street Shelter and Working Men's Home in Petticoat Lane was set up as a hostel for men. It housed 462 men, of whom 311 paid *3d* for their lodging and the rest *5d*. Rider Haggard described the shelter, and similar ones he also visited, as 'harbours of refuge for the unfortunates who find themselves on the streets of London at nightfall with a few coppers or some other small sum in their pockets. Many of these social wrecks have sunk through drink, but many others owe their sad position to lack or loss of employment, or some other misfortune.'[19]

The kitchen of a dosshouse near the docks.

The Spa Road Elevator at Bermondsey was a paper-sorting works. Vast quantities of paper were sorted into different kinds of material, after which it was pressed into bales by hydraulic machines and sold to merchants, an early example of recycling waste material. As Rider Haggard put it: 'The object of the Institution is to find work for distressed or fallen persons, and restore them to society. The Manager of this "Elevator", as it is called, informed me that it employs around 480 men, all of whom are picked up upon the streets.'[20]

There were also seventy men who lived on the premises, receiving board, lodging and a small wage. Accusations of 'sweating' were made against the Army for not paying them the 'union' rate, but most of the people 'rescued' by them and given jobs in the Elevator were entirely unemployable before the Army put them to work. Certainly the men themselves indignantly denied the charge of 'sweating'.[21]

At the Blackfriars shelter a free breakfast service was provided. Rider Haggard related how the Blackfriars shelter was 'the feeder of all the Salvation Army's Social Institutions for men in London.'[22] He added that 'from drunkards and Wastrels stained with every sort of human fault, or even crime, they are turned into God-fearing and respectable men who henceforward, instead of being a pest to society and a terror to all those who have the misfortune to be connected with them, become props of society and a comfort and a support to their relatives and friends.'[23]

Other projects which Haggard visited were the Army's home for boys at Bow Road, their carpentry workshop at Whitechapel, their maternity nursing home and maternity hospital. Among the most unusual of the Army's projects, at least at that time, was their Central Labour Bureau at Whitechapel. Haggard described how:

> hundreds of men apply there for work every week, of whom a great many are sent into the various Elevators and Shelters. The Army finds it extremely difficult to procure outside employment for these men, for the simple reason that there is very little available. Moreover, now that the Government Labour Bureaux are open, this trouble is not lessened. The hard fact is that there are more idle hands than there is work for them to do, even where honest and capable folk are concerned.[24]

They also sent many emigrants abroad, primarily to Canada, although a few were also sent to Australia. The Australians imposed far more restrictions on the type of people who would be allowed to emigrate than the Canadians did.

Another very unusual aspect of the Army's work was the Anti-Suicide Bureau. This project literally saved lives, the figures for 1909 in London alone showing that, out of a total of 1,064 potential suicides, all but twelve were persuaded not to take their own life. This forerunner of the Samaritans was introduced as long ago as 1904.[25]

The Army's work with children did not end with placing them in homes and finding employment for them. They even looked after them in death. In those days pauper funerals were an everyday occurrence. The young lived constantly in close proximity with death. One of the songs they sang at the funerals went as follows:

> There is a better world they say,
> O so bright!
> Were sin and woe are done away,
> O so bright!
> And music fills the balmy air,
> And angels with bright wings are there,
> And harps of gold and mansions fair,
> O so bright![26]

Another song, dating from the 1870s, was sung at Whitechapel, following cakes and tea:

> We are waiting by the river,
> We are watching by the shore,
> Only waiting for the angel,
> Soon he'll come to bear us o'er.[27]

In 1884 the Army began one of its most unusual operations, the 'Slum Sisters'. This began in a small way that year when a group of Salvationist women handed out flowers to women in the slum. Before long Emma Booth suggested: 'Why not take a room in one of the worst districts and send a few cadets to live there?' The young women had to dress like the people of the area in which they were living. Before long, they became involved in the lives of the local residents. Realising that the people of the rookeries needed practical help most of all, the 'Slum Sisters' set up what became known as the 'cellar, gutter and garret brigade'. By 1909 they had visited over 105,000 families and 20,000 sick people. Eventually they had to stop living in the rookeries themselves as they found that the constant noise and activity around them made it difficult for them to rest at night after their exertions during the day! The solution was to build what were known as 'Slum Settlements', of which there were nine in London compared with nineteen others in the whole of the United Kingdom (which in those days included the Irish Republic as well). This makes it clear to what an extent London predominated as the capital of poverty and how much worse the conditions in the rookeries were than those found anywhere else in the British Isles.

The 'cellar, gutter and garret brigade' spent a great deal of time in the early days of the project cleaning the homes of the dwellers in the rookeries. It cannot have been either easy or pleasant but it did make a difference to the lives of the people who lived there. The 'Slum Sisters' probably welcomed the gradual destruction of the rookeries as the conditions under which they worked in the new slum settlements that replaced them were altogether less arduous!

Haggard described some of the work done at the Hackney Road settlement:

> The Slum Sisters attached to the Settlement, who are distinct from the Maternity Nurses, visit the very poorest and worst neighbourhoods, for the purpose of helping the sick and afflicted, and incidentally of cleaning their homes.[28]

Haggard interviewed a sister at the settlement in Hackney Road, and reported the gist of her comments as follows:

> The Sister said in answer to my questions that there was a great deal of poverty in their district where many men were out of work, a number of them because they could find nothing to do. She thought that things were certainly no better in this respect; indeed, the state of depression was chronic. Owing to the bad summer of 1909, which affected the hop-picking and other businesses, the destitution that year was as great during the warm months as it usually is in the winter.[29]

The Salvation Army, whatever else may be said about it, clearly carried out all these and other charitable activities out of simple human kindness. Most of their projects were run at a loss and only a minority broke even. Booth may not have been the easiest man to get on with or even to like, but the organisation he founded did at least offer practical compassion to the helpless dwellers in the London rookeries. Rider Haggard, while finding the brass bands and the strident tone of the revivalism practised by the Army distasteful, admitted that he suspected that it was close to the spirit of how early Christianity might have been.

From the time that Asquith became Prime Minister in 1908, the government intervened more and more in areas where private charity had once been almost the sole provider. It was the beginning of the Welfare State and coincided with the end of the London rookeries. From now on the poor or supposedly poor would be placed in council homes at minimum rents. The abolition of the workhouse in 1928 by a Conservative government represented a visible break with the old system of 'public provision' for the poor. It is true that the National Assistance which replaced it was anything but generous, being not only means tested but frequently administered harshly, but at least it was a gift.

Baldwin, of course, who carried this measure through Parliament in 1928, was the first progressive leader of the Conservatives since Disraeli in 1880. He, perhaps as much as any politician of his time, laid the foundations of what became known in the 1950s and early 1960s as 'Butskellism', an ideology on which people of all three main political parties could broadly agree.[30]

Even though the conditions of the people in the London rookeries were poor from the 1630s onwards, and were at their worst from the 1830s to the early 1900s, there were always people and even organisations and institutions that showed them compassion and extended what was often known as 'the helping hand' to rescue or at least assist them to make their lives more bearable. These humanitarians were often ridiculed or condemned in their day, but we owe it to them that the lives of the rookery dwellers were not *worse* than they might have been.

Notes

1 John Stow, *Survey of London*, 1598.
2 William Shelton's will, 5 July 1672.
3 Records of Shelton's charity school trustees, 1816.
4 Elizabeth Saywell's will, 1705.
5 Ibid.
6 Middlesex Charities, record of Saywell's parochial school trustees.
7 Ruth McClure, *Coram's Children: The London Foundling Hospital in the Eighteenth Century*, Yale University Press, 1981.
8 Jonas Hanway, *A Sentimental History of Chimney-Sweepers in London and Westminster*, 1785.
9 Evidence of Sampson Stevenson to the Committee of the House of Commons, 27 June 1815, Rt. Hon. George Rose in the chair.
10 John Howard, *The State of the Prisons*, 1777.
11 Elizabeth Fry, Journal, 24 February 1817.
12 Elizabeth Fry, evidence to the House of Lords, 22 May, 1835.
13 Sir Robert Peel, amendment to the Municipal Corporations Bill, Committee of the House of Commons, 1835.
14 Ibid.
15 Motion by Joseph Hume, MP, 9 March 1837, House of Commons.
16 Motion by D.W. Harvey, MP, 9 April 1839, House of Commons.
17 Ibid.
18 See, for example, the Earl of Shaftesbury, 'The Mischief of State Aid', *Nineteenth Century*, vol. XXIV, December 1883. Shaftesbury certainly rejected the new economic ideas being put forward by Alfred Marshall and clung to the old *laissez faire* notions as to how the economy should be run.
19 H. Rider Haggard, *Regeneration: Being an Account of the Social Work of The Salvation Army in Great Britain*, Longmans, 1910.
20 Ibid.
21 Ibid.
22 Ibid.
23 Ibid.
24 Ibid.
25 Ibid.
26 *The History of the Salvation Army.*
27 Ibid.
28 Haggard, op. cit.
29 Ibid.
30 Butskellism was so called because of the close similarity of the views on most issues of Hugh Gaitskell, leader of the Labour Party, and R.A. Butler, one of the chief Conservative spokesmen.

11

THE DESTRUCTION OF THE ROOKERIES

During the eighteenth century private charity tried to help some of the inhabitants of the rookeries. When their living conditions became far worse under the Victorians, enlightened men and women campaigned hard for improvements. Some reformers began to call for the wholesale demolition of the rookeries rather than restoring their homes and supplying them with proper facilities. This policy appealed far more to the government than the alternative of reconstruction and repair. Many legislators were genuinely worried about the prospect of a huge underclass living in squalid conditions a stone's throw from the dwellings of the wealthy. Perhaps the destruction of the rookeries and the dispersal of their inhabitants offered a solution to the problem.

The first example of this was the Regent's Park development, carried out by John Nash between 1811 and 1825. His new streets, houses and shops wiped out the Oxford market on Upper Regent Street and also demolished the Swallow Street rookery in the process. Some of the St James section of Soho was also destroyed during these developments. Proper roads and sewers were essential features of Nash's plan. They achieved the desired effect of making the area attractive to wealthier leaseholders and tenants rather than the previous occupants, the poor.

Nash had not been concerned primarily with slum clearance but the example of his efforts was not lost on other developers. He had only dispersed the rookery dwellers to other locations but the new Regent's Park development stood as an outstanding lesson in how an area could be transformed. It was the first time that Parliament sanctioned a building development on the basis that it would include the demolition of a rookery area. Although at first his example was not followed, a precedent had been set and later on his ideas were taken up as a 'solution'.

Nash also proposed a scheme from Trafalgar Square to the site of the new British Museum building in Bloomsbury. This would have destroyed the rookeries of St Martin's Lane, St Giles and Bloomsbury itself. Such a vast project was too expensive and controversial for the aged Nash to carry out, though he built Pall Mall East, Trafalgar Square and the West Strand Improvements. The destruction of St Giles and its companion rookeries, however, was not to come until much later.[1]

A contemporary account of Nash's building projects was given in 1820. It remarked 'the progress made since the signature of the last treaty of peace in extending and beautifying London is almost miraculous.'[2]

The 1820s also saw the construction of the London Docks. This resulted in making nearly 2,500 people homeless as well as destroying one of the most beautiful churches in London, St Katherine's by the Tower. It created a wide range of new job opportunities but led to the beginnings of the expansion of the East End into a vast new area of slums. The massive influx of people streaming into London made the need to provide them with cheap housing an urgent problem. The combination of low wages, high unemployment and high rents meant that these early programmes of slum clearance simply displaced the poor into even more overcrowded conditions.

Central London in 1830 was still almost entirely residential. From the time of 'Gin Lane' in the early eighteenth century, the new suburbs slowly filled up with middle-class 'emigrants' seeking an escape from the poverty that surrounded them. This flight to the suburbs was only an option for the relatively prosperous before the introduction of public transport transformed the situation. George Shillibeer ran the first London 'omnibus' in 1829; the railways arrived in the capital from 1836. The use of these new forms of transport was for a very long time entirely beyond the means of the working classes. The majority of Londoners still lived and worked within 2 miles of the city centre.

By 1836 the new steam railways finally reached London. The opposition of the Whig government to any State interference with the economic life of the country prevented the building of railways except where the necessary funds could be raised through private capital. There was no attempt at central planning and what happened was a series of bargains between the railway companies and private landowners. The railways destroyed whole neighbourhoods in their search for land on which to build their stations and across which to lay their tracks. People were forced further away from the centre of London, almost accidentally creating new suburbs while destroying the central areas and making them ghost towns. The arrival of the railways did offer new employment opportunities, many of the dwellers in the rookeries labouring on the trackwork or station building, but their homes were slowly, inexorably, taken from them. They were forced out of the areas in which they had lived, often for hundreds of years, into even worse accommodation.

It was December 1836 when the London and Greenwich Railway Company first ran the new steam trains from Greenwich to Southwark. It swept through Southwark and Bermondsey, destroying vast rookery areas in its path. The whole character of the districts was lost as the railway ploughed on in its search for speed and communication. From now on the railways had rookery land squarely in their sights. They knew that it could be bought more cheaply than land in the fashionable areas and they also knew that they could claim to be improving the condition of the area. During the 1830s, Euston, Paddington, Fenchurch Street and London Bridge stations were constructed – eleven railway Acts were passed by Parliament in 1836 alone. The railways had arrived in London, and it would never be the same.

The 1840s saw the London and Southampton Railway build a new terminus at Waterloo, demolishing areas of Nine Elms and Lambeth in the process. When the Great Northern built King's Cross in 1852 they also destroyed the Battlebridge rookery. The building by the Metropolitan Railway of the world's first underground line between Paddington and Farringdon also swept away a number of rookery districts along the line, particularly in the area of each terminus. Saffron Hill and the insalubrious Paddington areas were gradually earmarked for destruction.

The railway companies made over 100,000 Londoners homeless. They neither paid any compensation to the evicted tenants nor provided them with alternative accommodation. The consequent pressure of overcrowding on the already crammed existing rookeries became worse. Appalled by the wholesale evictions, Lord Shaftesbury succeeded in getting an Act of Parliament passed in 1853 requiring railways to state how many people would be displaced if the work was carried out. The railways systematically evaded the new obligations laid upon them by the Act. As we have seen earlier, Octavia Hill described how the companies nullified the legislation by private bargains with landlords.[3]

The railways argued that they were not only providing new and improved transport for the people of London but also knocking down slum areas that were dangerous, dilapidated and insanitary. As for the inhabitants, they argued, entirely disingenuously, that they should move out to the suburbs and travel in to work by the new trains that the companies were providing. The poor could afford neither the rents in the emerging suburbs nor the train fares to travel from them in to work. It was not until 1874 that Parliament laid a statutory duty on the railways to provide alternative accommodation for those made homeless by their actions. By then two-thirds of the rookeries had already been destroyed.

In 1854, George Godwin protested against the demolition of the rookeries, one of the first voices to do so publicly. He complained that 'buildings have been cleared away, and those who inhabited them have been driven into equally unfit lodgings in other districts – a fact not to be lost sight of in considering the effects of the demolition of the dwellings of the poor without any provision for their reception elsewhere.'[4]

The Times protested in 1861 that the activities of the railways were simply destroying communities without abolishing rookeries. 'The poor are displaced, but they are not removed. They are shovelled out of one side of the parish, only to render more over-crowded and stifling apartments in another part. You may pull down their wretched homes: but they must find others.'[5] Ironically, in the very same year *The Times* produced an extraordinary editorial that attacked not only Shaftesbury for his attempts to preserve and renovate the rookeries, but even the Earl of Derby, the leader of the Conservative Party and a man who was three times Prime Minister, for his denunciation of the Saffron Hill clearances. It is a tribute to the influence of Shaftesbury that after years of lonely campaigning for a series of unpopular humanitarian causes he was now able to gain the support of the Leader of the Opposition. The editorial in question runs as follows:

There was a strange scene on Thursday night in the House of Lords. An old lounger at the bar of the House might have supposed that he had gone back 30 years, and was listening again to the old nonsense which vexed the ears of the nation in the days of his boyhood. Two noble Peers, each of great influence in his own far-extending circle, were successively addressing the House, and were repeating, in this last half of the 19th century, the commonplaces against Railways. Some of us can remember the lamentations of those days, – what misery the new invention would cause to inn-keepers and stagecoach proprietors; what widows and orphans would be ruined by the deterioration of turnpike-road bonds, how the breed of horses would be destroyed, how the art of driving four-in-hand would become extinct, how all the crops would be burnt up, how the towns that depended upon a stagecoach traffic were thrown into agonies at the idea of Railways coming near them; and lastly, but chiefly, how the rural parks and pleasant domains of the country gentry would be cut and carved by the dreadful iron roads, and how the privacy of their residences would be destroyed by those rushing, shrieking, steam engines. We had thought that these were buried follies, and that we had been too much ashamed of them even to put a tablet over their grave. Their ill deeds are sufficiently commemorated in the winding lines and inconvenient branches which are now made to connect towns with Railways from which they were at first so sedulously kept apart. The last use to which arguments against Railways were put was in the Roman States; but even the Pope himself gave them up at the last, and was asking for European capital when his fate came upon him. Nothing, however, is too foolish not to come into fashion again, and perhaps we ought not to be astonished to find even Lord DERBY and Lord SHAFTESBURY making speeches which Lord ELDON himself might claim as his own.

Lord DERBY's desire is to prevent the irruption of Railways into London. A clergyman has intrusted him with a petition, setting forth that he is incumbent of a parish which, if we take his description to be correct, must be an accumulation of human misery. Lord DERBY and Lord SHAFTESBURY tell us that there are many such parishes, and they cite the authority of Dr LETHEBY for those frightful truths which are already sufficiently known – and nothing can be so discreditable to a civilized country, – that human beings are huddled together in filth and squalor, and without distinction of age or sex, in ill-ventilate, ill-repaired, ill-drained, and ill-roofed dwellings. Unhappily, this is but too true. Why it should be so no one can tell. It cannot be from any special convenience in the locality, for these people must be labourers, whose work must lie in all parts of the great metropolis. It cannot be for cheapness, for the returns show that the inhabitants of these rickety dens pay upon an average a rent of £6 a year for a space of a thousand cubic feet, which, in proportion, is as much as a nobleman pays for his mansion in Belgrave-square. Perhaps it is the attraction of misery to misery and dirt to dirt. Such aggregations cannot be favourable either to public or to private morality. They must tend, not only to harbour, but to generate, dangerous classes. As we cut nicks through our woods, and roads through our forests, so it should be our policy to divide these thick jungles of crime and misery. Much already has been done to tempt these people to purer air and better habits. Thousands of cottages are springing up yearly in the suburbs which fringe the metropolis; model lodging-houses are being built; capitalists are well aware that there is no customer so profitable as the labouring man; but the multitudes, for bad reasons or for no reasons, cling to their old habits and to their old impenetrable haunts. The singular complaint of Lord DERBY and Lord SHAFTESBURY is not that these districts of wretchedness should be allowed to exist, but that Railways should be allowed to come in to open them up or to sweep them away. That a clergyman who has passed his life in ministrations amid such a population should complain that a Railway proposes to turn his whole parish into Railway lines, and to make him a sinecure pensioner, is not unnatural. He looks at the subject with the short sight of a man accustomed to live in darkness; but that Lord DERBY should call upon the Legislature to interfere to protect these fever preserves and these crime coverts is indeed strange. Stranger still does it sound to hear Lord SHAFTESBURY bemoaning the destruction of that dreadful rookery by Field-lane, which was the safe refuge of every London thief, and through the mysterious excesses of which the black volumes of the uncovered Fleet Ditch rolled, ready at any moment to hide the evidence of deadly crime. These are the dwellings of the labouring classes which we have heard two influential Peers describe in all their grossness, and yet desire to save. These are the dwellings which they would preserve, and for the preservation of which they would keep Railways out of London. Can anything be more absurd? Now that the centre of London is no longer the centre of manufactures, now that employment is dispersed over the great metropolitan province, it is convenient, and it is even necessary, that the habitation of the labourers should be likewise dispersed; and the Railways which come to thin these neighbourhoods are even more beneficial to the labouring man than they are to the classes above him. If there be a grievance, it is to that numerous class in London which lives by plunder alone, and which may be compelled to quit its accustomed haunts for others less hidden from the eyes of the police. If lodging a poor man did not pay, there might be danger that the labourer might be straitened for a lodging; but, while he pays the builder a better percentage upon his money than can be got out of a Prince, there can be no fear that the labourer will be unable to find a roof, even if a Railway should take his old house for a Station.[6]

The description of the position of Shaftesbury and Derby is an extreme caricature but it did represent a substantial body of opinion among the middle classes, possibly even a majority view. The growing criticism of their activities by influential members of Parliament began to concern the railway companies, particularly when it came from Derby.

The Earl of Shaftesbury, speaking of Cow Cross, an adjoining district of Clerkenwell, in the House of Lords, said:

In sixteen courts there I found one hundred and seventy-three houses, having five hundred and eighty-six rooms in all, and in them five hundred and eighty-six families; the number of persons was three thousand seven hundred and fifty-four, being an average of six and a half persons to a room. The rooms were from fifteen feet by twelve to nine by nine. They were low, dark, dismal, and dirty; so low, indeed, that it was with great difficulty I could stand upright in them, and when I extended my arms I could touch the walls on either side with my fingers' ends; in these rooms I found five, six, seven, eight, and even nine persons living.[7]

In response to the opposition that the railway-inspired clearances were beginning to attract, the Metropolitan Railway, always the most forward-thinking of the companies, suggested that a move to the suburbs might be a long-term solution to the problem. Charles Pearson of the Metropolitan, speaking to Parliament in 1855, complained that it was 'monstrous' that 'the poor are living upon ground that is worth £750 an acre per annum, when they might be transferred nightly in 20 minutes and back again to land that is to be obtained for £200 per acre.'[8] It was the Metropolitan Railway that introduced the first 'workmen's trains' from Paddington to Farringdon at 5.30 and 5.40

a.m. at a fare of 3*d* return. The idea became popular and was soon adopted by other companies. It undoubtedly helped to create new working-class areas in London that were not slums.

Peckham, Lewisham, New Cross and Battersea grew up around the railways in South London; Tottenham, Stoke Newington and West Ham around north and east London. The people who lived there, while still poor, lived in far superior conditions than those who remained in the squalid rookeries of inner London. Cheap trains were particularly popular in East London, where the entirely new phenomenon of the commuter was largely created by them. From as far north as Essex people travelled into the City of London on the cheap trains of East London. For the first time in history it was no longer essential for people to live within walking distance of their work – they could travel in by train instead.

Before the arrival of mass transit, travelling to work was only feasible within a 2-mile radius. This had forced the 'deserving' poor who were fortunate enough to be in regular employment to live in the rookeries with the 'undeserving', who relied upon casual work, street and door-to-door selling, credit and occasional charity or Poor Law relief. With the arrival of 'workmen's trains' and cheap trams, the working classes, encouraged by the destruction of their homes, moved out to Hackney and Islington, Fulham and Hammersmith, Wandsworth and Lewisham. The homes there were better built, in a cleaner environment and without the overcrowding characteristic of rookery dwellings.

As well as the effects of the railways the gradual improvements in the roads also contributed to the fall of the rookeries. The astonishing increase in population meant that the London streets were completely inadequate for the volume of traffic that passed over them. Nash had wanted to demolish St Giles as early as the 1820s but during the 1840s some of the worst slums in the area were cleared during the course of the building of New Oxford Street. The same fate befell the residents of Pye Street in 1851. The residents simply moved into adjacent streets, with the consequent increase in overcrowding but it was the beginning of a series of wholesale clearances that resulted in the majority of the rookeries being demolished by about 1900.

Most of the impetus for these developments came from the Metropolitan Board of Works, established in 1855. In some ways it was a kind of predecessor of the modern Greater London Authority. It had powers of compulsory purchase to obtain land needed for road developments. Much of the work it did was good, including the construction of many fine new thoroughfares. Perhaps its most impressive single operation was building the Victoria Embankment. Linked in with Bazalgette's pioneering scheme for a modern sewage system, it reclaimed land from the Thames and demolished hundreds of homes. The board was careful to build open roads wherever the housing density was high and to try to turn the adjacent land to purely commercial use. This enabled them to make thousands of people homeless without having any responsibility for rehousing them. Since the board was forbidden to own the land it had purchased, it was forced, after bearing the expense and labour of redevelopment, to sell it on to speculators.

The result of this early example of 'privatisation' was to make formerly undesirable areas of London suddenly attractive to property speculators. It was normal practice for the sites to go, not even to the highest bidder, but to the first bidder. Bargains were to be found for the quick-witted and unscrupulous speculator. The result was an entirely new kind of building in London. Victoria Street, long an area of desperate poverty, saw the construction of new blocks of luxury flats. It also saw a hotel and a new office block on the site. The poor were simply evicted and left to shift for themselves.

Inspired by the example of the board, the City of London decided to embark on an ambitious programme of new building. Smithfield, Billingsgate and Leadenhall markets were completely rebuilt, resulting in wholesale loss of jobs and widespread homelessness. The ancient rookery of West Smithfield fell at last. Saffron Hill and Holborn were largely demolished during the building of the new Holborn Viaduct, over 4,000 people being made homeless to enable its construction. The population of the City of London was cut from 129,000 in 1841 to 76,000 by 1871, 51,000 by 1881 and 37,000 thousand by 1891.

The Earl of Derby, speaking in the House of Lords of the parish of St Bartholomew, Moorfields, Cripplegate, said:

> The population of this parish amounts to four thousand five hundred odd, but I am informed by the incumbent that it may now be taken as exceeding five thousand. The number of houses in it does not exceed five hundred, which gives a proportion of nine or ten persons to every house in the parish. There is not a single gentleman's house in it, not a single large shopkeeper. The whole population is of the poorest class, the lower order of shopkeepers, costermongers, dock labourers, and others of the poorest order of the population. There are not ten families in it that occupy a single house, though the bulk of these houses contain only three rooms. In fact, to use the expression of the clergyman who called on me yesterday in reference to this subject, the aristocracy in the parish are those who can indulge in the luxury of two rooms; the great number of families have one room only, and in many cases there is more than one family in a room.[9]

In destitute Southwark, the board's architect was triumphantly claiming to Parliament that he had not only saved the board £200,000 by avoiding the local brewery but that he had also made nearly 1,500 rookery dwellers homeless. 'No inconvenience is anticipated and the Bill does not contain any provisions,' he remarked, adding, 'the houses are dense and mostly too crowded for health, comfort and convenience.'[10]

Parliament made little or no attempt to check the excesses of this earliest of 'quangos', even though taxpayers' money was being spent on vast public projects, including the purchase of the land to develop, and the assets were then being sold at knockdown prices to speculators. The purchasers had not been responsible for any of the costs incurred during development and construction of the new properties, nor did they pay the market rate for the land and buildings. They simply made an offer to the board, whose properties were invariably undervalued, sometimes as much as 90 per cent short of the market price, and made huge profits from the deal. Public assets were being sold to developers for private gain, often in a series of secret transactions involving bribery and corruption.

A particularly notorious scandal occurred in 1885, when the vestryman (local representative) for St Luke's Finsbury was found to have made £8,000 profit from the Golden Lane clearances. He also represented the St Luke's ward on the Metropolitan Board of Works. Although the scandal caused by his dealings forced the board to behave coolly towards him, he was re-elected to his position as a vestryman.

Even where no actual corruption was involved – as it frequently was – the effect of the transactions was to throw discredit upon the board. It became both unpopular and distrusted. Its disregard for the homelessness its own policies were creating finally forced even a reluctant Parliament to act. Before long, public dissatisfaction with the actions of the board led to calls for its abolition and replacement by a London-wide local authority instead.

The board was placed under a statutory obligation to rehouse the inhabitants they had made homeless. This belated measure was introduced at the moment that it tackled the most ambitious of all its projects, the Shaftesbury Avenue and Charing Cross Road developments. This new building work destroyed the slums of south Soho and almost the whole of the St Giles rookery. Partly from lack of funds and partly out of resentment at being forced to rehouse the inhabitants, the board saw to it that the smallest possible area of land and housing was made available to residents. They also made the rents of the new properties sufficiently high to make it impossible for the majority of the people who lived there to afford to remain in the area. It was a pattern of creeping gentrification, before which even the most notorious rookery of all was not safe. St Giles, with the exception of a small section of remaining dwellings, was now safely neutralised, and its population largely dispersed.

Where houses thronged with people had once stood, in their place now flourished music halls, theatres and other entertainment venues. It was at this time that the district became the capital of London's 'theatreland'. Shops, restaurants and places of entertainment flourished, but the citizens were simply turned out on to the streets, rehoused in accommodation that was only a marginal improvement on the rookery dwellings they had formerly inhabited.

This latest act of destruction was to be their last. After a scandal concerning the letting out of prime building sites in the Shaftesbury Avenue area, the government acted. Following an internal enquiry one of the Board's officials was disciplined. A Royal Commission followed, during the course of which it was found that two members of the board and a number of its officers had been guilty of dealing corruptly with public money for their personal gain. The board plaintively spoke of its great achievements and how sad it was that the actions of a few members, of whose dealings they were totally unaware, had sullied the proud name of the organisation. Parliament did not agree and in 1888 abolished the quango for good

The board could claim credit for the establishment of the London Fire Brigade, the building of a number of major roads and the acquisition and maintenance of no fewer than thirty parks in the area of the capital. The construction of the modern sewer network was perhaps their greatest single achievement. The board was replaced by the new London County Council. and elections for the new body were held in January 1889, resulting in a clear victory for the Liberals under Lord Rosebery. A further Act of Parliament in 1890 gave the LCC powers to buy and maintain parks and open spaces. They also began to develop the first electric tramways, not only offering a more efficient service than the old horse-drawn trams had done, but also extending the network across a far wider area of London. Like the Metropolitan Board of Works they also engaged in a vigorous policy of slum clearance. Once again their efforts to rehouse the displaced poor were hampered by the shortage of available land and the need to keep rates down. The financial constraints under which they operated can be seen from the fact that the LCC's net debt in 1893 was the same as that of the board had been in 1888.

Throughout the 1890s the LCC continued its programme of slum clearance. Even the toughest of them all, St Giles, fell before its relentless advance. It was still not easy for the council to replace the rookery dwellings with new homes but its perseverance eventually transformed the landscape of London. Their proudest achievement was the construction of the Kingsway tram subway. Powers to construct this were granted in 1902 and work began almost immediately. By 1906 the northern end of the subway was finished and in 1908 the entire link was opened for public traffic. This new road went up The Strand to Southampton Row, demolishing completely the rookeries in Clare Market and St Clement Danes.

Aware of the need to replace what they were destroying, at first they tried subsidising housebuilding by private contractors. Eventually they came to the reluctant conclusion that there was no realistic alternative to building homes for the people themselves. In 1900 the LCC purchased its first land for the purposes of building homes for the public itself. The era of council housing was born.

Admittedly, the 39 acres that the council bought in 1900 was not exactly in the rookery areas. The 'guinea-pig' site was Totterdown Fields in Tooting, South London. This purchase was followed by another equally suburban site at Norbury, also in South London.[11] It was not until they bought land in Tottenham and Hammersmith that the council even started to make any impact upon inner city poverty and overcrowding. Council housing of the same quality was simply not available at that time for the residents of St Giles and Saffron Hill, of Minories and Jacob's Island, of Pye Street Westminster or Berwick Street, Soho. Their time would come but not for many years as yet.

The Liberals, who had governed the LCC from 1889 to 1907, were finally voted out in favour of the Conservatives. By the time they lost office, the council's debt had risen from £18 million to £48 million. The rates had also risen by almost a third. Londoners voted for lower rates and less public spending. If it had not been for the piecemeal campaigns of slum clearance from 1820 to 1908 the rookeries might have survived. Even Saffron Hill managed to hang on in an attenuated form until the 1930s. However, they had been doomed as soon as the railway companies and the Metropolitan Board of Works saw that profits – both personal and corporate – could be made by demolishing slums and selling the land to developers or rail operators.

The LCC actively encouraged people to move out from inner London to the new suburban council estates. They offered workmen's fares on the council's trams, while the White Hart Lane estate in Tottenham was served by the Great

Jacob's Island, Bermondsey.

Eastern Railway's twopenny workmen's trains. The drift from London to the suburbs began. Cheap trains and readily available land led to the growth of the suburbs and the gradual decline of inner London as a residential area. It was not until the 1980s that Londoners began to flood back towards the centre of their city.

By 1900 the face of London had changed dramatically. Warehouses, office blocks, railway yards, stations and workshops replaced the houses that were once full of people. The 'respectable' working-class population moved out to a new ring of 'inner suburbs', either finding employment in the local area or commuting in to the City or West End. Those who remained as 'casuals' hung on in the central districts for as long as possible. They had no desire to move out to the expanding suburbs and could afford neither the rents to live there nor the transport costs to travel in to work. Those who could not or would not move out to the developing areas stayed on in the dwindling areas where rookery houses had not yet been demolished.

The coming of the First World War put a temporary end to casual labour as Britain enjoyed full employment for the first time since the Middle Ages. After the war was over new homes were built, the workhouse finally abolished and outdoor relief restored. The few remaining rookeries fell before the wave of modernisation in the 1920s and '30s. Those which were not destroyed were turned from residential to commercial use, and their inhabitants rehoused in council accommodation. A way of life that had lasted almost four hundred years was finally destroyed.

Notes

1   Sir John Summerson, *Georgian London*, Penguin, 1962.
2   Marquis De Vermont *and* Sir Charles Darnley, *London and Paris, Or Comparative Sketches*, 1823.
3   Octavia Hill, quoted in J.R. Kellett, *The Impact of Railways on Victorian Cities*, Routledge, 1969.
4   George Godwin, *London Shadows: A Glance at the 'Homes' of the Thousands*, Routledge, 1854.
5   *The Times*, 1861, quoted in: Francis Sheppard, *London 1808–1870: The Infernal Wen*, Secker and Warburg, 1971.
6   *The Times*, editorial, 28 February 1861.
7   Earl of Shaftesbury, House of Lords, 28 February 1861.
8   Charles Pearson, Metropolitan Railway, quoted in Sheppard, op. cit.
9   Earl of Derby, House of Lords, 28 February 1861.
10 Comments of the Board's architect quoted in Jenkins, op. cit.
11 A fascinating account of the Tooting development is given by the American visitor Booker T. Washington, 'London Through the Eyes of John Burns'. Washington was shown round the new development by John Burns, one of the leading figures in Labour politics from the 1880s to about 1910. The piece in question is given in: Walter Allen, *Transatlantic Crossing*, 1971.

CONCLUSION

The rookeries had an active life of nearly four hundred years. They arose as a result of the continual expansion of the population of London. The constant influx of people flooding into the capital in search of work created opportunities for property speculators to make money providing them with accommodation. When the homes were built landlords let them off to housekeepers, who in turn let them off room by room. The tenants themselves, faced with rising rents and a diminishing stock of houses, sublet the rooms into corners and living areas.

It is a common mistake to think that rookery dwellers had large families and thus contributed to the overcrowded state of their properties by their own actions. This is the exact opposite of the truth. They could not afford to support large families and the average household unit was a husband, wife and two children. It was the wealthy who had large families, not the poor.

Though crime and prostitution were common among rookery dwellers, most people worked hard at honest jobs. They were extremely versatile, engaging in any occupation that might enable them to earn sufficient money to survive. Throughout the seventeenth and eighteenth centuries figures for crime and prostitution declined steadily. It was under the Victorians that both rose sharply. Foreign visitors correctly identified the reason for it as the extreme poverty of the people.

Dwellers in the rookeries were not as poor in the seventeenth and eighteenth centuries as they became under the Victorians. Rents were lower, wages higher, the cost of living stable and employment less fluctuating. During the seventeenth century multi-occupation of dwellings actually declined. The latter half of the eighteenth century saw an increase in subletting but to nothing like the extent that occurred under the Victorians.

It was neither the houses nor the people but the surrounding environment that created the problems which beset rookery dwellers. Jacob's Island contained some of the most beautiful dwellings ever built for the working class, reminiscent of homes in Venice or Belgium. The district was even nicknamed 'Venice of Drains', the observation referring to the contrast between the beautiful homes and the insalubrious conditions in which they were situated. What made the area a rookery was the lack of fresh water. Surrounded on all sides by an open sewer, cholera struck the inhabitants while the exhalations of the local tanneries also poisoned the air.

Throughout London it was these environmental factors and not the houses themselves that caused the problems in the rookeries. Overcrowding was unpleasant but it was far worse under the Victorians than their predecessors. With the poverty rookery dwellers experienced, multi-occupation of dwellings was an economic necessity, not a choice. It was the government and local authorities of the day who forced the poor into overcrowded conditions. The common complaint by the authorities was that the rookery dwellers chose to live in overcrowded conditions and that the filthy state of their homes was the result of their own drunkenness, idleness and lack of cleanliness. These charges were indignantly refuted by opponents of the clearances, who pointed out that the majority of the dwellers would have chosen permanent employment over casual work if it was available. They also argued from the fact that positions on the railways, in spite of paying below average wages, were much in demand because they offered the possibility of a job for life. It was also pointed out that the poor were not responsible for the absence of drainage or fresh water in their dwellings and that it was an injustice to blame them for a squalor that was entirely beyond their control.

Even on the question of alcohol consumption, it was pointed out that the conditions in which they lived would tempt many persons into drinking as a temporary escape from their miserable existence.

The Victorians had many virtues but respect for the past was not among them. They had no concept of 'national heritage', instead being obsessed with the notion of progress. The beauties of art and architecture were to be observed in museums, galleries or other specially designated sites. It was impossible for the Victorians to value beauty over utility, art over science or money. Dickens's satire on the educational and social attitudes of his age in *Hard Times,* though exaggerated for dramatic effect, is not a caricature. The utter lack of interest in anything other than economic, scientific and technological matters really was characteristic of many, perhaps the majority, of middle-class people during the Victorian age. In their eyes clearing the rookeries and dispersing the people was progressive. They were the ultimate technocrats, believing firmly that science and technology could provide a solution to every problem. It was not until the passing of Victoria herself that the concept of national heritage dimly began to emerge into the public consciousness.

Now that the rookeries are gone and almost forgotten, perhaps the time has come for a fresh look at them. The social commentators of the time invariably concentrated on their defects, never upon their strengths. London has never again had the same deep and abiding community spirit it enjoyed before the destruction of the rookeries.

Commuting to work might have seemed an improvement in the nineteenth and early twentieth centuries but is now seen as a major source of stress. Most Londoners spend three hours a day travelling to and from work. Probably for this reason, from the 1980s onwards, Londoners began to desert the suburbs and move back into the areas of inner London that had been in decline for years. Former slum districts and rookery areas are now the most desirable and expensive addresses in the capital. Like their predecessors in St Giles and Saffron Hill, those Londoners who can do so now prefer to live as close to their jobs as possible.

This brings us to the crucial question – should the rookeries have been destroyed? Was, in fact, the whole programme of slum clearance a disastrous mistake? New roads and railways had to be built but a centralised planning system with an integrated transport policy would have created a better public transport system for London. It is still difficult to travel *across* London (east–west or west–east) by train. Rival companies deliberately laid their lines to inconvenience other operators. A responsible attitude by Parliament right from the start would have prevented this. Homes could have been saved, restored, renovated and fitted with proper sanitation. Communities could and should have been allowed to remain where they were, where many of them had lived for hundreds of years.

Developers seeking to turn the homes of the poor into luxury flats for the rich, railways concerned only with their own continuing expansion and the corruption of the Metropolitan Board of Works doomed the rookeries. Not only were ancient communities destroyed in the name of progress but a priceless and irreplaceable part of London's heritage was lost for ever. Other cities in the world have kept their ancient buildings, and the vibrant communities within them still survive.

It is largely the failure of vision by the Victorians, and in particular their lack of grasp of the essential part played by housing in the heritage of a nation, that leads foreign visitors to remark upon how utterly undistinguished the homes of ordinary Londoners are. Grand houses, royal palaces, luxury hotels and majestic churches there are in plenty, but the dwelling places of the people are poor things indeed. On the Continent, homes for the poor are full of character, just as those in the rookeries of London used to be. It is deeply to be regretted that they are no longer with us.

Appendix A

Medieval & Elizabethan Slums

Newgate Prison

The first slums grew up in the City of London and the areas immediately around it. The district around Newgate Prison was founded in the twelfth century and has the dubious 'honour' of being the first in London. It is perhaps surprising that the City of London, the wealthiest part of England, should have been the first area to generate slums. The rich merchants and traders who lived in their fine houses were only one side of the population of London, however – their fortunes relied on the efforts of a whole range of workers.

Quite why the area around Newgate Prison became the first slum is not altogether clear. Whether the very existence of a gaol in the area meant that only the poorer people would have chosen to live there or whether people who had family and friends imprisoned in Newgate chose to live near them is open to question. What *is* beyond dispute is that the reputation of the prison itself was appalling. Not only were the staff corrupt but the habitual brutality of both guards and inmates was so extreme that from time to time particularly horrific offenders were punished for their deeds. Prisoners who overstepped the mark were normally hanged; guards were generally simply dismissed. Rape of female prisoners was an everyday occurrence. As if the brutality of the regime was not enough, the squalid living conditions within the prison resulted in hundreds of deaths from disease. In the middle of the cells reserved for the worst offenders, those awaiting execution, ran an open sewer. Its foul stench not only infected the inmates but also those who lived and worked in the area.

Even the local clergy complained about the putrid smell and the consequent hazard to their own health. Soon the death rate from typhus in particular was higher in the vicinity of Newgate than any other area of London. In spite of all the complaints about the area nothing was done. Shopkeepers protested that citizens hurried into their shops and made their purchases as hastily as possible before making their escape. The local inhabitants complained that they could not stay long in the streets or even stand in their own doorways for fear of the poisonous Newgate air.

At least during the Middle Ages both the Church and wealthy citizens gave charitable relief to the London poor. Not only did beggars receive food from the gates of the churches and monasteries but even the servants of the wealthy gathered up the scraps after a feast and distributed them to the crowds of people waiting outside.

The Dissolution of the Monasteries by Henry VIII in 1539 was a disaster for the London poor. Once they had been deprived of the help they had formerly enjoyed from the monks they simply poured onto the streets in droves and begged at random. The result was a vast expansion of the slum population of London.

BRIDEWELL

Ironically this slum (and later prison) began as a humanitarian measure. When he was faced with the influx into London of some 12,000 desperately poor people from the countryside seeking work, Edward VI established Bridewell in 1550 as a centre of poor relief. Soon the impoverished immigrants became rowdy and even criminal. By 1553 the king was forced to abandon the idea of using Bridewell as a place of refuge for poor people. Instead he decided to turn it into a workhouse. Before long it became an actual prison in which the convicts were forced to perform hard labour as part of their sentence. As well as other thoroughly unpleasant and arduous tasks the inmates of Bridewell also had to clean out the open sewers that ran beneath their gaol.

Once again ordinary people flooded into the area and every inch of room and house space was taken up by lodgers. Most houses for merchants in the City at this time were built on four or five storeys and had ample space, natural light and ventilation. Houses in the rookeries were usually 15ft wide, densely packed and with frontages of 12ft. They were normally built on two or three storeys with three or four rooms in the building.

As the population of London continued to increase, alleys and courts, 'rents' and closes were built, built upon and built over. The normal construction material for houses at this time was wood which was of course cheap and quick to put up. In spite of its obvious hazards, because of its cheapness and the demand for new homes, the flimsiest and most unsafe wooden structures were erected as hastily as possible with no concern for the welfare of their inhabitants.

A contemporary poet and playwright, Thomas Dekker, gives a vivid account of the streets of London at this period, in the course of which he also reveals quite how unstable the new housing in the rookeries really was. Dekker says:

In every street, carts and coaches make such a thundering as if the world ran upon wheels; at every corner, men, women and children meet in such shoals, that posts are set up of purpose to strengthen the houses, lest with jostling one another they should shoulder them [down]. Besides, hammers are beating in one place, tubs hooping in another, pots clinking in a third, water-tankards running at tilt in a fourth. Here are porters sweating under burdens, there merchants' men bearing bags of money. Chapmen (as if they were at leap-frog) skip out of one shop into another. Tradesmen (as if they were dancing galliards) are lusty at legs and never stand still. All are as busy as country attorneys at assizes.[1]

EAST SMITHFIELD

Another area of the City that was rapidly turning into a rookery was the district around East Smithfield. This was just east of the Tower of London and began as a small settlement outside the walls of the City of London. It was given by King Edgar to thirteen of his knights as a reward for their services to him. In area it stretched from the south of Aldgate down to the River Thames.[2]

In 1229 Henry III granted permission for a fifteen-day fair to be held in the region. Merchants came from all over England to buy and sell their wares.[3] In 1236 it also became the site of the second Jewish quarter in London. It was known as 'Poor Jewry' to distinguish it from the existing and more prosperous settlement 'Old Jewry'.[4]

In 1348 the Black Death hit London. The churchyards in the City were soon unable to cope with the death toll and Edward III was forced to set aside a piece of land in East Smithfield to bury the plague victims. In 1442 Henry VI granted the right for the citizens of East Smithfield to hold yet another fair. This one lasted twenty-one days from 25 July. During the sixteenth century the authorities sold the right to hold this fair to the City of London.[5]

The most famous resident of East Smithfield was the poet Edmund Spenser. His father was a tailor from Lancashire but Spenser was born and bred in East Smithfield. He attended Merchant Taylors' School which in those days was an institution for 'pore scholars'.

Spenser not only learned to read and write there but also acquired a knowledge of Latin, Greek, French and Italian. Spenser demonstrated how scholars from poor backgrounds could overcome all the disadvantages of a slum upbringing and still go on to achieve success at university, in literature and even public life.

He became the most famous poet of his day and was showered with both money and fame as a result. Spenser was probably the first but certainly not the last slum dweller to achieve success. He actually referred to his upbringing in the following verses of one of his most famous poems:

> At length they all to merry London came,
> To merry London, my most kindly nurse,
> That to me gave this life's first native source;
> Though from another place I take my name,
> An house of ancient fame . . .
> Sweet Thames, run softly, till I end my song.[6]

St Katherine's by the Tower

Only slightly further east was the rookery of St Katherine's by the Tower. This was the site of one of the most beautiful medieval churches in London although the area it served was anything but salubrious. Most of the men in the area worked as sailors, hawkers, street traders, porters and dockers. Most of the women worked in public houses, domestic service, prostitution or petty crime. It also contained probably the largest number of pubs (known as 'beer houses' in those days) in the whole of London.

This was not only because of the huge consumption of alcohol by the citizens but because pubs were also the 'employment agencies' of their time. Masters would call at pubs to ask for hands and the workers in turn assembled there in hope of finding employment.

An area with such a high proportion of sailors among its population soon led to a whole industry springing up in ways to part the mariners from their money. It was very common for publicans to double up as receivers of stolen goods and to get a cut from prostitutes and pimps for allowing them to use their premises. If the sailors had not managed to squander their pay through the usual and relatively straightforward traps of drink and prostitution, the pickpockets, cutpurses and straightforward muggers were at hand to steal what remained. Fights between sailors and citizens in the area were frequent and generally bloody – they often ended up with fatal stabbings.

In spite of this the very existence of such a regular source of income drew poor people to St Katherine's like a magnet. It soon became filled with more and more people packed into small houses, let out room by room with as many as could be squeezed in together. Filth, disease, squalor and the appalling stench of sewage, rotting fish and decaying vegetables soon filled the air around and made it yet another dangerous rookery. The houses themselves were actually better than the average for rookery dwellers but the transient and semi-criminal population made the area extremely 'noisome', to use the contemporary expression. The area was furnished with stocks, pillory and a whipping-post, all of which were frequently employed in the punishment of the inhabitants.

St Katherine's was also home to a disproportionate number of immigrants. A survey of the population in 1572 revealed 828 Dutch, 69 French, 8 Danes, 5 Poles, 2 Spaniards, 1 Italian and 12 Scots. Many of the Dutch brewed beer and most of the French made hats.

WHITEFRIARS/ALSATIA

Even in the rookeries of Newgate and Bridewell it was always possible to find honest citizens carrying on their employment. The same was even truer of the East and West Smithfield and St Katherine's areas. However, the next of our slum districts, and the last one to spring up during the Elizabethan age, was almost entirely inhabited by the criminal fraternity. It was the district of Whitefriars, so called after the Carmelite church that had once stood on the spot.

Whitefriars was to be for a hundred years the most dangerous and lawless part of London. It stood behind the Savoy prison, between the Strand and the River Thames, bordering on Fleet Street and the Temple. Whitefriars soon became a notorious sanctuary for thieves, so far beyond the reach of law that it became nicknamed 'Alsatia' by analogy with the region of Alsace-Lorraine. This district was fought over by the French, Austrians, Prussians, Dutch and English but no one country was able to assert any kind of meaningful control over it.

For some obscure reason Londoners at this time did not like walking by the river. Their abandonment of the Thames left the waterside open to the criminal gangs who roamed around Whitefriars. Even the Watch, the local police force of the day, was afraid to enter the area. When they did so it was always in groups of at least five or six and even this was often not enough. Generally the citizens of Whitefriars would rally to the assistance of any of their brothers or sisters being sought by the law and drive away the Watch with sticks, stones and any other weapons to hand. The most notorious part of 'Alsatia' was Hanging Sword Alley. By 1673 the situation had become so serious that the Earl of Essex wrote to King Charles II protesting that 'they are become a reproach to ye Government, and look almost like petit rebellions, they going by 20 or 30 in a company breaking open houses even in the ye day time.'[7]

The king was aware of the problem but the absence of any kind of proper police force made it difficult for him to act. Everyone knew that the Watch could not subdue the bold and ingenious rogues who dwelt in Whitefriars. The only options open to him were sending in troops to maintain law and order or turning a blind eye. As he always did in the face of difficult choices, Charles II took the easy option.

Certain types of criminal soon became almost confined to Whitefriars. The 'rufflers' pretended to have served the king during the Civil War; they shammed injury and tried to swindle money out of former Royalist officers. The 'anglers' pushed a rod with a hook on the end through any open windows under cover of darkness. 'Polliards' and 'clapperdogeons' were beggars who used children to try to obtain money from bystanders. This particular scam became so profitable that children and even babies could actually be hired by the day from other citizens. 'Fraters' pretended to be collecting money for a hospital, and used forged documents to back up their claim. 'Whip Jacks' were men who pretended to be sailors and were always accompanied by a woman, whom they claimed to have saved from shipwreck. 'Strowling Morts' were women pretending to be widows, who usually worked with a male accomplice. 'Patricios' were bogus vicars, who performed unlawful but seemingly real marriage ceremonies in return for money. The top two posts in the hierarchy of villainy were the 'fencing cully', who received stolen goods, and 'the upright man', best described as the leader of a group of gangsters.

Hogarth, inevitably, immortalised the area in paint, where the ninth plate of 'Industry and Idleness' is set in Blood Bowl House, Hanging Sword Alley. It was not until the nineteenth century that the area was finally brought under control. Until then, as Macaulay remarked, even the warrant of the Chief Justice of England meant nothing unless backed by a file of musketeers.

Fleet Marriages

In addition to the 'patricios', there were also genuine vicars who were not too particular about the status of the bride and groom. They officiated at the area around the Fleet Prison, the Gretna Green of its day. 'Fleet marriages' were certainly dubious but were considered legally binding. It was extremely common for women to be drugged or made drunk and then married for their money. Drunken young men also woke to find themselves married to a woman they had only met the day before. It was not unknown for blackmail or even straightforward coercion to be used, particularly on young women.

'Patricios' also did a good trade in bogus marriages for the benefit of those men who wanted to seduce young girls but had to go through a form of marriage first. By employing a vicar who was not a genuine clergyman they could then repudiate the 'marriage' afterwards. Like the crime and violence, the dubious weddings of the Fleet became a scandal. Nothing was done about it, however, until in 1751 the Clandestine Marriages Act abolished the practice. After that couples had to go to Gretna Green to get married without the consent of their parents.

The main reason for the abolition of Fleet marriages was that too many young aristocrats were becoming ensnared by drink into unsuitable alliances. There were even rumours that some members of the royal family had contracted unsuitable clandestine marriages in the Fleet. There was considerable opposition to the Act and some very curious arguments were used at the time against its abolition.

Even now, some feminist historians condemn the Clandestine Marriage Act as an example of patriarchal tyranny. Curiously, at the time of its abolition, women rather than men lamented its passing and fought to keep it, so perhaps there is some truth in this claim.

Whitefriars was a rollicking, boisterous area, where drink flowed freely and sex was easily available. It became a kind of tourist attraction, particularly for young men from the aristocracy. In spite of the danger they still came for the 'experience'.

From the point of view of the inhabitants of Alsatia, the following charming lament survives, about a girl whose man has been hung for his crimes:

> Now my little rogue is gone,
> By the highways begs there none
> In body both for length and bone
> Like my clapperdogeon.
> Dumb and madman thou could'st play,
> Or a drivelling fool all day,
> And like a poor man thou could'st pray,
> Yet scraped with passes sealed away.
> When the evening hath been wet,
> For fire the hedges down did'st beat,
> Me then with stolen duck did'st treat,
> Or else a fat goose was our meat.
> Mallards then I could not lack,
> Bacon hung always at my back,
> Nor corn wanted in my sack,
> With good milk pottage I held tack.
> To thy dog and dish adieu,
> Thy staff and pass I ne'er must view,
> Though thy cloak was far from new,
> In it my rogue to me was true.[8]

Whitefriars continued to be a thorn in the side of successive kings. In 1697 William III finally demolished the houses and dispersed the inhabitants. Most of them simply fled to new rookeries, mainly in St Giles.

CLERKENWELL

Clerkenwell was another area of London that began to turn into a slum from early times. As early as 1422 Clerkenwell had been condemned as one of the most notorious 'Stewes', or brothels, in London. Throughout the Elizabethan age it continued to be a notorious centre of prostitution. Only Bankside in Southwark and, later, St Giles and the East End could match it for the number of women soliciting.

BANKSIDE, SOUTHWARK

This area was a slum from an early period of the Middle Ages. It was the leading centre for prostitution in London, and both wits and reformers complained that the Bishop of Southwark, who owned the land and houses in which brothels operated, was living on immoral earnings.

Notes

1   Thomas Dekker, *The Seven Deadly Sins of London*, c. 1600.
2   John Stow, *Survey of London*, 1598.
3   Ibid.
4   Ibid.
5   Ibid.
6   Edmund Spenser, 'Prothalamion', 1579.
7   Earl of Essex.
8   Anonymous, c. 1680.

Appendix B

Notable Characters
of the Rookeries

Several famous people were either born and raised or at least lived in the rookeries at some time during their lives. Hogarth and Turner, two of Britain's greatest painters, are so well known that mention of them here might seem superfluous. Instead, a small selection of some of the lesser-known but colourful characters who lived in the London rookeries will be given.

Joshua Sturges

Joshua Sturges lived at what is now the Blue Posts public house, on the corner of Hanway Street and the Tottenham Court Road. For many years he was the publican there, but his chief claim to fame was as a champion player of draughts (chequers). Not only was he a fine player but he also wrote one of the earliest manuals on the game, entitled *Guide to the Game of Draughts*, published in 1800 and dedicated to the Prince Regent. His epitaph read:

> Sacred to the memory of Mr Joshua Sturges. Many years a Respectable Licensed Victualler in this Parish; who departed this Life the 12th of August, 1813. Aged 55 years. He was esteemed for the many excellent Qualities he possessed, and his desire to improve the Minds, as also to benefit the Trade of his Brother Victuallers. His Genius was also eminently displayed to create innocent and rational amusement to Mankind, in the Production of his Treatise, on the difficult game of Draughts, which Treatise received the Approbation of his Prince, and many other Distinguished Characters. May his Virtues be rewarded in the next. Peace to his Soul, and respected be his Memory.[1]

JOHN MITFORD

John Mitford was born at Mitford Castle, Northumbria, into an aristocratic family. He served in the Navy under Hood and Nelson. His brother was Lord Redesdale; others, like John Mitford himself, became writers. A distant cousin, Miss Mitford, wrote *Our Village*; another relation wrote a history of Greece; yet another, Captain Meadows Taylor, wrote *Confessions of a Thug*; while John Mitford, generally known as 'Jack,' wrote 'hack work' for publishers in Seven Dials.

Mitford was best known in his time for one of his books, *The Adventures of Johnny Newcombe in the Navy*. After leaving the naval service he became a drifter. Towards the end of his life he lived either in the dosshouses of St Giles or slept on park benches. Burke states that 'during those years his appearance was so utterly ragged and offensive that even the regular users of these places shunned his company. When his lordship [his brother Lord Redesdale] provided him with clothes, to help him present a respectable appearance, the clothes were sold for gin.'[2]

While he was writing *Johnny Newcombe,* his publisher paid him a fee of a shilling per day. He wrote the work on the premises, fortified by a meal of bread and cheese and large quantities of gin. At night he slept on the grass in Bayswater fields and (apparently on rare occasions) washed himself and his clothes in the pond.

One of his publishers in Seven Dials found it impossible to get any work out of him without locking him in a cellar with a table and chair and a bottle of gin. Now and again, when the publisher cut off his 'gin' allowance, he went out on to the streets and exchanged his coat and shoes for another bottle. In December 1831, he died in St Giles Workhouse.[3]

Chaps warm themselves in the dosshouse.

'CORNER MEMORY' THOMPSON

John Thompson was born and bred in St Giles, where his father was a greengrocer. He acquired his nickname from having, for a wager, following his retirement to Hampstead, drawn a plan of the entire parish of St Giles entirely from memory. The plan included every pump, coach-turning and stable-yard and (the feature which led to Thompson's acquiring his nickname) the corner shop on every street. Apparently he had a photographic memory, since he also possessed the ability to read an entire newspaper overnight and then repeat it verbatim the following morning. He died in February 1843, at the age of eighty-six.[4]

'TIDDY DOLL'

Tiddy Doll was an eccentric seller of gingerbread. He plied the Haymarket dressed in brightly coloured and elaborate costume and wore a cap with a feather on it upon his head. He was present at every public hanging at Tyburn, selling his wares to the crowd, and became so well known that Hogarth drew him. Even his death was an act of theatre, drowning when a crack in the ice opened while he was catering during a Frost Fair on the Thames. A London restaurant is named after him.[5]

'ROMEO' COATES

Benjamin Coates acquired his nickname following a disastrous decision to hire the Haymarket Theatre for one night in 1810 and portray the part of Romeo in *Romeo and Juliet*. Observers described him as dressing 'in a cloak of sky-blue pink, profusely spangled, red pantaloons, a vest of white muslin, and a wig of the style of Charles II, capped by an opera hat.' As well as his ridiculous costume, he apparently also had a 'guttural' voice and every time he opened his mouth the audience roared with laughter. To make matters worse, his trousers were too tight and burst on stage. He became known as 'Romeo Coates' for the rest of his life.[6]

'LADY LEWSON'

A Mrs Lewson lived in Coldbath Square, Clerkenwell, until she finally died at the age of 116. Although she died in 1816, all her life she continued to dress in the style of the early eighteenth century, acquiring as a result the nickname 'Lady Lewson'. She lived in only one room of a large house, which was 'only occasionally swept out but never washed. She never washed herself, because she thought those people who did so were always taking cold, or laying the foundation of some dreadful disorder; her method was to besmear her face and neck all over with hog's lard, because that was soft and lubricating, and then, because she wanted a little colour on her cheeks, she bedaubed them with rose pink. The cinder ashes had not been removed for many years; they were very neatly piled up, as if formed into beds for some particular purpose.[7]

'Mad Madge'

Margaret Cavendish, Duchess of Newcastle, was one of the most original characters of the seventeenth century. She made her home in Clerkenwell and showed herself to have one of the finest minds of her time, in spite of her notorious eccentricity. Having sided with the king during the Civil War she found herself in exile but made an audacious return to England in 1651.

Margaret Cavendish never learned to spell properly and her grammar was also somewhat original. She proclaimed almost proudly that she did not 'understand grammar and the little she knew was enough to make her renounce it.' She also claimed that it was 'against nature for a woman to spell right.' Contemporaries considered her 'mad, conceited and ridiculous.' In spite of these peculiarities, in 1653 she burst into print with her first volume, a collection of verse entitled *Poems and Fancies*. The work attracted considerable attention and even won a certain amount of praise, though the more common reaction was ridicule.

In spite of this, she continued to publish, eventually producing twenty-two works during her lifetime. Two of them, *Poems and Fancies* and *The Blazing World* are, at least at their best, masterpieces. *The Blazing World* is both an intelligent and thoughtful attempt to reconcile the science and philosophy of her time and an anticipation of the much later genre of science fiction. She also made such remarkable comments as 'women live like bats or owls, labour like beasts, and die like worms,' an attitude which has led to her slow rediscovery by feminist historians. Her death in 1673, at the age of fifty, was a sad loss to English literature. 'Mad Madge' she may have been but she had the potential to be one of the greatest writers and thinkers of the seventeenth century.

Notes

1   Sturges's epitaph in Old St Pancras churchyard, sadly long obliterated.
2   Thomas Burke, *The Beauty of England*, Harrap, 1933.
3   Ibid. Burke's account is largely drawn from William Howitt, *Visits*, 1840
4   John O'London, *London Stories Old and New*, Newnes, 1926.
5   Walter Thornbury and E. Walford, *Old and New London*, 1883–1885.
6   Ibid.
7   W.J. Pinks, *The History of Clerkenwell*, 1865.

Appendix C

Population & Immigration

Table of Population, Metropolitan London*

1500	40,000–50,000
1563	93,000
1600	200,000
1650	400,000
1700	575,000
1750	675,000
1801 (First census)	958,000
1811 (Census)	1,139,000
1821 (Census)	1,380,000
1831 (Census)	1,656,000
1841 (Census)	1,945,000
1851 (Census)	2,363,000
1861 (Census)	2,808,00
1871 (Census)	3,261,000
1881 (Census)	3,830,000
1891 (Census)	4,228,000
1901 (Census)	4,536,000

Immigrants as a Percentage of the London Population, 1700

Age	Male	Female
15–24	61.3	55.3
25–34	67.2	69.3
35–44	75.4	74.5
45–54	81.5	78.6
55+	83.7	78.6

* In this table, Metropolitan London includes the City of London, Westminster, Southwark and the few London suburbs such as Spitalfields, Moorgate and Cripplegate.

Appendix D

Principal Rookeries

The City

1 Bishopsgate
2 Moorgate
3 Whitecross Street, Finsbury
4 Cripplegate
5 St Sepulchre
6 West Smithfield
7 Clerkenwell
8 Saffron Hill
9 Newgate
10 St Bride's
11 Bridewell
12 Alsatia, Whitefriars

The West End

13 Grays Inn
14 Lincoln's Inn
15 Bloomsbury
16 Holborn
17 St Clement Danes
18 Clare Market
19 St Giles-in-the-Fields
20 Berwick Street, Soho
21 St James's, Soho
22 Covent Garden
23 St Martin-in-the-Fields
24 Thorney Island, Westminster
25 St Margaret's, Westminster
26 Pye Street, Westminster
27 The Devil's Acre, Pimlico
28 Rents Buildings, York Street, Marylebone
29 St Mary's, Marylebone
30 Knightsbridge

THE EAST END

31   St Katherine's by the Tower
32   East Smithfield
33   Minories
34   Aldgate
35   Spitalfields
36   Shoreditch
37   Old Nicholl Street (The Jago)
38   Bethnal Green
39   Wentworth Street, Whitechapel
40   Shadwell
41   Limehouse
42   St George in the East
43   Stepney
44   Wapping
45   Mile End
46   Ratcliff Highway
47   Canning Town

SOUTH LONDON

48   Bankside, Southwark
49   The Mint, Southwark
50   Tooley Street, Southwark
51   Pearl Row, St George's Road, Southwark
52   St George's in the Borough
53   Red House, Old Gravel Lane, Borough
54   Kent Street, Borough
55   Jacob's Island, Bermondsey
56   Tanner's Yard, Bermondsey
57   Deptford
58   Rotherhithe
59   East Greenwich
61   Woolwich
62   Walworth
63   Newington Butts
64   Lambeth
65   Nine Elms
66   Battersea

NORTH LONDON

67   Agar Town, St Pancras
68   Battlebridge, King's Cross

BIBLIOGRAPHY

Numerous primary sources were consulted in the archives of Westminster and Camden Libraries, the London Metropolitan Archives and the Public Record Office.

CONTEMPORARY ACCOUNTS

Bardwell, William, *Westminster Improvements: A brief account of ancient and modern Westminster: with observations on former plans of improvement, and on the objects and prospects ... of the measures now intended to be pursued*, Smith & Elder, 1839

Beames, Thomas, *The Rookeries Of London*, Frank Cass, 1970 (1850, 1852)

Besant, Sir Walter, *Westminster*, Frederick A. Stokes Co., 1895

——, *London*, Harper & Bros, 1892

——, *History Of London*, Village Press, 1990

——, *London North Of The Thames*, Black, 1911

——, & Mitton, G.E., *The Fascination Of London: The Strand District*, Adam & Charles Black, 1902

Booth, Charles, *Life and Labour of the People in London: London North of the Thames: The Inner Ring*, Macmillan, 1902–3

Bosanquet, Charles F., *London: Some Account Of Its Growth, Charitable Agencies, And Wants*, Taylor & Francis, 1984

Boswell, James, *Boswell's London Journal 1762-1763*, Heinemann, 1951

Campbell, Robert, *The London Tradesman*, T. Gardner, 1747

Clinek, George, *Bloomsbury And St Giles Past And Present, with Historical and Antiquarian Notices of the Vicinity*, Truslove & Shirley, *c.* 1890

Dawson, Nancy, *Authentic Memoirs Of The Celebrated Miss Nancy Dawson*, 1762

Firmin, Thomas, *Some Proposals For The Implaying Of The Poor, Especially In And About The City Of London,* 1678

Godwin, George, *London Shadows: A Glance At The "Homes" Of The Thousands (The Rise of Urban Britain)*, Routledge, 1854

Graunt, John, *Natural And Political Observations Upon The Bills Of Mortality*, J. Martyn, 1676

Greenwood, James, *The Seven Curses Of London*, Taylor & Francis, 1984

Hanway, Jonas, *A Sentimental History Of Chimney-Sweepers In London And Westminster*, 1785

Hill, Octavia, *Homes Of The London Poor*, Frank Cass, 1970 (1875)

Hollingshead, John, *Ragged London In 1861*, Smith & Elder, 1861

Kennett, White, *The Charity Of Schools For Poor Children Recommended in a Sermon Preach'd in the Parish-Church of St. Sepulchers, May 16. 1706*, 1716

Maitland, William, *History And Survey Of London From its Foundation to the Present Time*, (2 Vols), T. Osborne, 1756

Mayhew, Henry, *London Labour And The London Poor*, Penguin, 1965

——, *London Characters and Crooks*, Hamlyn, 1969

——, & Binney, John, *The Criminal Prisons Of London And Scenes Of Prison*, L.C. Griffin, 1862

Mearns, Andrew, *The Bitter Cry Of Outcast London*, Leicester University Press, 1970

Parton, John, *Some Account Of The Hospital And Parish Of St-Giles-In-The -Fields*, Luke Hansard, 1822

Pember Reeves, Maud, *Round About A Pound A Week*, 1913

Shesgreen, Sean (Ed.), *The Cries And Hawkers Of London: Engravings and Drawings by Marcellus Laroon*, Stanford University Press, 1990

Sims, George R., *Here The Poor Live And Horrible London*, Garland, 1984

Stow, John, *The Survey Of London*, Sutton, 1994

Strype, John, *A Survey Of The Cities Of London And Westminster*, Churchill, 1720

De Vermont, Marquis, & Damley, Sir Charles, *London And Paris, Or Comparative Sketches*, 1823

Ward, Ned, *The London Spy*, Michigan University Press, 1993

Wilkinson, Robert, *Londiniana illustra*, 1814

SECONDARY SOURCES

Ackroyd, Peter, *London: The Biography*, Chatto & Windus, 2000

Alexander, Sally, *Women's Work in Nineteenth Century London: A Study of the Years 1820–1850*, Pluto Press, 1983

Arlidge, Abraham, *A Survey Of Hatton Garden*, London Topographical Society, 1983

Ashton, John, *The Fleet: Its Rivers. Prison And Marriages*, T. Fisher Unwin, 1888

August, Andrew, *Poor Women's Lives: Gender, Work And Poverty In Late-Victorian London*, Associated University Presses, 1999

Ausubel, H, *In Hard Times: Reformers Among The Late Victorians*, Columbia University Press, 1960

Beier, A.L. & Finlay, R.A.P., *The Making Of The Metropolis: London, 1500–1700*, Longmans, 1986

Beresford Chancellor, E., *London's Old Latin Quarter, Being An Account Of Tottenham Court Road And Its Immediate Surroundings*, Jonathan Cape, 1930

Bosanquet, Helen, *Social Work In London, 1869–1912: A History of the Charity Organisation Society*, Harvester Press, 1973

Bowley, A.L., *Wages in the United Kingdom in the Nineteenth Century*, Augustus M. Kelley, 1972

Brett-James, Norman G., *The Growth Of Stuart London*, Allen & Unwin, 1935

Burford, E.J., *Wits, Wenches And Wantons - London's Low Life: Covent Garden In The Eighteenth Century*, Robert Hale, 1986

Clark, Alice, *Working Life Of Women In The Seventeenth Century*, George Routledge and Sons Ltd, London, 1919

Cubitt, H., *Building In London: A Treatise on the Law and Practice Affecting the Erection and Maintenance of Buildings in the Metropolis*, Constable, 1911

Dale, T.C., *The Inhabitants Of London In 1638*, Society Of Genealogists, 1931

Davidson, Caroline, *A Woman's Work Is Never Done: A History Of Housework In The British Isles 1650–1950*, Chatto & Windus, London, 1982

Dyos, H.J., *Victorian Suburb, A Study Of The Growth Of Camberwell*, Leicester University Press, 1961

Earle, Peter, *The Making Of The English Middle Class: Business, Society And Family Life In London, 1660–1730*, Methuen, 1989

——, *A City Full Of People: Men And Women Of London 1650–1750*, Methuen, 1994

Esdaile, Katherine A., *St Martin In The Fields, New And Old,* Society For The Propagation Of Christian Knowledge, 1944

George, M. Dorothy, *London Life in the Eighteenth Century*, Penguin, 1966

Green, David R., *People Of The Rookery, a Pauper Community in Victorian London*, University Of South London, 1986

Hall, P.G., *The Industries Of London Since 1861*, Hutchinson, 1962

Handover, P.M., *Printing in London : from 1476 to modern times · competitive practice and technical invention in the trade of book and Bible printing, periodical production, jobbing &c*, Allen & Unwin, 1960

Heal, Ambrose, *Sign Boards Of Old London Shops*, Batsford, 1957

Herber, Mark, *Criminal London: A Pictorial History From Mediaeval Times To 1939*, Phillimore, 2002

Hind, A.M., *Wenceslaus Hollar And His Views Of London And Windsor In The Seventeenth Century*, Benjamin Blom, 1972

Hobson, J.A., *The Evolution Of Modern Capitalism – A Study of Machine Production*, Allen & Unwin, 1930

Irving, William Henry, *John Gay's London: Illustrated from the Poetry of the Time*, Harvard University Press, 1928

Jenkins, Simon, *Landlords To London: The Story Of A Capital And Its Growth*, Constable, 1975

Keene, D., *Cheapside Before The Great Fire*, Esrc, 1985

Knowles, C.C., & Pitt, P.H., *The History Of Building Regulations In London 1189–1972*, Architectural Press, 1972

Linebaugh, Peter, *The London Hanged: Crime And Civil Society In The Eighteenth Century*, Verso, 2003

Llewellyn-Smith. H., *The New Survey Of London Life And Labour*, Nine Volumes, P.S. King, 1930–5

Loveless, Leonard Charles, *The Story Of The Parish Of St-Giles-In-The-Fields, 1101–1931*, Verulam, 1931

Lucas, E.V., *A Wanderer In London*, Methuen, 1936

Macfarlane, Alan, *Marriage And Love In England: Modes Of Reproduction, 1300–1840*, Wiley-Blackwell, 1986.

Macmichael, J. Holden, *The Story Of Charing Cross And Its Immediate Neighbourhood*, Chatto & Windus, 1906

McMaster, John, *A Short History Of The Royal Parish Of St Martin-In-The-Fields*, London, W.C.G. Holder & Sons, 1916

Marryat, H., & Broadbent, Una, *The Romance Of Hatton Garden*, James Cornish, 1930

Marshall, Dorothy, *The English Poor In The Eighteenth Century, a study in social and administrative history*, Routledge, 1926

Mitchell, R.J., & Leys, M.D.K., *A History Of London Life*, Penguin, 1963

Morley, Henry, *Memoirs Of Bartholomew Fair*, Chapman & Hall, 1859

Mowat, Charles Loch, *The Charity Organisation Society, 1869–1913, Its Ideas And Works*, Methuen, 1961

Nevill, Ralph, *Night Life: London And Paris Past And Present with eight illustrations*, Cassell, 1926

O'London, John, *London Stories Old And New*, Newnes, 1926

Olsen, D.J., *The Growth Of Victorian London*, Penguin, 1979

Picard, Liza, *Restoration London*, Weidenfeld & Nicolson, 1997

Pimlott, J.A.R., *Toynbee Hall: Fifty Years Of Social Progress*, Dent, 1935

Pinchbeck, Ivy, *Women Workers Of The Industrial Revolution, 1750–1850*, Virago, 1969

Rasmussen, Steen Eiler, *London: The Unique City*, Pelican, 1960

Schwarz, I.D., *London In The Age Of Industrialisation: Entrepreneurs, Labour Force And Living Conditions, 1700–1850*, Cambridge University Press, 1992

Sekon, G.A., *Locomotion In Victorian London*, Oxford University Press, 1938

Shield, J., *The Effects Of Machinery On Wages*, Swann Sonnenschien, 1892

Sheppard, Francis, *London 1808–1870: The Infernal Wen*, Secker & Warburg, 1971

Shoemaker, R.B., *Prosecution And Punishment: Petty Crime And The Law In London And Rural Middlesex, 1660–1725*, Cambridge University Press, 1991

Stedman-Jones, Gareth, *Outcast London: A Study in the Relationship between Classes in Victorian Society*, Penguin, 1976

Stern, W.M., *The Porters Of London*, Longmans Green & Co., 1960

Stone, L., 'The Residential Development Of The West End Of London In The
    Seventeenth Century' in Malament, B.C. (Ed.), *After The Reformation*,
    Manchester University Press, 1980

Summerson, Sir John, *Georgian London*, Penguin, 1962

Tames, Richard, *Soho Past*, Historical Publications, 1994

Triggs, H.I., & Tanner, H., *Some Architectural Works Of Inigo Jones*, Batsford, 1901

Waller, M., *1700: Scenes From London Life*, Sceptre, 2001

INDEX

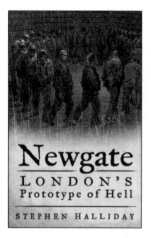
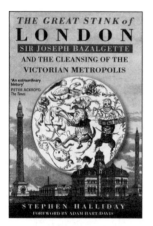
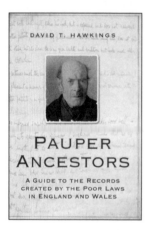

Cowboy Famous

Cowboy Justice Association
Book Four

By Olivia Jaymes

www.OliviaJaymes.com

Chapter One

The best part of Griffin Sawyer's day was the morning. He loved rising before dawn and sitting on the front porch of his home watching the sun come up while sipping on his first, second, and sometimes even his third cup of coffee. The peace and quiet were a balm to his solitude loving soul since he spent most of his waking hours dealing with the worst of humanity.

He usually had quiet at the end of the day too but nothing compared to this. He could remember the frenzy of activity and his mother's harried manner in the home he'd grown up in. She hadn't had it easy getting ten children up, dressed, fed and off to school but somehow she'd managed it. With a lot of help from the older children of which he was one.

Now, the only sounds were the rustle of the leaves and the muted quacks of a few ducks taking an early morning swim. No one was pulling on his sleeve asking for help to brush their hair, their teeth, or to get them more juice. He could be alone with only his thoughts for company.

But all good things had to come to an end.

Griffin heard the growl of an engine at the front of his home and then the clomp of heavy boots. He knew those boots as well has he did his own after the last few years. His deputy, Darrell "Dare" Turner, had come to pick him up for the monthly meeting with the town council.

Griffin had once asked his second-in-command how he got his nickname "Dare." The deputy had bravery and heart although it was usually covered up by a grouchy demeanor that had most people stepping lightly around the man. But nothing Griffin had seen Dare do had ever been foolhardy. He seemed to have a level head on his shoulders. Dare had simply scowled at the question and told Griffin the nickname had stuck in high school. No other details, which was just Dare's way.

"Are you ready to go?" Climbing the steps to the back deck, Dare wore the perpetual frown that furrowed his brow. Griffin had never figured out why Dare was always pissed off at life either but he could count the number of smiles he'd seen from the man on one hand.

"You wouldn't be so damn ugly if you smiled once in a while."

"No offense, but you're not my type," Dare answered flatly. His lips never twitched but Griffin thought he saw mirth in the deputy's eyes.

Laughter bubbled from Griffin and he had to put down his coffee mug before he spilled it on his clean uniform shirt. "Good morning, Dare. Want some coffee?"

"I wouldn't turn it down." Dare shrugged. "You're the one with the schedule."

Griffin lowered his legs from where he'd had them propped up on the deck and strolled into the kitchen through the sliding glass door knowing Dare would follow. They'd done this enough times to know the drill whenever Griffin's truck was being serviced. He ought to replace the ornery thing but he just couldn't bring himself to do it. It had been the first new truck he'd ever owned all by himself. He was the only one who had ever driven it.

"I've got my meeting but we have enough time to pour you a cup."

"Thanks. Was that Tina I saw barreling down your driveway as I was heading up here?" Dare asked, accepting the mug from Griffin.

Griffin's lips twisted as he remembered the conversation between himself and the woman he'd been dating the last few weeks. It had ended better than he'd expected but as usual she didn't understand. No one ever did.

"It was. I don't think I'll be seeing her anymore though."

Dare lifted the cup to his lips probably to hide a smile. "I guess she didn't get the memo."

"The memo?" Griffin filled his travel mug with coffee and a generous amount of cream. "What do you mean?"

"Everyone knows what you're like." Dare snorted and shook his head. "The female gossip is that you don't like women getting too fucking comfy here at your home. You like to sleep alone. You don't let them leave anything personal here or anything. Stuff like that."

Griffin turned away to hide his warm cheeks. He was particular about some things and it was true Tina hadn't appreciated that. Just this morning she'd used his fucking toothbrush because he wouldn't let her leave one here. Now he was going to have to stop at the store and get a new one. He knew it was hypocritical considering the places he'd had his mouth but he didn't like to share. His toothbrush or anything else.

"I like my space, that's all." Griffin took a drink of the hot liquid before turning back to his right-hand man. "Is that a crime or something?"

Dare lifted his hands in surrender. "Not to me. I don't blame you, personally. I like my space too."

"It's just they take over everything." Griffin sighed, still smelling the distinctive perfume Tina had sprayed on herself and half of the house. He'd have to open the windows to get rid of the stench. "Their female crap is everywhere and a man can't get a decent night's sleep with them draped all over you. And they talk. Always asking me what I'm thinking or feeling. Shit, maybe I'm not thinking or feeling any damn thing."

"You're preaching to the choir, boss man. The problem is they're always thinking something. Fuck, it's a wonder their brains don't explode from how much they're always thinking. That's not for me, man. You've got the right idea. Stay single and live alone."

Alone.

Griffin didn't want to apologize to the woman in his life constantly, but yes, he enjoyed being alone. He liked sleeping in his big bed by himself and drinking milk out of the carton. He liked having control over the thermostat and the television remote. If he wanted to eat ice cream for breakfast he could or maybe stay up all night watching a Clint Eastwood marathon. There was no one to bother, no one else's feelings that might get hurt. He only had to worry about himself.

"Shit, we better get on the road." Griffin glanced at his watch and grimaced. These meetings with the town council were never fun but they were necessary. Normally they were also uneventful but lately there had been a lot of wrangling over the budget. They wanted Griffin to cut a deputy and he was pushing back. They were too short staffed as it was.

He shoved his hat on his head and followed Dare out to the truck, his mind already moving past the events of the morning.

The woman who would understand Griffin simply didn't exist. There was no point in even looking.

This couldn't be happening.

Jazz Oliver stared at her cell phone in disbelief, blinking back the tears. She'd wanted that part. Badly. Desperately. She'd been in Hollywood for six years and the only thing she had to show for it was a few commercials, a bloody low-budget horror flick, and an impressive resume of waitressing jobs. Some unpaid bills too. She certainly couldn't forget those.

She was currently serving the breakfast crowd at Virgil's Waffle and Pancakes. There was more on the menu than just those two items but they did a big early morning business and she was loath to miss out on the tips.

"You've got customers at table three." Patty, another waitress and sometime actress, nudged Jazz. "You don't want to get Virgil's attention. He's in a mood today, has been all week."

Jazz grimaced and shoved her cell back in her pocket. Her boss had a rule about phones which most of them ignored but this might not be the day to push her luck.

Especially as she didn't have much luck to begin with.

"I didn't get the part." Even as she said it, the words formed a hard lump in her stomach. She'd been counting on that role. Born to play it, dammit. They'd passed her over and it hurt. She never got used to the rejection in show business. Her friends were constantly telling her she needed to grow a thicker skin if she wanted to be an actress in this town.

Patty, who'd had her share of disappointments, put her hand on Jazz's shoulder, her mouth turned down. "I'm sorry. You really thought you had it didn't you? I know how that feels, hon."

"I know." Jazz tried to push away the disappointment but fear wrapped around her heart instead. She'd really needed the influx of cash that job promised. She was swimming in a sea of red ink. "I shouldn't let these things bother me."

She tried to muster a smile despite what felt like the weight of the world on her shoulders. Patty was a good friend but she didn't seem to take the rejection as personally as Jazz did. But then Patty had a husband who made a decent living. Jazz, on the other hand, was already thinking about how she could possibly pay the rent and still have money to eat this month.

Like a robot on automatic, she went through the motions of waitressing, trying to keep a smile on her face when she really wanted to sit down and cry her eyes out. The customers didn't know or care about her problems.

"I need to talk to you before you leave," Virgil said as she shoved her tips deep into her purse and pulled on a sweater. "Just a quick meeting."

"Fine." She slung her purse over her shoulder and followed him to his office in the back of the restaurant. The other waitresses who had worked the morning shift, including Patty, were already there. Apparently he was planning to give everyone one of his usual royal ass chewings. Would today's be about upselling dessert or about keeping the patrons moving through their meal so he could turn over the tables faster?

"I'll tell the rest of the staff later," he began, his pockmarked features a ruddy tone that spoke of anger. "They've raised the rent here and I can't afford it any longer."

"What does that mean?" Patty asked, leaning against the door frame. "Are you moving to another location?"

"I'm closing," Virgil answered baldly, not bothering to soften the blow. "At the end of the day. I'm going to work for my father-in-law. So you're fired. Here's your final pay."

He shoved some envelopes their way and they all looked at each other disbelieving. This had to be some kind of joke. Luck this bad simply wasn't possible in one human being.

"Today?" Mary asked, her finger wagging under his nose. "Are you serious? Why didn't you tell us before now?"

"Because you would have walked out." Virgil shrugged. He didn't give a shit about his waitresses—Jazz had known that for a long time but this move seemed especially odious. Even for him.

Jazz grabbed the stack of envelopes from his desk and rifled through it to find her own before handing them off to Patty, anger churning in her gut. Jazz might be tiny in stature but Virgil didn't intimidate her in the least. "You're a real class act, you know that? A regular humanitarian."

She didn't bother to dial down the sarcasm in her tone. She had plenty of references available to get another crappy waitressing job. She didn't need his.

"I'm not running a charity here," he blustered.

"As of today, you're not running anything at all," Jazz retorted. "I'm out of here."

With her check clenched in her fist and her head held high, Jazz marched out of the restaurant, Patty and the others at her heels. Once on the sidewalk, Jazz paused, unsure as to what to do. She'd been planning to hit the grocery store on her way home but she wasn't sure she could afford food any more.

Mary pulled a credit card from her wallet. "The bars open and I'm buying. Or technically, my mom and dad in Virginia are buying."

"I always liked your parents. Lovely people," Patty giggled. "I'm in but only for sodas. Damn cold medicine means I can't drink. But I can be the driver for all of you."

The others parroted their agreement and Jazz didn't argue. No point in heading back to an apartment she could no longer afford. She'd have a few cocktails and drown her sorrows before going home. Sort of a last hurrah before facing the reality that she couldn't get away from.

She'd lost her job and the role of her dreams all within the space of a few hours. Things were definitely not going her way.

Chapter Two

"**A**re you drunk?"

Caitlin Dalton, Jazz's roommate and best friend stood in the living room with her hands on her hips and a disgusted expression. Caitlin's boyfriend, Tony Albright, was lounging on an easy chair with a grin on his face, presumably at the picture Jazz made in the doorway. She'd spent the afternoon drinking with her now unemployed waitress friends and she probably looked a funny sight still in her cheap, polyester uniform, her cheeks pink from the booze, her blonde hair askew from running her fingers through it in worry.

"I'm not drunk," Jazz denied, dumping her purse on the table beside the door along with her keys. "I'm tipsy."

"Can you feel your lips?" Caitlin demanded. "When you're drunk you can't feel your lips."

Jazz moved her mouth around and Tony's smile got even wider. "I can feel my lips. Don't have a cow."

"I'll get you some coffee. Patty called, by the way, and told us everything. About the part too."

Awesome. Patty, true to her word, had stayed sober as a judge all afternoon. She'd apparently informed Caitlin as to what a loser Jazz had become all in one day.

Jazz sank onto the couch cushions and kicked off her sensible tennis shoes she wore when waitressing and sighed in relief. She needed to soak in a hot tub and forget these last eight hours ever happened.

"I know I look ridiculous in this outfit," Jazz told Tony who was regarding her as if he were a kindly older brother and she a dotty younger sibling.

"The mustard color doesn't do anything for you," he responded. "So you got canned today?"

She winced at his plain speech but Tony rarely wrapped up his rhetoric in roses and moonbeams. He was a successful television producer-director and as such got to speak to people rudely. This was Hollywood after all, and Jazz was low on the totem pole while Tony was riding high.

"The restaurant is closing, so the short answer is yes. As for the part, well, it sucks. I would have been good in that movie."

Jazz had felt a symbiotic relationship with the role she'd been denied, had felt it was hers to lose. Every time she thought about the drunken, slutty child star who would be playing the part instead, she felt sick inside. But name recognition was everything and no one knew Jazz from Adam and Eve.

"Rogers is a decent director but he tends to the maudlin side." Tony took the cup of coffee Caitlin offered. "What will you do now?"

Jazz accepted the mug from Caitlin with a grateful smile and her roommate settled on the arm of Tony's chair. They'd been dating awhile and Jazz wouldn't be surprised to see the two of them get married. Because of his connections, Caitlin had landed a part in a soap opera.

"Get another job, I guess. Maybe two." Jazz's eyes filled with hot tears. She simply couldn't seem to catch a break in this town. She was already in debt due to her car breaking down. There had been no choice but to fix it. If she couldn't get to work and auditions, she couldn't earn money.

"Do you have any savings?" Caitlin asked, biting her lip. Until recently, she'd lived on a shoestring budget the same as Jazz.

"None." Jazz shook her head, misery winding its way through her abdomen and curling up like a heavy log while tears started to streak down her cheeks. "I have a big balance on my credit card because of the car repairs too. Plus all the other crap that waitressing doesn't pay for."

Something flickered in Tony's gaze but he remained silent and Jazz shifted her attention back to her roommate. The pretty redhead had a sad droop to her mouth and sympathy in her green eyes.

"You'll get another job," she encouraged. "A better one. You should try for one of those fancy ones in the Hills. Bigger, better tips, I bet."

"I need another job yesterday." Jazz tried to smile for her friend despite the feeling that the walls were closing in. She had few options at this point and crawling home to her family wasn't one of them. Whining wouldn't fix this either. She laughed but it didn't sound particularly happy. "Hey, maybe I could turn tricks on Hollywood Boulevard. Fresh air. Exercise. Meet new people. It's a cash business, I bet."

"How about two hundred and fifty thousand dollars?" Tony's abrupt question made her gaze swing to him. His eyes were intent but he didn't seem to be laughing at her.

"Who do I have to kill?" she joked half-heartedly.

"I'm serious, Jazz." Tony stood and walked over to the front window, staring at the street where a group of children were playing a game of kickball. "What are you willing to do?"

"Anything legal, I guess." Jazz wasn't sure she liked the gleam in his eyes. "What did you have in mind?"

Tony turned back to her and sipped at his coffee. "Have you heard about my latest project? I just had a contestant pull out and I need a replacement right away. It's thirty grand guaranteed even if you're ousted day one, but the winner gets a quarter million and great television exposure. You could get some solid offers from this. If you play your cards right."

Tony was a producer and director of reality shows or "unscripted" television as he liked to call it. He was dangling it right in front of her nose and he'd done it before. She'd always turned him down and told him she was a real actress.

But she'd never been this desperate. Thirty thousand dollars would make a lot of problems disappear, not to mention what two hundred fifty thousand could do. Lots of people had got their starts on reality television. Tons. Serious actors too. She'd think of their names later.

"I'm listening, Tony."

✧   ✧   ✧   ✧

"You can't do this. It'll be a disaster."

Griffin hopped up from his chair and paced the small room in City Hall that doubled as a conference area and the town council chambers. The room smelled of burnt coffee and stale pastries that a council member had brought. Griffin had declined when they'd offered him one.

He'd only been there for fifteen minutes but already things were on a downhill slide. He'd worked hard to create peace and harmony in Hope Lake and now they were throwing it away with both hands.

He simply couldn't allow it.

"Calm down, Sheriff." Otis McClintock, the owner of the local bar, waved at the chair that Griffin had abandoned after being told the news. "Let's talk about this. We understand you might have some objections but we're doing this for the good of the town. We're doing this to help you."

"*Help* me?" choked Griffin, his tone incredulous, his stomach churning with anger and frustration. "How will creating chaos help me? You're not helping, Otis. You're ruining everything I've worked for."

"You're being overly dramatic," Leroy Wilson, a third-generation rancher said dryly, relaxing back in his chair with a smile. "I don't think you can equate a reality show coming to town to chaos. You can handle it."

"I understand the sheriff's concerns," responded Alice Kennison, who owned the local grocery store and the one who had brought the pastries. She appeared to be flustered by all the emotion whizzing around the room. "This will certainly affect the citizens of Hope Lake. Perhaps we should have put this to a referendum."

"There was no time," Leroy blustered and sat up, making the chair legs squeak loudly in the room. "Besides, they elected us to make these kind of decisions. If we don't do this, we're going to have to cut the town's budget severely." His face purple with anger, he pointed to Griffin. "That's something you said we couldn't do. Well, now we've found another option and you don't like it either. Tough."

"Everyone calm down," commanded Otis, who stood to look Griffin in the eye. "I know this isn't perfect. I know this has the possibility of turning our peaceful little town into a sideshow but we don't have any choices left here, Sheriff. This town is broke. Busted. The economy sucks. I wouldn't be doing my job if I didn't find a way to solve our problems. This is a solution."

Griffin stopped pacing and scraped his hand down his face. What had been presented in the beginning of the meeting as merely an idea was looking more and more like a done deal.

"You want me to allow a bunch of civilians who have no experience to compete to become my next deputy? And I'm to do this all in front of a bunch of cameras? Have you lost your ever loving minds? Nothing good can come from this, Otis."

"On the contrary." Otis came out from behind the table and slapped Griffin on the back and smiled. "This is going to bring revenue to a town that sorely needs it. Maybe businesses will want to relocate here." That smile fell and Otis leaned in close, his voice soft. "This isn't about just you anymore. This is about every person in Hope Lake. The merchants are being starved out one by one. Are you going to stand in the way of prosperity? The production company has guaranteed us a payment of three hundred thousand. That doesn't even count the money they'll spend while they're here. Hell, the motel is already booked solid. Do you know how many deputies you can hire for three hundred thousand?"

Considering the piss poor pay? A hell of a lot. *Fuck a duck.* Griffin was cornered and he damn well didn't like it.

"Do I really have to hire the winner?" Griffin fell back into his chair, the anger draining away but the frustration remained. He might have to give in but he didn't have to be happy about it. When Dare found out he was going to be pissed off even more than usual.

Otis nodded and sat in the chair opposite. "The person who wins gets two hundred and fifty thousand plus a chance to be our new deputy."

"Why would anyone who had that kind of money want to be my deputy?"

"That could work to your advantage," Alice offered softly. "Maybe they won't even want the job."

"If they win they have to go through the academy. I'm not going to budge on this one. It's for everyone's safety."

Otis and Leroy exchanged a glance and then nodded. "Agreed. We assume most of the people who would be on a show like this are looking for a new line of work so they probably wouldn't have an issue with more training."

"Most? What other kind of people would be on the show?" Griffin finally popped open the soda can they'd slid in front of him before the meeting when he'd declined the coffee. A jolt of caffeine would be welcome about now.

"The kind that want to be famous." This time it was Alice who answered, her expression brightening. "People get on reality shows and act outrageous, and then they become celebrities. Don't you watch television?"

"Sports." Griffin shrugged. "I've got a TV if that's the question. A big one. I just don't spend much time watching it."

"You might want to turn it on and watch a few shows so you have an idea as to what goes on," Leroy replied. "I like the one where they sing and dance."

"My deputies don't need to sing and dance." Griffin's frustration was mounting again. "They need to be tough and smart and know how to deal with people."

"And you can test them on all of that." Otis patted the table. "The production company sent over a proposed schedule of events but said we could make changes." He pulled a thick stack of papers from a folder and pushed them across the table.

"How many people do I have to judge?" Griffin shuffled through the papers, eyeing the roster of so-called competitions. He would need to make some changes—that was for sure. It was clearly put together by someone who didn't have a fucking clue about law enforcement.

"Six, but you don't have to judge them. The viewing audience decides who stays and goes," Alice said brightly. Griffin was getting the idea that she liked this idea more than she'd let on in the beginning.

"I don't get to decide who I'm going to hire?" Griffin rubbed his temples where a major league headache was beginning to bloom. He was fucked and he knew it.

"Do what bosses have been doing for generations," Leroy laughed. "Make their lives so miserable that you're the last person they want to work for."

Griffin prided himself on being fair and treating his staff well. Torturing someone to make them leave wasn't a good plan. Shit, it wasn't even really a plan. If the winner was a nightmare, Griffin would just sit them down and tell them the damn truth. They deserved nothing less.

"Are you on board?" Otis asked, his expression full of hope. "We need your support, Sheriff. Everybody can benefit from this. You especially."

Griffin sat back in his chair and sighed. Resignation and defeat left a bitter taste in his mouth.

"You've left me little choice, Otis. Six civilians. No law enforcement experience. A competition for a butt-load of money in a tiny town in the middle of Montana. What could go wrong?"

•

Chapter Three

J azz's legs were cramped and her eyes gritty and tired. She reached under her bus seat for her purse and backpack, yawning and stretching. Tomorrow morning she'd need to do some yoga stretches to work out the kinks. They'd had a long drive from the Billings airport which had been minuscule compared to LAX, but was apparently the largest damn airport in the entire state.

She peered out of the bus window but couldn't see much of the town. Just some shadowed buildings and a deserted street. Almost midnight, it was pitch black and the few streetlights didn't seem to throw off much illumination. Levering out of her seat, she lumbered down the aisle with her heavy bag, her muscles and joints stiff from several hours in the air and on the road. The bus had been comfortable but she was ready to get some real sleep. Something she hadn't much of since she'd agreed to this crazy idea just two weeks ago.

She didn't want to be a cop.

Or a deputy.

Or whatever the hell she was here competing to be.

She just wanted a break in the cutthroat world of show business. Not asking for favors, she only wanted an opportunity to show what she could do. Hopefully this was her ticket to something better than waitressing and hoping her power wasn't cut off.

"Look at those stars." The woman who had sat across from her in the bus marveled as she gaped at the sky. A nice lady in her mid-thirties, her name was Peggy and she was from some little town in Illinois. Peggy and no last name, Jazz had been told sternly by one of the handlers. Only first names would be used to try and protect the contestants' personal lives, which was a joke. They would be outed on the Internet within minutes of the show airing, but if the handlers wanted to pretend otherwise Jazz wouldn't burst their bubble.

Jazz followed Peggy's gaze and was indeed shocked to see the vast number of stars in the inky black sky. She couldn't remember the last time she'd seen the Big Dipper, but there it was bright as day and easily discernible.

"Forget the stars, look at him," hissed Sandy, the pretty bru-nette standing next to them. In her early twenties and from New York City, she'd talked incessantly on the bus about how this show was going to change her life. She'd dropped out of college, bored and rudderless, determined to find an easier way to make a fortune and be famous.

At first with all the people milling about Jazz couldn't see what Sandy was talking about, but when Tony and Gordon stepped aside...

Jazz almost choked on her spit.

A tall, well-built man had his back to her. Faded jeans cupped a bitable butt and a shirt that looked like it had been tailored just for him emphasized his muscular wide shoulders. If this was what all the cowboys looked like around here Jazz was going to have to invest in a drool bib. He made the fussy, pretty boy men in L.A. that blew dry their hair and got manicures look pretty pathetic.

He turned around and her gaze went straight to a classically handsome face with a square jaw and narrowed eyes that seemed to take in everything around him. His dark hair was close-cropped, and on further inspection his nose appeared slightly crooked as if it had been broken once or twice. His lips were flat and Jazz couldn't help but wonder what he looked like when he smiled. Right now, his face was devoid of expression like the faces on Mount Rushmore.

"The only reason I'd kick him out of bed is to scr–" Peggy began.

"Ladies and gentleman," an older man standing next to the hot one began speaking, interrupting Peggy's most certainly ribald comment. "Welcome to Hope Lake, Montana. We hope you enjoy your time here. We know you're tired so we'll be checking you into your rooms in just a few minutes, but first I'd like to introduce myself and the man that you'll all get to know very well during your stay. I'm Otis McClintock, head of the town council, and this man is Sheriff Griffin Sawyer."

Otis slapped the sexy one on the shoulder and grinned. It was only then that Jazz noticed the gold star glinting in the light from the street lamps on his chest. He was her new boss.

Kind of.

"Is there anything you'd like to say, Sheriff?" Otis prompted, his gaze darting between the stony-faced sheriff and the contestants and crew. "This is your chance to give them a hearty welcome."

The sheriff crossed his massive arms across his chest, the material of his shirt straining at the seams. Damn, he had to work out several hours a day for a physique like that. He took a step forward but he still didn't smile. His eyes scanned the group as if he was trying to size each and every one of them up. She couldn't suppress the shiver that ran through her at the energy he radiated. He practically vibrated with intensity.

"Welcome to Hope Lake. As Otis said, I'm the law in this town and I take that very seriously. Each one of you will be tested both physically and mentally during this competition. Make no mistake…law enforcement is often dangerous. It can also be boring and frustrating, especially when dealing with a public that may or may not have the utmost regard for cops. I hold myself to the highest standard and I will hold you to that standard also. The people of this town deserve nothing less than your best. I will accept nothing less."

Alrighty then. So much for a pep talk.

Too bad the hunky sheriff was such a downer. It looked like he was planning on being some kind of drill sergeant and whipping them all into shape.

Two hundred and fifty thousand. Nationwide exposure.

She needed to keep her focus firmly on the goal. She was here to win, and if it meant doing pushups in the rain for the hot but cranky sheriff then that's what she'd damn well do. She'd seen his type in the movies and she could handle him.

Otis waited for a moment, but when the sheriff didn't say another word he nodded and smiled. "I have your room keys here. Let's just get you checked off this list and you can get some rest."

The contestants and crew lined up and the man checked them off on a piece of paper one at a time and handed them key cards. Hopefully she wouldn't have to share a room. Jazz liked her space in the mornings and evenings. Even though she had a roommate, she still liked the quiet when the apartment was empty or Caitlin was asleep.

Thanking Otis for her key, she threw her heavy backpack over her shoulder and waded into the sea of luggage that had been liberated from the belly of the bus. She'd tied a red ribbon around the handle so she could quickly identify hers. Grabbing the suitcase, she grunted a little at the weight. She'd packed practically everything she owned knowing she could be here for quite awhile. Luckily it was on wheels.

Everything was going fine until she had to pull her two ton bag up over the curb and onto the sidewalk. One try didn't make it and she had to give it a second go.

"Need help?"

The voice was rich and deep, sending tingles to her fingers and toes. Peeking from under her lashes, the handsome sheriff was looking down at her, his dark eyebrows furrowed. He was probably thinking that if she couldn't pull her own damn luggage – on wheels – she didn't have a furry rat's behind chance to win this competition.

Yep, he's impressed alright.

"I got it."

Giving one almighty pull, she heaved the suitcase onto the sidewalk trying to look like it hadn't almost yanked her arm out of the socket. How high were curbs in Hope Lake anyway?

"Let me help you."

She'd only let go of the handle for a moment but somehow she'd lost control of this interaction. It wasn't how she wanted to present herself, but that was the story of her life. He took off toward the row of doors that made up the motel and she had to jog to keep up with his long legs. She was barely five-two but he was easily over six feet tall and his shins alone were probably half a foot longer than hers.

He halted in front of door seven and waited for her to un-lock it. Jazz slid the keycard into the slot trying not to meet his eyes. She wasn't sure what she'd see. Scorn? Impatience? Amusement?

"You must have an anvil in that thing. It's a wonder you've dragged it as far as you have."

Jazz pushed open the door and slid her hand blindly along the wall looking for a light switch. He leaned across her and found it easily, the sudden brightness making her blink for a moment.

He smelled good. Really good. Kind of clean and earthy with a touch of…maybe citrus or spice. He rolled her bag into the middle of the room and then stepped back into the doorway as if his presence might frighten her. She ought to be afraid. In Los Angeles, she'd carried pepper spray and was always aware of her surroundings, but there was something about this man that made her feel safe. He was big and solid, looking like someone who carried his burdens easily. And he was the sheriff.

"Thanks. It's packed full since I'll be here for awhile."

She didn't know what else to say and he wasn't much of a conversationalist. She could hear the chatter of voices not far away but he'd only spoken the bare minimum of words. Letting her backpack slide to the floor, she almost heaved a sigh of relief out loud.

His lips quirked up in a half smile and in the light she could now see he had gray eyes, so light they were almost silver, fringed with thick dark lashes. She would kill for those lashes. Her own were blonde, pale, and scrawny, needing mascara for anyone to see them. One makeup artist on set had told her she needed to wear falsies but Jazz couldn't imagine putting glue that close to her eye.

"I was in Afghanistan for a year with only a backpack and a rifle."

"I left my gun at home." She tried to laugh despite the blanket of fatigue that lay heavy on top of her. "Men are lucky that way. You don't need as much stuff."

"I guess so. Well, good night." He turned to go but then paused. "Do you need anything?"

Trying to be a good host. Maybe he wasn't such a hard ass after all.

"Just a good night's sleep. Thank you, though." She realized she'd never introduced herself. "I'm Jazz, by the way. Jazz Oliver."

"Jazz? That shouldn't be difficult to remember. You're the first one I've met." His tone was tinged with amusement and she almost explained that she'd wanted something exotic and different. Something far away from the girl she'd grown up as.

But it was none of his business.

"That's the point," she answered lightly. "Good night, Sheriff."

The sheriff tipped his hat and was gone into the night, shutting the door firmly behind him. She toed off her shoes and stripped her clothes from her body. She ought to take the time to brush her teeth or comb her hair but she was exhausted in body and spirit. Tomorrow would be soon enough.

Jazz was here and there was no turning back. This show would make or break her career. No pressure. It only meant everything in the world to her. She wouldn't let anything get in the way of her dream. It was all she had.

Chapter Four

T he cameras had yet to roll and Griffin was already slightly pissed off, his legendary patience stretched thin. What should have been a quiet, pre-show meeting had turned into a three-ring circus with half the town pressing their faces onto the big picture window of the diner. The contestants and the producers had bought out the place for the morning so everyone could go over the rules of the game. Otis had informed Griffin that the sheriff and deputies were supposed to be there too.

That little piece of news was delivered after midnight last night. Otis withholding information until the last minute seemed to be a trend. Griffin hadn't learned he would be expected to meet the bus that carried the crew and contestants until a few hours before they arrived, so needless to say he hadn't been in the best of moods when Otis had dropped another bombshell. All Griffin had wanted to do was go home, eat some dinner, and get some sleep. That hadn't happened. He'd spent the evening in his office waiting for people he didn't even want to come to arrive.

His mood this morning hadn't improved with a few hours of sleep and a couple of cups of coffee. He'd driven up to the diner and seen the crowd of people waiting and almost turned the truck around and kept driving. If yesterday had been peaceful and calm, today was going to be the opposite.

With no end in sight.

Now Griffin, Dare, and Adam were sitting at a table fighting the urge to disperse the crowd and tell the Hollywood types who had tried to order *espresso* for fuck's sake that this whole idea was off.

"I like espresso," Adam said, taking a deep drink of his coffee. Blond haired and blue eyed, he was handsome enough to be one of the actors in the show. He'd been a deputy for almost six months and so far seemed to know what the hell he was doing. He did his job and didn't take any crap without being an asshole.

"Drink your fucking coffee," Dare growled, an even deeper scowl scoring his features. Blunt and to the point, the deputy hated anything disorderly. The crowd outside was being managed by the junior deputies and none too well. Griffin might have to lash Dare to the table to keep him seated. "How long is this supposed to last? I've got shit to do."

"We've all got shit to do," Griffin growled. "As of now, we're in hell. But we're in this together. Got it?"

"Speak for yourself." Adam grinned and signaled for a refill. "I think this is really cool, personally. I can't wait to see myself on television. Don't you want that?"

"I could go happily to my grave and never see myself. Hell, they put that waterskiing squirrel on TV so it don't seem like such an accomplishment really." Griffin hated the crowds and the noise. The next few months weren't going to be easy.

"I saw that on YouTube. Still, it is cool. I'm going to record the shows on my DVR."

"Shut the fuck up," Dare snarled but Adam just laughed. Everyone knew how Dare was and nobody took his bark seriously. He was always in a bad mood—it didn't matter what was going on.

Griffin studied the six contestants over the rim of his coffee cup. He'd been given a short bio on each one of them and had made sure to memorize the names with the faces. They all came from diverse backgrounds but no one stood out as possible deputy material except for one.

Wayne. In his mid-thirties, he was retired military which was usually a good sign. Watching him, Griffin noticed the man was an observer, not saying too much. That was also a good sign. He would be one to keep an eye on.

Then Danny. A construction worker in his late twenties, he grinned a lot and seemed more interested in showing off for the females and the producers than doing any real work. A man like that could get someone killed in a dangerous situation.

Levi. A laid-off software engineer, but there didn't appear to be anything soft about the man. Around forty, he had the rough around the edges look of a man who had seen some bad shit but came out the other side. Unfortunately, he didn't have any military or law enforcement experience. If he could learn quickly, he might be a candidate.

Peggy. Mid-thirties and newly divorced, her bio said she was here to prove something to herself. She would certainly be tested by the demands of the job. At least she didn't stare down at her fucking phone every second of the day.

Like Sandy. A tall brunette in her early twenties, she was quite vocal about wanting to make her life "easier." She'd dropped out of college because it was "hard" and "useless". If she thought this was going to be a cakewalk, Griffin had bad news for her.

Then there was the tiny Jazz Oliver. She probably shouldn't have told him her last name, but they'd all been tired last night.

She didn't even reach his shoulders she was so little. A breath of wind could blow her away. And that pretty blonde hair and angelic blue eyes wouldn't intimidate a toddler. No way would she be able to handle a deputy's job, but then it wasn't his place to question the recruits they'd sent.

Shit, he didn't even get to choose the winner. All he could do was put them through their paces and hope that the right one was selected. His money was on the cute little Jazz to go first. She might not even make it through the morning. Griffin had a wild day planned that should shake up these tenderfoots.

"Ahem." The producer slash director, Tony Albright, cleared his throat and stood at the head of the room, not seeming to notice the throng of people pressed to the window and entrance. "Let's get started, shall we? We wanted to go over the rules and schedule quickly so that everyone is on the same page. Gordon?"

Gordon Schofield, a slightly younger but pale-faced man and Tony's assistant, handed him a tablet and the producer swiped at the screen a few times.

"Here we are. First, please remember that physical violence towards each other is strictly forbidden. Anyone breaking that rule will be immediately disqualified. Sex, on the other hand," Tony grinned, "is completely okay. Especially romance for the cameras. Remember, drama raises interest, and interest raises the ratings. There's a bonus in it for everyone if the show goes Top Ten."

Griffin inwardly groaned at the producer's words. He'd been right when he'd told Otis that nothing good could come from this. Was the money really worth it?

Tony droned on about the rules, of which there weren't many. The little tidbit that they'd signed a waiver absolving the production company and the town of Hope Lake should they receive physical or mental damage or even death was actually good news. At least he wouldn't be sued when this was all over.

"The show will be a standard thirteen episode season. Each week we will film Saturday through Thursday. That will be edited down to a one hour show aired on Friday night. At the end of the airing if it's an elimination week, the viewers will see phone numbers and a website where they can vote. By the next morning, we'll know who is going home. We'll film you leaving and show it the next week at the beginning of the show. However, you won't be going anywhere. You'll stick around this area until the finale. Remember, some weeks we may or may not have someone going home. Some weeks more than one person might get the boot. We'll keep changing it up to keep the viewers guessing. The last four weeks of the challenge will be the final two contestants competing directly against one another. That's where we'll get some merchandising going with team t-shirts and so forth. Also, there will be lots of bonus footage on the website, so flash those pearlies, people. Remember we're trying to make great television here."

Tony's voice boomed in the small area and the contestants and crew nodded, murmuring among themselves.

"Keep this in mind. You don't necessarily have to be the best to not get voted off by the viewers. Be interesting. Be compelling. Whatever you do, don't be boring. You'll get booted off in a heartbeat. Now let's quickly go over the schedule of challenges."

Tony ran through the competitions, a much different list than what Griffin had been given at the beginning. Luckily the producers were open to making changes and Griffin had availed himself until the original plan was barely recognizable.

"I'll turn things over to Sheriff Sawyer now. If you have any concerns, please let us know." The assistant tugged on Tony's sleeve and whispered something into his ear. "Oh yes, Gordon just reminded me. The competition starts right now so we'll need your cell phones. No contact with the outside world for the next three months that is not supervised. Gordon, pass the box around."

The six contestants looked none too happy about handing over their phones but they did it one by one. The box was folded shut and shoved under Gordon's arm while Sandy complained loudly. Her hands were fluttering and her cheeks were red as if she didn't know what to do with herself if her phone wasn't in her fingers.

"Sheriff?" Tony nodded toward him. "They're all yours. Let them know what this week's challenge is going to be and then we can go film the arrival of the contestants first."

Griffin walked to the head of the room, trying not to outwardly show his frustration and cynicism about the entire situation. This wasn't their fault. It wasn't their problem that he had a desk full of work and deputies that were going to have to pull double shifts for weeks while they were here. It was his job to make all of this work somehow.

"Today we're going to do the obstacle course. All recruits need to be able to complete it within five minutes. That's a goal to work toward. I don't necessarily expect that today or even by the end of the week. Myself and Deputy Turner will be working with all of you this morning. Then this afternoon we'll start working in your handbooks. Here in Montana we use several, but for this short period we're going to concentrate on police procedure which will include arrests, searches, interviews, and privacy expectations. Any questions?"

Danny raised his hand with a grin. "When do I get my gun?"

Everyone laughed but Griffin and Dare.

"You don't," Griffin retorted. "Deputies in Training are not issued firearms. Now are there any more questions?"

This time they all shook their heads and kept their mouths closed. Good. They were beginning to understand what they needed to do. Close their mouths and listen. Learn.

Griffin stepped back so Dare could take charge. Griffin almost felt a little guilty that he was putting them in his second in command's hands on the very first day.

Almost.

"Recruits!" Dare bellowed, making a few people cringe as the sound reverberated off the walls. No one could pull off that narrow-eyed scowl like Dare. A few people looked like they wanted to dart away and escape.

But there wouldn't be any of that.

"Recruits!" he yelled again. "Line up single file at the door! No talking! No whining!" The contestants sat motionless as if they couldn't believe what was happening.

"Move it!" Dare hollered and Griffin thought his ears might bleed. But it got their attention and the entire room shifted, the only sound the scraping of chairs on the tile.

"You're a total bastard," Griffin whispered low. "I think they peed themselves."

Dare just shrugged, his expression implacable. "This is the least of their problems today. If I don't have all of them puking up their breakfasts by ten in the morning, I've failed."

Chapter Five

The obstacle course didn't look that bad.

It didn't look like fun either.

There was crawling under nets, climbing walls, hurdles to jump, a rope to swing over a large muddy area and a few other items to ruin their day. It reminded her of a boot camp fitness class she'd signed up for a few years back. Jazz was glad that staying in shape was part and parcel of being an actress these days. She didn't want to embarrass herself in front of the cameras. Or the sheriff and his deputies.

Sheriff Sawyer, out of uniform and dressed in blue sweats and matching tank top, was currently wearing an expression that clearly showed he wasn't impressed with his so-called recruits and she couldn't really blame him. Sandy was complaining about losing her phone. Danny was busy trying to charm Sandy and all the other pretty female crew members. Wayne was lagging behind the entire group and constantly had to be herded as he would wander away if they weren't watching. Peggy had taken one look at the course and almost burst into tears and was being comforted by Levi. His eyes had gleamed when he'd gotten a look at the challenging obstacles. It looked like he was ready to go for it.

Jazz was in Levi's camp. The sooner they did it the sooner it would be over. She needed to practice and do the best she could. On Thursday she would be competing with the other five and only the winner would be safe from elimination.

She had to win.

The cameras were stationed along the course as the competitors warmed up and stretched their muscles. Despite some morning yoga in her hotel room, Jazz was still a little stiff from the traveling yesterday and the last hour hadn't helped. She'd spent most of it waiting around while the production crew filmed the contestants "arriving."

They'd all been cleaned up with hair and makeup which wasn't going to help them in the least now. Jazz's three coats of mascara were going to run and turn her into a raccoon no matter how waterproof the package said it was. It was hot and there was going to be sweat. End of story.

"Line up and we'll let you go one by one, giving the person ahead of you some time. We don't want you to bunch up. For this first run just take your time and get familiar with the course," the scowling Deputy Turner said. Jazz wondered if the man ever smiled. He appeared to be mad about basically everything all the time. Maybe his tightie whities were way too tight.

Trying to muffle her giggle, Jazz got in line behind everyone but Wayne. As usual he was pulling up the rear.

Danny went first, diving down so he could crawl under the netting on his belly. When he cleared that obstacle, he grabbed the rope and sailed over the mud pit without a problem. The climbing wall was where he found an issue. Already winded, he didn't have the strength to pull himself up and over. Bent over with his hands on his knees, he sucked in some air and then stepped back to try again.

This time the handsome sheriff leaned over and said something to Danny before he got a running start. Whatever it was, it must have made a difference because he easily cleared the wall and was on to the rest of the course.

"What do you think the sheriff told him?" Wayne asked, his brows knitted together. "Whatever it is, I want to know too."

Levi went next, and despite having a supposed desk job he made the course look damn easy. Well, crap.

Peggy struggled and required coaching from the sheriff and deputy, as did Sandy, and then it was Jazz's turn. She took off at a run and dove to the grass, banging her knees and elbows on the ground. Bruising easily, she was sure to have some black and blue marks from this activity.

Grunting as she propelled herself forward on her belly, her ponytail got caught in the netting overhead. Jazz cursed and reached up to free herself but a set of larger, rougher hands were already there. His palm gently pressed on the back of her head so her nose was millimeters from the dirt.

"Keep your head down and use your hands, elbows, and feet to push yourself along. Don't worry about looking up."

His commanding tone left her in no doubt he knew what he was talking about. Keeping her head down, she managed to clear the net and sprang to her feet.

"Easy. Pace yourself this first time out, Jazz."

The sheriff was following her along the course and she wasn't sure if she was glad or annoyed. Having him watch her so closely was slightly unnerving, but if he could help her compete then it would be worth it.

"Get a running start for the rope swing."

Jazz paused about ten feet from the mud pit before speeding up. She grabbed the rope and sailed over the muck but landed awkwardly, stumbling and having to right herself.

"Are you okay? You look like you twisted your ankle. Do you need a medic?"

Geez, he was right next to her wearing a concerned frown. After last night's issues with her luggage, he must think she was a total weakling. Wiping the sweat from her brow, she shook her head.

"I'm okay."

"Now for the wall, you're going to want—"

"I've got this," she interrupted.

Determined to show him she wasn't useless, she lunged at the wall six foot wall built with logs but missed grabbing the rope and landed in a heap on the ground. The dirt and grass stuck to her damp skin and her knee was scraped and bleeding.

That was certainly impressive.

Muttering every curse word she knew under her breath, she pushed to her feet, ignoring the throb in her knee and the protest of her now sore bottom. There was no doubt about it. She was going to be a giant bruise when she was done today.

A strong hand wrapped around her arm and helped her stand.

"Will you take some advice now or are you going to be stubborn?"

The little blonde's chin was lifted in challenge as if she was planning to toss his help back in his face. She'd already done better than he'd expected and certainly better than the other two females. He hadn't got a good look at her figure last night or this morning but dressed in shorts and a t-shirt her body was toned and a little distracting if he was honest.

Something flickered in her eyes and her shoulders dropped in defeat. "I'll listen."

Griffin admired her gumption and go-getter attitude, but she was plumb going to wear herself out on this course if she didn't listen to a few tricks.

"Use your legs. Power up as high as you can and climb trying not to pull yourself up. Your arms will be tired and the monkey bars are next."

Jazz chewed on her lip and nodded before taking a few steps back so she could get a running start. Her movements graceful, the second time she got over the wall without much fuss. She was probably going to be sore later from her fall but at least she'd completed the first three obstacles. He'd seen much worse in his time.

The monkey bars were difficult and she struggled as he tried to coach her regarding momentum. Eventually her shoulders gave out and she had to move on to the balance beam stretched over a pool of water. He'd seen men throw the challenge right here so they could land in that cool water on a hot day. This one, however, skipped right over the four by four without so much as a wobble.

Damn good balance.

Grinning now, Jazz sailed through the tires lifting her knees and then crossing the finish line. His misgivings had been premature. She was a fighter and he admired that. She didn't give up but had wisdom enough to know when to let someone help her. It was a rare combination.

He was going to have to keep an eye on her.

She collapsed onto a bench next to Peggy, giggling and smiling, looking way too attractive. He needed to keep his mind on business and stop looking at pretty young women. Young being the operative word. He'd seen her bio and she was twenty-seven to his thirty-six.

Too young, and way out of bounds. No matter what Tony might say. Griffin wasn't going to have sex for the cameras and the American viewing public. She was cute and that was the end of it.

Her knee was still bleeding but the last guy, Wayne, was already blundering through the course having issues on the very first obstacle. His bio had said he was a former Marine with no medical issues, so no way should he be having problems. It looked like he'd never exercised in his life.

Griffin nodded to Dare to intervene when Wayne landed on his ass in the mud pit after an attempt to swing over it on the rope. The deputy helped the man up and tried to coach him through it. After several tries, the former military man gave up and walked around it, heading for the wall.

"How about a tip for this one?" Griffin asked. Wayne was scowling worse than Dare but Griffin was used to dealing with people who weren't very damn happy.

"This is stupid," Wayne spat. "Why do I need to know how to do something like this? I don't enjoy wasting my time."

Griffin's brows shot up at the contemptuous tone. Had Wayne spoken to his drill instructors that way during basic?

"Agility and speed are important for an officer," Griffin replied, not going into the gory detail that he could have added. "Now the best way to do this is to use your legs."

He continued explaining but it was clear Wayne had tuned him and everyone else out. The former Marine was being pouty, for fuck's sake. Griffin was starting to have some doubts about this man's bio. And if his was wrong? What did that say about the others? Was the producer deliberately misleading Griffin about these contestants?

He and Tony were going to have a chat. Misinformation could put someone's life in danger and Griffin wouldn't allow that to happen. It was his job to keep these six people safe.

Jazz needed to get to a phone. When Tony had told her she would be cut off from family and friends, it simply hadn't sunk into her brain what that meant. Giving up her phone had been painful to say the least. She wasn't addicted to staring at it all day like so many people, but it was a lifeline to her agent. Jazz had been on several auditions and she needed to know if she had any paying jobs when she returned to L.A.

From her spot on the bench, she could see into the make-shift tent next to the obstacle course. A phone sat on the table next to a few bottles of water and some first aid supplies. She needed to slip into the tent, grab the phone, call her agent, and then replace it before anyone was the wiser.

Call me Ninja Jazz.

Her palms sweating and not from the heat, she sidled casually into the tent. Grabbing some band-aids, a bottle of alcohol, and a few cotton balls, she settled into a metal folding chair and smiled at Deputy Turner. He nodded to her as he chatted with Peggy but his attention was clearly on the other woman who was asking for advice about the monkey bars.

As Jazz dabbed alcohol on her knee, the two of them exited the tent leaving her all alone with the phone. The burn of the alcohol made her hiss but she slapped a band aid over the wound and quickly grabbed the phone, shoving it under her shirt just as the sheriff entered.

His gaze went straight to the now empty space where the phone had sat and then to her. Never a good liar, she probably had "guilty" stamped on her forehead.

Shit. Shit. Shit.

"I was just coming to check on your scraped knee. Good, I see you put a bandage on it."

The sheriff reached for a bottle of water and twisted the top off before handing it to her. She had no choice to reach for it and her hand visibly shook until she wrapped her fingers around the cool plastic.

"Thank you." The words came out scratchy and tinged with guilt but he simply sat down in the other folding chair and opened a bottle for himself.

"Looks like you're still shaken up from the course. You should drink some water and rest a little before trying it again."

Again? They had to do it again? Holy fuck.

"I'm okay. I just need something to drink." She held up the bottle and took a big swig from it, the frosty liquid sliding down her parched throat. It did nothing to calm the trip of her heart as the sheriff regarded her closely. She swallowed hard and fidgeted in her chair under his intense gaze. She bet criminals didn't last long in his interrogations. She was ready to spill her guts and he hadn't even asked her a question.

"So why did you steal my phone?" he asked, his tone soft. He didn't sound accusatory, mostly just curious, as if he was asking directions.

Her chest tightened and her stomach flipped. Wiping her palms on her shorts, she licked her lips nervously. She was an actress and it was time to pull out some skills.

"I don't know what you mean."

The sheriff chuckled and lifted the water bottle to his full lips, swallowing down half the contents. "You know exactly what I'm talking about. Tony laid down the rules this morning and already you're breaking them. I'm just wondering what's so important you'd risk getting kicked out the first day."

Jazz rubbed the back of her neck, wet with sweat. She didn't enjoy lying. She especially didn't like lying to this man who already may not have the best impression of her so far.

"I need to call my agent," she admitted with a sigh of resignation. "I had several auditions before I left Los Angeles and I was hoping to have work when I get back. It's how I pay the bills. I'm an actress. When Tony said we'd be cut off, I guess I didn't really process what that meant."

The sheriff pursed his lips in thought and then nodded before standing up. "An actress, huh? I'll leave you to it then. Just leave the phone on the table when you're done. I'll keep people out for ten minutes, but after that you're on your own."

Shock rippled through her and her hand went reflexively to where the phone was nestled. "Really? You're not going to tell on me?"

This time he smiled and she finally got to see what he looked like when he wasn't stone-faced. Holy smokes he was gorgeous. He probably had women lining up just for a date. Or more.

"I won't rat you out. I have other ways of making my point." Now he was grinning and she was beginning to worry. "Looks like your first patrol will be with me. Tonight. Be ready and in uniform at four o'clock at the station. I'll let Tony and Dare know."

"With you?" she echoed. "Tonight?"

"Yep. We're short of deputies but it's really bad now that Dare and I have to spend so much time with the show. I have to take a shift tonight since my usual guy worked during the day. Four to midnight. Don't be late."

"But we have class at eight in the morning," she gasped finally realizing he'd cornered her nicely. She couldn't protest without revealing what she'd been doing in the tent.

"We're going to miss some sleep." The sheriff nodded as if this was an everyday occurrence. "Welcome to the wonderful world of small town law enforcement. I'd get used to it if I was you. Ten minutes, Jazz."

He ducked out of the tent before she could argue. Not that she had the time. She'd need every second of the few moments he'd allocated to her. She pulled the phone from under her shirt and typed out her agent's number. Crossing her fingers, she prayed for good news.

She hung up just as her time elapsed, depressed and deflated. Nothing. Nada. Zip. At this rate, her best chance of getting a job was winning this show and working as a deputy.

Groaning, she got to her feet and headed out of the tent. It was going to be a long day and even longer shift tonight. Going out on patrol with her sort-of boss on her very first day didn't sound like a good idea in the least.

She simply couldn't catch a break.

Chapter Six

It wasn't the most boring thing Jazz had ever done in her life but it was definitely in the top ten or so. In the last hour of patrol with the sheriff they'd driven around, checked on a few homes and businesses to make sure the doors were locked, and pulled over a truckload of teenagers for going a few miles over the speed limit. He hadn't even given them a ticket. Instead, she'd sat in the SUV while he chatted with them and gave them a good-hearted warning about the dangers of speeding and driving while intoxicated.

If this was what his job entailed, he was wildly overpaid.

But then again the cameraman Jerry sitting in the backseat doing nothing but filming them might qualify for that title as well. He'd only said one sentence when he'd joined them in the SUV.

"Forget I'm here."

If only she could.

"Thirsty? Hungry?" Griffin asked, taking his eyes off the road for only a moment to glance her way. "I'm going to stop and get a quick bite at the diner."

The diner was on the main road, and based on the food she'd had this morning not a bad place to eat. It had a typical decor of Art Deco design with old Coke signs on the walls and a jukebox playing country songs for a quarter. She hadn't eaten since noon and she was starving. They'd spent the afternoon going over police procedure and she hadn't had a chance to grab a bite before patrol.

"I could eat."

He didn't say anything else until they were seated in a back booth and had ordered a couple of iced teas and cheeseburgers. He'd exchanged pleasantries with the waitress before pulling his hat off and placing it on the vinyl seat next to him. Jerry sat in the booth across, the camera aimed directly at them. Apparently he didn't get to eat but the waitress did promise to bring him a glass of ice water.

"Why don't you call me Griffin, okay?"

His expression and body language were relaxed and open, not uptight and tense as it had been earlier in the day. He really was a startlingly good looking man with his dark hair and light eyes. Sitting across from him, she could study his features up close without it seeming strange. In addition to his crooked nose, he had a small scar on his chin. Quelling the urge to trace it with her fingertips, she instead tried to get him to talk about himself.

"Thank you, I will. So Griffin, why don't you want all of us here? Don't like reality television? Or should I take it personally?"

If she'd surprised him, he didn't show it. "Am I that transparent? Guess I'd never make it as an actor, would I?"

The waitress slid their teas in front of them and disappeared into the kitchen.

"Actually, you've done a pretty good job of hiding it but I study body language. Yours clearly says that you're not comfortable with all this. How come?"

Griffin sat back and rubbed the scar absently. She'd have to find out how he'd acquired it. "It's nothing personal. You seem like a nice woman. All of you do. But I like things quiet in my town. Hell, you'd probably call it boring. I like being able to go fishing in the mornings and visit the schools. Talk to the kids. I just like things peaceful."

"And it's not peaceful anymore?" she asked, trying to draw him out further. She liked listening to him speak, his voice deep and controlled.

Griffin grimaced. "Did you see the crowd of people gathered to watch the obstacle course this morning? Or the mob around the sheriff's station this afternoon? I have a feeling it will only get worse before it gets better."

He was probably right. If Tony had his way, they would draw crowds from miles around. It made for better ratings.

"Then why do the show?"

"Money," he replied flatly. "The town desperately needs the money. They've been pressuring me to cut a deputy and we're short-handed as it is. I'd like to hire a couple more people but there's been a real budget crunch since the economy tanked. Believe me, I didn't want to agree but I had no choice. Shit, Tony wants to *interview* me. Ask me about my life."

From the grim line of his jaw she could see the truth of his words. He would do it but he didn't have to be excited about it. Pretty much every guy Jazz knew would be thrilled about being on television. Griffin Sawyer was different and she kind of liked it.

"You could be a star if you wanted to," she challenged. "You've got the looks. Why not?"

He looked at her like she had three heads and six arms. "Are you kidding? That sounds like hell to me. I don't want people sticking their nose into my business." He tilted his head and gave her an appraising look. "Is that what you want? You're an actress, right?"

"Attention doesn't bother me." Jazz shrugged, not wanting to explain the childhood that had shaped her. "I like acting. I like pretending to be someone else."

If only for a little while.

"Not for me." Griffin shook his head. "I'm quite happy with who I am."

"I am too," she argued, sitting straight up in the booth. He'd misunderstood. "It's not like that."

One eyebrow rose slightly but he didn't push. "I didn't say you weren't happy. I only said I was. Touchy, aren't you?"

She wasn't about to answer.

"So what are we going to do tomorrow?" Jazz held her breath, waiting for him to change the subject back to happiness and all that entailed.

He grinned, obviously knowing what she was doing but letting it slide. She kind of liked the fact that he didn't feel the need to be right all of the time or to needle her into admitting her deep dark secrets. He was content to let people be. It was a refreshing change.

"I'm going to let you look through some cold cases. Each one of you will get to choose one to work on."

An assignment. That might be something she could sink her teeth into better than running an obstacle course. "What's a cold case?"

"A case that has gone unsolved for an extended period of time. No new leads to follow up on. The trail has gone cold."

The burgers were placed in front of them and the heavenly smell of chargrilled meat and deep-fried potatoes made her stomach growl. Griffin laughed and popped a fry into his mouth.

"I'm hungry too. We need to eat quickly and get back on patrol."

She was just finishing the last bite of her burger when the radio on his shoulder beeped. He answered in short, clipped tones, obviously understanding the cop shorthand used by the dispatcher. One thing was clear—they were on the move. Finally something was actually happening.

Griffin threw some money on the table and grabbed the two to-go iced teas from the waitress. He'd obviously eaten here a time or two.

"We need to go."

Jazz fumbled for some cash in her pocket. "I just need to—"

"Relax, I've got it. We need to hustle, Jazz."

She didn't like the idea of him buying her a meal but the urgency in his voice won out. She slid across the booth and headed straight for the door trailing right behind him, hurrying to keep up, Jerry jogging behind her. They climbed into the SUV and he turned on the sirens and lights as they backed out of the parking lot.

"I want you to stay put in the truck. Got it? I don't want to be worrying where you are and if you're all right. That goes for you too, Jerry. This is a show about Jazz, not a show about crime."

Jerry grunted and she couldn't tell if he'd agreed or not. Jazz nodded but then realized all his attention was focused on the road considering they were going over a hundred miles per hour. Adrenaline kicked in and her stomach fluttered at the unknown. She'd seen cops work on television but tonight she would be up close and personal.

"Don't worry. I don't want to get in the middle of whatever we're heading toward. By the way, just what is the trouble? A robbery or something?"

"I wish." His jaw was tight and a pulse beat at his temple. "Domestic disturbance. I've been there way too many times."

She had no frame of reference for that, didn't know what to say. Her father and mother had never argued, their relationship close and loving to the point of cutting everyone else out. Even after her father had died, her mother hadn't used physical violence against Jazz. No, her mother had used a much more effective weapon to batter Jazz's psyche. Jane Oliver had simply ignored Jazz as if she didn't exist.

Griffin pulled up in the driveway of a lovely ranch style home in an affluent suburb, slamming on the brakes and swearing under his breath. A sobbing woman, her eyes already starting to swell and turn purple, was trying to exit the house through the front door but a larger, red-faced man had a hold of her hair and was yanking it hard. His expression of sheer glee at the pain he was inflicting made Jazz wish she hadn't promised Griffin to stay in the car. She'd like to smack that look right off his face. Bullies like that needed to be taught a lesson.

Her pulse pounded in anger as Griffin jumped out of the truck in a flash, yelling at the man to stop and step away from the woman. A string of obscenities fell from the suspect's lips, clearly not scared of any consequences from his actions. Before she could catch her breath, Griffin had the man down on the ground and cuffs slapped on him. She gaped at the sheriff's efficiency. There had been no long, drawn out struggle. No arguing. Just one smooth movement to the cushion of the grass.

Clean and simple.

Barely winded, Sheriff Griffin Sawyer was a total badass. Jazz had seen fearless stunt men jump from a car going eighty miles an hour or set on fire for the cameras, but they wouldn't have been able to take a man down to the ground in less than three seconds flat.

Impressive.

"Holy hell, I wouldn't want to meet the good sheriff in a dark alley." Jerry whistled under his breath.

The suspect was bellowing loudly and the altercation had attracted attention from the neighbors who were peeking out from behind their drapes.

Sadly not one of them had come to the woman's aid. The woman needed to find new friends and neighbors, although one of them must have called 911 at least.

Tires squealing, a vehicle pulled in behind theirs. Deputy Dare hopped out of his truck, dressed in jeans and a t-shirt but sporting a badge and his gun belt, and lifted the crying woman to her feet.

"Easy there, Alexa. I've got an ambulance coming to check you out," the deputy's voice was soft and soothing, his usual scowl softened with kindness. Jazz was seeing why Dare was Griffin's second in command. Griffin himself was still holding the belligerent, howling man on the ground trying to get him to calm down. The window of the truck was down and Jazz could smell the alcohol wafting off the abuser from six feet away.

"Fuck you, Sawyer, you motherfuckin' cocksucking cop," the man growled, thrashing on the hard pavement. "This is between me and my goddamn wife. She was asking for it, I tell you. She hit me."

Wow, this guy was a real charmer. He didn't appear to have a scratch on him that wasn't self-inflicted. Griffin had been careful to make sure the man wasn't injured while cuffing him.

"Tell me another one, Lane. You and I meet like this too often," Griffin muttered between clenched teeth. "I'm placing you under arrest."

Alexa, still sobbing, shook off Dare's help and fell to her knees beside Lane and started pushing at Griffin's arm. "No! Let him go! You're hurting him. He didn't do anything."

There was more crying and wailing before Griffin and Dare wrestled the couple to their feet, the man still yelling about police brutality and the woman screaming and crying about how everything was so unfair. The EMTs had shown up at some point and the battered and bruised woman rejected being taken to the hospital, but the man complained loudly of how he'd been injured by his wife and he'd had no choice but to defend himself.

Griffin and Dare managed to get the couple to quiet down so the EMTs could do their job. The woman was cleaned up and given a few butterfly bandages for a cut on her forehead. They wanted her to have stitches but she adamantly refused. Checking out the man, they shrugged at the absence of any real injuries, declaring him fit and heading back out into the night for their next call.

Now the real haggling began. Griffin and Dare wanted to arrest Lane but Alexa kept swearing she wouldn't press charges. Lane blamed everything on his wife but didn't want her to go to jail. Jazz wanted to smack some sense into both of them. How Griffin managed to keep his temper in check she had no idea.

Finally he cut off any more conversation with a wave of his hand.

"Dare, take Lane into custody for drunken disorderly and resisting arrest. Mrs. Atwater you can bail out your husband tomorrow morning after ten."

The wife moaned and wailed as if her husband was being dragged off to war or Siberia.

Dare nodded, his expression stony. "Alexa assaulted you, boss. You have cause to take her in as well."

Griffin sighed and brushed the clinging grass off his uniform. "I know, but this situation is bad enough, don't you think? No sense in making it even worse. Thanks, by the way. I didn't expect you."

"I heard the call on the scanner. I don't live far and we've been here enough to know what to expect. It was no big deal to help out." The burly deputy clapped a hand on Lane shoulder. "Let's go sober up, buddy. You'll feel worse in the morning."

Dare led the man to his truck and put him in the backseat before driving away. Griffin was still trying to convince Alexa that she needed to press charges for domestic battery but the woman kept shaking her head.

"He doesn't mean it, Sheriff. He's real sweet when he's sober. It's the alcohol that makes him act like that. He loves me. I know he does."

"The alcohol has control more often these days." Griffin's tone was calm and controlled but she could see the tension in his shoulders. "There's a shelter in Harper, Alexa. I can take you tonight."

"Leave my home and husband? I could never do that." The woman sounded scandalized. "Tomorrow everything will go back to normal. You'll see. Lane will apologize. He loves me."

The kind of love Jazz had grown up with was looking better and better. Her mother might have ignored her but at least she hadn't beaten the crap out of her. Finally Griffin got Alexa back into the house and returned to the SUV, climbing into the driver's seat. He sat there for a moment and then turned to Jazz.

"Thank you."

"Thank you for what?" Jazz asked, not sure if he was being sarcastic. He had a strange look on his face she hadn't seen before – half sad and half exasperated.

"Thank you for doing as I asked and staying put. It allowed me to concentrate on dealing with Lane and Alexa. As you can see they're a handful."

Jazz wrinkled her nose in distaste. "I have to admit it was all I could do not to march out there, smack both of them, and haul Lane off to jail. You've got the self-restraint of the Dalai Lama."

Griffin snorted and smiled a little. "No one has ever compared me to the Dalai Lama, that's for sure. Seriously, I'm glad you didn't give into that impulse. Lane is unpredictable when he's drinking and Alexa can be too. I don't want any of my deputies-in-training to get hurt. Especially not the first damn day." He tapped her on the nose. "By the way, we may not have covered it yet, but we don't smack our suspects no matter how much we want to."

"As I said, I admire your restraint." Griffin started the car and backed out of the driveway while she clipped her seatbelt closed. "I take it you and Dare make frequent visits here?"

"Too frequent. It's worse around the holidays. Summer is usually a quieter time." Griffin rubbed the back of his neck. "It's escalating, which worries me. I used to come out here every couple of months, then every month, now it's every few weeks."

From the way Griffin was speaking freely, he appeared to have forgotten Jerry in the backseat getting all of this on tape. Jerry too seemed to understand that he needed to sit in the shadows and stay quiet.

"She doesn't seem to want to leave. Does she have money of her own? Family?"

"She's got a sister in Bozeman but I'm not sure they're all that close. As for money, hell, I don't know those kind of details."

Jazz looked around the upper middle class neighborhood as it zipped by her window. "I didn't expect a call like that in a neighborhood like this."

Griffin glanced at her quickly. "You thought it would be in some rundown neighborhood? I hate to shatter your illusions, but domestic abuse crosses all socio-economic boundaries. This is not a movie, Jazz. This is the real thing."

"All these well-kept houses with their green lawns and pretty flowers. It makes you wonder what they all hide. Or at least it makes me wonder."

"You sound like you might have an idea what goes on behind closed doors. Want to share?"

She glanced back at the cameraman in the backseat and Griffin seemed to pick up on her thoughts.

"Turn off the fucking camera," Griffin ordered in a tone that couldn't be ignored. It appeared to work pretty well on the young man in the back seat. He dropped the camera to waist level but shook his head at the same time.

"I'm not supposed to do that," he protested. "I'll get in trouble."

Griffin pulled the SUV off on the side of the road. "Then get out."

"What?" Jerry shrank from the car door as if he could be magically sucked out of the vehicle. "You can't leave me here, dude."

Jazz studied Griffin's profile, trying to see if the man sitting next to her was truly serious about leaving Jerry to walk back to the hotel. In the waning light he appeared to be ready to do just that.

"I'm the law in this town and I can do anything I want. Secondly, I'm not going to leave you here. I'm just asking you to stand on the side of the road while we talk. It you want to stay in the vehicle you know what to do. Shut the fucking camera off. You got your titillation for the evening already. Just be sure to get Lane and Alexa to sign a release before you show that tape to anyone."

Indecision warred across Jerry's features but finally he sighed and pressed the button on the side of the camera. The green light went dim.

"Tony is going to kick my ass."

Griffin looked Jerry up and down. "You can probably take him. I think he was wearing nail polish."

Laughter bubbled up and Jazz couldn't hold it in. "That's not uncommon in Hollywood. Men get manicures."

Griffin was looking at her like she was crazy again. "What for?"

"For about thirty dollars," she giggled. "Seriously, haven't you heard the term metrosexual?"

"No," he said shortly. "Honestly I'm afraid to ask what that means."

Even Jerry was laughing now. "Men who care about how they look and dress."

"I don't even know how to respond to that," Griffin retorted.

The radio crackled and the fun was over. Griffin turned on the sirens and lights and pulled out into traffic.

"You can turn that camera back on. We're headed to another call." Griffin glanced at Jazz. "You can answer my question another time."

This time Griffin's expression and body language were relaxed. "Where to now?"

"Mrs. Mulvaney's cat Snowball is up a tree again. She wants me to climb up and get it down."

He was smiling now.

"For real?"

"For real," he confirmed, looking over his shoulder at Jerry. "Mrs. Mulvaney is going to be very excited about being on television so be sure to get her in every shot."

With the sun going down, they headed to the other side of Hope Lake to rescue a cat. Saved by a feline, Jazz wouldn't have to explain her thoughts or past to Griffin.

For now, anyway. She had a suspicion that once the sheriff honed in on something he would be like a dog with a bone. Relentless.

And she wouldn't—no—couldn't let him in. He was too attractive, too dangerous, too wonderful. Jazz already liked Sheriff Griffin Sawyer far too much.

Somehow, some way she had to avoid him. She had her future planned and nowhere was there a small town sheriff in that plan.

Chapter Seven

Griffin dropped the stack of manila folders into the middle of the conference table. He had all of the contestants in the interrogation room of the station to begin going through cold cases. Each person would select one case to work and belong to them solely. Griffin or one of the deputies would help and guide them but ultimately the contestant would lead the investigation.

It had been a compromise with the producers, who had wanted Griffin to give them "real" law enforcement work. He hadn't wanted to do anything of the sort but had conceded that he couldn't keep them in the classroom or on the obstacle course forever. Some of these cases were decades old and weren't so much cold as downright frozen. It was doubtful any of them would find a new lead but it would keep them busy.

"These are cold cases."

Griffin pointed to the pile in the middle of the table and tried to forget the camera was capturing his every word and movement. Last night when he'd been with Jazz he'd forgotten. There was something about the cute blonde that made him think of only her. When she was in a room, his gaze naturally went straight to Jazz first. Maybe it was that charisma that people talked about when speaking about people in show business. Whatever it was she'd taken up some real estate in his brain. He wasn't sure what to do about it or even if he needed to do anything about it.

"Look through them. Decide which one you'd like to take ownership of. Remember, whichever one you choose will be your case. We'll help and guide you, of course, every step of the way but try to pick a case that you find interesting or fits with a particular strength or knowledge base you may have."

They were all looking at him again as if they were statues. This group had a bad habit of needing to be told things more than once.

That could get you killed when you were a cop.

"Go ahead and get started."

This time the six of them moved and pulled folders off the stack one by one. There wasn't much sound in the room except the turning of pages and a few murmurings.

"Sheriff, can I speak with you?"

Tony, the producer and sometime director was standing there with his shadow, Gordon the assistant producer, who seemed to do all of the real work. Tony liked to tell people what to do but didn't like to get his manicured hands dirty from what Griffin had seen. If Gordon wasn't around, Tony would be up shit creek without a damn paddle.

"Sure, we can go to my office."

Griffin led the two men across the hall and waved for them to sit down while he took the chair behind his desk. Tony gave Griffin a smile that was probably meant to be encouraging but came off kind of smarmy.

"We just finished watching the dailies from yesterday's shoot and I have to say it's even better than I'd hoped for. The footage of you and Jazz last night was particularly spectacular."

Griffin didn't trust Tony as far as he could throw him, and even less at the moment. Just what was this guy trying to say? Did he want Griffin to let the contestants carry guns and wrestle suspects to the ground?

Not going to happen.

"That's good...I guess," Griffin said carefully. "Right?"

"It's excellent," Gordon enthused, then went silent when Tony gave him a quelling look.

"What we're trying to say," Tony said, scowling at Gordon, "is that there seems to be some chemistry between you and Jazz. The screen crackled with it when you were talking. We'd like to keep that going."

Yep, his instincts had been right. Tony was up to no good.

"And what do you mean by *keep it going*?"

"Viewers love characters they can root for and they love nothing more than to cheer for love."

"And?" Griffin prompted. He was going to make this son of a bitch say it out loud. "What does that have to do with me and Jazz going on patrol last night?"

"It's obvious you two are attracted to each other," Gordon broke in before Tony could speak. "Go with it."

Tony glared at Gordon but didn't correct him. Griffin stroked his chin and gazed over their heads as if he was actually entertaining these thoughts.

"Go with it," he repeated. "What did you have in mind?"

This time Tony was the first to speak. "Take her out on dates. Spend time with each other. If something naked happens, it's all the better. We wouldn't film that part, of course," he added hastily when Griffin sat up in his chair. "Let the audience watch you two fall in love. They eat that shit up."

There was no fucking way Griffin was going to sex up Jazz for the cameras. No matter how much he was attracted to her.

"What if we don't fall in love?" Griffin asked. "What if we end up hating each other?"

Tony's face split into a grin. "That's almost as good. Tension and animosity make for great television. Besides, I don't expect you two to really fall in love." The producer snorted in derision followed by Gordon. "Just ham it up for the cameras a little bit. After all, when this is over Jazz is heading back to L.A. and her career. It would be a bad idea to fall in love for real."

Nice of Tony to worry about Griffin getting his poor country boy heart broken.

Griffin nodded and the two men looked excited but he quickly dashed their hopes. "No can do, I'm afraid."

"No?" Tony repeated the word as if he'd never heard it or didn't know what it meant. "What do you mean *no*? This is a great opportunity, Sheriff."

Griffin leaned forward in his chair, his gaze affixed to the men. "For whom?"

Tony's mouth opened and closed a few times, his face turning red. Finally he pulled himself together enough to answer.

"Okay, fair enough. It would be great for the show, therefore great for me. But it's also great for the town. They get a cut of the profits. It's a win-win, Sheriff. Think about it."

Griffin was shaking his head but Tony and Gordon had already stood to leave as if they didn't want to hear any more objections.

"Don't say no yet. Just mull it over. We'll talk later." Tony said as he and his assistant scurried out of the office. Griffin was left sitting at his desk feeling frustrated and a tiny bit pissed off. He'd known something like this would happen but nobody was fucking listening to him these days. It was enough to make a man head for the nearest fishing hole and drown some worms.

Now there was an idea. A morning on the lake at the back of the house. A couple of beers and peace and quiet. Sheer heaven.

He sighed pulling his thoughts back to the present. Might as well just cowboy up and get his work done. Griffin stood and strode to the office door, sticking his head out.

"Wayne, you're up!" he bellowed into the quiet hall. He had no doubt they could hear him in Interrogation since the door was open. "Bring the case you've selected and let's discuss it."

No fishing, no fun. Only work.

Well, at least he'd put the kibosh on pretending to fall in love with Jazz. She really was the perfect woman to get involved with though. She wasn't sticking around so the relationship would have a definite expiration date. There would be no messy endings, just a mutual *so long, it was fun* when things were done. Two people having some fun for as long as it lasted or until the woman started wanting to smother him.

Perfect, except for the cameras.

That was something Griffin simply couldn't get past.

"So what case have you chosen?" Griffin asked Jazz.

They were sitting in his office and he'd called in the contest ants one by one. She was last and she was pretty sure she knew why. Tony and Gordon had pulled her aside earlier to talk. Sure they'd discussed it with the sheriff as well, Jazz wanted to dig a hole and jump in. Embarrassed was too weak a word for how she felt.

Mortified.

That fit better. She could only hope Griffin didn't think the whole illusion of them pretending something was going on between them was her idea.

She would admit – to herself at least – that she'd barely slept last night. Her head had been full of images of Sheriff Griffin Sawyer and that was the least of her problems. Vividly remembering how good he smelled and how his body emanated a comforting warmth had given those pictures true life. They'd tortured her until the wee hours of the morning when she'd finally dozed off exhausted and confused.

There was something about Griffin that got to her. Maybe it was the aura of command that surrounded him or the calm and controlled way he dealt with issues. Maybe it was the way he filled out his blue jeans and t-shirt. Either way she was in deep shit and she'd only been in town for less than forty-eight hours.

Crap.

"This one." Jazz watched Griffin's expression closely but he gave away nothing. If he was upset it didn't show. "It sounds interesting. The victim especially."

When Jazz had read the file about Casey Charlock, she'd known this was the case she had to have. Her fingers had gripped the file tighter and tighter as Jazz had read about the neglected daughter that had gone missing. The mother hadn't bothered to report Casey gone. It had been a friend who had eventually alerted the sheriff. Fast forward a few weeks later and her body was found in a ravine. She'd been beaten and strangled. They'd questioned her boyfriend but he had an alibi and others lacked motive. The case had grown cold and no new leads had been turned up for ages.

Griffin perused the file and his brows pulled together. "Are you sure, Jazz? This is one hell of a case to take on. I pull this file down when I have time and try to make some headway. So far there's nothing. I'd hate to see you bang your head against a wall.

Jazz wasn't sure she was ready to talk about her own childhood, but the expression on Griffin's face made it clear he was unsure about letting her work on this. She needed to make him understand.

"Let's just say I feel a kinship with Casey, okay? I'd like to work on it." He was still frowning but more from concern than anything. "Please?"

He rubbed his chin but finally nodded and sighed. "If this is what you really want. I'll help you all I can. There's not much here, honestly."

"I saw that they didn't have much for forensics although they managed to get DNA from under her fingernails. There were no footprints at the scene, no fingerprints."

"That was just for starters. It was a cluster from day one. You haven't learned this yet but the longer a case goes unsolved the less the chances are that it ever will be. The first forty-eight hours after Casey disappeared were of utmost importance and we missed those due to her mother not reporting her missing. It didn't get any better from there."

Griffin laid out the grisly crime scene photos on his desk alongside each other. "Did you look at these? Are you sure you can take something like this? It's not a pretty sight, Jazz. What this monster did to Casey was an ugly thing. She fought to live and it showed."

Jazz swallowed hard, a lump forming in her throat. She had looked at the pictures and they'd made her sick to her stomach to see what one human could do to another. It had only made her more determined to find Casey's killer. The girl deserved some closure.

"I have a pretty strong stomach. I didn't read the autopsy report though. Just the police notes."

The corners of Griffin's mouth turned up slightly. "Mine and Dare's notes. We tried to do right by Casey but in the end it wasn't enough."

"I'm sure you did all you could," she replied, trying to erase the lines in his forehead and the unutterably sad expression on his face. It was clear that this case had made an impression on Griffin, that it still affected him even now.

His lips flattened into a line and his gray eyes were a cold, flinty black. "It wasn't enough." He scooped the photos back into the folder and closed it. "I'll schedule some time for us to go through each piece of evidence. You can also re-interview some of her friends and family. Well, her mother anyway. She didn't have any other family."

"Thank you." She cleared her tight throat knowing she needed to discuss the other subject hanging over their heads. "Um, did Tony and Gordon talk to you today?"

Griffin instantly turned guarded, his shoulders tense. "Yes. Did they talk to you too?"

Jazz chewed on her lip and nodded. "They did. I just wanted you to know it wasn't my idea."

Her words came out all at once and she rubbed her damp palms on her blue jeans. She didn't want this man thinking she was, well, interested in him...that way. Even though she was. Sort of. She just didn't want him to know that. A little old-fashioned, Jazz preferred the male to make the initial moves. Of course that explained why she didn't date much.

"I never thought it was." Griffin was relaxed and smiling now. "Tony doesn't seem like the type who is looking for a lot of input from others. I'm guessing he likes the ideas to be his own."

This sheriff could read people well.

"If it isn't his, he'll find a way to take credit for it." Jazz laughed and felt the tension drain away. Griffin Sawyer was a really down to earth guy. "I make it sound bad but he actually is a pretty nice man. He's just ambitious, that's all. He's dating my roommate."

Griffin's eyebrows shot up in surprise. "Is that how you got on the show?"

"It is," she nodded. "I was having a bad day. A very bad day. I got fired from my crappy waitress job and lost out on the part of a lifetime. I was in debt due to major car repairs and behind on my bills. This opportunity was a godsend, honestly. Tony said it might lead to some job offers, but I know I have to stay on the show long enough to be noticed. Getting kicked off early won't help my career although I will be debt free. That is a relief."

Griffin seemed to study her for a long time before speaking. "You need to get noticed to get acting jobs then?"

"It's really the only way." Jazz shrugged. "I haven't had much luck the regular route. I'm starting to get pretty discouraged."

"And more camera time would help you?" he persisted, his gaze pinning her to the chair. The answer seemed damn important to him. She felt her heart start to pound in her chest at the mere suggestion that he might be willing to pretend to be involved with her.

"Yes, why do you ask?"

Was he really thinking about saying yes to Tony's proposal? An image of Griffin and herself locked in a passionate, naked embrace flashed in front of her eyes and she had to take a few breaths to keep her pulse under control.

"I told Tony and Gordon no." His lips twisted into a wry smile. "Not that they listened. I hope you can understand why I can't do it. It just wouldn't be—well, ethical. Not to mention it's not a good idea to get involved with someone that kind of works for me. In a way."

Jazz exhaled slowly, trying not to show her disappointment. He was right of course, and if she'd learned anything about him in the last thirty six hours or so was that he was as solid and honest as a summer day. Pretending anything wasn't his style.

"It's okay. I understand. It wouldn't be right."

"I hope you're not upset." Griffin had leaned forward in his chair and wore an earnest expression. She wasn't upset because she'd never really truly believed he would do it. But deep down she was kind of disappointed that she wouldn't be spending any extra time with him. She was attracted to the sheriff.

A whole hell of a lot.

"I'm fine. Honest. It never occurred to me that you would do it. I was shocked when Tony and Gordon brought it up. Tony will do anything for ratings."

"It wouldn't be the right thing to do," Griffin replied. "What kind of man would I be if I pretended something that wasn't true?"

Normal? Like everyone else?

"Most people wouldn't have been as honest as you are. They would have done it." It was all she could think of to say and it sounded pretty awful. Maybe she needed to re-think the people she surrounded herself with.

"Hell of a way to live," he said briskly, picking up the file and holding it out for her. Apparently their conversation was at an end. "I'll talk to Tony and Gordon again and make it clear. Will you be around later this evening? We can go through the evidence if you have time."

It seemed sort of surreal. She'd just had an honest conversation with a man and he didn't get all bent out of shape or anything. Griffin Sawyer had acted like a bona fide adult. A real man. She could get used to this. Apparently she'd dated way too many baby-men in Hollywood. Griffin was setting a brand new standard and he wasn't even her boyfriend.

"Th–Thank you, that would be great," she stuttered, still overcome by his straight shooting honest attitude.

She took the file and stood ready to make her getaway. She didn't need him to see how much he affected her. It would only make them both uncomfortable. "I'll be at the hotel studying my handbook later. Do you want to call me there and I can come here? Wait. They took the phone out of my room."

"I know the manager of the hotel. I'll call the office and they'll knock on your door. How does that sound?"

"Sounds perfect. I'll see you then."

Griffin nodded, his attention already moved from her to the paperwork on his desk. She slipped out of the door and headed back to the interrogation room.

She would look through the evidence with Griffin tonight and get a feel for this new case. And it wasn't a date. He wasn't interested in the least.

All she had to do was keep telling herself that over and over again.

Chapter Eight

Griffin was almost out of the door to head to his meeting with the other nearby sheriffs when Dare flagged him down.

"Got a minute?"

Griffin took a quick look at his watch and nodded. "If it doesn't go much longer. I've got a meeting with the guys at the roadhouse. What's up?"

For the first time since he'd known Dare the deputy didn't look pissed off. Instead he looked lost, as if he didn't know where to go or what to do. He had Griffin's full attention. He'd never seen Dare look that way and honestly it worried him.

"It's...well, shit, Griffin, It's a family thing. I got a call this morning and my dad had a heart attack. He remarried after he and my mom divorced and she passed away from cancer a few years ago. He doesn't have much family."

Dare paused as if he'd run out of words. Griffin remembered when Dare's stepmother had died. He also remembered that Dare had some tension with his father which might explain why Dare wasn't at the man's bedside. Either way it was none of Griffin's business how his deputy dealt with his family and Dare sure as hell wasn't coming to Griffin for advice. He probably needed time off and was afraid to ask for it with everything going on.

"Of course you can have some time off—" Griffin began.

"That's just it," Dare cut him off. "It's not just time off. I need to resign."

Griffin inwardly reeled as if he'd been slugged with a two by four. "Resign? What the hell for?"

Dare scraped his hand through his hair, his lips a grim line. "Dad's not doing well and my stepsister doesn't have anyone to watch over her. She's a teenager, and according to the social worker that called me, if family doesn't take over they'll put her in foster care until she's eighteen. That's months away."

"Then take a leave of absence until your dad is better. Shit, don't resign," Griffin argued. Dare was one of the best deputies in Montana. Griffin would hold the job open as long as it took. "I don't want to lose you. I'll wait, man."

Dare's shoulders lifted. "Sheriff Barkley wants to retire, Griffin."

Sheriff Lionel Barkley had been the head lawman in Dare's hometown for at least the past thirty-five years. Rumor was that Barkley was planning to die with his boots on so to speak and it looked to be true. The man had to be at least seventy years old, hunchbacked and mean as a snake.

"Retire, huh? Didn't see that one coming."

Griffin was helpless to stop this train from flattening him. There was no way he would get in the way of Dare getting his own town. Shit, he deserved it and then some.

"No one did. He's been talking about it for months. Called me last fall but I was happy here. But with dad and everything…"

Dare's voice trailed off as if in apology but he didn't have anything to be sorry for. Griffin appreciated that the deputy had stayed on as long as he had, especially if he'd been courted by his own town.

"Aw, fuck. I understand. You've got some pay coming for unused vacation time. Let's sit down and talk about this when I get back. How long do you think you can give me? A week?"

Dare nodded. "I'm sorry about this. I know it's the absolute worst time this could happen."

"There would never have been a good time so it might as well be now." Griffin shrugged as if it didn't matter but his mind was already whirring as to how they were going to cover shifts. "I'm happy for you although I'm sorry about the circumstances. I hope your dad pulls through."

"I'm hopeful. As soon as I'm off the clock for today I'm going to go visit him, but I'll be back in tomorrow. The doctor said he's stable but unconscious so my sitting by his bed wouldn't change anything."

Griffin never doubted Dare's dedication to the job, but his words underlined that there were indeed issues in the Turner family. "If you need more flexibility let me know. Family comes first."

As close to a smile as Dare ever allowed himself crossed the deputy's face. "You'll just be covering those shifts yourself, boss. We're stretched as thin as ice in April."

Griffin slapped Dare on the back and grinned. "My dad always used to say that idle hands do the devil's work. He always respected a man who put in an honest day's work and then some."

"Your dad would know. How many brothers and sisters you got again?"

"Nine. Four brothers and five sisters." Saying it out loud never ceased to amaze Griffin. They should have put his family on a reality show but thank god they never did. "And we grew up in a three bedroom house with one bathroom."

Dare pushed the brim of his hat up and chuckled. "Holy shit. That explains a whole bunch about you."

"It explains why I don't mind taking a piss outside. Now I need to get on the road. I'll be back by dinnertime. Can you pull the evidence for the Casey Charlock case, by the way? Jazz chose it as her cold case and I want to review the evidence with her."

"Will do. And thanks for not blowing a gasket."

"Wouldn't have made any difference now, would it?" Griffin turned on the heel of his well-worn cowboy boots and made straight for his truck. His day was turning out to be a real doozy. He couldn't help but long for a quiet lazy afternoon on the lake.

But he sure as shit wasn't going to get it.

The smell of stale beer and sweat coiled around Griffin as he walked through the now quiet roadhouse. In just a few hours the place would be filled with people stopping in for a cold one after working all day. The jukebox in the corner would be rocking and the air would be filled with cigarette smoke but at the moment the only sounds were the other men laughing and popping open a soda can. The roadhouse wasn't allowed to serve alcohol outside of business hours, not that the men would have drunk it anyway. They were on duty.

Griffin pulled out a chair, sank into it with a sigh, and caught the cold can that Seth slid down to him.

"What did I miss?" Griffin asked with a smile. Just being around his friends made him feel better. He trusted these men more than anyone else in the world, and he knew they trusted him. They'd seen some rough times but they'd always pulled together.

"I was just giving Logan some shit." Reed laughed and took a swig of his soda. "He's too fucking happy. It gives me the creeps."

Reed Mitchell was the slickest, coolest son of a bitch Griffin had ever known. He made everything look easy – the job, women, fishing. Fuck, Griffin had never seen anything Reed wasn't good at. And the kicker? Reed didn't give a shit either way.

He didn't care if women chased him. Although they did.

He didn't care if he was the best shot of them all. But he was.

Reed was also the most mysterious. Griffin had known him for over five years and yet didn't know a damn thing that was truly personal. Reed played it close to the vest without being an asshole about it. The men knew that was what he wanted and they all respected it. Once Griffin had been having some drinks with Jared and Logan and they'd speculated about Reed's past, coming up with ever increasingly outlandish tales. Logan had postulated that Reed had been some sort of spy and Jared thought Reed might be a genius on the run from foreign governments. Or several ex-wives.

They'd probably never know.

"You hate familial happiness," Seth Reilly countered with a grin. "You should talk to a shrink about that. It's a flaw in your character."

"One of many, I fear," Reed mocked and then shuddered. "All this conjugal bliss makes me break out in hives."

Jared Monroe sat back and stretched out his long legs, a smile playing on his lips. "As long as it's not contagious I'm fine with it."

"Not looking to find a good woman and settle down? Man wasn't meant to walk alone." Tanner Marks nodded as he studied the men around the table. "A good woman can be the making of a man."

"And a bad one can be his undoing," Griffin replied. "But then you're so happily married you can't even think straight. It's all that sex. It messes with your mind."

Tanner chuckled and popped a potato chip into his mouth. "I'll go to my grave crazy but well laid, thank you very much."

"A man can have sex without marrying a woman these days, Tanner." Jared snagged the bag of chips from the middle of the table and pulled them toward his end. "Trust me on this one. I know."

Jared certainly did know. His story was serial monogamy. He'd date one woman until she started to squawk about marriage and kids and suddenly Jared would have a new one on his arm. Generally the ladies lasted twelve to twenty-four months tops. All of them beautiful and all of them successful. Jared's standards for perfection were way too high for anything else.

"Can I interrupt with a little bit of business?" Griffin queried. "Dare resigned today. He's moving back to his hometown, Valley Station. He's going to take over for Sheriff Lionel Barkley."

The whole room seemed to erupt in talking all at once until Tanner pounded his fist on the table to bring them back to order.

"Hell, that's a surprise. Never thought I'd see the day Barkley would retire. I figured he'd go at his desk wearing a gold star."

"I think we all thought that but the town will be much happier having Dare," Logan said. "He's going to have a mess to clean up just like I did, God help him. And I know you're going to be sorry to see him go. That puts you in a real fix doesn't it?"

"You have no idea," Griffin groaned. "We're already short resources. I'm fucked."

"Dare or no Dare I heard you're screwed. Is it true about the television crew? Come on, you can tell us the truth," Seth cajoled, wearing a shit-eating grin.

Swearing under his breath, Griffin took another drink of his soda. He should have known that this wouldn't stay a secret. He carefully explained the reasoning of the town council, adding that he hadn't really been given a choice.

"So maybe you'll get a decent deputy out of this." Jared shrugged. "I may be able to help you though. I got a call from an old buddy in the Army. He's been a cop in Chicago but wants a more small town life. I don't have the budget to hire anyone but I can have him call you if you're interested. I can vouch for him. Hard worker and honest. He'd be a good addition I think if he can get used to the slower pace."

"Have him call me," Griffin replied immediately. "What's his name?"

"Trace Hadley and I'll call him tonight."

For the first time today Griffin thought things might be looking up for a change. He cleared his throat to get their attention. "I brought up Dare leaving for a reason. He's getting his own town and it's within the hundred and fifty mile radius of here. What do you think about inviting him to join the group?"

The other five men looked around at each other as if to see if anyone had any objections but all nodded their assent. Tanner, the unofficial leader of the group, slapped the table. "Looks like we've added a seventh to our group. Let Dare know he's welcome."

Seth leaned forward. "Since we're talking about adding...Evan Davis has left the Marshal Service." There was a stunned moment of silence before Seth continued. "They'd put him on desk duty since the shootout where he got hurt. That's not what he signed on for and he was pretty sick of it. He's now the sheriff of Marywood just about a hundred and seventy-five miles from here. It's a little out of our usual radius but I'm sure he won't mind the drive."

Logan shook his head in disbelief. "Never thought that guy would quit. They must have really screwed him."

Griffin had the same thoughts but hadn't voiced them. Marshal Evan Davis had seemed to be dedicated to the job. For him to leave it must have been bad.

"Anyone opposed to adding Evan?" Tanner asked, his voice booming over their murmurs. No one spoke up and Tanner pounded the table twice. "Passed. Looks like we've added two people today. If they even want to join us, of course. Shit, we might need to add a table."

Reed drained his soda can and tossed it in the trash. "Tell the new guys they bring the snacks."

"We take turns," Tanner contradicted. "Now who had new business?"

"Now wait a minute." Logan's face was split into a grin. "I want to hear more about Griffin's pretty boy face showing up on television."

Griffin flipped Logan the bird. "It's a fucking nightmare, asshole, just as you would expect. I spend all my time babysitting a bunch of civilians who don't know one end of a gun from another—well one does, but the others...shit. I don't have enough manpower as it is and now I've got cameras following me around. I'm lucky one didn't follow me here." Griffin stared hard at each of his friends. "Give me any more shit and I will bring the cameras next time. You can share in my hell."

Jared held up his hands in surrender. "I for one don't want anything of the kind, so consider my lip zipped on the subject. I will offer assistance if you have issues with crowd control. I have a few junior deputies that could use the experience."

Tanner looked around the room after Griffin thanked Jared for the offer but all the men had shut their mouths. They weren't stupid. "So? New business?"

Griffin raised his hand and sighed. "I'm re-opening a cold case. Casey Charlock."

Tanner frowned. "That young girl whose body was found in a ravine after being missing for a few weeks? Do you have a new lead? That's good news."

"No new lead." Griffin shook his head, hating to bring up the reality show. Again. "I'm letting the contestants work on cold cases. Jazz chose this one. I wasn't thrilled about it but it seemed to be important to her."

"Jazz?" Jared arched an inquisitive eyebrow. "Who is Jazz and since when do you make law enforcement decisions based on what's important to pretty girls?"

"How do you know she's pretty?" Griffin quickly shot back but felt the cut of Jared's query. Griffin was making decisions based on Jazz's feelings and it made him nervous. He shouldn't like her so much. Or be so attracted to her.

Fuck.

"Because you wouldn't give a shit what she wanted if you didn't want to go to bed with her," Jared replied with a chuckle. "Blonde, brunette, or redhead?"

"Blonde," Griffin answered grudgingly. Maybe he was letting his dick do the thinking when Jazz was around. Opening up the Casey Charlock case with no new leads was only going to upset a lot of people in town. Nothing was really going to change.

Yet he couldn't forget the look on Jazz's face when she'd shown him the file she'd chosen. When she'd said she had a kinship with Casey there had been a look in her eyes...

Fuck, he was getting soft in his old age.

"Blonde and buxom?" Reed leered. "Lucky you."

"Not lucky me. I wouldn't have a relationship with someone I'm supervising. No way."

"I got involved with Presley," Seth offered. "Look how that turned out."

His buddy wasn't helping in the least.

"Yes, *look how that turned out.* You don't get enough sleep, you change diapers, fix bottles, and never get any time to yourself. Doesn't sound like much of a deal to me." In fact it sounded awful to Griffin. He'd already done his time changing diapers and fixing bottles, not to mention a bunch of other things he didn't want to repeat.

"I don't want any time to myself," Seth laughed. "I guess that's the difference between you and me. Alone wasn't that much fun."

"That's where we're different," Griffin echoed, wanting to change the subject. "I'm re-opening the case. I may need some of your connections at the federal level for the forensics."

"I thought there wasn't much there," Jared said.

"There wasn't but maybe the FBI lab might be able to find something the state lab couldn't. I'm open to any suggestions."

"I can give my buddy in Quantico a call." Jared tapped his chin. "I might have a connection at the NSA I could check. He might be able to pull her emails and phone calls."

Everyone knew Jared had done something super-secret when he was in the military but not exactly what it was. He joked he'd have to kill them if he told them.

They all wanted to live more than they needed to know.

"Thanks. I'll be honest, guys, this case has never ceased to bother me. There has to be something, anything out there that could help us. Casey deserves justice."

His friends nodded soberly and Griffin knew they were all thinking about their own cold cases. Every lawman had that one case that wouldn't leave him alone. Casey Charlock was his.

Maybe this time he could close the file once and for all. But first he needed to get his head out of his ass regarding Jazz. She was off limits and he needed to remember that, especially as they would be spending time together for this case.

He could look, but no way could he touch.

Chapter Nine

Barney the cameraman was in the corner of Griffin's office trying to be unobtrusive, but Jazz could see the sheriff's gaze keep flickering that direction. She felt badly for him, really. It was clear he wasn't comfortable in front of the cameras. He only seemed relaxed when they were absent or he forgot they were there.

He also looked exhausted. Dark circles under his eyes and his broad shoulders seemed slightly hunched with fatigue. He was working some really inhuman hours from what she could tell. Even last night he'd sent her off to bed while he wrote up his paperwork for the shift. God only knew what time he got to bed. Deputy Dare had mentioned that Griffin had come in before dawn. There was a distinct possibility he'd never slept at all.

"I know you've seen the photos in the file but there are more in here. Much more graphic. Can you handle it?" Griffin asked, his voice low.

The room was silent except for the hum of the air conditioner. The other contestants were back at the hotel and the day shift had gone home. There was only the two of them, the cameraman, and Deputy Adam in the outer office.

Jazz nodded yes but inside she wasn't so sure. She'd seen the words of the medical examiner – death by strangulation. The pictures in the file had been mostly from a distance and been more concentrated on the crime scene than the body or the wound.

He lifted the lid from the cardboard box and set it aside before digging in and pulling out several plastic bags.

"These were the clothes she was wearing that day. The medical examiner found a few hairs on her shirt that were consistent with Casey's mother."

The jeans looked muddy but otherwise normal. The blouse however had a vivid reddish-brown stain that could only be blood. Jazz felt her stomach lurch slightly but she took a few deep breaths and it settled down.

"Margaret Charlock was a suspect?" Jazz asked as she carefully accepted a stack of photos from Griffin. These were indeed more graphic as he had warned but instead of feeling sick Jazz felt her anger grow. A young woman had disappeared and then been found murdered. Her mother hadn't really cared much, if at all. If she had reported her missing right away, could Casey's life have been saved? The injustice done to this pretty young woman made Jazz pissed as hell.

She felt his large hand warm and strong on her shoulder. A zing of electricity ran through her body and she stiffened at the unwelcome awareness his touch brought. Her attraction to him was a non-starter. This was all about work and she needed to focus on the case. She needed to focus on Casey.

"Are you okay?" he asked. "Your face looks a little red. Why don't you give me those photos back? They're kind of grisly. I've been doing this a long time so I'm used to it."

"No, it's not that." Jazz shook her head, wondering what he would think about her messy emotions. He always appeared to be in control. "I'm mad. What was done to her makes me angry. Shit like this should not happen."

Griffin studied her for a moment, and then to her surprise smiled. "Good. That's not a bad emotion to have when you're doing a job like this. We should be angry about what happened to Casey Charlock. A pretty girl just nineteen years old heads home from work and is never seen alive again. Keep that anger handy, Jazz. It can be your fuel when you haven't had enough sleep, the clues dry up, and the case is going nowhere."

"Did you sleep last night?" she asked softly, their gazes seeming to collide and hold. Those silver-gray eyes didn't look as hard and tough as they usually did. Griffin Sawyer looked almost...vulnerable.

"I got a few hours," he answered shortly, the moment between them gone as quickly as it had come. "In answer to your first question, yes, Margaret Charlock was a suspect. But we were never able to connect her with the murder. Casey lived at home so having a few of her mother's hairs on her shirt wasn't exactly a smoking gun."

"Did she have an alibi?"

Jazz sifted through the photos and found one of the young woman smiling and laughing, sitting next to what must have been a good friend, their arms draped over each other's shoulders.

"It's hard to say. The medical examiner had difficulty narrowing down the time of death exactly. Margaret Charlock was out and about the entire day her daughter died. She's a real estate agent so she probably had opportunity. For me, the question is did she have motive? We couldn't find one."

Jazz held up a picture of Casey with a young man at Christmastime. There was a decorated tree in the background and Casey wore a bright red sweater and bell earrings.

"Is this her boyfriend?"

"It is. Buddy Meltreeger. She'd been dating him for about nine months from what he said. From all accounts they seemed pretty happy. Until they weren't."

In the photo they did seem happy. But Jazz knew that pictures could deceive.

"They were fighting?"

"They were typical teenagers. Breaking up and getting back together, a real on and off type of relationship. Buddy said they were in the off stage when she disappeared."

"Has he ever been arrested? Any anger issues?"

"No, and none that we know of. His friends speak highly of him and all he's ever had were a few speeding tickets. Not that unusual for a young man who likes souped-up cars."

"So we have no suspects?" This was going to be harder than Jazz had imagined. She wanted to give Casey closure but it wasn't going to be easy.

"I didn't say that." Griffin plucked the photo of Casey and Buddy out of Jazz's fingers. "Buddy isn't perfect. He likes to drink and party. There were rumors of him being a little too friendly with other females."

"In other words your typical horny teenage guy," she replied dryly. "Hardly a motive for murder."

"True. Margaret Charlock isn't out of the woods either as far as I'm concerned. The fact that she never reported her daughter missing is a big red flag for me. What was she covering up?"

"Maybe she just didn't give a shit." The words tumbled out of Jazz's mouth before she could stop them. She bit her lip hard to keep from saying anything else. She'd gone and done it now. Opened up the proverbial can of worms.

"You and I are going to have a talk about that statement someday, but I can see today isn't the time or place," Griffin stated. "You let me know when you're ready."

Her mouth fell open and she forgot what she was going to say. He'd shocked her completely.

"It's your own business, and there's obviously a story there, but I respect your privacy, Jazz."

"I've never met anyone like you."

More words she couldn't seem to control. What was it about this man that made her say things better left unsaid?

"I've never met anyone like you either." Now he was smiling and she felt her heart start to pound in response. "How did you get the name Jazz anyway?"

That was a pretty easy question. Comparatively.

"My real name is Janine. But when I went into show business I wanted something different. Something no one else would be named."

His eyes narrowed and his gaze seemed to look deep inside her. "You wanted to become someone different than Janine."

It wasn't a question.

"Yes." She shifted uncomfortably in her chair. She hated discussing anything outside the official bio she used professionally. "I guess so."

He just nodded and reached back into the box, not probing further. Her breathing went back to normal but her pulse still hammered. She was getting used to it. His proximity seemed to do funky things to her equilibrium.

They reviewed the rest of the contents and it was late in the evening before they were done. Even Barney was yawning and stretching his stiff back and arms. Remembering how Griffin had cornered her about her name in front of the cameras made her want to run and hide. They'd both forgotten they were being taped. She couldn't let that happen again.

"Shit, I'm beat," Barney said, grabbing his black leather supply bag and tossing it over his shoulder. "See you in the morning."

The cameraman practically ran out of the door obviously hoping they wouldn't find anything else to do. Jazz's stomach growled loud enough to get Griffin's attention.

"You need to eat," he pronounced. "I'm sorry I kept you so late."

"It's no big deal." She slung her purse over her shoulder and started to back towards the door. "I'm probably going to head to the diner." She sucked in a breath and gathered her courage. She wasn't ready for the evening to be at an end. "Want to join me?"

She held her breath in hope, butterflies flying merrily in her abdomen and making her a little nauseous. The more time she spent with him, the more time she *wanted* to spend with him. It was a vicious cycle but damned if she wanted to stop.

"I'm too fucking exhausted to eat. I need to get some sleep." Griffin yawned and she tried to push away the disappointment. "Tomorrow we'll go talk to Casey's mother. Have your questions ready."

Always back to business with him. Well, screw him—she could do that too.

"I will. Thanks."

She turned and flew out of his office and then out of the station heading straight for the diner. The message was loud and clear from Sheriff Sawyer. He wasn't interested and that was that.

She needed to concentrate on winning the contest and finding Casey's killer and not on the sexiest man she could remember seeing in…well, her whole damn life. No sense getting her panties all bunched up about a man that didn't even see her as a woman.

Focus. She wouldn't allow herself to be distracted from what was really important. Her career.

Chapter Ten

Jazz sat next to Griffin in the SUV while Barney took up most of the back seat with his camera and sound equipment. They were heading to the edge of town where Margaret Charlock lived in one of those planned housing communities were all the homes looked the same except for a few variations. It was a neighborhood perfect for the bland and colorless woman Griffin had first met nine months ago.

Griffin had finally gotten some quality sack time last night after he'd shut off his mind from thinking about Jazz and Casey and the contest. And Jazz.

Shit, he was in deep with this woman and he barely knew her. At one point last night when she'd shyly asked him if he'd slept he'd wanted to lean down and kiss her full pink lips. Pull her into his arms and see if her curvy body felt just as good against his as it looked. Her expression had been so serious and concerned. He couldn't remember the last time someone had been truly worried about his well-being. Other than his mother. You'd think after ten kids she'd be immune to a stuffy nose but every time he got a cold she acted like he had one foot in the damn grave.

Keep your mind on business. Not the glimpse of tanned cleavage just peeking out of her dark red blouse. Or her dainty feet with their shiny cherry red toenails ensconced in a pair of white sandals.

"Are you ready for this?" he asked, more to get his mind out of the gutter than to actually get the answer. He'd already looked over her proposed questions and deleted a few and added his own. If she had been more seasoned or had any law enforcement training whatsoever outside of the last few days, he would have proposed they play good cop/bad cop. But that was out of the question at this point.

Jazz was obviously nervous, plucking at the denim of her jeans and chewing on her lower lip. For someone who acted in front of the camera for a living, she couldn't act cool about this.

"I think so. I'm worried about doing something wrong," she admitted, her eyes wide. He felt something lurch in his chest and swung his gaze away from those guileless blue topaz eyes and back to the road.

"You'll be fine. We'll do this together. Just remember what we went over. Never lose your cool, and never act like you don't believe her. Always be her friend. Get her to trust you. That's when they say things they wouldn't normally say. If anyone needs to get tough, I'll do it. Got it?"

"Got it. I–" Jazz started to say something else but Griffin's swearing interrupted her.

"Shit, what now?" he said to no one in particular, bristling with frustration. It was bad enough being on camera all the damn time, then Dare quitting—now something was wrong with the truck. The check engine light was illuminated and he pulled the vehicle off onto the shoulder. Ignoring the inquiring expressions of both Jazz and Barney, he hopped out and opened the hood. Damn cars these days were all run by computers but it might be something simple.

A quick perusal showed a leak in the evaporative system of the vehicle. A crack in one of the hoses could cause an increase in the pressure in the gas tank. Not good. The thing was this was no crack in an old hose. This was a clean cut as if from a knife.

Someone wanted them to have to pull over. Griffin had a pretty good idea who that was.

He slammed the hood shut and swung back into the driver's seat, ignoring Jazz's question about what was wrong. He was too pissed to answer at the moment. Instead he got on the radio and called for a tow truck and eyed the cameraman in the rearview mirror. Finally, he took a deep breath to rein in his anger and turned to the woman beside him.

"Grab your stuff, we're going to have to walk from here. It's only a couple of miles."

Jazz frowned but did as he asked, sliding out of the passenger seat. To Griffin's amusement, Barney did the same, the heavy leather bag hanging from his shoulder and clearly weighing him down. Not in the best of shape to begin with, there was no way the man would be able to make the two mile hike with all that equipment.

But that wasn't why he wasn't going.

"You're staying with the vehicle, Barney. Someone needs to be here when the tow truck shows up."

Barney started to protest but Griffin waved away any arguments the man might have had. But he was going to make sure the cameraman knew why he was staying.

"Let's step over here for a minute and talk."

Jazz was watching them both with interest but Griffin had to hand it to her—she didn't ask a lot of questions or try to interfere. She let him pull Barney aside where it would be hard to hear them talk but she could still clearly see them.

"I'm going with you." Barney's jaw was set in a stubborn line but Griffin didn't give a shit. He didn't like being manipulated. At all.

"The fuck you are," he said softly, keeping his voice low but with enough depth that Barney would know Griffin was damn serious. "Funny thing about that leak. It looks like a clean cut on the hose. You wouldn't know anything about that, would you?"

The telltale red stained cheeks on the portly cameraman told Griffin everything he needed to know. Barney stammered but couldn't seem to get any words out.

"I assume this wasn't your idea," Griffin grated. "Tony and Gordon?"

The man flushed a deeper crimson and nodded. "They wanted you and Jazz to have to spend time together."

"Well, that's exactly what we're going to do. But you won't be there. Tough luck."

"C'mon, sheriff. Cut me a break. Tony's already crawled up my ass this week. I need this job."

"Who would you rather have mad at you?" Griffin gave the man his most steely, intimidating stare. The one he'd perfected in the military when he was in the Middle East. "Me or Tony?"

Barney swallowed hard and his red cheeks turned pale. "Tony."

"I'm glad we've come to an understanding. I'll be having a talk with your boss, don't worry. I'll let him know how little I appreciate stunts like this."

Griffin didn't waste any more time. Turning away, he motioned for Jazz to follow him and they started trudging on the side of the highway. She didn't speak for a long time and then finally she stopped and placed her hand on his arm, sending a rush of heat through his body.

He almost cursed out loud at the unwelcome tingling her fingers evoked. She was part of this circus that was fucking with his life and that meant she was trouble. Capital T.

"What happened back there?" she asked, her head tilted to the side in question, her long blonde hair falling over one shoulder. He quelled the urge to reach out and see if the strands were as silky as they looked. "I have a feeling I missed something."

"I'll tell you later," he growled, still pissed off and frustrated at the interlopers who were trying to mess with his life and his town. There wasn't an amount of money in the world that was worth all this shit as far as he was concerned. "Let's get a move on. She's expecting us."

"You will tell me, Griffin Sawyer," she vowed, her eyes sparkling with challenge. "Something is definitely going on."

Something was going on and Griffin was going to nip it in the bud. Now. No one was going to push him together with Jazz just for ratings or money or whatever the fuck their reasoning was. She was off limits.

He was her fucking boss, for Christ's sake. He didn't go around dating or fucking his employees.

Well, shit. Now he had an image of them rolling around naked in his giant king sized bed together. He willed his cock to behave behind the button fly of his jeans and concentrated on how the sun was setting in the west. Hell of a way for the day to end.

"I'll tell you everything, Jazz. Just as soon as we question Margaret Charlock. Deal?"

"Deal," she echoed. "You're a very strange man. Do you know that?"

"Hollywood, you don't know the half of it."

"And whose fault is that?" Her laughter echoed in the silence. She had a nice laugh. Not too loud and not too soft. Just right, really.

"Mine," he readily agreed. "Things are complicated, that's all."

"You don't want us here," she stated succinctly. "I get that."

"I like you, Jazz. I just don't like having a camera stuck in my face all the time."

"Is that why you made Barney stay behind?"

Griffin laughed at the naive question. "Nope. Barney stayed behind for a completely different reason. Now let's get going."

They hurried their pace as they walked side by side on the shoulder of the deserted road. Griffin would tell her what was going on later. She'd said Tony was a pretty good guy but Griffin had his doubts. If he was capable of this, what else was he trying to manipulate for his own ends?

Griffin was determined to find out.

✧ ✧ ✧ ✧

"I don't know what we have to talk about," Margaret Charlock said as they all three sat down in her beige living room. Jazz inwardly shuddered at the impersonal furnishings devoid of any semblance of individuality. There wasn't even a photo of Casey anywhere that Jazz could see. The room could have belonged to anyone anywhere in the world.

"We want to make sure there's nothing we missed," replied Griffin, settling himself on the oatmeal colored sofa with only slightly darker throw pillows. "We appreciate you speaking with us today."

Margaret folded her hands in her lap and waited for their questions. At forty years old, she was an attractive woman with short auburn hair and a trim figure. Her face was carefully made up with a skillful hand and her clothes were stylish but as bland as the living room. It was almost as if the woman wanted to fade into the background of life wearing earth tones.

"I am tired after working all day," she said pointedly. "If we could get this over with I would be glad."

"As I said we appreciate your cooperation." Griffin nodded toward Jazz. "This young woman is Jazz Oliver, one of my deputies in training. We're both going to be asking you a few questions."

The woman's eyes narrowed and her cheeks turned pink. "I've heard about the reality show being filmed in town." Her hands seem to flutter around and finally landed on the sofa cushions. "You're not filming this, are you?"

"No. We're not filming or recording," Griffin assured her. She seemed somewhat mollified but still nervous.

Griffin nodded for Jazz to begin. Taking a deep breath, she steadied her voice and tried to control her madly beating heart. This was worse than opening night jitters.

"Mrs. Charlock, when you gave your statement to the police you said that Casey and Buddy had broken up. Were they in contact with each other at all?"

"Not that I know of, but Casey was an adult and I didn't interfere in her life." Margaret shook her head but her right hand had swung up to cover the base of her throat. "She had lots of boyfriends. I didn't pay much attention, honestly."

That statement caught Griffin's attention apparently. "Was she dating anyone else at the same time she was dating Buddy? Or afterward?"

The woman's hand stayed right where it was giving Jazz a front row seat to a woman who just might be lying. She at least felt vulnerable. Her body language was screaming it even if she didn't verbally say it.

"She dated a lot," Margaret insisted. "There were always boys hanging around. I didn't get all of their names."

"She dated someone after Buddy?" Jazz asked, watching the woman closely.

"I really don't know for sure." Margaret shook her head but her gaze was darting around the room as if she didn't want to look them in the eye. "My daughter lived her own life."

Anger churned in Jazz's gut at the indifferent statement from the clearly non-grieving mother.

"She was nineteen," Jazz snapped. "Still a teenager. I doubt she *lived her own life* by choice. She was a young girl who needed her mother."

Margaret's mouth fell open and a cold expression crossed her face. "Are you questioning my parenting? Who do you think you are?" the woman said frostily.

If Griffin had any ideas about halting this line of questioning, Jazz never gave him a chance. She was too far gone to remember his instructions despite the warning bells ringing in her own ears.

"I'm someone who understands your daughter, that's who. She was *nineteen*, Mrs. Charlock. Not far from a child and she lived under your roof. Are you saying you have no idea what she did the last few days of her life? That you haven't given it any thought since she died?"

"That's enough, Jazz," Griffin cut in, his voice sharp and commanding. Her voice died but the righteous anger she'd felt was still stirring inside. The back of her neck was hot and she could hear her pulse pound as if someone with a snare drum was sitting and playing in this colorless living room.

"I'm sorry about Ms. Oliver, Margaret. She's still in training and can get carried away. Please continue. We appreciate your understanding."

Jazz doubted Margaret Charlock appreciated anything about them at the moment. Her face had turned a peculiar shade of purple, probably with anger, and her shoulders seemed to shake.

She jumped to her feet and went over by the sliding glass doors to look out, ignoring both of them. Griffin's lips had formed a grim line and Jazz knew she was in for an ass chewing when they left. She'd done the opposite of what he'd asked but being friends with this woman simply wasn't something she was capable of doing.

"The last day I saw Casey she said she wanted me to meet someone. A new boyfriend." Margaret's fingers plucked at her strand of pearls, her body turned away from them. "I don't remember his name, if she ever told me, which is why I never mentioned it before. What's the point? You can't find someone without a name. I don't even know what he looks like." She finally turned toward them, her expression mutinous. Whatever small cooperation they'd had at the beginning was long gone. "Now I'd like you to leave."

Griffin stood, pulling Jazz up with him, his hand under her elbow. She could feel the tension in his frame as they stood side by side. "Thank you, Margaret. We appreciate the help and we'll call if we have any more questions."

"Do that," she replied, her tone brittle. "But I doubt we have anything more to discuss. Let my daughter rest in peace, Sher-iff."

"That's exactly what I aim to do, ma'am."

Griffin tipped his hat and guided Jazz to the door so quickly she almost stumbled trying to keep up. The door swung shut behind them and they walked silently to the end of the driveway where a patrol car waited, complete with Deputy Adam as a driver. Griffin hustled her inside the vehicle and it smoothly pulled away from the curb. Once they were away from the house, Griffin turned to her, his expression stormy.

Uh oh.

"What in the hell were you doing back there? What were you thinking?"

Boy, did he sound pissed. Mental note. Don't upset the sheriff.

"I was thinking she was a lousy mother. And she was lying. I could tell."

"You could tell," he repeated. "You're some expert in lying as well as an actress?"

She ignored his sarcasm.

"She was being evasive. As an actress I study body language, and when a person does this," Jazz placed her hand over her throat. "That means they feel the need to protect themselves. They're worried about something. They could be lying."

"She was lying when she said she didn't know anything," he admitted but didn't look all that damn happy about it.

"Exactly! I helped."

Griffin shook his head grimly. "Helped? I'm not sure I'd call it that. You had some dumb luck. It could easily have gone another way, Jazz."

"But it didn't," she insisted. "I may not have done what you said but it worked. Admit it."

"I admit nothing," Griffin retorted, frustration in his tone. "You better hope that this lead pans out because after what you pulled in there she will never – I repeat – never speak to us again. On or off the record. Shit, Jazz. It's not just this, can't you see? What if we'd been in a dangerous situation? You need to listen to me and do what I tell you. Failure could get you killed. As in dead."

Shit, now she felt kind of crappy. She's been too emotional to think logically.

"So you guys got a lead in the case?" Deputy Adam's question broke in to the conversation and let Jazz off the hook from responding to Griffin.

"Kind of. We need to do some more digging." Apparently Griffin was done chewing her out and was now tapping a note into his phone. He barely spared a glance for his deputy. "We need to talk to Casey's friends again. If anyone knows the guy's name it will be one of her girlfriends."

"So there was another guy?" Adam persisted. "But you don't know his name? That's too bad."

Griffin scowled at Adam and then returned his attention to his phone. "A temporary setback. Drop us at the station, okay?"

"Sure, boss. The station. This sure is exciting. A lead in a cold case."

"Can you just drop me at the hotel?" she asked Adam with a smile.

"No, take us to the station," Griffin contradicted. "We're not done yet, Jazz."

He wanted to yell at her some more? Delightful.

"I'm kind of hungry—" she began.

"Don't worry, I'll feed you," he answered smoothly. "We have a lot to discuss."

Shit. Shit. Shit.

Jazz knew exactly what the sexy sheriff wanted to talk about. She'd revealed just a bit too much when questioning Margaret Charlock and now she was going to pay the price.

Whoever said the truth hurts had really hit the nail on the head.

Chapter Eleven

J azz's stomach growled at the intoxicating smell of tomatoes, cheese, and garlic. With barely a word directed toward her, Griffin had picked up his old truck at the station, bundled her in it, stopped off at the only pizza joint in Hope Lake for some takeout, and he was now driving down the main road out of town. Not wanting to rock the boat further, Jazz hadn't asked any questions about where they were going or what they were doing.

At least he was planning to feed her before he killed her.

Pulling off the main drag, Griffin drove slowly down a dark dirt road, the truck jostling her with every dip and pothole. She was just about to ask him where the hell he was taking her when they pulled into a clearing with a darling log cabin at the center. The porch was lit up along with a lamp in the front window.

"How cute," she exclaimed. "Who does this belong to?"

"Me," he answered shortly, grabbing the pizza from the backseat and making a beeline for the house. She pushed open the truck door, muttering under her breath about gentlemanly behavior and stubborn cowboy cops. At the top of the porch stairs, he stopped and whirled around, a frown on his handsome face.

"Did you say something?"

"Uh, no." Jazz shook her head, trying to hide a smile. "Must have been the crickets."

"Right," he snorted and turned back to open the door, switching on a few more lights as he walked to the back of the large room where the kitchen was located.

"You don't lock your door?" she asked, following close on his heels.

For the first time in hours he smiled. "Who's going to break into the sheriff's house?"

"Someone stupid?"

He laughed as he pulled a stack of paper plates out of a cabinet. "They'd have to be. I've got cameras all over the place. I can see what's going on here from my laptop or phone at every minute of the day."

"Paranoid much?"

"Just realistic. My siblings sometimes like to drop in unannounced to go fishing. This way I know what I'm coming home to."

"How many siblings do you have?"

She accepted the two cans of soda he'd pulled from the refrigerator and followed him as he pushed open the sliding glass door to what appeared to be a back deck.

"Nine. Have a seat."

He'd flipped a switch and the large back patio was illuminated with what seemed like a thousand twinkle lights. To her shock, the back of the house overlooked a huge lake that shimmered under the moon and the lamps. It was absolutely beautiful and she sunk down into a chair at the table for six and drank in the peace. There was no sound but a few crickets and the croaking of a frog.

"This is gorgeous but, holy shit, I had no idea there was a lake back here. If the lights were off I could have just walked right into the water without realizing it. I might have drowned."

"I think you're being a tad dramatic." Griffin opened the pizza box and nudged it towards her so she could go first.

Maybe he was more of a gentleman than she'd given him credit for earlier.

Pulling two pieces from the large pie, she bit into the slice and hummed with pleasure. Good pizza.

Griffin smiled at her approval and helped himself to a couple of slices. "The guy that owns the pizza place really knows his stuff, doesn't he?"

She nodded in agreement and they ate in silence until their stomachs were full. Popping open her root beer, she sat back in her chair with a satisfied sigh.

"So you have nine siblings. What was that like?"

She'd always wanted a brother or sister. It would have been nice to have the company, almost like a built-in best friend.

Griffin took a swig of his own soda. "Crowded and loud. There was never enough of anything. Space, food, money, toilet paper. Nothing. It was an economics lesson in the scarcity of resources."

"I'm sure it wasn't that bad," she denied. "It must have been fun having all those brothers and sisters around. I would have loved to have been brought up in a big family."

"Which part do you think was the most fun?" he taunted. "Changing their diapers? Giving them a bottle? Getting stuck at home babysitting when I wanted to be out with my friends? No, wait, it had to be the part where all twelve of us lived in a three bedroom house with one bathroom. It got so bad when my sisters became teenagers that my dad dug an outhouse in the back yard."

Bowled over by his vehemence, she exhaled slowly. "Clearly I've hit a nerve."

"I'm sorry." Griffin's lips twisted into a wry smile. "It's just that everyone thinks that growing up in a big family is like on television with *The Brady Bunch* and *Eight Is Enough*. It's not even close."

"So you don't get along with your family?"

That seemed to surprise him. "I love my family. They're wonderful people. What makes you think I don't get along with them?"

"Um, because you just said growing up was a version of hell?"

He chuckled and stood from his chair, leaning on the deck railing and looking out over the lake. "As long as I don't have to share my bedroom or bathroom, I think my family is awesome. The best. My mom and dad were great parents and we all turned out okay."

"But you had to help out a lot? Were you the oldest?"

Suddenly she wanted to know everything about him. His childhood. His teenage years. Every single detail.

"The third oldest. I had an older brother and sister. Mom just loved babies so she kept having them. Dad must have too, I guess. They used to laugh and say they were fielding a baseball team. They loved us and did their best to make sure we had what we needed. It wasn't easy. Dad owns the auto repair shop in town so we were never rich by any stretch. Mom had been a school teacher but after the first baby she opened a home daycare business in our renovated garage. Lucky me, I got to be around even more kids then."

"Three bedrooms and one bathroom couldn't have been easy," she remarked, trying to draw him out further. "I never thought of myself as lucky not having to share anything."

"It wasn't bad with the first six of us. It was the last four that really squeezed us in. My parents kept saying they were going to buy a new house but they loved living on that piece of property away from town. Then Dad said he was going to build a bigger house, but there always seemed to be other things to do and spend money on. The two youngest still live at home. They have their own rooms so they're probably not in a hurry to move out."

"So they come here to fish? Your brothers and sisters?"

"They come here to escape." Griffin chuckled and tossed his soda can into a garbage pail. "They come here for the same reason I bought this place. Peace and quiet. Can you feel it, Jazz? The whole day falls away when I sit back here in the evening or have my coffee in the morning. Nothing matters but the silence. You can hear yourself think. That's not a common state, honey. And I have it. It belongs to me."

She could feel what he was talking about and how important it was to him. This place did have a magical quality to it that seemed to soothe the soul. She could imagine him sitting out here with a beer after a long, hard day, his feet propped up on the railing, a smile on his face.

She could imagine herself sitting next to him, their hands entwined. Not talking but just absorbing the tranquility.

Don't go there.

Pushing away the intimate thoughts, she instead concentrated on the words he'd left unsaid.

"You couldn't hear yourself think growing up?"

He turned to stare over the lake, his broad shoulders and back facing her. "Rarely. I find that I like living alone. I like having my space. I suppose as a woman that bothers you. I find that most women think that a man alone is a problem."

Pushy know it all alpha male.

"My, oh my, we do make assumptions, don't we?" Jazz laughed at his challenge. He might like to fish, but this little guppy wasn't dumb enough to take the bait. "I think maybe, just maybe you've met the wrong women. As for myself, I have a roommate so I love it when I'm home alone. I love the peace and quiet. Probably because that's all I had growing up."

He turned and crossed his arms over his chest, a smile playing on his lips. "The wrong women, huh? Let me ask you a question. You're dating a guy, okay? And you go back to his place to have sex. When you're done what do you do?" He held up his hand. "Let me answer that question for you. You want to cuddle and then fall asleep. Maybe even talk about your feelings. You steal all the covers and insinuate yourself into the middle of the bed, draping yourself over him so he has to lie still so you can sleep. Then you want to spend the night. That's what you do," he stated.

By the time he'd finished, Jazz was laughing so hard her ribs hurt. Man, Griffin had some issues he needed to work on.

"First of all, I make sure to bring the guy back to my place so I have control of the situation. Second, when we're done I usually hint for him to leave, honestly. I mean, don't get me wrong. Sex is great and everything and I love mixing it up in the middle of the bed, but when it's over it's over. He either needs to go home or we need to retire to our neutral corners of the mattress. I'm not much of a cuddler if you want to know the truth. I'm too fidgety. And I can't sleep with some guy wrapped around me either. Shit, you're like freakin' furnaces and I wake up all sweaty. Yuck."

His shocked expression made her laugh all the harder, her giggles echoing in the dark. He shook his head as if he didn't believe a word she'd said, which he probably didn't.

"That hasn't been my experience. I mean, at all. I'm not sure if you're telling me the truth or saying something you think I want to hear."

"I have no clue what you want to hear," Jazz declared. "But I do know why women do that stuff to you."

His eyebrows shot up and he leaned forward so his palms were flat on the table. "You have my undivided attention. Do tell."

"You're a catch, Sheriff Sawyer. You're gainfully employed. Honest and hard-working, which believe me is damn near impossible to find in a man. You're also tall, dark, and handsome. Shit, I bet you have to beat them off with a stick. These women are trying to become a fixture in your life without you noticing. They want to end your lonely bachelor existence," she said dryly. "They want to get married and make you the groom."

Even in the dim light she could see a dark streak on his cheekbones. She'd embarrassed him.

"I don't make all that much money and my brothers are better-looking than I am."

That was saying something because Griffin Sawyer was hot. Or maybe his personality just made him seem that way. At this point she wasn't sure anymore.

"Fuck, and modest too. I'm surprised the ladies in these parts aren't camped out on your doorstep. Is there anything wrong with you?"

Griffin straightened up and smiled. "Sure is. I don't like women invading my space. I don't like sharing. I don't like taking care of anyone. You know, all those things that people in relationships do."

"You should see someone about that then," she shot back, enjoying his good mood. He didn't take himself too seriously and wasn't conceited in the least. Living in Hollywood she'd known her share of men that were completely stuck on themselves.

"It's not a problem. For me." Griffin shrugged and sat back down at the table across from her. "Now let's talk about your issues."

She'd thought she was home free but he'd only lulled her into a false sense of security.

Jerk.

The tiny little blonde wore an outraged expression much to Griffin's amusement. Despite her questions about his hectic childhood he'd never lost focus of the reason he'd brought her here. They needed to have a chat about her animosity toward Margaret Charlock. If this was going to be a recurring issue during the investigation he needed to know about it now.

"I don't know what you're talking about."

Her cute elfin chin was lifted in bravery but her lips were trembling. She knew exactly what he was talking about and she wasn't leaving here until they had it out.

"Yes, you do," he replied calmly, not budging an inch. "C'mon Jazz, we need to discuss this. I brought you here away from the cameras and the prying eyes of the town so we could talk privately. It's time."

Wringing her hands together, she chewed on her lips and seemed to mull his words over. He stayed quiet letting Jazz gather her thoughts, not hurrying. He'd learned a lot of patience as one of ten children.

"I'm an only child," she finally said, the words coming out in a rush. He'd noticed she did that when she was nervous. He didn't want her to be nervous now but he needed to know what was bothering her.

"Okay," he said slowly, keeping his voice soft. "I figured that when you said you wished you'd grown up in a large family. Was it lonely, Jazz?"

Blinking several times as if to hold back tears, she was quiet again, pondering his question. Eventually she nodded, her gaze going over his shoulder, looking past him and out at the lake.

"Yes. I was alone a lot. Except when I was at school. I had a lot of friends there. I was popular and was involved in the drama club. I liked school."

He digested her words and tried to form a question that sounded non-threatening but still got to the heart of what he needed to know.

"I bet you were popular. A pretty little blonde like you must have had a bunch of boyfriends. Were you a cheerleader?"

She smiled, her gaze still far away, and nodded. "I was. I was senior class vice-president too."

"Prom queen?"

Jazz shook her head but her smile didn't falter. Whatever memories she was thinking about at the moment were good ones. "Abigail Dennis was prom queen. Much prettier than me. And she was senior class *president*."

Griffin heartily doubted that this Abigail person was better looking than Jazz.

He hated to take the smile away but he had a terrible feeling his next statement was going to do exactly that.

"Your parents must have been very proud of you."

Her smile vanished.

"They were busy."

Griffin felt his heart start to ache in sympathy. His Jazz was wearing a sad little expression and it was all he could do not to pull her onto his lap and hold her until she smiled again.

His Jazz? What the fuck was he thinking? She wasn't his any-thing except deputy in training.

"They were too busy for you weren't they, honey?" he asked gently. He could see the parallel lines between Casey's life and Jazz's clearly now. This was why she'd wanted the case. This was why she wanted to bring justice to Casey.

"They should never have had children." Jazz's voice sounded small in the silence. "They loved each other so much there just wasn't anything left for anyone else."

As part of a big family, Griffin knew love wasn't like a pie with bigger and smaller slices handed out to a few lucky people. Love was like a giant rubber band that kept on stretching, making room for everyone. Love compounded on itself expo-nentially. His parents hadn't run out of love with ten children. They'd had more than enough for their family.

"Did they hurt you?" His voice grated and he winced in-wardly at the awkward question as a few tears fell from her eyes.

"No. Never. Not once." Jazz shook her head and the deck lights made her tears shiny on her cheeks. "They just...ignored me. I had all the things I could want. I just didn't have parents. My friends thought it was cool that I had so much freedom. I was jealous that their parents cared what time they came home and who they were with."

Pulling her attention from the lake, she finally looked at him, her expression crumpled. He'd brought this on and he would have to deal with the aftermath, but he'd had no choice.

"I don't remember them ever hugging me." Reflexively, she pulled her knees close to her chest and wrapped her arms around her legs as if to hold herself close. He had to fight the urge to wrap his own arms around her. He swallowed the lump that had taken up residence in his throat upon hearing her sad story. How could her mother and father not adore her? She was everything lovable and then some.

"They weren't cruel." Griffin could see that Jazz felt the need to defend her parents which was normal. She probably blamed herself as children often did when their parents divorce or abuse them. He'd seen it often enough in dysfunctional domestic situations.

"Do you talk to them?"

Jazz shook her head, more tears silently falling. He'd never seen a woman cry so quietly and it made him wonder how many times she'd cried alone in her room so her parents wouldn't hear.

"Father died when I was fifteen and Mother never really recovered. She paid even less attention to me then. As soon as I'd saved enough money after graduation I left for Hollywood. Mother barely noticed. At the beginning I'd call home but she'd make an excuse to end the conversation quickly. She didn't really want to talk to me. She wanted to be left alone. So that's what I did."

A ball of anger lodged itself right in the middle of his chest. Jazz's stupid, self-absorbed parents were idiots. They'd had the love of their daughter and they'd thrown it away. If there was any justice in the world…shit, who was he kidding? He'd been in law enforcement and the military long enough to know that justice – true justice – was a rare thing.

Maybe together they could find some for Casey.

He reached across and swiped at her tears, her skin warm under his fingers. Rising from his chair, he scooped her up into his arms and sat back down with her on his lap. He let her cry, simply rocking her back and forth and stroking her silky hair.

"That's it, honey, cry it all out. Things will look better when you're done."

He didn't know that for sure but his sisters always seemed to feel better after a good cleansing cry. He didn't know why it worked but it did.

Eventually the tears stopped and she sniffled and scrubbed at her cheeks. Her eyes had a liquid sheen to them as she gazed into his for a long time. A connection, tenuous but real, built between them stronger with each passing moment. It pulled at him, tugging him closer to her emotionally and physically. It wasn't a shock when their lips met.

Quicksilver. A frisson of electricity shot to every part of his body, making his hands tremble as he pulled her closer. Her warm but intoxicating scent wrapped around them, making him slightly dizzy while the heat of her body burned through the fabric of his clothes. Instantly every nerve inside of him was awake and vibrating with tension.

He couldn't have said if she'd made the first move or if he had but at this moment it was a meeting of equals. The kiss was a give and take unlike anything he'd experienced. She didn't just receive but delivered a bounty of pleasure as well. She tasted of tomato sauce, garlic, and something that was so intrinsically Jazz he would know it anywhere.

Sixty years from now when he was old and gray he would remember the feel and the taste of one Jazz Oliver. They'd been building towards this moment since that first night he'd help her with the luggage. The kiss was more than momentous. It was inevitable.

And it scared the living bejesus out of him. Not to mention it was wrong. Very wrong.

He pulled away and her fingers tightened on his shoulders for a second before loosening. Their lips parted, their breath coming in ragged gasps. He wondered if her heart was galloping at the same pace as his and decided it was. Her lids were sleepy and her mouth swollen, and she had that well-kissed look that made a man crazy with lust.

He was not immune but he didn't have the luxury of lifting her into his arms and carrying her into his bedroom. It couldn't happen.

Her fingertips traced his chin and jaw, making it difficult for him to speak. Every instinct inside of him was screaming for them to join together in mutual satisfaction. It was a physical pain to reach up and capture her hand, pulling it away so she couldn't touch him.

"Jazz. We can't." His voice sounded like a shovel being dragged across asphalt. He had to push the words past his tight throat.

Her brows pulled together and her head tilted slightly. "What do you mean we can't?"

She was whispering as if there were people or cameras. There was no one to stop him from doing something wrong. He only had himself to make things right.

"You're a deputy in training, honey. I'm practically your boss. It wouldn't be right to take advantage of you that way."

She smiled then, that smile that women got when they knew they were right and the man was wrong. "Maybe I'd be taking advantage of you, Sheriff."

He disentangled himself from her arms, lifting her up and placing her in her own chair. He couldn't think straight when she was so near. His cock was swollen and pressed against his fly and he stood and walked a few steps away to get some much needed space and air.

"Other people wouldn't see it that way, Jazz. I have a professional standard to uphold."

The smile disappeared and her lips pressed together. "A professional standard?" she echoed. "That sounds like bullshit to me. It sounds like you just don't want to get involved. Afraid I'll want to spend the night, Griffin?"

"It's not bullshit." The haze that had wrapped around them was rapidly disappearing, leaving them both raw and unprepared for reality. "I'm the sheriff of this town, honey, and as such I have a leadership role. It wouldn't be right for me to start something with you while you were under my supervision. That shit might not mean anything to you in Hollywood but it means something here. All I have is my integrity."

Jazz hopped to her feet, her breath coming hard and fast. "I hope your integrity keeps you warm at night, Sheriff. Now please take me home."

He'd fucked this up and handled things all wrong. With a past like hers, Jazz would see his pull back as a rejection of all that she was. If she only understood it was far from it. It was one of the hardest things he'd ever done, breaking their kiss and stopping the tidal wave that seemed hell bent on washing them away and into the nearest bed.

"Jazz," he tried again, keeping his voice soft. "I want you, Hollywood. Make no mistake. You're fucking perfect and if things were different I'd make love to you all night long in every way possible. But–"

"Fuck you, Griffin," Jazz interrupted, her voice sounded broken and close to a sob. "I'm not buying whatever it is you're selling. I get the message loud and clear so stop worrying. Let's go."

Without a backward glance, she turned on her heel and disappeared into the house, presumably heading for the front door. Griffin sighed in defeat, vowing this wasn't the last word on the subject. He'd give her time to calm down and then talk to her again. She'd already been emotional talking about her parents and then this. She needed a chance to decompress and calm down.

With a grim sigh, he followed her, grabbing his keys from the kitchen counter on the way out. She was already sitting in his truck by the time he got to the front door. When he swung into the driver's seat, she averted her head so she was staring out of the window.

"You've got this all wrong, honey, and this conversation isn't over. I know it. You know it. And my hard cock and blue balls know it. I didn't want to stop back there."

She didn't reply or even turn to acknowledge his words. Turning the key in the ignition, the engine came to life and he headed back toward the main road.

This wasn't over by a long shot. He'd talk to her again tomorrow and make her understand. Just because he wanted something didn't mean he could reach out and grab it whenever it suited him. Grown men didn't do that. Real men respected boundaries.

And right now there was a giant fence with a "no entry" sign on Jazz Oliver.

Chapter Twelve

Jazz sat down on one of the benches that ran alongside the obstacle course and shielded her eyes from the bright sun. It was competition day on the show and each contestant was going to run the course. For real. The person with the best time couldn't be eliminated this week. Right now, Danny was chatting with Sandy while Levi and Wayne hung out near the tent.

Griffin was trying to corral the large crowd that had come to watch today. Every day the crowd had grown larger and today was no exception. Every deputy Griffin had was on duty and a neighboring sheriff from another town had even given a few men on loan. It was easy to see that Griffin was not happy with the loud, raucous throngs that had taken over his town. For a man that loved his peace and quiet this had to be hell.

Tony and Gordon were working the crowd, trying to get them excited and cheering for the contestants. Hoping neither of them noticed that Jazz was alone, she tried to not capture anyone's attention, ducking her head and pretending to tie her shoes. She knew the producer and his assistant wanted to know what was going on between her and the sheriff. One minute things had been warming up and now it was a veritable arctic zone.

The last few days had been excruciatingly awkward between Jazz and Griffin. She knew it was all her own fault but she always had trouble admitting when she was wrong. This time wasn't any exception to that.

He'd tried to explain the next morning, but still upset after a sleepless night she'd shut him down quickly. She'd known she gone too far when his expression closed and his gray eyes turned flinty and cold. He was pissed as hell at her stubborn attitude.

And she didn't know how to make it better. Once she'd calmed down and realized he had a point about them getting involved it had been too late. She'd screwed up and now he thought she was a real bitch.

"God, it's hot out here."

Sandy plopped down on the bench next to Jazz, a bottle of water pressed to her forehead.

"It is warm today. I'll be glad when this is over," Jazz replied awkwardly. She liked Sandy just fine but had found the two of them had little in common. Their conversations this week had grown shorter, especially as Sandy had begun to spend more time with Danny and Wayne. Jazz had found she had more of a rapport with Levi and Peggy.

"This whole thing is just stupid." Stupid was one of Sandy's favorite words. The bus ride was stupid, the hotel was stupid, the food was stupid. And so on.

"It's just the first of many challenges. I think we're all going to be disappointed today except for Levi. He's probably going to win."

Sandy gave Jazz a smug mile and leaned back on the bench. "I'm not worried."

Jazz frowned, not understanding Sandy's nonchalance. After her performance today she should be concerned. "We all need to be worried if we don't win."

"I'm not going anywhere," Sandy declared with a giggle and then pranced away toward a cameraman.

"Wait—"

"Are you ready, Jazz?"

Deputy Dare's voice broke into Jazz's query. It was the deputy's last day of work and he'd been thoroughly embarrassed with a gigantic cake at the sheriff's station. There had been a lot of back slapping and funny stories told but all in all everyone seemed sorry for him to go. Dare included. She didn't know what he had planned but he had the demeanor of a man that was headed to war or something like it.

"I'm ready. Any advice?"

Jazz tugged on the leather gloves that would keep her palms from being ripped to shreds and steeled herself for the challenge. She'd need a miracle to beat Levi but stranger things had happened.

"Yeah, keep your ass down when you crawl under the net."

She glanced over her shoulder at her generous curves and grinned. "I'll do my best but I can't promise anything."

She would have sworn on her own life that the surly deputy almost smiled. Instead he nodded and escorted her to the starting line. Sandy, Danny, and Wayne had already made their runs posting fairly lousy final scores. Jazz had a real chance if she could edge out Peggy. Levi was easily the frontrunner today and he would be going last.

"Don't be in too much of a hurry and be careful," Dare said as she stretched her muscles in readiness. She was anxious for this to be over. "The penalties are what killed the others so having a clean run will help you. Got it?"

She nodded and focused ahead of her, waiting for the starter's pistol. Her heart was beating a mile a minute and she only hoped she could run that fast.

"On your mark. Get set."

A loud blast in her ears and she was off. Diving to the ground, she remembered to keep her ass low and she easily cleared the first obstacle. Focusing her energy, she smoothly moved to the next, careful not to incur a penalty. Everything she'd learned in the last week came together and she crossed the finish line feeling like she'd won. She'd given it all she had, holding nothing back.

She was sucking in air when Deputy Dare walked up next to her. "Great run, Jazz. That's a personal best for you. Here's some water."

He handed her a cold bottle and headed off to the starting line where Peggy was waiting to take her turn. Gulping down half of the bottle, Jazz collapsed on the bench, her elbows on her knees. Levi smiled and sat down next to her.

"Wow, you were amazing. That was awesome."

In the last week she'd learned several things. One was that Sheriff Griffin Sawyer was like no man she'd ever met. Honest, good, and hardworking. A man a woman could depend on. The second thing she'd learned was that Levi was cut from the very same cloth. He was currently in the middle of a nasty divorce, and for the life of her Jazz couldn't think of a single reason a woman would want to rid herself of a great guy like him.

He said it was because he didn't have any money. Jazz simply thought the woman was crazy. Just like Griffin, Levi was a catch.

"Thanks. I wanted to give you some competition." She laughed and set her now empty water bottle on the ground.

Levi grinned and patted her hand. "You did that and then some. I'm going to have to run my best today. That's the way it should be."

"Couldn't let you just waltz away with the win."

Levi lifted his gaze to the other competitors and gave her a wry smile. "You're someone I wouldn't mind losing to, Jazz. You've worked damn hard this week."

"So have you." She paused before plowing forward into 'none of her business land.' "You really want this deputy job, don't you? I mean really, not just the money or the recognition. You want the job."

His expression grew serious and he nodded. "I do. This is my chance for a new start. I did everything I was supposed to and it didn't work out. I studied hard, got good grades, went to a good school, and then got a good job that paid well. Married a beautiful woman, got the house in the suburbs and the three car garage. That's where it all went bad. Next thing I know my software job has been shipped overseas. Then the two subsequent jobs, the same. Wife gets tired of financial instability and leaves, cleaning me out. House goes into foreclosure and the wife sleeps with my best friend. He's employed." Levi rubbed his chin and shook his head, but he didn't look bitter despite everything that he'd been through. "I'm tired of chasing the supposed American dream. It's time for my dream. When I was a kid I used to pretend to be a cop, now I have a real chance to be one. This is my shot."

His reasons sounded so much better than her own. If he'd asked her why she wanted to win, what could she say?

I want to be a star.

So people will love and approve of me like my mommy and daddy never did.

Jazz wasn't naive or stupid. She knew why she was doing the acting thing. She loved the applause and the adulation. Inside she was still that little girl trying to get her parents' approval. Funny thing, it had never occurred to her at eighteen there might be a better and easier way to get that love and approval, but she was thinking about it now. Look at the lengths she was willing to go to for this dream. Would it be worth it?

Somehow she doubted it.

"You're up, Levi."

Griffin was standing up in front of them, or at least his worn cowboy boots were. She let her gaze wander up his tall frame all the way to his handsome face. He was wearing his usual cowboy hat that shaded his features but she could see his expression was guarded as if she might go into a tirade right then and there.

"Good luck, Levi," Jazz said as he bounded to his feet, a smile on his face. If she couldn't win she sure wouldn't mind if he did. He deserved it, really.

"Thanks, Jazz. I'm off."

Levi jogged towards the starting line and Griffin turned to walk away as well.

"Wait. Griffin, I need to talk to you, okay?"

He halted and lowered himself onto the bench not saying a word. The ball was in her court.

"Listen, I'm sorry. Really sorry. I can be a real bitch sometimes and the other night was one of those. I didn't understand in the moment but I get what you were saying. I just wasn't very happy about it."

He didn't look at her, his eyes following the line of people crowded around the course. "I wasn't happy about it either."

He wasn't going to make this easy.

"Are you mad?"

A corner of his mouth tilted up. "Nope."

"You aren't saying much."

This time he turned to look at her. "There isn't much to say, is there? I'm not mad. I'm frustrated. Sexually and otherwise. But this game has to play out before anything can happen."

"Maybe I'll get voted off tomorrow night."

There was a part of her that hoped she would. It would free them from the confines of a professional relationship and plunge them into a personal one. But if she did get voted off, she couldn't win, probably wouldn't get any acting jobs, and to top it off wouldn't help find Casey's killer.

Shit.

"You don't mean that." Griffin was shaking his head in denial. "I know you want to win."

"Two hundred and fifty thousand would be life changing for me," she replied, thinking of the acting lessons she could take with that kind of cash. She had a feeling making love with Griffin would be life changing as well. She certainly wasn't going to be the same when she got back home no matter what happened between them.

"For most people." Griffin chuckled before standing and nodding towards the course. "Watch."

The starter gun went off and Levi flew off the line. Jazz watched in awe as he easily navigated every obstacle and crossed the finish line. No one had to tell her he'd won and was safe. It was clearly obvious. Levi was one step closer to his second chance.

And Jazz?

She was one step closer to possible elimination.

The good news was Jazz didn't hate Griffin anymore. The bad news was nothing was going to change in the near future. Tony and Gordon, who seemed connected at the hip these days, had walked up to Griffin eating breakfast at the diner and told him that it was Sandy who had been voted out.

If Griffin's cock and balls had been voting things might have been much different. As it was, blue was going to be the color of the day. Again.

He shouldn't be unhappy that she was still in the game. This was what she wanted. Her dream was on the line from what she'd told him. Winning meant a lot to her and he wasn't about to start rooting against her. He truly wanted her to be happy.

But what had seemed so clear a week ago was looking much different now. Just seven days ago his biggest problem had been a loss of quiet and privacy. Now his best deputy had quit, his town was overrun with loud, rude looky-loos, and his nuts were in a knot all because of a pretty blonde with a great smile.

"Buy me breakfast?"

That smile was standing right in front of him and his heart lurched in his chest.

Fuck.

"Sure." Griffin nodded and she slid into the booth opposite him looking beautiful this morning. Not appearing to be wearing a shred of makeup, she still managed to look pretty with her big blue eyes and dimpled cheeks.

"I saw Tony on the way in." Studying the menu, she didn't meet his gaze. "He asked to talk to Sandy. Does that mean what I think it means?"

Sandy had come in dead last in the obstacle course the day before but hadn't seemed to mind in the least. She'd joined Danny at the local watering hole where the two of them had drowned their sorrows with beer and whisky right along with a late arriving Wayne. All three of them had done poorly in the challenge and they all knew they were on the chopping block.

"It does. Tony and Gordon just told me. How is Sandy this morning? Adam said she, Danny, and Wayne closed down the bar last night."

"Surprisingly alert. She met up with me as I was walking here this morning. Said she was hungry."

"I doubt she'll be shocked or anything," Griffin assured her. "She had to see this coming."

"I'm not sure about that. She was really cheery when I saw her. Happy, like she didn't have a care in the world. She was like that on the day of the competition too. Said she wasn't worried."

"Maybe she's decided she doesn't want to compete anymore. She—"

Whatever he'd been about to say was drowned out by yelling coming from right outside the diner. Tony, Gordon, and Sandy were standing on the sidewalk right in front of the big window in full view of the diners and half the town screaming at one another. Sandy waved her arms, wildly gesticulating, while Tony and Gordon's faces turned purple. Whatever was being said, it was clear that Sandy was not taking the news well.

"Uh oh," Jazz intoned. "This is bad. Very bad."

It took her a minute to realize she was talking to no one and Griffin was up and out of the booth. He hit the door moving fast and stepped between Sandy and the producers, pushing them further apart. She couldn't hear exactly what he was saying but she could hear the deep commanding tones he used whenever he was in full-control mode. It worked like a charm and voices quieted although Sandy didn't look any happier. Jazz thought the young woman would look sad but if anything she looked angry. Clearly she'd never believed she was going to be voted off.

Whatever Griffin was saying seemed to penetrate the emotions and the three of them headed down the sidewalk walking briskly. Griffin re-entered the diner and scowled at the crowd that had gathered around the window.

"Sit the hell down," he barked. "There's nothing to see."

He was still mumbling under his breath when he sat back down. "People have plumb lost their damn minds in this town."

"And it's all our fault," she added with a grin, trying to get him to smile.

He rolled his eyes and smiled as the waitress filled his coffee cup and took their orders. Pancakes for her, and bacon and eggs for him.

"It's not all your fault," he finally conceded when they were alone again.

"But most of it is."

This time he smiled widely. "Yeah, most of it is." He sipped his coffee and eyed her over the rim. "What are you doing today?"

Jazz shrugged. She hadn't thought far into the future considering it could have been her given the old heave-ho this morning. She probably needed to study her handbook but wasn't really looking forward to that.

"What did you have in mind?"

"Tony and Gordon are going to be busy shooting Sandy's exit today. I thought you and I could drive over to Corville and question Casey's old boyfriend, Buddy. What do you say?"

"I say yes. When do we leave?" she asked eagerly. If she couldn't have Griffin, then maybe she could help solve the cold case.

"After breakfast," he laughed. "And I have to make a stop along the way—I hope that's okay."

"Sure it is. Where are we stopping?"

"My parents' house. My dad needs a hand fixing a few shingles on the roof. It shouldn't take long. A few nails and we'll be on our way. I would do it before I picked you up but their place is on the way. It would save us an hour."

Not willing to admit she was dying to meet his family, she smiled in agreement. "Then it only makes sense. We'll stop off there first."

"Thanks for being so flexible."

Jazz dumped some sugar into her coffee. "That's me. Flexible. Does Buddy know we're coming, by the way?"

"No, and I'd like to keep it that way. I've talked to the sheriff over there, Logan Wright. He's the one who told me where Buddy was working and hanging out these days. He knows we're coming into his jurisdiction and he agrees that it's best if we surprise Buddy."

"Lucky guy," Jazz joked.

"If he was lucky he never would have gotten into this situation to begin with. No, I'd say Buddy Meltreeger is one unlucky son of a bitch. And until we find Casey's killer, this cloud of suspicion is going to hang over him for the rest of his life."

"Then let's go find out who did it."

Winning the competition was becoming less and less important with each passing moment. Higher priority was bringing Casey's murderer to justice. Spending more time with Griffin wouldn't be all bad either.

Especially if they were naked.

Chapter Thirteen

Griffin snagged his keys from the top of his desk, hurrying to meet Jazz at his truck. He was anxious to talk to Buddy and see if they could learn anything new from him. Perhaps he'd known Casey had been seeing another guy.

"Boss, you're going to want to see this." Adam was holding up a magazine in the air. Griffin sighed with frustration. Adam was a good deputy but he seemed to think that Griffin was interested in the same things. He didn't give a shit about the latest royal gossip or what Brangelina was doing these days.

"I'm on my way out, Adam. Can it wait?" Griffin tucked his sunglasses in his shirt pocket and moved toward the door.

"I don't think so. There's an article in this magazine about you and Jazz. Well, really about the entire town and the show. I think you better take a look."

"What?" Griffin roared, snatching the glossy pages from Adam's fingers. A quick perusal of the photos and contents, and Griffin's worst fears were realized. Someone was giving this rag information about the show and the contestants. The real stars of the article appeared to be himself and Jazz though. There was a large color photo of them standing close together with a lurid headline about him, her, and a pair of handcuffs.

White-hot anger burned inside of him and his fingers crumpled the papers before tossing them into the trash. It was where shit like that belonged. He dug his wallet out of his back pocket and shoved some cash into Adam's hand.

"Go buy every fucking copy you can find."

His deputy looked down at the money and then up at Griffin. "Um, boss, will it really make any difference? Those magazines are all over the country and probably online too. Buying them up in town isn't going to matter."

"Just fucking do it."

Adam scuttled out the front door of the station shaking his head. Griffin knew he was being unreasonable but he didn't know how to handle the overwhelming fury coupled with the total inability to control the situation. He was helpless to do a fucking thing about it, and could only sit back and watch this nightmare unfold.

Griffin retrieved the wadded up tabloid from the trash. He was going to take great pleasure in shoving it up Otis McClintock's ass. Maybe Tony's too.

Everything Griffin had predicted was coming true.

Griffin stomped out of the station, his expression like black thunderclouds. Jazz watched him yank open the driver's side door and slide in next to her, slamming it shut with a growl. Whatever he was pissed about had happened in the fifteen minutes since she'd last seen him. He'd been fine when he walked out of the diner.

He tossed a crumpled up magazine on the seat between them and fired up the engine, throwing the truck into gear. She reached for the ball of paper, smoothing it out so she could see if this was the source of his fury. One look and she knew that it was. A picture of the two of them was front and center along with a suggestive headline. A week ago she would have given her right arm for publicity like this.

Today all she could feel was ashamed of her industry. Griffin Sawyer was a private man and this had to be sheer torture for him.

"I'm sorry," she said softly.

He slammed on the brakes and she had to brace herself on the dashboard, the seatbelt snapping her back in her seat. Luckily they were on the open road, the town a half a mile behind them.

"Did you do this?" he asked incredulously, his cheeks red with anger. "You sold me out for...what, Jazz? Some fame? A part in some movie?"

"No!" she exclaimed, placing her hand on his thigh, squeezing the hard muscles. "No! I didn't do it. I swear. I was only saying that I'm sorry it happened to you, that's all. Honest, Griffin."

She felt his tense muscles relax under her palm and he scraped his arm across his grim features. This was one unhappy man and Jazz didn't have a clue how to make things better.

His head fell back on the seat and she heard him exhale slowly as if trying to control his emotions. "I'm sorry I blew up like that. I know you wouldn't do this to me."

"Did you think I had?" It hurt to ask the question but she had to know.

Griffin shook his head before sitting up and putting the truck back in gear. "No, it never occurred to me until you said you were sorry. Then I flew off the handle."

The truck picked up speed and Griffin looked calmer although still upset. "Do you know who leaked this stuff?"

His lips were tight and he didn't answer for a long moment. "I assume it was Tony and Gordon. For publicity."

"I don't think it was Tony." Jazz shook her head as she paged through the story and pictures. "I heard him talking to Caitlin – my roommate – once about the editor of this particular journalistic tome. Tony can't stand him. I don't see that he would give someone he hates an exclusive."

"Then who?" A muscle was working in Griffin's jaw.

"A contestant? Maybe someone from the town? Could have been someone in the crew as well. Is it important? It's done and out there. There's nothing you can do about it."

Griffin was shaking his head. "No one from town would have those kinds of contacts. At least I don't think they do. And it's not over and done with. I could sue."

"On what grounds? You're on a television show. That makes you a public figure. You can't sue them for invasion of privacy."

"I could sue them for libel. They're making it sound like we're involved," he said grimly.

"Griffin." Jazz used a gentle tone, not wanting to rouse his ire further. "They didn't make anything up. There is this…thing that's between us. You can see it in this picture. It's what Tony and Gordon were talking about." She paused, not sure what words to use. "It shows."

Griffin rubbed his temples with his left hand, letting his right hand rest on the wheel. "Shit, I know. But goddammit, I never wanted to be a public figure. It's out of hand, Jazz, and I can't stop it."

That was what this was really about. He'd lost control and an alpha control freak like Griffin wouldn't like this one little bit.

"You're right, you can't," she agreed, using her best no non-sense tone. "All you can do is ignore it and go about your business."

He grunted and shifted in his seat. "Easy for you to say. This has probably happened to you before. Hell, you're probably glad it happened. This helps you, doesn't it?"

He didn't sound accusing. He sounded more exhausted than anything.

"I've never been in a tabloid before. And yes, this could help me. But I still wish it hadn't happened. I don't want to get something at your expense. I'm not that selfish."

"I wasn't saying that you were, but this is a good thing for you, right? Honestly, I'm not trying to be a jerk. I'm sincerely asking because I'd like to think that something good is coming from this fiasco."

"I admitted it could help me, but I'm still not happy about it. I know this sucks for you."

She put every ounce of sincerity she could into her voice and he must have heard it. His entire body seemed to relax and the corners of his mouth quirked up.

"I hope you get the role of your dreams from this, Jazz. I really do."

She believed him, but suddenly she was having a great deal of trouble even picturing that part of her dream. Hollywood seemed very far away at the moment. Just a fuzzy image in the back of her mind.

She'd heard you could get lost in La La Land and start thinking it was real. Now that she had some distance, she could see that nothing she'd been doing in Los Angeles had been all that real or important. What she was doing now might be the most important thing she'd ever done in her entire life.

"We'll see. Now tell me more about your family." Jazz wanted to change the subject. "Will I meet your parents today?"

"You will. As for what I could tell you, I don't know. You can ask them anything you want when we get there although I doubt you'll get a word in. Mom will be talking your ear off wanting to know about Hollywood and if you've met Channing Tatum."

Laughter bubbled from Jazz's lips. "Never met him but he is hot. Is he your mother's favorite?"

"She's seen that *Magic Mike* movie a hundred times," Griffin groaned. "It's embarrassing as hell. My sisters come over and they crowd around the TV."

"I think I'm going to like your family. They sound fun."

"You have a strange idea of fun, Hollywood."

"Probably, and I like it when you call me that, by the way."

"Call you what?" Griffin turned down a dirt road lined with trees and slowed way down due to the ruts in the road.

"Hollywood. You'd think it would sound condescending, but when you say it, not so much."

Pulling up in front of a ranch style home with white siding and pink and red flowers in the yard, Griffin put the truck in park and twisted around so he was facing her.

"I need to watch my mouth. I don't want to say that in front of other people, but I can't seem to help myself."

"That's because I'm sugar sweet," she said, tongue firmly in cheek.

Griffin chuckled and pulled on the door handle, letting the hot summer breeze into the truck.

"You can't even act sugar sweet which is just fine by me. I think that kind of a woman would be boring."

"And I'm not boring?" Jazz let him open her truck door and help her down. An older version of Griffin was coming out of the garage waving and smiling. He could only be Griffin's dad.

"Far from it." He captured her fingers with his own and a tingle shot up her arm and to further places south. "Come meet my folks."

It felt very intimate but somehow right to be here with him meeting his mom and dad. But then so far everything felt right with this man. It was going to be a long twelve weeks if she lasted until the end of the show. Slowly but surely she was falling for him. Lord knew she admired him too. She'd never in a million years thought she'd meet anyone remotely like him. Hadn't even thought they really existed if she were honest.

But he was all too real.

Griffin's parents were everything Jazz could have hoped for and more. Liam Sawyer had slapped Griffin on the back, shook Jazz's hand, and then promptly put his son to work on the roof. The mother, Linda Sawyer, had salt and pepper hair but was still quite attractive. It was easy to see where Griffin got his devastating good looks. If he looked half as good as his father when he was in his sixties...holy Toledo. The family should have all become actors or models with their strong bone structure and easy smiles.

Jazz and Linda were sitting on the front porch drinking lemonade and chatting while Liam shouted directions from the ground up to Griffin on the roof. From the increasing brevity of Griffin's answers, it sounded like he was getting tired of being bossed around. Apparently Liam was well aware of it because after the last order, he'd given Jazz and Linda a wink and a grin.

"How long will you be in Hope Lake?" Linda asked, offering another cookie. Jazz was always watching her weight but they were the best damn oatmeal cookies she'd ever tasted. She simply couldn't resist.

"Another eleven weeks if I make it to the end of the show. Even if I get voted off I might hang around. The producers want everyone to stick fairly close to this general area. We're all in the finale show."

Linda's green eyes twinkled and she had a knowing smile. "Hang around here? Not much going on compared to California."

The banging of the hammer overhead stopped and Jazz heard Griffin swear under his breath.

"Oh, I don't know about that. There's one or two interesting things." Jazz looked up at the porch ceiling and smiled.

"Good luck." Linda leaned forward and whispered. "My boy is a hard case. I fear that it's our fault."

"He definitely has a few issues," Jazz whispered back. "But he's a good man. You did a good job, Mrs. Sawyer."

"Thank you, and call me Linda, please."

"I will, thank you. These cookies are criminally good. The best I've ever had."

"I'll give you the recipe," Linda beamed at the praise.

"I don't really cook much for myself."

"I'd take her up on that offer. Those cookies are famous in five counties and she keeps that recipe under tighter control than the gold at Fort Knox." Griffin had come down from the roof and was standing on the porch. Damn if he didn't just about bring her to her knees. At some point he'd stripped off his shirt and the hammer hanging from his belt loop pulled his jeans low on his hip bones. His shoulders, slick with sweat, were muscled and wide and his abs were tight with ridges that made her want to trace them with her tongue. She couldn't stop her gaze from wandering just a tad further south and her mouth went dry at the impressive bulge behind his fly.

She ran her suddenly sweaty palms down her jeans and then lifted her heavy hair off of her damp neck. Griffin was watching her closely waiting for her to say something.

What were they talking about?

Cookies.

"Then I better take that recipe." Jazz had to drag her gaze away from Griffin's half naked body to be able to form sentences again. "Thank you."

Man, she had it bad. In her entire life she'd never lusted after a man the way she did this one. If this went on for another eleven weeks she'd be a drooling, mumbling mess.

"I'm going to go clean up, then Jazz and I can get on the road. We have a lot to do today." Griffin grinned and headed toward the door but stopped right next to her.

Leaning down, he whispered only for her to hear, "Saw you look."

Whistling a lilting tune, he tromped into the house with Jazz still sitting there with a scarlet face and a racing heart. She couldn't imagine what Linda and Liam must think of her.

"Can I give you some advice?" Linda asked. "You look like you could use it."

Jazz nodded slowly but a trifle unsure she was making the right decision. It might be advice she'd rather not hear.

"You're going to have to toughen up if Griffin's the one you want. He's one of ten and they were all hard on each other growing up. Teasing became a sport to those kids. You're going to have to get a thick skin because he's one of the better ones at it."

Was he the one she wanted? She definitely wanted him, but *the one?* That was simply setting herself up for heartache.

"I don't think he wants to be the one." Jazz answered by deflecting Linda's advice back on Griffin. She wasn't ready to inspect her own feelings and motivations that closely. Not today. Maybe never.

Linda snorted and waved her lemonade glass. "He doesn't know what he wants. He thinks his life is perfect just the way it is. What it is is empty," she stated, slapping the glass down on the table. "If you want him you're going to have to play his game. Give him what he thinks he wants, Jazz. He'll find out that it's not pretty quick. The problem is he's spoiled."

Liam, obviously a wise man, had disappeared somewhere into the garage leaving Linda and Jazz all alone.

"Spoiled? He doesn't seem spoiled at all to me," Jazz denied. "In fact he's one of the best men I've ever met. Honest, loyal and all that stuff."

"I didn't mean that way," Linda replied, her voice dry. "I meant by women. They dance to his tune because they want him to fall in love with them. What they don't realize is he will never fall for a woman who does that. He needs a woman who doesn't make things too easy. And no, I am not talking about sex."

Her cheeks grew warm and Jazz's fingers tightened on her glass. She didn't want Griffin to fall in love with her. "I think you've misunderstood my relationship with your son. It's not serious or anything. I'll be going back to Los Angeles eventually."

The thought made her miserable though. Nothing there glittered anymore the way it had before she came here.

"I don't think so but if that's how you want to play it, we will." Linda sipped at her lemonade and reached for another cookie. "So tell me what you'll do when you get back home."

Jazz and Linda spent the rest of the visit talking about movies, television, and Jazz's roommate Caitlin. Linda knew who she was as she watched the soap opera Caitlin was currently in. The time passed quickly, and before she knew it Griffin had joined them once again.

"Ready to go?" She watched as he drank down a large glass of lemonade practically in one gulp and grabbed several cookies.

"I'll get a bag for you." Linda slapped at her son's hand but her face was smiling. Jazz couldn't help but feel a tightening in her chest at the love she saw between mother and son. It was an expression Jazz had often dreamed of being on her own mother's face.

That dream had long passed.

Jazz stood quickly, suddenly feeling like she needed to go. Seeing this close, happy family unit had been harder on her than she'd bargained for.

"I'm ready," she said, brushing off the crumbs from her jeans and avoiding Griffin's gaze. She didn't need to be interrogated by him at the moment and those gray eyes saw way too much.

"Then we should get on the road," he agreed, accepting the plastic bag of cookies from his mother. He leaned down and kissed her cheek and she gave him a big hug.

"Try to come to Sunday dinner and bring this charming young lady with you."

"I will if you make fried chicken." Griffin put his hand on the small of her back to lead her down the stairs. Her skin tingled through the fabric where it touched and her pulse skipped a beat.

He helped her into the truck and she tried to control the heat that swept through her body at his very nearness. Her knees almost buckled as the scent of his skin wrapped around her.

The one? Did she really want Griffin Sawyer to be the one? He wasn't even looking for the one.

What an ugly freakin' mess she'd walked right into, all because she wanted to be a star.

Chapter Fourteen

"Buddy Meltreeger has been keeping his nose clean since Casey Charlock's death," said Sheriff Logan Wright. Griffin and Jazz were sitting in his comfortable living room and drinking iced tea. "No more speeding up and down Main Street. No more closing down the bars on Friday and Saturday nights. It appears he doesn't want to bring himself to my attention."

Jazz kept sneaking looks between Griffin and Logan over the rim of her glass. While Logan was all blond and blue eyed gorgeous with a gleam of the devil inside, Griffin was the epitome of tall, dark, and sexy with the aura of hardworking and responsible. They were like opposite sides of a really hot coin.

"Logan, Mark is not behaving." A female voice from the hallway made all three of them turn their heads. "Melissa is tearing her hair out."

An attractive brunette stood in the doorway, her own hair askew. A pencil was stuck into her ponytail and there was some sort of stain on her t-shirt that was paired with plaid pajama pants. She looked like she hadn't slept in days.

"Are Mark and Melissa your kids?" asked Jazz, wondering if the poor woman had been up with sick children the last few nights.

Logan grinned and stood to wrap his arms comfortingly around the woman. "Mark and Melissa are our fictional characters and sometimes they give Ava a hard time." He winked at Jazz and Griffin before kissing the obviously lucky woman on the forehead. It was clear he adored her. Stain or no stain. "She's almost done with this book and on a deadline. Honey, you need to get some rest. They're not going to behave until you do."

"I only have about twenty thousand words left," Ava replied, her eyes looked a little unfocused. "I can't stop now."

"If you want those words to make any sense you'll go to bed right now and get some rest."

Ava looked indecisive, but apparently Logan knew how to handle her. "If you sleep now, I promise to make you some pizza and cheesecake for when you wake up."

"I am tired." She smiled and headed back down the hallway leaving a grinning Logan in her wake.

He settled back down on the couch. "Sorry about that. It gets a little weird around here when Ava's getting to the end of a book. I'm used to it but I'm sure it looks strange to others."

"Your wife is a writer? That's so cool. I've always wanted to do that," Jazz enthused.

"She is, and a damn good one too. She'd be happy to talk to you about it when she's done with the book," Logan offered. "Maybe she can give you some tips."

"I wouldn't want to bother her," Jazz protested but Logan waved her worry away.

"She loves doing it. Talking about writing is almost as much fun for her as actually writing. I'll give Griffin a call when she's done and maybe we can have you guys over for dinner."

Feeling her cheeks warm, she ignored the intimation that she and Griffin were a couple.

"That's very kind of you," she replied instead.

"You should have known Logan before he married Ava. Kind is not how you would have described him," Griffin laughed.

Looking at the stunningly handsome sheriff, Jazz had a few ideas of the adjectives she might have used.

"Perhaps I would have described him the same way I describe you," she teased.

Logan laughed, the sound booming in the air while Griffin frowned. "She's got your number, Griff. You may have met your match."

Griffin growled but didn't say much else. Jazz was actually coming to like his stubborn, ornery growls. He only used them when he didn't have the words to express himself.

It was kind of cute. Like a giant, sexy teddy bear.

"Anyway, do you need me to go with you when you question Buddy?"

Griffin shook his head and finished off his iced tea. "It's your day off. Besides, I think you promised pizza and cheesecake not five minutes ago. I'd hate to be you if Ava wakes up and there's none here."

Logan stretched out his long legs. "She's going to sleep probably through morning. She's been up for about thirty-six hours straight. I have time to run to the store and there's a great new bakery in town. I'll pick up a cheesecake there."

"I think we'll be okay on our own. I'll call you if I need you. Deal?" Griffin stood and Jazz followed suit. She was ready to finally talk to Buddy and find out his story. Did he know that Casey had been seeing someone else?

"Deal. Let me know if there's anything else I can do."

Jazz and Griffin bade Logan goodbye, hopped into the truck, and got back on the road. No words were spoken during the drive and only the sounds from the radio kept it from being completely silent. She wasn't used to being with someone who didn't talk. About themselves. All the time.

"You're very quiet. Is anything wrong?"

He flashed her a smile before turning his attention back to the road. "No. Should there be? I'm a quiet guy, honey. I only speak when I have something to say. When I do have something to say, believe me, nothing will stop me."

She thought about that for a minute and decided she liked it. It was straightforward, just like him. No drama.

"And you don't have anything to say now? Not even about Logan giving you a hard time?" she teased.

"Logan gives everyone a hard time. It wasn't that long ago he was known as the biggest male whore in Southern Montana—hell, maybe the entire state. Now that he's a happily married man, he likes to act like his past never happened and that he's pure as an angel's tear."

Jazz giggled at the image he painted. "Uh, nothing about Logan makes me think he's innocent. He may be married but he's got bad boy written all over him. Or former bad boy in his case."

"Do I look like a bad boy?" Griffin was laughing as he pulled into the parking lot of a local coffee shop.

"Not in the least," Jazz answered instantly. "You're the guy in the movies that everyone follows when the shit hits the fan. A born leader."

He rubbed his chin and contemplated her words. "I think I like that. Does that guy get everyone to safety?"

"As many as he can. Sometimes he has to sacrifice himself though."

"Don't like the sound of that." He put the truck in park and pushed open the door. "Are you in the mood for a fancy coffee?"

"I guess." Jazz shrugged and frowned as he came around to her side of the truck to help her out. "I thought we were going to talk to Buddy. What are we doing here?"

"Buddy has a weekend job here according to Logan. If I've timed this just right, he should be getting off work in about fifteen minutes."

"Is there anything else I don't know?" she asked as they entered the dimly lit establishment. Several tables were filled with people tapping away at their laptops while others lounged on overstuffed couches. The muted sounds of their conversations mingled with the clinking of glassware and the occasional ring of the bell over the door.

"Yep, and you're about to find out." Griffin placed his hand under her elbow and led her to a small table in the far corner. They settled into chairs and a young man bustled over to take their order. "I like fancy coffee drinks."

"Can I—Oh shit, not again," the young man groaned. "Why can't you leave me alone?"

"I'll have an iced white chocolate mocha with the dark chocolate shavings on the top. Jazz?"

"Uh, the same?" Griffin looked like completely unperturbed at the negative vibes rolling off Buddy Meltreeger. He looked slightly more mature than the photo in the case file, but all in all he hadn't changed much.

"Listen, I'm not getting you anything," Buddy hissed, leaning forward. "Get out of here and leave me alone. I didn't do anything."

"We want to talk to you," Griffin replied reasonably. "If you didn't do it, you need to help us find who did. Otherwise this is going to follow you around for the rest of your life. Do you want that? I want whoever did this. I don't have anything personal against you, Buddy."

Several expressions flitted across Buddy's face until he got to acceptance. Finally he nodded. "I get off work in a few minutes. I'll talk to you then."

"Don't forget our coffee," Griffin reminded him.

The young man's eyebrows shot up in surprise. "You were serious? Dude, teenage girls come in after school and order that drink. You really want that one?"

If the remark bothered Griffin it didn't show. "I'm secure enough in my manhood." He held up two fingers. "We'll both have one."

Buddy shuffled back behind the counter and Jazz took in Griffin's smug expression. "I guess I did learn something I didn't know before. You have the coffee palate of an adolescent cheerleader."

"So?" Griffin asked with a grin. "As for my beverage choice, I have a bit of a sweet tooth."

"A bit? That drink is going to have so much sugar in it I'm going to have to run a marathon to burn off the calories. I don't normally eat or drink things that have that many calories in them."

"Why?" He looked genuinely confused. "You had cookies today."

"I'm an actress. The camera adds ten pounds."

His heated gaze ran up and down her body sending warmth straight to her toes and fingers. "You'd look just fine if you gained ten pounds."

"I'm considered fat for an actress," she sighed, knowing it was back to rice cakes and grilled chicken breast tomorrow.

Letting herself go while she was here was a bad idea. It would just make it all the harder when she got home.

"You're considered perfect here in Montana," Griffin retorted. "Damn woman, cut yourself some slack. Live a little. You never see a tombstone with the words 'Gee, I shouldn't have eaten that last cookie' on it."

Buddy slid the two drinks in front of them with a "Be right back." Jazz sipped at her drink, her face hot with embarrassment.

"You're good for my ego but it's not that simple. I need to lose weight," she argued. He just didn't understand the pressure she was under. Show business was full of gorgeous women and they were all vying for the brass ring.

"A man doesn't want to lie on top of a bag of bones." Griffin kept his voice low so no one else could hear them, thank the Lord. "Drink your iced coffee. In fact, I'm going to order you one of those rich desserts in the display case."

"Then it's a good thing you and I aren't lying anywhere together," she replied, her tone chilly. She didn't like to be reminded that his integrity was more important than them shagging like there was no tomorrow. She understood it, but she didn't have to like it.

"Yet."

Heat bubbled through her veins at that so simple one-word and the promise it held. With each passing day her desire for him was growing stronger. How could she ever last eleven more weeks? Maybe she would get voted out sooner. Much, much sooner.

"Okay, I've only got about thirty minutes." The legs of the chair scraped on the floor as Buddy sat down. "I'm supposed to meet my friends at the bowling alley."

"Then we'll get right to the point." Griffin introduced Jazz and her role before posing the first question.

"Did you know Casey had a new boyfriend after the two of you broke up?"

Red stained the young man's cheeks but he nodded affirmatively. "She said she did when I called her one night but I knew she was lying."

"How do you know she was lying?" Jazz queried, watching the boy's face closely for any tells.

"Because Casey lied all the time. About everything. She lied about shit that didn't matter," Buddy declared. "Casey Charlock, sweet as she was, was the biggest liar I've ever known in my life."

Griffin wanted to throttle the red-faced kid. "Why in the hell didn't you ever say anything?" he asked incredulously.

"I dunno." Buddy shrugged, his expression abashed. "My mom and dad always said to never speak ill of the dead. It seemed a crappy thing to do to call her a liar. I did care about her, Sheriff."

Rubbing his suddenly throbbing temple, Griffin reined in his anger and frustration. Buddy Meltreeger was only twenty-two. In the eyes of the law an adult, but really still a child inside.

"What made you change your mind and tell me now?" he asked between gritted teeth.

"I guess now that's she's been gone for so long it doesn't feel all that terrible to say it out loud. She wasn't a bad person." Buddy's voice had an urgent quality. "She just lived in a fantasy world. Probably because of her mom."

Griffin flicked his gaze quickly to Jazz to make sure she was alright with this line of questioning. Ever since her crying jag at the house, she'd seemed more centered but this might send her off the end again.

"Can you clarify that statement about her mother?" Jazz asked softly but clearly.

"Casey's mom was one stone-cold bitch. She really didn't give a rat's butt about Casey and the feeling was mutual. She was only living there until she could save up some money and go to college. Supposedly. But I found out from her friend Tonya that Casey was blowing all her money on new clothes and shoes. And she hadn't even looked into schools. So that story was another bullshit line. One of many."

"What were the others?" Jazz fiddled with the straw in her drink. Her expression looked calm but she was jiggling her foot under the table.

She wasn't the only one who studied body language.

Buddy grinned as he scratched his chin. "There were a bunch of them. Her dad was going to buy her an apartment in New York City and she was going to move there and work for Donald Trump. Hell, I doubt Casey ever met her dad. Ever. And then there was the story about how she'd been chosen by a talent scout to go to Hollywood and be a model."

"A talent scout? Do they even have those anymore?" Griffin pulled out his notebook and started scratching notes as quickly as he could.

"No, I don't think so. Besides, Casey was about my height. No way was she going to be a model." Jazz was shaking her head, her brows furrowed. "You said that Casey and her mom didn't get along very well. Did they ever argue?"

"Not that I ever saw." Buddy shook his head. "That would have required effort from her mom and that sure as shit wasn't going to happen."

Griffin paused and looked Buddy right in the eye. "I going to ask you a question and by God you better answer me honestly. Do you think Margaret Charlock had anything to do with Casey's death?"

The young man's expression grew solemn. "No, I don't. Casey's mom didn't care enough about her to kill her. It was like she was invisible."

"So who do you think killed her then?" Jazz's follow up question came quickly on the heels of his answer.

"I can't think of anyone I know that wanted her dead. She was a fun girl even if she did like to tell a few whoppers now and then. Everyone knew it and ignored it. If you needed something, Casey would be right there to help you. Like I said, she was sweet. But I guess she could have lied to the wrong person, maybe. Maybe she pissed someone off. Anything can happen."

"The wrong person," Jazz echoed softly. Her gaze was far away somewhere, her brow knitted in thought. The vibration of Griffin's phone in his pocket pulled his attention from Jazz and Buddy. He frowned at the screen when he saw it was Adam. He knew better than to bother Griffin during an investigation.

He pressed the Accept button. "What?" he barked. "I'm working here, Adam. We talked about this, remember?"

Griffin listened, growing more appalled by the second. When he rang off he stood, wanting to get out of there as quickly as possible.

"What's going on? Are we leaving?" Jazz reached down for the purse she'd tucked under the table.

"Yes," he answered shortly. "Sorry, Buddy. Police business. Thanks for the time. We'll be in touch."

Griffin knew he was being rude just blowing the young man off like that but they needed to get back to Hope Lake. Now. He hustled Jazz out to the truck and swung into the driver's seat.

"Where's the fire?" Jazz asked, a little breathless at the way he'd dragged her out of the coffee shop. "Why are you in such a big hurry?"

"We need to get back to town right away." The engine roared to life and he backed out of the parking space. "Sandy was found dead this afternoon by a couple of fisherman. Her body was dumped on the far side of the lake."

Chapter Fifteen

I t hadn't been easy to convince Jazz to hang out at his house while he went to the site of the body. He'd finally had to lay down the law by telling her she was basically still a civilian and would have to sit in the truck if she went with him. Possibly for hours. Faced with that amount of boredom she'd finally given in, although he wouldn't describe it as graceful.

Dropping her at home had made more sense than taking her all the way back to the motel and then circling back to the lake, but it made him kind of nervous. Jazz was all alone in his house. She could rifle through his clothes, movies, books, and even personal papers if she was determined. It felt so intimate. He didn't have anything to be ashamed of but it felt like he was really putting himself out there for her to judge.

What if she found him lacking in some major way? And why did he care? He'd never cared what a woman thought of him before.

"Did you touch the body?" Griffin asked Irwin Nichols, one of the men who had come to the lake to fish and instead found Sandy dead about five feet from the water's edge. The area was surrounded by several trees but hardly private. The killer had to have been desperate to dump a body pretty much out in the open albeit far from a main road.

Irwin shook his head, his face still pale from his gruesome discovery. Sandy's body looked none too pretty. "No way. I barely kept down my lunch, Sheriff. We called the station the minute we saw her, poor girl."

"Good job. I just want to review this. You didn't see anyone or any vehicle, correct?"

"It was just me and Turk. Shit, we never expected this. Who would do something like this?"

That was the question of the hour. Griffin had given the body a cursory inspection without actually touching it, and one thing was clear—Sandy had put up a hell of a fight. She hadn't gone down easy which meant her killer had been more powerful. Probably a man.

The state forensics team had arrived, taking over from the coroner who had pronounced her dead, and were now processing the body and the scene although Griffin doubted the lake was the actual kill location. The grass seemed mostly undisturbed whereas a struggle would have crushed the vegetation all around. No, the murder had taken place elsewhere and the body was dumped here.

It made finding the perpetrator harder. But not impossible.

"I don't know who would do something like this, Irwin, but I plan to find out. Can you and Turk go with Adam to the station? He's going to type up your statements and I want you to review them to make sure every single detail is correct, okay?"

Irwin nodded and followed Adam and his friend to a squad car. Griffin turned his attention back to the crime scene taking in the possible points of entry and exit. Luckily any driving not on the dirt road would show in the tall grasses. In addition, carrying a body in on foot would show deep prints on the banks.

Walking over to one of the crime lab SUV's, Griffin spotted Layla Wallace. She'd been one of the techs that had processed Casey's crime scene and a few others. Friendly and open, she was often more forthcoming than some of the others who rarely spoke and looked at Griffin as if he were some backwoods bumpkin sheriff.

"Hey, Layla. It's good to see you on this one."

Layla was labeling a brown paper bag but still smiled at his greeting. "I bet you say that to all the forensic technicians."

"Hardly. Most of them won't give me the time of day," he replied. "I'm hoping you're going to tell me something that's going to help me."

Layla tucked the bag into a suitcase filled with the evidence she'd collected. It looked like a hell of a lot more than they'd been able to get with Casey but then this was a fresh crime scene. The coroner estimated that Sandy hadn't been dead long before she was found, perhaps less than an hour. "You know what I tell you is conjecture at this point. I don't know anything for sure until I get to the lab."

He knew she needed to cover her ass and respected that.

"I get it. Tell me what Layla thinks."

Her eyebrow, complete with a gold earring piercing the skin quirked up, but she nodded thoughtfully and leaned on the vehicle. She looked like a biker chick with her piercings and tattoos but she knew her shit backwards and forwards.

"That girl put up a fight. I got scrapings from under her fingernails. Her clothes were torn and her panties were bunched up and her skirt was around her hips. Could be from sexual assault or just from being dragged. I've already put a note for the medical examiner to do a rape kit. She had bruising on her inner thighs and I got a good picture of what might be a useful print. She also had bruising on her arms and face. Looks like the doer smacked her around a little before he strangled her. We have ligature marks on the neck."

"Any idea what he used?"

"Not at the moment but I'm still working on that. I need more time."

Layla shut the back of the SUV and dug her keys out of her pocket, indicating question time was over.

"I appreciate the help. Thanks," he said gratefully. Anything that could give him a head start was appreciated at this point. Sandy was basically a stranger in Hope Lake and he didn't have a clue why anyone would want to kill her. Had someone followed her here? Was it a resident? Or was she a random killing?

Pulling his phone from his pocket he pressed a few buttons. Jared's voice came on the line almost immediately.

"Hey, asshole. What's up?"

"Can't you ever greet someone normally? Don't answer that. Listen, I need some of your computer wizardry. I got a dead woman here. She's only been in town about a week and I know almost nothing about her."

"And you want me to find out everything about her," Jared stated. "Right down to what shampoo she uses."

"Exactly. I have to figure out who might want to kill her."

"It's gonna cost you," Jared warned with a laugh. "Nothing in life is free."

"I'll take my chances." Jared was just blowing smoke. He loved hacking into places he wasn't supposed to be. "Let me give you the particulars. I also need some background done on a few others."

Griffin recited Sandy's full name, age, and last known location which were all on the bio he'd been given at the beginning. Hopefully it would be enough although Jared was known to make miracles on occasion. In addition he gave Jared the names of all the competitors plus Tony and Gordon. Maybe there was a link somehow.

"Got it. It's a tall order. It may take a few days."

"I know. Just let me know when you have something," replied Griffin, his attention already pulled in another direction. Tony was striding up to the crime scene with a determined look on his face.

"Will do." Jared hung up and Griffin shoved the phone back in his pocket, bracing himself for what was to come. Although it was clear that Tony already knew what had happened, it was still never a pleasant job to talk about the details of a murder with someone who knew the deceased. Especially as Tony was a suspect in Griffin's eyes. Tony and Sandy had been arguing just this morning.

"Sheriff." Tony came right up to Griffin, invading his personal space as if to intimidate him. Griffin wasn't that damn easy to intimidate. In fact, the producer didn't give Griffin cause to worry in the least. He was just too much of a pretty boy. He'd never want to mess up his manicure. "I want to see Sandy."

Now that was a strange request, but this guy was in show business so who knew what was normal and what wasn't. He'd have to ask Jazz later.

"I can't allow that." Griffin held up his hand. "Her body is already being prepped for transfer to the nearest medical examiner. Also this is an active crime scene. I can't have you tromping all over it ruining possible evidence."

"She's not a body, she's a human being," Tony puffed, his face turning a funny shade of red. "I'm responsible for her while she's here."

"I apologize. Sandy is being prepped to be moved. And I still can't let you in. But since you're here I need to ask you a few questions."

"What kind of questions?" Tony was frowning and trying to edge past Griffin. He had to step in front of the producer and place his hand on Tony's arm to keep him still.

"Where were you between eleven and one today?" Griffin watched Tony's expression closely. There was something about this guy that made Griffin think twice.

"I was in my room on a conference call with the network. Why? Wait. You don't think I had anything to do with this, do you? I didn't do this!"

Tony's voice rose above the others talking and everyone came to a halt for a moment and looked their way. Swallowing hard, the producer shook his head, his once red skin pasty white. "I didn't hurt Sandy. I liked her. She was a nice girl. I could never hurt anyone, Sheriff. Never."

This time his voice was softer but it quivered with fear. Griffin's gut was telling him the man spoke the truth, but with a killer you couldn't be sure. Some of them were so slick you could be convinced of anything by them.

"How well did you know Sandy?"

Tony's hand rubbed his chin and then the back of his neck. "Not well. I met her during auditions in New York a few months ago."

"I thought you lived in Los Angeles." Griffin grabbed his notebook from his pocket and found a fresh page, noticing the notes he'd made about Casey's murder earlier. Now he had not one but two open homicides at once and low resources. It was damn hard to do right by these victims when he couldn't even staff at normal levels.

"I do, but I travel all over. Both of us do, really. Gordon and I scout locations for our reality shows months in advance and do some auditions. That's where I met Sandy."

"Did you date her?"

Griffin was using "date" as a euphemism for something far more animal and Tony seemed to get the idea at once. The producer shook his head vigorously but sweat had popped out on his forehead. Not a good sign.

"I'm dating Caitlin, Jazz's roommate," the man said, pulling a handkerchief from his pocket and mopping his brow. "I'm not a cheater."

"So if we check for sperm we won't find any of yours then? Are you sure? I can get a warrant for your DNA." Griffin looked down at the now wilting man who was hanging his head. Tony looked up at Griffin and then closed his eyes and sighed.

"I had sex with her last night and this morning, and a few times during the week," Tony admitted in a small voice so unlike his denial a few minutes earlier. "But I didn't kill her, Sheriff. Sandy and I just had one of those on-set things. Casual and uncomplicated. Have a little fun and at the end everyone goes their separate ways with no hard feelings. It has nothing to do with how I feel about my girlfriend."

Griffin despised men like this. Men who made excuses for their lack of character and expected everyone else to make allowances.

But it didn't make him guilty. Not yet anyway.

"No hard feelings, huh? That isn't what I saw or heard this morning. It seems Sandy was very pissed off at you. From what I heard, you'd promised she wouldn't be voted off the show and she would be in the final two."

Tony looked like he might cry, his expression tragic and pale. "I may have said I would help her but the viewers control who gets voted off. If she thought that she misunderstood."

"Yeah, I just bet she did." Griffin closed his pad with a snap. "I'll have more questions for you down at the station."

"Am I under arrest?" Tony was visibly shaking now.

"No. Do I need to place you under arrest? You aren't thinking of skipping town, are you?"

Griffin didn't trust these show biz types any farther than he could throw them. Jazz not included in that. He'd already decided she was someone he could rely on and trust.

"I just talked to the network. They've decided to cancel the show due to this horrible tragedy. They don't want to be seen as cashing in on a young girl's death. I was planning to round everyone up and get them on the next plane home."

Jazz, gone? Griffin didn't like the fact that he responded so negatively to that thought but now wasn't the time for deep introspection.

"First of all, no one is leaving town. Until I get everyone's alibi and confirm it, you are all suspects. Everyone stays."

Tony nodded, obviously not in the mood to argue. "I'll have to call the network again. They're expecting me back tomorrow."

"You do that." He couldn't resist asking. Jazz had really hoped to win. "What happens to everyone since you have to shut down? All that prize money. Does that mean no one gets it?"

"The insurance company will make sure all the crew, the town, and the network gets paid. The contestants as well. They'll probably just take all the prize money and divide it five ways. They'll all come out okay."

And Griffin wouldn't be obligated to take any of them as a deputy. He should be jumping for joy but it was hard to be happy about anything when a young woman's life had been snuffed out long before her time.

"I'll need to talk to everyone, Tony. All the contestants and all the crew."

The producer nodded again and pulled out his cell. "I'll call Gordon and tell him to get everyone together. Do you want them at the station?"

It was as good a place as any. He'd start with the contestants and work his way through with the help of his deputies. They might just get done by tonight.

"Yes. Competitors first. If they have any proof of their whereabouts, now would be the time to produce it. Except for Jazz. She has an ironclad alibi."

"What's her alibi?" Tony was punching in a text and scowling at the phone.

"She was with me all day."

This time Tony looked up and nodded. "That is a damn good alibi. Wish I had it. I was right about you two, wasn't I?"

"Shut up, Tony," Griffin responded, not willing to play the man's games today of all days.

This time a killer wasn't going to go unpunished. If he couldn't solve Casey's murder, then by God, he'd solve this one.

The click of the door roused Jazz from where she was dozing in Griffin's man-sized leather recliner. Rubbing her eyes, she pushed the chair closed with her legs and watched as one very tired sheriff shut the front door, kicked off his boots, and made his way into the living room.

"Did I wake you?"

"I was just dozing a little. What time is it?" The sun was down and the room had grown dark with only the flickering of the television for light. Griffin pulled off his hat and sent it sailing across the room to land on the dining table.

"Damn, I'm beat. I didn't think we'd ever get through those statements. You're going to have to come to the station tomorrow, Jazz, and give one too. I let it slide tonight because you're not a suspect. But you might know something that could help us."

That got her attention. Sitting up straight in the chair, she stretched out her stiff legs with a yawn. "Is everyone on the show a suspect then? That's terrible."

"They were at the beginning of the evening but luckily several people do have strong alibis so we were able to cut down the number of suspects in a few hours. That helps a great deal. Levi and Peggy were with Adam studying their handbooks so we can cross them off the list. The crew was having lunch in the diner and there were witnesses so I've marked them off as well." Griffin cushioned his head with his hands and stared up at the ceiling. "That leaves Wayne, who can't seem to account for his whereabouts at all. Very fishy. Also Tony and Gordon. Tony says he was on a conference call with the network part of the time but I don't have corroboration of that yet. The rest of the time he's not sure of what he was doing, which I find odd. Gordon says he was with Tony the entire time. Now that I believe considering the way he has his nose stuck up Tony's ass twenty-four seven."

"So Tony's your main suspect? Maybe someone from town did it." She hated to point the finger at people she didn't even know but she couldn't imagine Tony killing anyone. Just having him under suspicion was going to upset Caitlin.

"I'm concentrating my efforts on Tony, Wayne, and Gordon until someone tells me that Sandy had contact with anyone else. I've impounded Tony and Gordon's rental car and I'm doing background checks on all the contestants."

"Including me?" Jazz got up from the recliner and sat next to Griffin feeling the heat from his body.

Griffin nodded, his gaze capturing her own. "Even though you have a solid alibi, I can't treat you any differently than the others. It wouldn't be right."

"I don't mind. I don't have anything to hide, but damn, there's that integrity again," Jazz sighed. "All that honorable stuff is keeping me celibate."

His silver-gray eyes seemed to glow in the dim light. "About that. You'll probably find out tomorrow but the network has cancelled the show. They don't want to be seen as cashing in on Sandy's death. Tony said the insurance company will probably just split all the prize money between the contestants."

The news wasn't completely unexpected. She'd wondered today as she'd waited for Griffin just what the network and producers would do. Canceling the show was one of the options she's considered. The money would come in handy but she would miss out on the exposure, although she'd been thinking about that less and less these past few days.

"You won't get a new deputy," she said, not wanting to think about leaving. There was nothing holding her here now.

"I'm going to make Levi an offer. But I'm more worried about you. Are you okay about this? I know you wanted to win."

His hand curled around hers and their fingers entwined, sending streaks of heat to her extremities and making her nipples bead behind the lace of her bra.

"You know I never really wanted to be a deputy. I'm fine with the network canceling the show. I'm disappointed but that just means I need to work extra hard at getting another break."

It sounded kind of depressing when she said it. Going back to her empty and fairly vacuous life wasn't as appealing as it had been only a few days ago.

"I hope you get it." Griffin's voice was soft and it sent shivers up her spine. Just being near to him was doing dangerous things to her equilibrium. He could arouse her with just a few words or gestures without really trying.

"Your mother stopped by earlier," Jazz said, unwilling to discuss her career and the goals she'd set for herself when she was only a teenager. "She left a roast chicken in the refrigerator and a few other things. She heard about Sandy and thought you might work late. Said that you don't take care of yourself very well."

Griffin chuckled, his lips curving into a smile. "I probably don't, but then I always know she'll drop off a chicken or a pot roast. Did you have some?"

"It seemed weird to make myself at home like that, eating your food and using your kitchen."

"I told you to make yourself at home," he reminded her.

"I thought that meant to watch television or maybe sit on the deck. I didn't think it meant eat my food, look through my closets, and take a nap in my bed."

His callused fingers slid from her hand up her thigh and for a second she couldn't breathe. Her pulse began to pound in her ears and she had to swallow hard to be able to speak.

"Did you look through my closets?"

His mouth was close to her ear now and she was literally shivering with arousal at his nearness. Clamping down on her emotions, she inwardly shook herself trying to control her runaway heart.

"No. I didn't nap in your bed either." Her voice sounded rusty and choked, and she almost swallowed her tongue when he began to nuzzle her hair. This Griffin wasn't one she was familiar with at all. Was he playing with her?

"Now that is a real shame. I would have liked to come home to you in my bed, Hollywood," he said deeply. She pulled back in shock as his words began to penetrate her addled brain.

"What about your integrity?"

Without answering her, he quickly levered to his feet and gave her the most wicked grin she'd ever seen. She yelped as he scooped her up and her world turned decidedly upside down. Tossing her over his shoulder, he gave her bottom a playful slap as he strode into the bedroom. She was unceremoniously tossed on the king-sized bed and barely able to catch her breath before Griffin's large body was coming down on top of her, flattening her into the mattress.

"Honey, the show is over. I'm not your boss anymore, if I ever really was. So we can do dirty, raunchy things together all damn night and my integrity is securely intact. I've been looking forward to this since Tony told me the news."

She stared up into his face, so sexy and handsome. He was grinning from ear to ear and she could feel his very hard cock up close and personal as it pressed into her belly. If he was as big as he felt, she was in for quite a night. There was only one thing left to say.

"Thank you, baby Jesus. Let's get naked."

Chapter Sixteen

Horndog Griffin was quite different than honorable, sheriff-in-charge Griffin. Bottom line?

He was much more fun.

After several minutes of long kisses and rolling around on the comforter getting it all wrinkled and messy, she tugged at his shirt trying to pull it free of his pants. His fingers stayed her movements even as he pressed a soft kiss to the base of her throat, wringing a groan from her lips and sending a streak of lightning straight to her pussy.

"Easy, honey. We got all night. We've only kissed once before tonight and I don't want you to miss out on the buildup."

He had to be out of his fucking cowboy mind. They didn't have time for that. She needed him now. Right now. It felt like her body was on fire, the flames licking at her skin and sending a flush of arousal from head to toe. They'd only kissed and she'd gone up in flames.

She slid her hands under the cotton of his shirt and explored the warm skin and play of muscles under her palms. "I want you now, Griffin. I can't wait."

"We've waited this long, we can wait a little longer," Griffin chuckled against the sensitive flesh of her ear while one of his hands glided down her body and cupped her bottom, giving it a little squeeze.

"I thought men were always supposed to be in a hurry," she breathed, barely noticing when he popped open her jeans and pulled down the zipper.

"I think you've been hanging out with the wrong men, honey," Griffin replied with a smile and then he didn't say anything at all. His mouth was too busy kissing the skin he'd exposed on her abdomen. He licked and nipped his way down to where the zipper ended before tugging at the denim material to slide them down her legs.

Cool air hit her overheated flesh and she sucked in a breath as he tossed the pants to the floor. Pushing her thighs apart with his wide shoulders, he pressed wet kisses from her toes, up her calves, along her inner thighs, and over her abdomen until he was stopped by the barrier of her blouse. She was writhing and twisting on the bed as he started the process all over again with her other leg, unerringly finding every sensitive or ticklish spot on her lower half.

Her hair was tangled and her breath was ragged when he paused from torturing her to slowly unbutton her shirt one button at a time. It felt like the air was being sucked directly out of her lungs as he bared her inch by excruciating inch.

"You're driving me crazy," she choked.

He picked up her hand and placed it on the denim of his fly where his hard cock pulsed under her fingers. She rubbed the fabric until he closed his eyes and growled,

"I'm driving myself crazy."

"Don't. I'm ready for you."

She doubted she'd ever been this wet before in her life. The crotch of her panties had passed damp a long time ago and the honey was starting to make her thighs sticky.

"It will make it even better if we hold back. Just a little bit, Hollywood. But if you're that needy, I'll take care of you."

Needy was a good word. Greedy was too.

Griffin hooked his thumbs on the sides of her panties and slid them down her legs before tossing them over his shoulder without another glance. She'd have to hunt for those later but for now the room seemed to spin as he traced patterns on her lower abdomen with his tongue. Grabbing his head and tangling her fingers in his short, dark hair, she held on for dear life against the tidal wave of pleasure as that naughty tongue slid through the dark blonde curls and straight down to her swollen clit.

His tongue swirled around and around the nub while her insides quaked in response. The tension began to build deep within her and she crumpled the sheets as her fingers clutched the cool fabric. Tighter and tighter her arousal coiled even as he pressed first one thick digit and then another into her pussy.

"So tight, honey. I can't wait to be inside of you."

He whispered the words and his hot breath caressed her clit, making her toes curl. It was too good, too intense and her entire body felt as if it was strung taut and ready to snap at any moment.

His fingers caressed her from the inside as his tongue played games on the outside. He lapped at the top of the swollen button, and her legs shook and shifted farther apart.

"Ready, honey?"

He didn't expect an answer apparently, which was a good thing as she couldn't have formed a word to save her life. Everything she was feeling had overwhelmed her conscious deliberate thought. All she could do was respond and react to his sensual ministrations. Moving his fingers in and out, his mouth covered her clit and sucked gently while using his tongue to tickle the sides.

The explosion was instantaneous.

White and colored lights danced behind her lids as the coil inside her unwound, unleashing a torrent of pleasure so exquisite it took her very breath away. It was not like any orgasm she'd ever experienced, but then Griffin Sawyer wasn't like any other man. She should have known he'd be expert at the give and take of pleasure. He was damn fine at everything he did.

He kissed his way to her mouth by blazing a heated path up her body before capturing her lips as if in victory. Her limbs heavy with languor, her heart racing in her chest, she'd give him this win but it was only a battle, not the war. Her goal was to make him feel as good as she did right at this moment and she wouldn't be deterred.

Wrapping her arms around him they kissed, hot and urgent. She could feel the heat of his hard cock sear her skin through the heavy denim of his jeans. When she wrapped her legs around his lean waist and ground against him, his dick jumped behind his button-fly. How he could hold himself in check at this point was beyond her, his self-control like iron.

"Oh God, that was intense," she breathed.

"Now that's what I like to hear. You like playing games, baby? I like to play games in the bedroom too." Griffin chuckled and nipped at her shoulder, making her shiver in his arms before levering up and tugging at her open blouse. She rose up so it would slip off her arms and then reached around to pop open the fasteners of her bra but his fingers beat her to it.

"Sincere, hard-working Sheriff Sawyer likes to play games?" Her voice was husky as the lace and satin bra slid down her arms and off. He tossed it on the growing pile of clothes on the floor, not even sparing it a second glance. Every bit of his attention was focused purely on her. The sensation was a heady one.

Jazz wasn't a virgin. She'd had sex before with various men, although not in near the numbers that some of her friends had. In those past encounters she'd always felt as if she were in competition for the man's attention. Maybe from the demands of his cock, or his phone, or sometimes from his own ego. Not tonight. Every bit of Griffin Sawyer was with her. He wasn't thinking about tomorrow morning or his work schedule. He was here totally in the present.

"I most certainly like to play games. How about we play the 'strip game'? I ask you a question and if you answer it correctly, I'll take off a piece of clothing."

Laughter bubbled from her lips. She'd never seen Griffin act silly and goofy but this was nice. He didn't take himself too damn seriously.

"I don't know about this. What kind of questions are you going to ask me?"

His head dipped down and he captured a nipple between his lips, licking and nipping at it until she was moaning and writhing underneath him. When he finally lifted his head, he went to work on the other until it was a tight bud and she was breathless and begging for a reprieve. Her empty pussy clenched, wanting and needing to be filled and only Griffin would do. She clutched at his broad shoulders and wriggled her hips in provocation.

Sliding down her body, he dropped kisses along her torso and thighs before coming to a standing position on the floor in front of her. Leaning back on her elbows, she enjoyed running her gaze up and down his gorgeous body even though it was fully clothed. Peggy had been right that very first night.

The only reason a woman would kick Griffin Sawyer out of bed would be to do it with him on the floor.

Maybe they could do that next time. This time would be on the very comfortable bed.

Griffin played with the first button on his shirt and gave her a smile that took her breath away. "First question. What two colors mixed together make purple?"

What was this? Preschool? Her mind was already fogged with arousal and desire and he wanted her to think?

Shit. She blinked and tried to remember playing with paints as a kid.

"Red and blue."

"Winner, winner," Griffin chanted, popping each button open way too slowly. When he pulled the material apart to reveal his perfect male chest she had to bite her lip to keep from running her tongue over those perfect abs. He tossed his shirt aside and moved his hands to the buttons of his jeans.

"Question number two. Name a mammal that lays eggs." His smirk made her want to hurl a lamp in his direction, but she could tell that he wouldn't be swayed from this little game.

"I swear when this is over, I will kill you," she hissed. "Slowly and painfully. Mark my words, Sheriff."

"I'll take my chances, Hollywood. Now answer the question."

"Platypus, you asshole. Now strip." Her voice had risen slightly but it sounded more strangled than pissed off. Griffin laughed and popped open each button on his fly and pushed the jeans down to his ankles before kicking them away. Clad only in a pair of black boxer briefs and white socks he should have looked ridiculous. Instead, he looked delicious, better than any of those male models that flocked together in Los Angeles, primping and preening for the cameras. This show, while frustrating as hell, was *only* for her. The public wouldn't get to see this. Ever.

"Now for question thr–," he began but didn't get any further. Unable to take it any longer, she sat up and grabbed the front of his shorts, pulling him toward her until he laughingly fell on the bed next to her. She tugged at the last layer of fabric between but he obligingly put his hands over hers and shed the briefs along with his socks, letting them fall to the floor.

His impressive cock bobbed against his stomach, a pearly drop of pre-cum on the purple-red mushroom head. The thick shaft was decorated with a complicated map of dark veins and she couldn't resist the urge to trace them first with a fingertip and then with her tongue.

Groaning, his fingers tangled in the strands of her hair but he didn't try and direct her movements, content to let her explore. Running her tongue from base to tip, she swirled her tongue around the head over and over, his salty taste bursting on her tongue. Reversing direction, she headed for his balls, already drawn up tight to his body and laved the crinkly flesh until he cursed and moaned.

"Shit, honey. I'm going to blow if you keep that up."

Griffin's voice was hoarse and rough, and as tempted as she was to keep torturing him, she wanted him inside of her even more. She reluctantly pulled back and his arm swung across the bed to reach into the nightstand. Rolling on a condom, he lifted himself up so he was hovering above her, his cock nudging her slit. She gripped his biceps and slid her knees further apart. He was a big man—all over—and she was suddenly more than a little nervous.

"Are you okay, honey? You don't look too sure about this." His lips lightly played with her own but she knew the question was sincere. If she'd changed her mind, he'd pull away, no matter what it cost him.

"I'm a little nervous," she confessed, looking down between them at his length and girth. She hadn't done that well in school but the math wasn't adding up. "Uh, you're not a small guy, Sheriff, but I'm a small woman."

He barked with laughter and it made his cock bob. "Honey, I'll take this as slow as you need me to. I promise we'll fit together just fine."

Nodding, she closed her eyes as he began to push forward, stretching muscles she hadn't used in a while and rubbing sensitive spots she hadn't known she had. She exhaled slowly as he carefully pulled back and then pressed forward gently. With each stroke he gained more purchase until finally he was in to the hilt. Her toes curled at the unimaginable feeling of being completely filled by him.

"Open your eyes, Hollywood."

Reluctantly she lifted her heavy lids only to find those silver eyes focused directly on her. He watched her every expression as they slowly fucked, the power and speed building with each thrust.

"You feel so good, honey. So good."

He whispered praise and dirty talk in her ear while they flew to new heights together, her body moving closer and closer to orgasm as he pistoned in and out. Her nails scored his back and her legs wrapped around his hips, holding him as closely as possible. She'd never felt this close to another human in her life, never understood when people talked about becoming *one*. But they were one as they moved in unison, letting instinct take over and pushing logic away.

Tomorrow she might wonder at the intelligence of her decision but right now was all that mattered.

With each thrust his groin rubbed against her swollen clit until she exploded with pleasure. Crying out his name, she gave herself over to the waves that battered her already spent body. When he followed her over the cliff, she watched entranced as he threw his head back and groaned her name. The cords on his neck stood out in stark relief and his teeth snapped together, showing off his square jaw. He was in a word…beautiful.

His forehead came down to rest on hers as their breathing became less ragged. Eventually he rolled off of her and padded to the bathroom only to return in less than a minute and pull her close.

"Honey, that was one hell of a ride."

"Is that some kind of cowboy after sex talk?" She punched him playfully in the shoulder. "I guess I'll take it as a compliment."

"It's meant as one." Griffin kissed her temple and pushed a few errant strands of hair off of her forehead. He was quiet for a moment. "Did you say there was chicken in the fridge?"

Giggling, she rolled to her side and ran her fingers up his chest, watching the play of muscles in fascination. "I did. Are you hungry? I am too."

In fact, now that he'd mentioned it, her stomach felt distinctly empty and it gnawed at her insides. She wouldn't be able to sleep until she was fed.

He sat up in bed and swung his legs over the side searching, probably for his shorts. She grabbed his arm and put her other hand on his cheek, cupping his jaw.

"Wait for just a minute." She screwed up her courage, wanting to say something but so used to men being jerks she hesitated. But this was Griffin and if he was a jerk she hadn't seen any sign of it. It was time to extend a little bit of trust to the male species. "You were worth the wait."

She held her breath while he seemed to consider her words, her heart thumping in her chest. A slow smile bloomed on his face and her stomach fluttered in response.

"You too, Hollywood. Never had a better night, if we're telling the truth here."

"Me too. It was..." She really didn't have the words to describe what had passed between them. She only knew that everything was different. Did he know it?

"Yeah," he nodded in agreement. "It was something, wasn't it? I knew you were trouble the minute we met."

"You did not," she denied even as he handed her the scrap of panties he'd tossed away earlier and then his shirt. It smelled like him and she happily slipped her arms into the oversized fabric, somehow still warm from his body. "You thought I was too flimsy to carry my own luggage."

"Yep, trouble." He stood up looking like a Greek god in nothing but those shorts. Holding his hand out, he helped her to her feet. "Let's get some dinner. I've worked up an appetite."

Maybe she was imagining it and everything was still the same. As she passed by the mirror she sneaked a look at both of them.

They looked the same.

They talked the same.

They were in the same house and going to eat the same chicken in the very same kitchen.

Maybe everything, all the emotions she'd felt only minutes ago, was an illusion. And if they were, where did that leave her?

Leaving, that's where. If nothing had changed, then there was nothing to keep her in Hope Lake. And it wouldn't take long to figure it out. Tomorrow morning at the very latest.

Chapter Seventeen

Sunlight streamed in the bedroom windows telling Griffin in no uncertain terms that it was later than his usual rise and shine. It didn't matter that he'd put in a sixteen hour day yesterday or that he'd probably do it again today. There was a killer to be caught and it wouldn't happen with him lazing around in bed, no matter how pleasant it might be.

He rolled over onto his side and looked at the woman he'd made love with last night. Jazz had scooted over to the far side of the bed leaving at least a foot of space between them, but he could still smell the fresh scent of her hair and feel the warmth of her skin. He didn't know if she'd moved away because she'd wanted to or because she thought he wanted her to, but he didn't like it.

To his surprise, he liked the feel of her body snuggled with his and the way her silky golden hair tangled around him. At one point last night, while he'd been inside her tight little cunt, he'd buried his face in those tresses and let himself breathe deeply. There was something about her that stirred him like no one else.

Lying on her side, her pretty face towards him, she looked like an angel peacefully sleeping. He simply couldn't allow that to continue. He might have a million things to do today but the very first thing he was going to do was Hollywood.

He reached across the sheets and slipped his fingers between her legs, unerringly finding her clit. Brushing it with his thumb, his slipped a finger inside her already wet channel. Had she been dreaming naughty thoughts while looking sweet and innocent? He had to admit the dichotomy turned him on. Angelic on the outside but sinfully carnal on the inside. It was a dynamite combination that had made him hard enough to pound nails with his cock last night.

That same dick was awake and aroused as her lips parted and a small moan escaped. Her lashes fluttered but he stopped stimulating her long enough for sleep to win once again. Then and only then did he start up the rhythm with his thumb and fingers. The button swelled under his ministrations and she moaned again, this time louder.

"Griffin." Jazz said it so softly he almost missed it. She knew it was him even in sleep.

Something inside his chest twisted and tightened and he slid across the bed to press his lips to hers. Capturing her pink mouth, he took his time exploring every nook and cranny, finding the spots that gave her the most pleasure. She'd been robbed in a way, their relationship not following a normal path. Any other time they would have dated, kissed, maybe even necked on his sofa before making love. His hands would have wandered all over her sexy curves and he would have catalogued every area that made her moan or even sigh. Instead, they'd had a heated coupling that he'd tried like hell to slow down. He'd simply wanted her too much.

But this morning, although his need for her raged, he could more easily control it. They could take their time, caressing and stroking, making love in an unhurried fashion. Sometimes he liked it fast and hard, but this morning he planned to take his time and enjoy himself thoroughly.

He pulled back and her eyes slowly opened, getting used to the bright sunlight. She smiled and then gasped as he moved his wandering fingers that were now clasped tightly between her thighs.

"Oh Griffin," she sighed.

"Oh Jazz," he teased before bending his head to tease a pouting pink nipple with his tongue. "Good morning, baby."

"Oooooh, it is a good morning isn't it?" Jazz wriggled but he threw his leg over her keeping her prisoner on the mattress. Giggling, she writhed under his tongue but her hands went to the back of his head, holding them there before sliding down his arms.

He quickly rolled away to grab a condom, trying to rip open the package but she wanted to help. Within seconds, they were both laughing like teenagers in the backseat of a car on Saturday night. Griffin positioned himself on his back and motioned for her to saddle up.

"Ride me. Give me a show, Hollywood," he urged.

He wanted to see her above him, her body naked for his enjoyment while her tight pussy hugged him. She hesitated for a moment but he reached for her, helping her straddle him with her thighs. Her cheeks and chest were pink but something inside must have overrode her innate shyness. Lowering herself down on his already aching cock, she closed her eyes and let her head fall back, her lips parted in a groan.

The tension in his lower back and balls was already building too fast and he gripped her hips to slow her movements and make it last. Her snug cunt stretched to accommodate his size but wrapped him in a singeing wet heat.

Lifting her long golden hair off her neck with her arms and rolling her pelvis, Jazz rode up and then down, over and over. The pressure built until he thought the back of his head would surely blow off. Sweat formed on his skin as the temperature between them zoomed into the stratosphere.

Jazz was so fucking gorgeous with her long golden hair falling over her shoulders and playing peek-a-boo with her pale pink nipples. They were both breathing fast, their moans and groans echoing off the walls.

The pleasure was too much and it would only be a few moments before the dam burst and he shot his seed into the barrier. He reached between them and found her clit, rubbing it with his thumb until her back stiffened and her pussy clamped down on his cock. Her hands went to his thighs, the nails digging into the flesh as she leaned back, thrusting those luscious breasts into the air.

As her orgasm carried her away, his own exploded through his balls and out of his cock. He could feel his dick swelling, her pussy growing even tighter and he sucked air into his lungs as the world tilted on its axis.

So fucking good.

When she collapsed on his chest, he stroked her back, their bodies covered in a fine sheen of sweat. He nuzzled the top of her head and reveled in the feel of her velvety soft skin under his fingers and the delicious weight of her torso.

He felt the loss of her heat immediately when she rolled away, looking up at him. Her blue eyes were soft and her smile made his heart ache and his stomach twist. She was a dangerous woman but he was beginning to not care. Nothing had prepared him for Jazz Oliver.

"We better get up," she said softly, her expression one of regret and he knew his own reflected the same feeling. "It's going to be one crazy day."

For the very first time in Griffin's life he wanted to stay in bed. Specifically he wanted to stay in bed with this woman. The emotion stunned him with its almighty strength. He couldn't have wrestled it away with sheer brute force, but could he negotiate with it?

There were too many reasons not to get involved. The first one was that Jazz would never stay in a tiny backwoods town in Montana. She was born to be a star. She had that indefinable something that made her sparkle. It was only a matter of time before she hit it big and then she'd forget all about the affable sheriff she'd had a tumble with once upon a time.

A sour taste in his mouth at that thought, Griffin pulled himself up and out of bed, grabbing a robe from the bottom bedpost. Tossing it to her, he snagged a pair of boxers for himself. Time to stop mooning over things that could never be and get back down to what was real.

Work.

"You go ahead and shower and I'll start some breakfast."

Turning on his heel and exiting the bedroom, he resisted the urge to look back over his shoulder at her delightfully tousled appearance. He needed to keep his eyes firmly focused on the future, and that future would never include the woman in his bed. Even if by some bizarre circumstance she would stay, he couldn't do the whole "love" thing. He wasn't meant for the give and take of a real relationship.

He'd forgotten it for a few hours but it was back firmly in the forefront of his mind. He wouldn't let it go again.

✧ ✧ ✧ ✧

Griffin had retreated inside himself, Jazz could tell. Sitting out on the back deck, they were sharing breakfast and acting normal. But something between the time they'd been in bed and when he came out of the shower had changed. He was holding a piece of himself back almost as if he couldn't allow himself to be happy.

"Do you eat this every day?" Jazz eyed the thick bacon and scrambled eggs mixed with cheddar cheese sitting on the plate with a piece of toast slathered in real butter. "It'll clog your arteries. You'll drop dead at forty."

"I'm healthy as a horse," Griffin boasted, digging into his eggs. "My father ate this for breakfast and my grandfather too. He's over eighty and on his second wife."

"In that case maybe I'll just drop dead at forty," she retorted but had to admit the breakfast was delicious. "You're a good cook though."

Griffin laughed and shoveled more food into his mouth. "You've pretty much seen the extent of my culinary skills. I can also cook chicken and steaks on the grill. End of story. Can you cook?"

Wrinkling her nose, Jazz thought of the rare times she would make something in the kitchen. "Kind of. Does spaghetti or macaroni and cheese count? Oh wait, I can make hot dogs. You just boil them, right?"

"Griffin!" a voice called and then a young man bounded up the deck stairs, a newspaper in his hand. He had to be Griffin's brother, the resemblance was that strong. "Damn, bro, I was pounding on the front door. Couldn't you hear me?"

"No, I have the sliders closed. I don't like to let bugs in the house." Griffin sat back in his chair. "By the way Jazz, this is Price, my brother. Price, this is Jazz. Now what brings you here this early in the morning?"

"It's not that early and I know who she is. The whole damn town knows." Price tipped his hat. "Pardon me, ma'am. Griff, have you seen the papers this morning or the far end of your driveway?"

Griffin's eyes narrowed and his body stiffened. "No, I can't see the end of the driveway from the house. It's too far. Why? Is there something I need to see?"

Standing slowly, he moved toward the doors but Price caught his arm. "You can't go out there unless you're prepared. The property across from yours is covered with reporters. Shit, there has to be at least a dozen and a few satellite trucks too."

Griffin muttered under his breath and rubbed his chin. "Son of a fucking bitch. What are they doing here?"

"You're the goddamn sheriff, bro. There's a dead girl that was on the television and they all want to know who did it. I don't suppose you know?"

"It hasn't even been twenty-four hours," Griffin argued but his brother cut him off.

"Like they give a shit. They all know Jazz is here too." Price tipped his hat again. "Pardon me a second time. It's no one's business what you two do but it looks like at least three major news networks are making it their business."

Jazz buried her face in her hands, her heart sinking. Griffin was a private man and this was going to send him over the edge. Whatever good they'd had last night and this morning was about to be blown all to shit.

"Fucking hell," Griffin cursed. "What's in the paper that I don't want to see?"

Price handed it to him with a grimace. "There's an editorial in there from Councilman Leroy Wilson questioning whether you're up to the job, so to speak. He says that we need a new sheriff because you couldn't catch Casey Charlock's killer, now this girl. Oh, and that you have sexual dalliances with suspects."

"Jazz is not a suspect!" Griffin exploded, his normally calm demeanor shot to hell. A muscle was working overtime in his jaw and his face had turned red. "She was with me at the time of the murder. Son of a bitch. Son of a fucking bitch."

Griffin perused the paper as Jazz's stomach twisted in her gut. Her appetite completely gone, she pushed her plate away, unsure how to make any of this better. Griffin threw the newspaper over the railing and into the water.

"Leroy Wilson can kiss my lily-white ass," he pronounced flatly. "He wants me to be a fucking hero with no budget and no trained deputies. He couldn't find anyone else to be the sheriff of this backwater piece of shit town for what they pay me. If he wants my badge he can fucking have it."

"Calm down, Griffin." An older gentleman with a lined face and silver hair was climbing the deck stairs. "No one wants your badge, least of all me. Leroy's just blowing off steam like he always does. He likes to stir things up, you know."

"Hey, Otis." Price shook hands with the older man. "You make it okay through that line of reporters?"

The man named Otis smiled and sat down in Griffin's recently vacated chair. "I pointed my truck in the direction I wanted to go and heaven help those who get in the way. They moved."

Otis held his hand out to her. "Hello, my dear. Councilman Otis McClintock. You must be Jazz Oliver."

"I must be," she answered weakly, shaking his hand. "How bad is it?" She nodded toward the front of the house. Somewhere at the end of Griffin's long driveway were a bunch of reporters hell-bent on getting a story.

"It's bad. I fear you are not going to get to leave here without your picture being taken. Is that a problem? I heard you're an actress. Isn't there a saying about no such thing as bad publicity?"

Once glance at Griffin's thunderous expression and she knew there wasn't anything she would do to keep them both out of the papers. She didn't care what opportunities it cost. Nothing was worth the misery he was obviously in.

"I'm not sure that saying is accurate," she said quietly, watching Griffin carefully. Right now he had his back to all three of them and was staring over the placid lake. Finally he turned around, his features set in stone.

"Do I have your support, Otis, to run this investigation as I see fit? I won't tolerate any interference from the council members. I mean it."

Griffin's tone was one that brooked no nonsense and Otis seemed to pick up on it. He nodded vigorously even as he picked up an abandoned piece of toast and bit into it.

"Of course, of course. This is your baby. I just need one favor."

"What's that?" Griffin asked suspiciously, one eyebrow lifted in question.

"Find the person that did this quickly. Today, if possible. Every day that passes makes us look more like some pissant town with a Barney Fife sheriff. People don't want to visit or open businesses in places like that."

Jazz's eyes went wide at the Barney Fife comment but as usual Griffin showed amazing control. He barely batted an eyelash but his teeth were gritted together in anger.

"Might I remind you that it was *you* who brought these people here? It was *you* that said nothing bad would happen. I told you that I was understaffed but no one fucking listens to me around here."

Otis stood and brushed the toast crumbs from his shirt. "Make this go away," he said bluntly. "I've got deals in the works and this is putting them in jeopardy."

"Are you threatening Griffin?" The incredulous words popped out of Jazz's mouth before she could stop them. He looked like somebody's grandfather, for heaven's sake.

"Of course not." Otis smiled charmingly, but this time Jazz wasn't in the mood to be swayed. "I simply let him know how important it is to get this cleared up as soon as possible. I love Griffin like a son."

"I've seen how you treat family," Griffin snorted. "Count me out. But the message is received. No one wants this put to bed more than I do. Soon. If you want to be any help, call your buddies in Missoula. I need our evidence to go to the front of the line at the state lab. We can't do much without it. This murder will be solved by forensics. No one is lining up to confess."

"Consider it done." Otis bowed his head and headed toward the stairs. "Thanks for breakfast and good luck getting out of here. Do you want me to call Adam or anything?"

"I'm the goddamn law in this town. We'll get out of here."

Otis chuckled and disappeared around the corner of the house. Griffin pointed to Price.

"You stay here with Jazz. I'll get the nosy bastards outside to follow me into town by promising them a statement. When they're all gone, get her out of here."

Jazz stood up to protest. If anyone should throw themselves on the sacrificial altar it was her. The show was the reason all this had happened. She might not have personally brought the show here but she was a part of the problem.

"I'll get them to follow me," she urged. "You stay here. I can deal with this."

"You can deal with this?" Griffin was looking at her like she was insane. "You said before you've never even been in a tabloid until now. This is my town, and you're my responsibility, Hollywood."

"I don't want to be your responsibility," she bristled, not liking that term in the least. "I can—"

"Easy, honey. I meant that in a good way." Griffin held up his hands in surrender. "Let me take care of this."

"Uh, can I suggest something here?" Price broke in. "I'll drive my truck to the other side of the lake and wait for you there. You take your boat and escape across the water. I'll drive you into town and you can pick up one of the SUVs there."

"That's the first smart thing I've heard all morning," Griffin sighed. "What about the press though? What will they do?"

"Eventually they'll figure out they've been tricked and they'll head into town," Jazz responded. "Then we'll have a whole new problem trying to duck them."

"Why would we do that?" Griffin's brows were pulled together in a frown. "We've got nothing to hide. I'm not ashamed that I spent the night with you. Are you ashamed of me?"

"No, not at all," she denied and his expression cleared. "I was just thinking of you, that's all."

"The genie is out of the bottle, honey. No sense in trying to stuff it back in. It just makes us look like we have something to hide." Griffin ran his fingers through his short cropped hair. "While we're in town we need to get your stuff from the hotel."

"Why?" She wasn't following Griffin's train of thought clearly. There was no other hotel in Hope Lake to move her to, not that it would make any difference. They'd find her no matter what.

"You're checking out. I can't protect you when you're away from me. You'll stay here until this madness is over."

Was the man that didn't like women interfering and getting their things all over his house asking – no, telling her that he wanted her to move her stuff in? Even if it was only for a short time? This was personal growth for Griffin Sawyer.

"That means that I'll have stuff in the bathroom." She tried to suppress a smile but couldn't quite manage it. "I might have stuff in your closet too. I may even want to watch something on television."

"For the love of fucking God, let's just get your stuff. But just so we're clear, I control the thermostat," he warned, his tone disgusted as Price burst into laughter.

"Holy shit, she knows what you're like, bro," he said, holding his sides and a grin on his face. "I can always take her to Mom and Dad's if you can't handle having a female guest."

Griffin did that growling thing again where he didn't know what to say, or maybe he knew but the words were too rude. He pointed to the stairs and Price loped off with a wave.

"Give me about twenty minutes then get in the boat."

Griffin's grim expression didn't change as he scooped up the plates and headed into the kitchen.

"Come inside," he commanded. "And wipe that smile off of your face. It's not that damn funny."

Unable to control her mirth, she trailed after Griffin, her hand covering her mouth but it failed to mute the gales of laughter. She was about to move in – albeit temporarily – with the most avowed bachelor she'd ever met.

And it was that damn funny.

Chapter Eighteen

"Have we heard anything from the lab? If not, give them another call. Also, bring me those statements we took yesterday from the contestants and crew. I want to go through them again."

Griffin barked out orders as he and Jazz walked through the station. They'd managed to escape the house without tipping off any reporters but it was a short-lived situation. He would have to make some statement to the press today about the state of the investigation.

"Sit here, Hollywood, and I'll have Adam get your statement."

Adam bustled over from the coffeemaker. "I'm on it, boss. I did call the crime lab and we're tenth in line, and the statements are on your desk."

"Phone again in a few hours. Otis is supposed to call in a few favors from his friends in the capital. Jazz, give Adam your statement and then I'll have him drive you to the hotel to check out."

"Do you always do this?" Her head was tilted to the side but she was smiling.

"Do what?" He really didn't have time for twenty questions today.

"Order everyone around like a general. Does this usually work for you?"

The little vixen was actually laughing at him again. She'd already made it known that she found their situation amusing. She should be damn grateful that he felt responsible for keeping her safe from the press but mostly she seemed to find it funny. He was the one that was going to be sharing his home for the foreseeable future but no one seemed to care about his sacrifice.

Of course he could send her to his parents' house but then the press would just hang out there and Griffin wouldn't put his mom and dad through something like that. No, she would have to stay with him and he would just have to bite the bullet and deal with it. It probably wouldn't be for that long.

"Yes, it does work," he responded before turning to Karla, his administrative assistant. She ran the office and took his messages. Not well, but then like most people in this office, Griffin had taken what he could get for the money. Maybe he could use some of the television cash and hire more office help. "Karla, do I have any messages?"

The tall and skinny brunette shoved a stack of papers in his hand. "Several. By the way, I quit."

It was only with her words that he even noticed that she had her purse slung over her shoulder and a sour expression.

"What do you mean you quit? What's wrong today?"

Karla had various complaints, mostly to do with the hours, working conditions, and the pay. She didn't like her desk. She didn't like the sound of a ringing phone. She didn't like talking on the phone. And she didn't like making coffee.

"I've been dealing with a phone ringing off the hook since the minute I got here," she huffed.

"That's your job," he reminded her tightly. He had damn near come to the end of his patience and that was saying something.

"Not anymore. You don't pay me enough to do this." Turning on her heel, Karla was out the door without a backward glance.

"Good riddance," Adam muttered. "What a royal bitch. I didn't want to say anything, boss, but that woman was simply unpleasant in every way she could be."

Griffin sighed and rubbed the back of his neck in frustration. "You should have said something before. She was walking a thin line with me anyway. If I knew she wasn't treating you guys well I would have let her go."

"She's gone now." Adam shrugged and sat down next to Jazz who had silently watched the exchange. "Let's get going, Jazz, so you can get out of this craziness."

Griffin left Adam and Jazz to it and went straight back to his office, closing the door behind him. Flipping through the messages, he had a few from the local news reporters that he knew personally and a few from journalists he'd never heard from before. He picked up one message and started to smile. Jared. Hopefully he had some information that would help the investigation.

Picking up the receiver, Griffin punched in a few numbers and waited for Jared to answer.

"Monroe."

"Hey, it's Griffin. I got your message. Tell me something good, buddy."

"I'm about to tell you something you are not going to like," Jared warned. "That guy Wayne you had me check out. You said he was ex-military. He's not ex-anything. His real name is Wayne LaDuke and he's employed by *The Latest* magazine. You know the one where you and Jazz are front and center? Looks like you've got a fox in the henhouse."

Griffin clutched the phone tighter in his hand, wishing it was Wayne's neck under his fingers or maybe even Tony's. He didn't like being made a fool of and those two had done a number on him. Griffin had known in his gut there was no way Wayne could have been in the military but he'd trusted Tony's bios. How many of them were smoke and mirrors?

"I know just what to do with a fox. Anything else?"

"Yeah, that Tony guy, the producer-director? Seems he's got something of a temper. He's been arrested twice for domestic battery with a former girlfriend. Charges were dropped, and from what I've been able to find the network buried the story."

"That's very interesting. Seems like I've got a couple of people I need to talk to again."

"I don't envy you this case. It's hard enough to solve a crime but to do it with a bunch of reporters watching you? That's bullshit."

Griffin couldn't agree more but the situation was what it was. "I know, but there's nothing to be done now. No sense closing the barn door if all the horses are out. I've got to make a statement to the press sometime today too. Shit, I hate this. A week ago my life was normal."

"Normal is a state of mind," Jared retorted. "Listen, I need to run. I've got a full workload here and all this research as well."

"I really appreciate your help. I owe you a steak dinner at King's."

"You bet I'll collect. See you."

Jared hung up and Griffin sifted through the rest of the messages. They could all wait. He stood and opened his office door to yell for Adam to bring in the current suspects for a second interrogation but was shocked to see Jazz at Karla's desk.

Cradling the phone between her head and shoulder, she was typing something into the computer.

"What's Jazz doing?" Adam was standing at the printer hopefully completing Jazz's statement. "Is that her statement?"

"Yep, all she needs to do is sign it." Adam grinned and puffed out his chest with pride. "She volunteered to stick around and help in any way she could so I put her to work at Karla's desk. I think she's doing a pretty good job."

If Jazz hadn't yelled at anyone or made bad coffee she was already doing better than Karla ever had, but this kind of work probably wasn't her idea of fun. He waited until she hung up before leaning down so his palms were on the desk, their heads close together.

"Hollywood, what are you doing?"

He kept his voice low. His business wasn't everyone else's business.

She looked up, merriment in her eyes. "Helping. What does it look like? No wait, don't answer that. I'm not sure I want an honest answer. I don't really know what I'm doing but I do have some rudimentary computer skills and I'm good with people. So far I've answered three phone calls and no one yelled or anything."

"Okay, I know what you're doing—why don't you let me in on the why you're doing it."

"You need the help." Such a simple statement but it made Griffin's heart twist in his chest. Her expression was honest and direct, those blue eyes wide and innocent. She simply wanted to make his day a little easier.

"Are you sure you want to do this? I can have Adam take you back to the house," he offered, trying to give her an out. She didn't have to do this if she didn't really want to.

"And just sit there doing nothing or watching television?" Jazz wrinkled her cute little nose. "No, thank you. I'd rather be busy. Are you okay with it?"

Her uncertain expression about did him in. He smiled reassuringly and patted her hand. "Of course you can stay. I'm thankful for the help. It's going to get crazy around here."

She nodded as the phone rang again and he turned his attention back to Adam. "Get Tony Albright, Gordon Schofield, Danny Molton, and Wayne LaDuke, better known as Wayne Larker, in here. I want to talk to them. Bring them in the back door."

"Sure thing, boss." Adam dropped the statement on Jazz's new desk and picked up his keys from the file cabinet. "What are you going to do about the reporters outside?"

"I'm going to make a goddamn statement, that's what I'm going to do," Griffin grated. If he gave them some information, they just might leave him alone. "Now."

Adam scurried out of the front door and Griffin stood there thinking about what he was going to say. And not say. A great deal was riding on his ability to hold things together around here and keep control.

"Are you really going to make a statement?"

Jazz's soft voice pulled his from his unpleasant thoughts. "I have to. They're like rabid dogs out there. They won't be satisfied until I throw some raw meat at them."

"Raw meat? I'm not sure I like the sound of that, Griffin." Jazz tapped a pencil against a pad of paper, her expression one of concern. "Do you want me to be there with you when you do it?"

"Yes, both you and Levi. Maybe Peggy as well. You know, in the military they would have called this a diversionary tactic."

"Diversion?"

Griffin smiled as his thoughts became clear in his mind. He knew what to do and say. He had Uncle Sam to thank for it.

"Call the hotel and get Levi and Peggy here. I'm going to give the press some homework. I might as well put them to work since they're here."

"You're starting to scare me."

Laughing at the dry tone in her voice, Griffin simply shook his head. "On the contrary, for the first time today I'm starting to think clearly. Just watch, Hollywood. Today we throw the dogs a bone and let them keep busy fighting over it."

Hopefully they would take the bait.

Griffin stood at a makeshift podium in front of the sheriff's station. Surrounded by reporters holding out microphones along with a couple of satellite trucks and cameras, he appeared to be calm, cool, and completely in control. Jazz, standing just behind him and next to Levi and Peggy, couldn't help but admire his self-possession. If this bothered him, and she was pretty sure it did, it didn't show in the least.

"Do you know why we're here?" Levi whispered in Jazz's ear.

"It's exciting just to be on the news. I hope my mother sees this," enthused Peggy. "This is really cool."

Jazz wasn't as convinced. She'd always dreamed about being in the spotlight, but now that it had happened it wasn't nearly as exciting as she'd imagined. In fact, having all these cameras stuck in her face really kind of sucked. It wasn't glamorous at all.

"I'm not really sure," she admitted. "Griffin wanted us here while he makes a statement about the case."

"Poor Sandy," Peggy sighed. "So young and pretty."

"Poor sheriff." Levi nodded to where Griffin was waiting patiently while the crowd milled around him. Citizens of the town must have heard what was going on because the throng was growing exponentially. "He's under a microscope. No one should have to solve a murder under those conditions. Especially not a private man like him."

"Can everyone quiet down?" Griffin's deep commanding tones boomed from the microphone and the crowd quickly hushed. He held up a piece of paper and began to speak. "I have a short statement and then I will take a few questions."

You could have heard a pin drop on the pavement. He had their complete and undivided attention.

"My name is Sheriff Griffin Sawyer and I have been a resident of Hope Lake my entire life except for a couple of trips to Afghanistan. I have been the head lawman for the last five years. If you want to know anything more about me, my biography is on the town website."

There were a few murmurings and Jazz was sure several people had just pulled out their phones and were searching for more information about the handsome sheriff.

"Yesterday afternoon the body of a young woman, Sandy Dunham, was found by two local men. Preliminary time of death from the coroner is estimated to be around noon. The medical examiner has not given an official cause of death but there were ligature marks around her neck and defensive marks on her body. Any DNA or trace evidence found has been sent to the state crime lab. Yesterday my deputies and I interviewed the contestants, producers, and crew of the show. After confirming the details, we were able to eliminate several people as suspects including the crew and the three contestants you see behind you. The investigation will continue today as we talk to persons of interest and receive information back from the lab."

Griffin raised his head from the statement and looked out over what must look like a sea of faces to him.

"I will take a few questions." A dozen hands shot up and voices rose until he held up his hands. "*One* at a time or this press conference comes to an end."

Griffin pointed to one of the men in the first row. "How about you start?"

"Sheriff Sawyer, you say these people have been eliminated. On what basis?"

"Solid alibis," Griffin replied, his expression flat but serious. "Levi Collins and Peggy Stahley were both with Deputy Adam at the time of the murder in the station house behind me. Jazz Oliver and I were in another town investigating another case. Next question."

A woman pushed to the front, a microphone held out. "Sheriff, are you and Jazz Oliver having an affair?"

If Jazz had expected Griffin to be angry she was disappointed. Not a flicker of emotion crossed his features. It was as if the reporter had asked him the price of milk. It was that crazy patience and control he'd learned as one of ten kids.

"I don't see what that has to do with the investigation but I'll answer it anyway. Neither Jazz or I are married to other people, so the answer is no, we are not having an affair."

"But are you sleeping together?" the woman persisted. "She was seen entering your home last night and no one saw her leave."

This time an eyebrow lifted just a little and his silver eyes turned a flinty charcoal. He leaned forward so his lips were close to the microphone. "I'm only going to say this once so I want to be very clear. Jazz Oliver is under my protection. You can twist and turn that any way you want. You will anyway. Let me say something else while I'm at it. Hope Lake is my town. These residents depend on me to protect them, and nothing will keep me from doing that. If any of you get in the way, or harass the good people of this town, the information flowing from my office to you will come to a halt. A complete stop. Do we understand each other? Good. Next question."

The crowd pressed forward and questions and answers were volleyed back and forth. The reporters seemed slightly more subdued after Griffin had given them the evil eye speech and no one referred to anymore hanky or panky—the questions focused on the investigation.

"One more question, Sheriff." A tall man in the back raised his hand. "What was the motive for this murder?"

"We don't know yet," Griffin stated flatly. "That is still a question unanswered. Why would anyone hurt this young woman?"

The man scribbled frantically on his notepad and Jazz began to see Griffin's genius. The press was going to dig into the background of Sandy, of course. If there was any dirt, they would find it, but that wasn't the important thing. Griffin had given them something to grab and work with. He'd given them a bone to chew while he got on with the investigation.

Griffin held up both hands and took a step back. "No more questions. Thank you."

Voices rang out with additional queries but Griffin ignored them all, corralling Jazz, Levi, and Peggy into the station. He pointed to the coffee machine and then back to the front door.

"Help yourself to some coffee while the reporters disperse. Unless, of course, you want to be in the papers or on TV. If so, you're free to go."

Jazz watched him head back to the interrogation room and she hurried to catch up with him, wrapping her hand around his heavily muscled arm.

"Wait. Where are you going?"

Griffin chuckled and smiled, those gray eyes no longer cold and hard. "While all the press was out front, I had Wayne, Danny, Tony, and Gordon snuck in the back entrance for a second session of questions."

Jazz slapped her forehead at his underhanded yet ingenious moves. "It wasn't enough that you sent them off to find someone with a motive for Sandy's murder. You also tricked them."

"Are you taking their side?" he asked with a widening grin and she shook her head. "I don't need them sticking their nose into my case. All of these men might be innocent and I don't want their lives torn apart by an overzealous reporter."

"As I said, you are really starting to scare me."

"I take that as a compliment." He touched the brim of his hat in a mock salute. "Can you order some lunch from the diner? Just call there, they know the drill. Add whatever you want too. I'm going to be hungry when I'm done."

Jazz decided she never wanted to tangle with Griffin when it came to the law. She'd stick to answering the phones.

He was too smart, too devious, and way too sexy.

Chapter Nineteen

G riffin's interrogation with Danny had been boring but fruitful. With hardly any pressure, the young man had finally admitted to where he was midday yesterday. He'd been locked in his hotel room with one of the waitresses from the diner and they hadn't been playing board games or watching television. Adam had been dispatched to the restaurant to bring the confused female to the station.

Griffin personally questioned her in his own office away from Danny. The trembling and crying girl admitted the deed and fearfully asked if anyone needed to know. It was a good question as the waitress was dating a young man over in Harper and had been for quite awhile. When Griffin asked why she'd put her relationship in danger, she'd said she simply wanted a "brush with fame" as she'd phrased it.

Acknowledging the situation she was in, Griffin told her he'd try and keep it out of the press but it would go in the official case file. Hopefully none of the reporters would care what Danny's actual alibi was, only that he had one.

Wayne was the next one brought into the room. Drinking a cup of coffee, the man sat across the table from Griffin, his expression one of extreme annoyance. Apparently he'd been in the middle of something when he'd been called to the station.

Too fucking bad.

"Do you have any objections to this interview being taped and then transcribed?" Griffin asked.

"No, let's just get this over with. I have things to do." Wayne's fingers were drumming on the table top in a testy manner.

"I'll try to be as expeditious as possible." Griffin pressed the record button on the laptop. "For the record, state your name, please."

"Wayne Larker."

"Do you want to stick with that answer?" Griffin leaned forward and made sure their gazes met. After a long moment, Wayne looked down at the table.

"My name is Wayne LaDuke but it seems you already knew that. Not bad for a small town sheriff."

"I do what I can," Griffin answered, keeping his own words brief. This wasn't about him and all about Wayne. "Tell me where you were and what you were doing between eleven and one yesterday."

Some internal struggle crossed the man's face but he finally blew out a long breath and slumped in his chair. "I was filing a story with my magazine over in Springwood. The coffee shop there has Wi-Fi."

"Was it another story about me and Jazz?" Ice dripped from his voice and Wayne winced before answering.

"No, this one was about Danny and the waitress he was see-ing," he said, still staring at the table but at least the tapping of his fingers on the wood had ceased. Anger churned up Griffin's stomach acid and he had to swallow down the rising bile in his throat.

"That young girl is going to be in your rag tomorrow?" he asked, keeping the pressure up with a hard tone to his voice. This man didn't give a shit about the lives he played with, only caring about the payday at the end.

Shifting uncomfortably in the chair, Wayne nodded. "That and the murder. Shit, it's my job, Sheriff."

Every cell in Griffin's body wanted to tell this man how sickening his actions were, how selfish and self-centered he was. But Griffin had too many years of practicing control to let it out. Instead he pushed away his disgust and continued the interview. His personal emotions were a luxury he couldn't afford right now.

"Do you have anyone who can verify your whereabouts?"

Wayne looked up and nodded vigorously. "Absolutely. My editor and several people in the coffee shop. I ate there too. Cheesecake."

"How did you even get there and what phone did you use? Tony took all of your phones."

"I borrowed one of the crew trucks. They were all hanging out in the diner and no one was using any of them. All the keys were just sitting out on the production table in the office after they filmed Sandy's departure."

"The office? You mean the hotel room they're using as a center of operations?"

"Yes, that one. No one was in there so it was easy, really."

Wayne tugged at his collar as if it was too tight. Good, he should be uncomfortable considering what he'd pulled.

"And the phone?" Griffin asked, trying to keep the man focused.

"The box of phones he took from us are in that office unguarded. I slipped in, got the keys and my phone, went to Springwood because I heard it's the biggest town around this area, filed my story, then slipped everything back before anyone noticed. Everyone was upset about Sandy so no one noticed me."

Incompetence reigned. So much for keeping the competitors isolated and all that shit. Jazz hadn't needed to steal Griffin's phone. She could have stolen her own.

"I'll check out your story," Griffin nodded. "Now tell me what you know about Sandy and don't leave anything out."

Wayne heaved a put-upon sigh but began to speak. "According to what I've been able to find out, which isn't much, is that Sandy is a college dropout who picked up her life and moved to New York to become a famous actress on Broadway. She's never had an actual part and from what I've heard has no discernible acting, singing, or dancing talent."

"Then what does she have?" Griffin asked, giving Wayne a hard look but silently cursing Tony. This didn't sound like the cheery, sunshine filled bio that Griffin had read.

"Balls. Not real ones," Wayne amended hastily. "She's got confidence. She's one of those people who can walk into a room of millionaires and think they're inferior. That they'd be lucky to know her."

"So she had rich boyfriends?"

Wayne shrugged. "She's been photographed with some real estate tycoons. They'll be in the paper tomorrow."

"I want those pictures." Griffin's fingers tapped on the table. "Here in this office. Have your magazine send them to me. Today."

"Yeah, whatever. Can I go now? That's all I really know." Wayne spread his arms wide as if he was helpless.

"One more question. Were you and Tony in on this together? Did he put you on the show to get publicity?"

"Fuck, no. Tony and my editor do not get along. Don't know the whole story but they pretty much hate each other's guts. I had to get on the show just like everyone else. *Now* can I go?"

"I'll call over to Springwood and confirm your story. Don't leave Hope Lake in the meantime," Griffin warned, although he was pretty sure the reporter was telling the truth.

"I won't," Wayne laughed. "This is the story of a lifetime."

Griffin shot the man such a look of dislike his smile immediately disappeared and he swallowed hard, his Adam's apple bobbing.

"I mean, I'll just go back to my hotel room and read," Wayne said quickly, his skin pale.

"Right. You'll just read." Griffin didn't believe it for a minute but if the man was innocent, and Griffin was pretty sure he was, there was nothing he could legitimately do to stop him from reporting on the happenings in town or on the case.

Griffin stuck his head out of the door and motioned for Adam to escort Wayne out of the back entrance. Three people were sitting on the bench outside of the interrogation room, Tony, Gordon, and someone Griffin had never seen. Wearing an expensive suit and carrying a briefcase, the person could only be a lawyer.

"You're next," Griffin said pointing to Tony. "Let's go."

Tony stood right along with the man in the suit. Griffin knew where this was going. Tony had lawyered up. The man held out his hand.

"I'm Ambrose Tell, an attorney from Beverly Hills. The network asked me to be here to make sure that Tony and Gordon's rights weren't being infringed upon."

Suuurrre. Just looking out for their rights.

Griffin shook the attorney's hand and ushered them both into the office with Gordon trailing behind. Ambrose put his hand on Gordon's shoulder and smiled. "I'd like my clients to be questioned together, if you don't mind."

"I do mind, actually," Griffin worked to keep his voice even despite the ever growing frustration he was feeling with this case. Every time he thought he'd found a lead the only place it sent him was a dead end. "It's common practice for each person of interest to be interviewed separately."

"And they were yesterday, I believe," the lawyer responded smoothly. It was probably why he was making hundreds of dollars an hour. "But I'm afraid I can't allow that to happen today. Together or nothing."

Making sure his features didn't reveal the argument raging inside of him, Griffin eventually nodded curtly and opened the door wider so they could all enter the room. He needed to talk to Tony and if that meant Gordon had to sit in, so be it.

While the three men settled into their chairs, Griffin stuck his head around the corner and hissed to get Jazz's attention.

"Pssst." Jazz looked up, her expression puzzled. "Did anything get delivered for me?"

Her face relaxed into a smile and she picked up a stack of envelopes and handed them over. "Just ten minutes ago. What are they?"

"Leverage," he said and twisted around, looking through the papers one by one. With a satisfied smile, he re-entered the interrogation room and sat across the table from the three men.

"So," he began, letting his gaze wander to each man and back again. Tony looked nervous, tugging at his collar, the attorney looked cool and calm, while Gordon looked angry as if he didn't want to be there. "I haven't been able to nail down your alibis for yesterday. Tony, according to your own network, you were on the phone from eleven to twelve. That still gives you time to commit the murder."

"I didn't kill Sandy," Tony rasped, sweat popping out on his forehead. "I liked her. She was a good kid."

"Then tell me where you were after the phone call." Griffin needed to keep the pressure on Tony, never letting the man relax or feel comfortable.

"He was with me," Gordon interrupted. "We were in Tony's room going over the schedule for next week. That's what I told you yesterday. Stop badgering him."

The shorter man's face was red, his hands in fists. It appeared Gordon was very protective of his boss.

"Is that true?" Griffin kept his attention on Tony, barely glancing at Gordon. It would be his turn eventually.

Tony nodded eagerly. "Yes. I just don't keep track of the time very well. That's Gordon's job."

The attorney stood, his chair making a scraping sound on the worn linoleum. "Are we done now, Sheriff? Both men have iron-clad alibis."

Griffin looked from one man to the other and smiled. "What they have are each other. Each man is swearing the other was with him without any outside corroboration. That might be a strong alibi in Beverly Hills, but here in Montana it's just words."

Ambrose's cool facade slipped slightly with a tightening of his lips as he sank back down into the chair. "Do you have any more questions?"

"I do indeed. Gordon, did you know that Tony had a sexual relationship with Sandy as recently as yesterday morning?"

The brighter red shade of Gordon's face answered the question. The assistant had known and had maybe even helped to cover it up.

"I did," Gordon answered carefully. "It was consensual."

"Never said it wasn't." Griffin turned back to Tony. "Now, can you tell me about your two arrests for domestic battery?"

Tony's face turned purple and he went to stand, but Ambrose patted him on the shoulder and told him to calm down.

"That was supposed to be erased from my record. How did you find that out?"

"We're not as backwoods here as we appear," Griffin replied, keeping his tone cool. "Let's talk about those incidents."

Ambrose placed his hand on Tony's just as he was going to speak. "I don't think any prior acts are germane to this discussion. Next question."

"No, I want to answer this," Tony protested. "I didn't do anything wrong. Lena was crazy and she'd attack me. Then she'd call the police and tell them I assaulted her. I was only defending myself."

How many times had Griffin heard that very same whiny tale? Too many to count. He didn't believe it this time either.

"So your explanation is that a woman who was five feet one and less than one hundred and ten pounds hurt you so badly you had no choice but to hit back? That's your story?"

"It's the truth," Tony swore. "Ask Gordon. He met Lena. He knows what she's like."

"It's true," Gordon nodded. "Lena would go after Tony with kitchen knives. She was insane."

Was Gordon covering for his boss? It sure seemed like it at the moment. But Gordon couldn't rig an entire crime lab.

"I have a warrant for your DNA, Tony," Griffin held up one of the envelopes. "A lab tech is going to be here in about fifteen minutes to collect it."

Tony turned and gave his attorney a frantic look. "Can they do this?"

Griffin slid the envelope across the table to Ambrose who quickly scanned the contents. "It appears the warrant is in order."

This time Tony did stand up, the chair flying backwards. He paced up and down the small room, his breathing becoming increasingly ragged.

"I admitted that Sandy and I slept together. What do you need my DNA for?"

"Sandy fought her killer, Tony, and she had skin underneath her fingernails. Will your DNA match, I wonder?"

"No," Tony said forcefully, coming to a halt. "I didn't hurt her. I swear as God is my witness. The last time I saw Sandy she was alive."

"Then you won't have any problem giving us a sample. If you're innocent it won't match," Griffin replied reasonably.

Tony rubbed his forehead and nodded. "Fine. Whatever. Is that all?"

Sliding the second envelope over to the lawyer, Griffin shook his head. "Not quite. I also have a warrant to impound and search all the vehicles belonging to the crew. That means your rental and all the trucks and vans." Even Ambrose didn't look happy this time as he perused the warrants. "And lastly, I have a warrant to search the rooms of Tony and Gordon."

Tony groaned and leaned back against the wall, looking up at the ceiling. "There's nothing to find. I didn't do anything. God, this is worse than any movie. I'm being railroaded for a crime I didn't commit."

"If you didn't do this, the best way to clear yourself is to co-operate and let the lab do their job."

"Sure," Tony snorted. "That's probably what you say to everyone. Right before you arrest them."

Griffin stood as well, wanting to make sure Tony understood what was going on very clearly.

"Listen, I don't get a commission if I arrest you. I get paid either way. I want to find the killer. The real killer, not just a notch on my belt. That's not good enough. The only way to get justice for Sandy is to find out who really did this. If it's not you, then fine. This is not a personal thing. This is about Sandy. Got it?"

The man swallowed hard and nodded. "Got it. What happens now?"

"You stay out of the way while your room is being searched. You give up your DNA quietly when the lab tech comes to get it."

Ambrose cleared his throat. "And Gordon?"

Griffin leveled a gaze at the assistant, still unsure as to where he fit in all this mess. "I tried to get a warrant for his DNA as well but I was turned down. Not enough probable cause. That could change if I find something in his room. In the meantime, he needs to cooperate and not leave town."

"Fine," the attorney answered briskly. "Do we wait here?"

"Yes, and then Adam will escort you out the back entrance. There's no need for the press to get a hold of any of this. Although Wayne has probably called his office and told them everything."

"What about Wayne?" Tony asked, his brow furrowed. "What do you mean?"

"You didn't know? Wayne's a reporter with *The Latest.*"

If Griffin had doubted Wayne earlier when he said Tony wasn't involved, there was no doubt now. Tony and Gordon both looked astonished. To Griffin's surprise, Tony turned on his assistant immediately.

"You little worm! Did you know? Did you? Did you set me up?" Ambrose had to stand hastily and keep Tony from going after Gordon. There was that nasty temper again.

"I didn't know," whined Gordon. "I didn't."

"Then you're incompetent. You're supposed to check out the contestants. When we get back to Los Angeles, you can clean out your desk. You're fired," hissed Tony, a small amount of spittle landing on his chin. The pretty boy producer wasn't so good looking at the moment.

Gordon cowed in his chair while Ambrose tried to calm the producer down. A seasoned attorney would know this little display of emotion was not helping his client in the least.

"I'll leave you three alone. I think you have plenty to discuss."

Griffin turned and exited the room, closing the door behind him with a small smile. The first step was to shake up Tony and Gordon walking in lockstep with each other. Whenever Griffin encountered alibis that were co-dependent like this it made him very suspicious.

Something was there and Griffin was going to get to the bottom of it.

Tony had motive. Covering up an illicit relationship, plus a violent past.

But did he have opportunity? Only Gordon really knew.

The next step was to find the crime scene and the vehicle Sandy had been transported in. Maybe Jared might come through with more details as well. Heck, even the press might come up with motive. All the lines were in the water—he simply needed a few fish to take the bait.

Chapter Twenty

"**C**an I use your phone after dinner?" Jazz asked Griffin. "Tony still has mine. I need to call my friend Caitlin. I'm sure she's heard about all this by now. She's got to be freaking out."

They were both staring into the refrigerator trying to figure out what to eat for dinner. It had been a long day at the station but Jazz was glad she'd been able to help out. It was a heck of a lot better than sitting around waiting for answers.

"Tony doesn't have your phone—the crime lab does. I was able to get a warrant for everyone's rooms and the phones too."

"Will I get it back?" Jazz sighed as she thought of her brand new phone being pulled apart and ruined by some guy in a white coat.

"You will, I promise." Griffin turned at the sound of the doorbell pealing insistently. There were a few reporters camped out at the end of the long lane to the house, but most had turned in for the night. Besides, she doubted they'd come right up to the front door and ring the bell.

Griffin shrugged and looked outside the window before breaking into a grin. "It's my friend Reed and it looks like he brought food."

Pulling open the door, Griffin ushered in a tall handsome man carrying several takeout containers. The smell of fried chicken made Jazz's stomach growl and she pressed her hand to her abdomen in embarrassment. If the two men noticed, they didn't act like it. Slapping each other's back and smiling, they led the way to the deck while she grabbed plates, silverware, and paper napkins from the kitchen.

It was another beautiful night, the air warm and soft. A small breeze kicked up and tousled her hair and cooled her skin. Their visitor stuck out his hand with a smile.

"I'm Reed Mitchell, and you must be Jazz."

"I am," she nodded. "It's nice to meet you."

Jazz couldn't stop her gaze from going back and forth between the two men so similar and yet so different. Both had dark hair, although Griffin kept his cropped short while Reed's was slightly longer with some strands falling over his forehead and a few curls at his neckline as if he was due for a trim. Both had the square jaw and impressive physique that made women's heads turn and their panties damp.

But it was Reed's eyes that caught her attention the most. Steel blue, they were guarded and wary. This was a man who was either hiding something painful or trying to keep something painful from happening to him. Perhaps both. Yet at the same time he seemed to carry himself with the utmost confidence, a pure male swagger to his step.

All that emotional unavailability paired with a face and body like a god, he had to have women following him around with their tongues hanging out. Females were suckers when it came to a testosterone laden hunk with baggage.

"As nice as it is for you to bring dinner, I have a feeling you're here for something else," Griffin said as he handed out cans of soda. Jazz opened the containers and steamy goodness wafted from the styrofoam all the way to her nose. They passed around the food and filled their plates as the crickets chirped in the background along with the occasional splash from a fish or duck.

"I figured you hadn't had time to eat with everything going on. I saw your press conference on television today. You handled it well. It's still a clusterfuck though. Excuse me, Jazz," Reed apologized ruefully. "Sometimes I forget I'm around a lady."

"I've heard and said most dirty words, so curse away." Jazz lifted a forkful of fluffy mashed potatoes to her mouth and almost groaned aloud at the deliciousness. Starch and butter were so damn good.

"Jared asked me to help," Reed continued. "I've been looking into your victim's past and found out some very interesting things."

Griffin wiped his mouth with a napkin. "Do tell. Was she a drug dealer or something?"

Putting his fork down on the plate, Reed shook his head. "She was a high school dropout who kicked around living on the dimes of rich, older men. Married ones, mostly. They'd get her a place to live and a credit card and she was all set. Until she'd inevitably try to blackmail them for more money. She'd threaten to tell their wives to get the big payoff. Then she was off to the next victim."

"So she wasn't an actress on Broadway?" Jazz shook her head in disbelief. If this was true, Sandy had missed her calling. She would have been a great actress. No one had had a clue.

"That's what she called herself." Reed shrugged his shoulders and buttered a roll. "I think she even went on a few auditions from what I could dig up but that wasn't the point. She went there to meet successful people who had connections."

"And she never went to college?" Jazz passed Griffin a roll before going back to her own dinner. It was sad to hear that Sandy's life had been one scam after another. Jazz hadn't gotten close to the girl, but no one deserved to die the way she had no matter what they'd done.

"The closest Sandy got to college was an apartment near NYU." Reed pushed away his now clean plate. Jazz was always amazed at how much and how quickly men could put food away.

"If she was blackmailing Tony, that would give him motive," Griffin observed, drinking the last of his soda.

"If," interrupted Jazz. "Who was she going to tell? Tony and Caitlin aren't married. All Caitlin would have done is dump Tony's ass. It's not like they had three kids and a house in the hills."

"Maybe she threatened to tell the network." Griffin had leaned forward, his fingers steepled in thought. "I'm sure the bigwigs don't want their producers playing hide the weasel with one of the competitors."

Almost spraying ginger ale she'd just guzzled, Jazz clapped a hand over her mouth. She choked and coughed as she tried to swallow the cool liquid and giggle at the same time. Both Griffin and Reed slapped her on the back.

"Hide the weasel?" Jazz wiped the tears from her eyes with the napkin. "Holy shit, don't say things like that when my mouth is full. Since when did you become funny?"

"I've always been funny."

"I think she means funny haha, not funny strange," Reed retorted, a huge grin on his face. "But to your point, that could be construed as motive. He would want to protect his position at the network. When do your forensics come back from the lab?"

"Hopefully soon. My gut tells me I'm not going to get a confession. I'm going to need DNA and trace evidence to find the guilty party."

Reed glanced at his watch and grimaced. "Shit, I need to get going. I promised one of my deputies to cover their shift tonight."

They all stood and Jazz started to gather up the plates while Griffin talked to Reed softly. Not sure what they were saying, she carried the dishes into the kitchen and began to load the dishwasher.

"A woman who does dishes? She's a keeper." Reed shoved his hat back on his head. "Let me know if you need anything. I've got my cell on me twenty-four-seven."

"Thanks for dinner and the information." Griffin walked Reed to the door. "I'm guessing the tabloids would have dug this up eventually but I don't have time to waste."

"None of us do. Have a good night."

Reed clomped down the porch steps and Jazz heard the growl of a truck and then the hum of the engine as it disappeared into the night.

"You two were whispering." She closed the dishwasher and walked back to the deck to gather up the empty food containers. They all must have been hungry because there was very little left. "Can I ask what you were talking about, or would that fall into the nosy interfering female category?"

"He asked me if I needed help keeping the press away from you. In my experience, Reed is extremely protective of females. I told him we were okay for now but I would keep the offer in mind. I trust you'll let me know if the reporters start to hound you."

Griffin took the styrofoam from her hands and shoved it into the trashcan, pushing it down before closing and tying it off.

"He seems like a nice man. I didn't see a wedding ring so I assume he's not married. Has he ever been?"

Maybe a woman had put that pained look in Reed's eyes. Even a man like him could be hurt.

Griffin spread his arms wide and chuckled. "Who the hell knows? Reed never, and I mean never, talks about his past. I'm told he mentioned sisters once, but that's it. He could have been pulling our legs. All of us know absolutely zilch about Reed before the day we met him. If we found out he was grown in a lab until the age of thirty we wouldn't be shocked. Or maybe he hatched from the egg of an alien. All I know is he is the most secretive son of a bitch I've ever met. He's also one of the nicest guys. He'd give you the shirt off his own back if you needed it. He's just that way."

"What *do* you know about him?" Jazz's mind was whirling, thinking of a million possible scenarios for the handsome sheriff.

"Only what he's dropped in passing. He was in the military like pretty much all of us. We know he did tours in both Iraq and Afghanistan. We know he came back about six years ago and had a job offer with Homeland Security but he turned it down. He likes steak and pizza, Steven Seagal movies, and motorcycles."

"That's it? How can you even call yourself friends? I know everything about Caitlin and she knows everything about me."

"That's because you're women. Men don't need to talk about their feelings and eat ice cream, honey."

Jazz blew a raspberry and Griffin laughed as he carried the trash bag into the house. He'd already explained to her the folly of leaving food outside when there were wild animals all around.

"So how do men bond?" she asked, locking the door behind her out of habit. "Beer, poker, and cigars?"

Griffin double bagged the trash and placed it in the garage right outside the kitchen door. "Personally I like fishing, hunting, and checking out women's racks."

"Guns and boobs, huh? How typical," she chided but her pulse was already beginning to speed up at the gleam in his eyes. She'd seen that very same look last night and this morning.

Hallelujah.

"Speaking of awesome racks, Hollywood, I like that yours is purely factory original."

Jazz rolled her eyes and looked down at her chest. "Do you know how many times people in the business have told me I should have my boobs done? I've lost count, that's how many."

Griffin finished washing his hands at the sink and dried them on a towel. "That would be a real shame. They're perfect just the way they are. Perfect size, perfect shape." He tossed the towel away and placed his hands on her hips, letting then slide upward until they were cupping her breasts. Streaks of heat went straight to her pussy and her nipples tightened under his palms.

"They wouldn't be better…bigger?" She had to swallow hard to speak as his thumbs brushed the tips making them ache and harden even more.

"No way." Griffin shook his head and then lowered it, placing a kiss on each taut peak through the fabric. "They wouldn't fit with your frame."

Part of her wanted to ask him what he meant by that, but then he slipped his arms around her and pressed his lips to hers and she forgot all about it. He took his time with the kiss as if they had all night, and they actually did. It was still early, the sun not quite down. They could explore each other to their hearts' content for hours and still get a good night's sleep.

His lips traveled across her jaw to her ear where he nibbled on the lobe. Giggling, she slapped lightly at his arms but he just pulled her even closer until the heat of his body penetrated her clothes. She could feel the outline of his hard cock against her belly and she rubbed herself against it until he groaned.

"I saw you brought some of those girly bath liquids. How about a soak in the tub?"

She loved soaking in a bubble bath and had brought along a bottle of suds in the hope the hotel had a big tub. Unfortunately the motel in Hope Lake didn't fall into that category but Griffin's tub certainly did. It wasn't jetted but it was plenty large enough for the two of them. It was sweet of him to offer as he probably didn't hang out in a sweet-smelling bath very often.

"You'll smell like citrus," she warned him. "Specifically oranges. Can you handle it?"

"It's better than purty flowers," he groaned. "I can handle it if you're there."

She let her hands glide up his muscular back loving the way he felt, so firm and strong. "I'll be there alright. Last one there's a rotten egg."

She dashed toward the bathroom but a long arm snagged her around the waist and lifted her up and over his shoulder. She was destined to never enter the bedroom under her own steam. Beating on his lower back with her fists, she waggled her legs to try and distract him but as always he was goal-oriented. Before she knew it, she was being gently placed on her feet in the middle of his bathroom.

"Strip, Hollywood." His voice was gruff with arousal and she could clearly see the ridge pressing against the fly of his jeans Her mouth watered at the thought of driving him crazy with her lips and tongue.

He twisted the handles on the faucet and the tub began to fill. She grabbed her bath bubbles from the cabinet under the sink and poured a generous amount into the steamy water.

Immediately the churn of the water began to create a creamy foam that she couldn't wait to lie in and relax.

She shucked off her clothes but he still beat her into the tub, relaxing back and beckoning for her to join him. Stepping into the hot water, her tight muscles loosened and she breathed a sigh of relief as she lay on top of him, her back to his front. He seemed to need the silence so she didn't speak as he turned off the faucets and then picked up a washcloth, running it over her already sensitive skin.

Goosebumps broke out as the rough material slid over her shoulders and down to her breasts. She arched her back as he made ever tightening circles around and around until the nap of the fabric abraded her already hard nipples, sending arrows of pleasure straight to her pussy and clit. Moaning her approval, she luxuriated in her arousal and her eyelids drooped keeping the world at bay. There was nothing but his talented, giving hands and the sound of the water lapping against the sides of the tub.

"You are so fucking beautiful."

Heat swept through Jazz at his hoarsely voiced words. She rarely felt beautiful in a town where everyone was gorgeous. Talented makeup artists and hairdressers could wave their wand and make her look good for a few hours but in her everyday life…she was just Jazz. Hips too wide. Boobs too small. Lips too thin. Legs too short. She'd heard it all in the last several years.

But this man thought she was beautiful. Griffin was the type of man who would never say something he didn't truly mean.

"So are you," she said because she honestly thought he was. It wasn't only his physical appearance that was impressive—although it was—it was his heart. The way he loved his family, and the way he took care of his town. Even the way he wanted to protect her from the bogeymen in her life.

His lips near her ear, he chuckled and slid the washcloth down over her belly to her clit, already swollen and aching with need. Taking his time, he rubbed slow circles around the nub, never breaking the rhythm that was surely going to send her over. Shuddering with pleasure, she braced her legs on the edge of the tub, letting them fall open.

"Men can't be beautiful," he chided, pressing a kiss to the damp skin of her shoulder.

"You are," she insisted, the words coming out as a half-groan. "And men can be beautiful."

He didn't answer her this time. Instead, he increased the pressure on her clit until the room spun. Grabbing hold of his powerful thighs to stay steady, she teetered on the edge of release.

"Come for me, Hollywood. It's time, honey."

His voice was deep and rich and his hands were doing magical things. At some point the washcloth had drifted away and his callused fingers were rubbing the sides and top of her clit.

"Griffin."

She didn't know if she whispered or screamed his name but her climax hit hard and fast. Water sloshed over the sides and onto the floor as her body bucked with each wave of pleasure. He crooned soothing words as she let it take control, giving herself up to it until it left her weak and wrung out.

Curling into his arms, he wrapped them protectively around her, capturing her lips with his own in a carnal kiss of promise. There would be more pleasure to come.

He lifted up slightly in the water and she moved to the end of the tub as he dug for a condom from his pants pocket. Jazz let her gaze wander lazily down his masculine frame taking in every curve and dip of his muscles.

Rivulets of water ran down his torso and across his ridged abdomen tempting her to follow that silver trail with her tongue. The coil inside of her tightened in response at the sight of him hard and ready. She pulled up onto her knees and pressed their wet bodies together, his impressive cock sandwiched between them.

"My turn," she whispered as she kissed a path down the hard planes of his chest and stomach. Engulfing the head of his cock in her mouth, she sucked him in as far as she could take him.

His fingers twisted in her hair and a groan was torn from his throat as she tightened her lips and moved up and down the shaft while her tongue traced the veins and bumps. His cock seemed to pulse and swell in response and a heady feeling of power swept through her. Giving Griffin the kind of pleasure he gave her was a satisfying feeling. The more she gave, the more she received in return.

His hands wrapped around her upper arms and he tugged her away, his breathing ragged and harsh.

"I need you bad, Hollywood. Are you ready for me?"

She'd been ready from his first touch. Now she was desperate for what he could give her. He guided her so she was bent over the edge of the tub, her torso cushioned by a thick towel. She heard the crinkle of a wrapper and then his strong fingers on her hips as he guided his thick cock inside.

Griffin started slowly at first, and then when she wriggled her hips in impatience, he pulled back and thrust in hard and fast. It took her breath away and started the immediate build toward another climax.

Gripping the edge of the tub, she braced herself as his thrusts sped up giving her exactly what she needed. The spring inside of her coiled tighter and tighter as each stroke rubbed a sensitive place inside of her. Realizing he'd found her sweet spot, he went after it relentlessly until her whole world turned upside down and sideways. Waves of heat and pleasure curled her toes and made her shake and shudder.

Griffin tumbled over the edge right along with her, a string of expletives falling from his lips. She could feel his cock as it jerked inside of her, his hot seed filling the condom and sending another shock wave right to her core.

They stayed locked together for a long time, their breathing returning to normal. When Griffin finally pulled away, he trailed his lips down her spine making her shiver and quake. He quickly ran the washcloth over both of them before helping her to her feet. Wrapping a towel around her, he leaned down with a smile and kissed the tip of her nose.

"Go lie down, honey. I'll clean up in here."

Her knees like jelly, she managed to somehow make it from the bathroom to the bed. Tossing the towel aside, she slid between the cool sheets and closed her eyes. She loved times like this when it felt like they were the only two people in the world. Pulling the covers up to her chin, she luxuriated in the cocoon they'd created around themselves. No reporters. No suspects. No town council members.

Just her and Griffin.

Jazz sighed with contentment as she watched Griffin stride out of the bathroom wearing nothing but a smile. She had big plans for them tonight and they'd only accomplished a small portion of her list so far. She reached for him as he joined her on the bed, snuggling into his arms.

Letting the silence surround them, she could hear his even breathing and feel the slow rise and fall of his chest. He'd been working so hard. It was good he was getting some rest. Her plans could wait for another time.

Sleep, however, didn't come easy to Jazz. She lay awake replaying every conversation with Tony she'd ever had. Could he really be a killer? Then she thought about Casey Charlock, who still waited for her justice. Would Jazz be here when that happened? Would it ever happen?

Eventually she gave up and headed out to the deck with Griffin's cell phone. It was time to bite the bullet and talk to Caitlin. Her friend deserved to know what was going on. She just wasn't going to be very happy about it.

Chapter Twenty-One

Griffin sat in his office and looked out over the station, quiet and subdued after all that had gone on a few days before. He needed the peace, his nerves and patience stretched thin from working a case that had suspects but no real evidence.

It had been two days since he'd questioned Tony and Gordon. Two very long days. No amount of pleading phone calls to the state crime lab from Otis could hurry them along. Griffin was starting to think something was wrong with the evidence that had been collected. Even the reporters were bored and spent most of their time hanging around the diner drinking coffee and eating homemade pie. A few had even left town, chasing a flashier, more exciting case.

In the meantime, another slick, expensive attorney had arrived from California for Tony. Calling into the station on his arrival in town, the man had handed Griffin his card with a smug smile and said that his client was no longer answering questions. If Griffin needed to know something, he could submit questions in writing and possibly Tony would take the time to answer them.

But probably not. It didn't matter anyway. There wasn't anything to be asked until Griffin heard from the lab.

"Do you have a minute?" Jazz stood in front of him looking so damn beautiful he wanted to throw her down on his desk and have his way with her. She was the only good thing in his life right now. Having her support these past few days had meant everything to him. He hadn't even minded how she'd taken over his bathroom.

The first day she'd kept her makeup and things all neat in a little purse, but by the second day they'd began to migrate onto the vanity and onto any flat surface in the shower. When they'd left the house this morning, there had been no less than a dozen items on the counter by the sink and at least four separate bottles or jars in the shower. One had been shampoo and the other conditioner. He had no idea what the others were but if she needed them then there wasn't much he could do about it. Besides, she was always so pretty how could he complain?

"Sure, come on in. I was just looking at the map of the area around the site where Sandy's body was found, trying to think of where the murder might have taken place."

"Any ideas?" Jazz leaned over his desk and he could smell the clean fragrance of her skin. His cock stirred and he had to shift in his chair to relieve the pressure. He probably ought to get used to being semi-aroused whenever she was around. They made love every night and every morning, each time better than the last.

It wasn't the sex that drew him in but her easy to be with manner. She seemed to understand instinctively when he needed quiet, not nattering on and on about nothing. She was happy to cuddle when he was in the mood but just as content to sleep in her own space. There were no demands he cater to her preferences. They simply compromised when they didn't agree. No pouting or emotional blackmail.

But that didn't mean he was in love. He'd know if he was. Not yet. It was too soon and he wasn't ready. Being in love meant things would change, and damned if he was ready for that. Couldn't things go on the way they were?

"I've got a few ideas. Here." He pointed to an old hunting shack to the north of town. "And here." He moved his hand to the west, pointing to the Rinehart ranch. "The one to the north is an old cabin that a lot of hunters use. It's isolated so no one would hear anything and definitely off the beaten path. The one road leading to it can barely even be called that. It's basically two tire tracks in the dirt and brush."

"And the other?" She peered more closely at the map, her brow knitted in concentration.

"That ranch used to belong to the Rineharts."

"Used to? Who does it belong to now?"

"The bank. It was foreclosed on about a year ago. Remy Rinehart held on as long as he could but in the end he sold off all the horses, livestock, and any heavy equipment and moved out. They haven't had a buyer for it yet. The only thing is the house isn't far from the road. The hunting cabin would be more private."

Griffin tapped the map with his finger, frustration tight in his gut. He was missing something, something important. Police work wasn't much like in the movies. It was usually boring stake outs, mindless sifting of paper clues, and the hope that forensics would find something. Mostly it was old-fashioned grunt work.

That was where he was sitting. His suspect had motive and opportunity, but there was no physical evidence linking him to the crime. That meant Griffin had to work twice as hard to find that link.

"But the killer would have to know about the cabin, right? How would Tony know about it? He's been here less than two weeks."

"True. That's why I've requested a warrant for the Rinehart place." Hopefully he would have it this afternoon.

"What about the cabin? You didn't get a warrant for it?"

"I don't need a warrant for the cabin. It's open for anyone to use. I'll stop there on the way to my meeting and look around. If someone's been up there recently, I'll be able to tell."

In fact, he'd asked Reed to meet him there. His friend had a keen eye for detail around crime scenes and might see something Griffin missed. He had to admit he didn't hold out much hope though. In the last two days he'd searched every line shack, tent, and abandoned structure in a twenty mile radius from where Sandy's body had been found. Today he'd decided that he had to expand his criteria for possible kill sites, which was when he'd taken a look at these two properties.

"You're heading out to a meeting?" Jazz had a cute little pout going on but he knew better than to think she was really upset. She'd actually shocked him with how independent she was, spending her free time while he was working with Levi. He would be heading to the academy in a few weeks and was working with Adam until then. Wayne was also hanging around town trying to dig up dirt on anyone and basically making a nuisance of himself. Peggy and Danny had left when they had been cleared from suspicion.

"My sheriffs' meeting. What will you do today?"

Jazz still helped out part time in the office but he really needed to get someone full time. While she was good at the job, he didn't think it excited her much. She was probably itching to get back to her life in Los Angeles. A thought he didn't like to ponder too often.

Jazz reached across his desk and placed a sticky note near his elbow. "I was thinking about going to talk to Tonya and see what she knows about this maybe imaginary boyfriend Casey had. You know I haven't forgotten her."

Griffin picked up the square piece of paper with an address scratched across it. Jazz had been looking in Casey's file again. "I know you haven't, honey. I don't want you to think I have. I think about her every day. It's just a cop has to work a case when it's hot."

"I know. That's why I was thinking I could go talk to Tonya since you can't spare anyone right now."

Her expression was hopeful and Griffin was loath to dash her hopes. He held up the address. "Can you even find your way there by yourself? This is in Springwood."

"If I can find my way around the Los Angeles freeway system, I think I can manage to find a small town off a main road. So I can go?"

He could see how important this was to her, and despite his conflicted feelings he finally nodded. "But," he warned, "you cannot go as someone from my office. I can't lend you one of the SUVs since you're no longer a deputy in training. You'll have to take my truck. Also, you cannot present yourself to Tonya as anyone official. You can tell her how you came to see Casey's file and ask if you can talk to her. If she says no, then that's that. You turn around and come back, got it?"

"Got it." Jazz nodded, a gleeful smile across her face. "How about you draw me a map?"

Griffin comforted himself with the knowledge that technically there was no way he could stop one civilian from talking to another civilian. Besides, keeping Jazz busy while he worked this case seemed like a damn good idea. If she wasn't bored, she wouldn't be thinking of reasons to leave Hope Lake.

"Can I interrupt for a moment?"

Gordon's voice pulled Griffin's attention from the woman across from him to the doorway where the man stood uncertainly. Shifting from foot to foot, the assistant producer looked as if he'd like to be anywhere but where he was standing.

"Sure, Gordon. How can I help you?"

It was too much to hope for that the man was here to rat out his boss. Maybe he too had a big-wheel lawyer coming to town. Griffin had to give the man credit though. Even in the face of all this shit, Gordon hadn't crumbled. All Griffin had to do was sit in the same diner as Tony and the producer practically dissolved into tears.

"I have Jazz's check from the insurance company. Actually it's really just a receipt for what they deposited into her account." Gordon held out an envelope to Jazz. "I gave Levi his already. Everyone else's has been mailed."

Griffin really didn't give a shit how the others were getting their checks. He only cared that now Jazz had her money and freedom. She could leave at any time.

"Thank you," Jazz said softly, reaching for the envelope. She gazed at it and then up at Griffin. He knew she was thinking the same thing he was.

"Uh, well, okay. I'll go now." The uncomfortable silence must have jarred at Gordon and he turned and exited the office quickly.

Her finger ran under the lip of the envelope and she extracted a single sheet of paper. Her hands trembled slightly as she read it, folded it, and then stuffed it back. Her color was high and she pushed the envelope into her purse.

"Are you okay?" Griffin couldn't stop himself from asking the question. She looked a little sick to her stomach, actually.

"It's just more than I thought."

"That's good, right?" She deserved the money. He knew she needed it.

"It just feels so strange. My entire adult life I've worried about every dime. As of today I can breathe a little easier. I'm not sure how to react."

"How about acting like you're happy?" He smiled, hoping she would follow suit. She seemed to be in something of a daze. The check must have been a whopper. He was pretty sure she was worth ten of him now.

Smiling tremulously, she took a deep breath. "I am happy. I can easily pay off my credit card and sock away a robust rainy day fund, although Los Angeles is an expensive place to live. It won't last long."

"You could live somewhere cheaper." *You know, like Hope Lake.*

"New York isn't any less expensive. Any place people want to be, well the cost of living is going to be high. And I don't have any acting jobs to go home to."

Ouch.

Griffin decided to simply put it out there. He didn't know where their relationship was going but he knew it was too soon to see it end. "Then you don't have to be in a hurry to leave."

"Don't you want your bathroom back?" she teased. "Or the rest of your bed? Or the remote?"

His own words were coming back to bite him in the ass. "You're not much trouble," he answered lamely. Not knowing what to say, he said the first thing that came to mind.

"Now there's what every girl wants to hear. That she's not much trouble." Jazz was openly laughing at him now. "Don't worry, Griffin. I'm not trying to slip into your life under the radar and make myself indispensable. I'm sure better women than me have tried and failed. Your bachelor existence is safe."

Those were the words he'd always longed to hear from a woman. Every woman but her, that is. He'd spent so many years avoiding relationships that now he was thinking he might want one he didn't have a fucking clue how to make it happen. What could he say?

Do you think you might want to stick around and see what happens?

Just what every girl dreams of hearing. Not. To make matters worse, he was no Prince Charming. He was pretty sure that damn prince had never gutted a fish in his life. Was there such a thing as a camouflage crown?

"Here are my keys." Griffin dug his keyring from his pocket, changing the subject back to work. It felt comfortable and a damn sight safer. "Let me draw you that map."

Pushing thoughts of relationships, scary commitment, and possible love aside, he concentrated on getting Jazz ready to talk to Tonya. What they had or what they could have was going to have to wait, at least for now.

"You're late," stated Logan as Griffin and Reed strode into the roadhouse. "Didn't you get my texts?"

"We did and then ignored them," Reed laughed. "We were on our way already. Don't get pissy. We stopped off and took a look at the hunting cabin north of Hope Lake."

"And?" Tanner prompted, leaning forward to grab one of the sodas from the middle of the table. "Any luck?"

Griffin shook his head in disgust and frustration. He was sick and tired of coming up empty at every turn. "Another bust. The place looked like it hadn't seen another human being in forever. Everything was covered in a thick layer of dust. Nothing disturbed or out of place either. It's not our scene. That leaves the Rinehart place. If it's not our kill site then I'm plain out of ideas."

"You'll get this," Seth assured him. "We'll help all we can."

Sighing, Griffin popped open a can of soda and shook his head. "It pisses me off that someone can stroll into my town, commit a murder, and then laugh behind my back."

"Doubt he's laughing," commented Jared, who was sitting at the end of the long table. "He's probably scared to death of being caught. He'll trip up and you'll get him. But you need to stop making this personal. That will get you nowhere."

Griffin rubbed his temple where a headache had bloomed after his conversation with Jazz. It seemed like he couldn't do anything right lately. "You're right, but sometimes it feels personal."

"Unless your half-brother kills your father because the man murdered his own wife, and then your mother…no, it's not personal."

It was good Logan could kind of joke about what happened to him. Of course, having Ava was a major consolation prize.

"When you say it that way," Griffin laughed as his phone started vibrating and beeping with an incoming email. "Shit, sorry about that."

Pressing a few buttons, his heart started to pound as he looked at the sender. The crime lab.

Fucking finally.

"It's the lab. Hold on, let me read the report."

He opened the attachment and scanned the contents. A myriad of emotions began to churn in his gut as the results of each test were revealed one by one.

"Well," Reed prompted. "What does it say?"

Taking a deep breath, Griffin read the report. "Tony Albright's DNA matches the sperm collected from Sandy, but does not match the skin under her fingernails."

"So Albright's not your guy." Tanner's mouth turned down. "Sorry, man."

Griffin kept reading. "Hairs and blood belonging to the deceased were found in the back of one of the crew vans. While crew fingerprints were found, neither Albright's nor Schofield's prints were found."

Logan frowned. "Wait. So one of the crew did it? But I thought they all had an alibi. Although the killer could have worn gloves, so the lack of evidence could be meaningless. And who is Schofield?"

"Gordon, the assistant. And the crew do have solid alibis," Griffin said grimly. "But there's more."

"The DNA under the deceased's fingernails was placed into the system for comparison and it matched another sample."

"Excellent." Jared slapped the table top with a grin. "Who's our killer?"

"The unknown assailant of Casey Charlock."

Griffin placed the phone down and looked around the room at five of the best lawmen he'd ever known. They looked as sucker-punched as he felt.

"Say that again," Tanner said. "Casey and Sandy were murdered by the same person? How is that possible? Casey was killed months ago and these people came into town recently."

"So someone in Hope Lake killed them both?" Seth's expression was puzzled, his gaze darting back and forth as his mind worked on the question. "But why? What do the two women have in common? This doesn't make any sense."

That was true. Or was it? Casey and Sandy were both attractive young women who had been strangled and their bodies dumped away from the kill site.

"I don't have any evidence that Sandy had any interaction with the people of Hope Lake. None at all. So if someone from the reality show killed Sandy then they had to be in Hope Lake when Casey was killed," Griffin intoned, mostly to himself. Something was niggling in the corner of his brain. Something he couldn't quite put his finger on. What was it that Tony had said that day?

Gordon and I scout locations for our reality shows months in advance...

"Jared? Do you have your laptop with you?" Griffin's mind was going a mile a minute, his body pumping with adrenaline.

"It's in the truck. What do you need?"

"I need you to check out Gordon Schofield's credit cards. See if he was anywhere near Hope Lake at the time of Casey's murder. Hell, while you're at it, see if there are any unsolved murders in the towns where he's visited in the last couple of years."

"I'm on it." Jared disappeared out of the front door of the roadhouse but Griffin didn't need the computer search. He knew with a growing certainty deep in his gut what Jared was going to find.

Unbeknownst to Griffin, Gordon had been in Hope Lake nine months ago scouting the location. He, for whatever reason, had killed Casey and now Sandy. Gordon was a stone cold killer.

Chapter Twenty-Two

G riffin's map in hand and the radio blaring, Jazz drove the truck down the almost deserted road. It was midday and the sun was high in the sky. A great day for a drive. It was such a luxury to be on roads that didn't boast of bumper to bumper traffic and exhaust fumes. She could get used to something like this.

That was the elephant in the corner of the room she'd been ignoring this week. Since coming to Hope Lake and meeting Griffin, her life in California wasn't looking all that great. The chances of her ever making it in show business were slim, and even if she did would that make her happy? Being here and followed by the press had shown her that notoriety wasn't the glamorous, wonderful thing she'd thought it would be. It turned out she was more private than she'd ever believed.

Living with Griffin also hadn't been the ordeal she'd imagined. For all his bluster about not liking his routine messed with, he was pretty laid back. They found common ground easily, both of them knowing when to give in. If something was important to Griffin, Jazz would gracefully let him win. But when he saw that something was important to her, he would defer to her wishes.

Damn it all, she was pretty sure she was in love with him. She didn't want to be because it was all too complicated and messy but she might not have any choice.

He simply might be *the one*.

The engine coughed and sputtered and the truck began to slow down, losing acceleration quickly. A glance at the dashboard had her cursing a blue streak. The gas gauge showed empty but she could swear she started out with three-quarters of a tank. What kind of mileage did this thing get?

Pulling the truck off to the side of the road, she put the vehicle in park, all the while muttering under her breath. She reached into her purse for her phone but then groaned in realization. Her phone was at a crime lab in Missoula.

Well, shit.

Pushing open the driver's door, she walked around to the back of the vehicle to look into the bed of the truck for a gas can. Climbing onto the back bumper, she was able to see the completely clean – and empty – truck bed.

Double shit.

The sound of an oncoming car had her jumping down to the ground and waving her hands. Maybe she could flag down a motorist and use their phone to call Griffin. She wasn't stupid enough to get into a stranger's car although everyone she'd met since coming to Montana had been very friendly and helpful.

Elated as the car slowed down, she was surprised to see Gordon behind the wheel. He had a briefcase on the seat beside him but was dressed casually.

"Hey!" she greeted him as he rolled down the passenger window so she could lean in. "I'm so glad to see you. I think I ran out of gas. Can you let me use your phone?"

"I can do you one better. I think I have a gas can in the trunk that's full. The rental agency was very thorough. Gas stations are far apart in Montana."

Jazz performed an internal fist pump. She could get back on the road right away and still talk to Tonya. There was an exit just five miles up the road. She could fill up the tank the rest of the way there.

Gordon popped the trunk and rummaged through its contents. "Yes, here it is. Nice and full."

She walked to the back of his car where Gordon was holding up a gas can. "I can't thank you enough," she sighed, letting some of the tension drain from her body.

"I'm sorry, Jazz. But I can't let you talk to Tonya."

She didn't have time to react to his knowing about Casey's friend and where she was going. Gordon reared back with the metal can and swung it forward, catching the side of her face and temple. The world spun as pain exploded in her head and her hands went out instinctively to keep herself from going down. Her heart thumped in her chest and sweat broke out over her entire body as she struggled to stay conscious.

Her fingers clawed at the solid metal of the car but she could feel herself falling as if in slow motion. The breath was sucked from her body and her vision turned a mottled gray before spots of black danced in front of her eyes.

Griffin pulled his SUV in front of the hotel and hopped out. His friends were right behind him having offered to help in Gordon's arrest. Griffin hoped the man would come along quietly, without any fuss, but he'd been doing this too long to count on it. Having some extra hands that were highly experienced to boot could only help. If Gordon tried to run, they'd be right behind him.

When Jared had searched for unsolved murders of young women, there had been several in towns that Gordon had visited. The dates from his credit cards matched up to the time frames of the crimes. There was a good chance Gordon Schofield was a serial killer.

Griffin could only be glad that Jazz was out of town talking to Tonya. If the arrest didn't go well, she would be far away from any danger.

He stopped at the hotel office to talk to the manager who hadn't seen Gordon in over an hour and the room had been empty when the maid cleaned. Griffin told the manager to stay put while they visited Gordon's room, but if he wasn't there they would need the room unlocked.

"Tanner, Seth, and Logan, you guys take the back in case he tries to run. We'll take the front. Hopefully I can arrest him without any problems."

The three lawmen rounded the building as Griffin, Jared, and Reed approached room number five cautiously. Pulling his gun from its holster, he shoved himself against the building on one side of the door frame while Jared and Reed did the same on the other side. Griffin reached out his arm and knocked loudly.

"Hope Lake Police," he yelled through the door. "Open up."

There was no sound from inside the room. Griffin knocked and announced himself again, waiting silently and not moving. Finally Griffin shook his head and lowered his weapon, frustration and adrenaline pumping through his veins, but steps behind him made him raise it again. His adrenaline surging, he whirled around and came face to face with the hotel manager.

"Whoa, it's just me," the man joked, holding his hands in the air. "The maid just stopped by the office and said she saw Mr.

Schofield driving west not long ago. Do you still want me to open his door for you?"

"Yes, please." Griffin relaxed, blew out a breath, and holstered his weapon.

"What kind of car was he driving?" Griffin would put out a BOLO for the whole county along with the warning that Gordon could be armed and dangerous. A man facing multiple murder counts wouldn't want to be arrested.

The manager frowned. "One of those nondescript rental cars. White. Four doors. Maybe a Ford or a Chevy. Mid-sized. Can I help in any way?"

"Just keep your eyes open. If you see him, call the station. Do not engage him. He might be dangerous."

Brows raised, the manager nodded and unlocked the door. "All these show business people seem a little strange."

Reed sidled up next to Griffin, holstering his weapon. "What do you want to do now? Where do you think he was going?"

"I don't know but my gut is telling me that we should follow him. He might know the area a little bit having scouted here nine months ago, but we know it like the back of our hands. If he's moving west there are only so many routes he can take. He might even be headed to the Rinehart place."

Seth, Tanner, and Logan joined them, their expressions grim. Jared leaned against the brick facade of the hotel, stroking his chin.

"The Rinehart ranch? That's the abandoned ranch west of here isn't it? What's his connection to that place?"

"I think it might be where he killed Casey and Sandy. He needed somewhere private to do the deed and I've looked everywhere closer to the dump sites. He might be re-visiting the scene, you know, getting his kicks from it. I'm trying to get a warrant to search the place."

Tanner gave Griffin a twisted smile. "If we see his car there, I think you've got probable cause, buddy. What's the plan?"

"After we search his hotel room for any clues, we all head out in three groups of two. That way each group can investigate one of the possible routes he might have taken. I'll take the one to the Rinehart place."

Griffin was already thinking of every possible scenario as to how this might play out. The more he thought about it, the more he was glad these five men were here. His deputies were good but this was a completely different league.

Griffin's phone buzzed and he dropped a few swear words as he dug into his pocket. It was Adam. Again. Griffin really needed to have a talk with him.

"Sawyer."

"Boss, it's Adam. I think you may want to head out here. Levi and I are west of town and we found your truck on the side of the road."

That wasn't possible. Jazz had taken his truck to Springwood.

"It's probably not my truck. Jazz borrowed it to talk to a friend of Casey Charlock's. Run the plate and find out whose it is."

There was a pause and for a moment Griffin thought the call had dropped.

"That's just it, boss. It's definitely your truck. Keys are in the ignition still and Jazz's purse is sitting on the passenger seat. Maybe the truck broke down and she started walking."

Griffin's truck was always in the shop these days but if Jazz had abandoned the vehicle and started hoofing it, why on earth would she leave the keys and her purse?

It didn't make any sense and Griffin didn't like it at all. Something wasn't right. A deep sense of foreboding was building inside of him, his gut screaming that Jazz was in trouble. She wouldn't have walked away like that.

"Have Levi stay with the truck and you go farther down the road and see if you can find her. We're on our way in the meantime."

Griffin hung up and stared at his phone cursing that he hadn't replaced Jazz's cell with something, even a cheap throwaway. It had been foolhardy to send her on a road trip without one and that was his fault. He fucking knew better.

He shoved his cell back in his pocket and scraped his hand down his face. If anything happened to Jazz he didn't know what he'd do.

"My truck is abandoned on the side of the road and Jazz is gone. Keys still in the ignition and her purse on the seat. Pair that with the fact that Gordon was headed in the same direction and you've got a situation I don't like in the least. Instead of splitting up, we need to head there and see what we can find. Let's go."

The six of them made for their vehicles as fear began to take root in Griffin's gut. What if Gordon had Jazz?

"Relax, man, we'll get this guy." Logan headed for his truck with Jared right behind him.

"Relax," Griffin muttered. "He's always fucking relaxed."

Reed slapped Griffin on the back as they all headed out to the vehicles. "Logan has a point. Tension is not going to help you at this juncture. You, me, him—we all know what we have to do. Let's just go do it and get it done."

Griffin couldn't agree more.

Jazz's head, face, and body ached as her eyelids slowly lifted. A shaft of light hit her pupils and she groaned at the pain that pierced her skull. Shutting her eyes against the harsh sun shining through the wooden slats of the roof above, she waited for a wave of nausea to pass before opening her eyes again, her brain sluggish as she took in her predicament.

She was lying on a hard floor, bruised and battered from Gordon's rough handling. It was hot and still, the aroma of dirt, sweat, and gasoline heavy in the air. Experimentally moving her arms and legs, she found her wrists were bound together behind her but her legs were free.

A tidal wave of images flooded her as she remembered how she'd gotten here. Running out of gas. Gordon hitting her with a metal can. Throwing her in the trunk. At some point she'd lost consciousness and now she was a captive inside…a barn or stable? The floor was dirt and concrete with a large stack of hay bales but there didn't appear to be any animals or people.

Her heart accelerating, her gaze darted around the large open room looking for an escape route. The door was in front of her, wide open but was Gordon waiting on the other side? She couldn't stay here and wait for him to kill her, she had to take action. She needed to find a way to escape and the first thing was getting herself untied.

There was no doubt in her mind that Gordon intended to kill her, whether it be now or later. When she'd last seen his face right before she'd passed out, his eyes had an empty, glassy look in them. It was as if nothing human resided there and it had given her chills. If she didn't do something fast she was going to be dead.

He was trying to keep her from talking to Tonya which could only lead Jazz to believe he had something to do with the Casey's murder. Was he the talent scout that was going to make Casey a star that Buddy had spoken of? Perhaps Casey had been telling the truth about that. Jazz knew that Tony traveled to locations so it wasn't much of a stretch to think that Gordon did also. He could have met Casey and promised to put her in the movies or make her a supermodel.

Carefully and quietly, she levered to a sitting position, wincing as her head pounded and her stiff muscles and spine protested. Pulling at the rope wrapped around her wrists appeared to be futile. It moved loosely on her sweat-slicked skin but she couldn't see what she was doing to untie the knot. Heart pounding and stomach twisting with desperation, she slid her hands under her butt and then down her legs, leaning forward so her body was essentially folded in half. Bending her legs slightly, she was able to push her bound wrists from the back of her body to the front.

All those years of yoga and Pilates had finally paid off. She'd have to give her instructor a big kiss when she got out of here.

If she got out of here. Alive, that is.

Taking a few deep breaths she lifted her arms, the rope wrapped around her wrists, and began to tug at the knot with her teeth, heart beating so loudly she thought he might hear. If Gordon found her trying to escape it would not be good.

Able to find some purchase at last, Jazz gritted her teeth together hard on the rope and gave it one mighty tug. The knot finally loosened and she was able to wriggle her hands free. Her relief was short-lived however. She needed a weapon in case Gordon was outside this building. A few heavy rakes and shovels were hung on the wall right behind her and she started to rise and grab one when she heard footsteps.

Falling back down on her already sore ass, she balled up the rope in her fist and placed her hands behind her back. If this was Gordon coming, he didn't need to know she'd managed to get loose.

He walked in carrying two large metal gas cans but stopped when he saw she was sitting up. Scowling, he set them down and walked a few steps toward her.

"You're awake," he said unnecessarily, his tone conversational. "I was hoping you'd stay unconscious. Fire is a terrible way to go I would imagine."

He said it as if they were discussing the weather or maybe how the Yankees were going to do this year. He didn't really look or sound any different. Completely non-threatening in appearance at the moment, this man was planning to murder her in cold blood. She took a few deep breaths to calm her nerves and steady her voice. She'd heard stories of people who had talked their way out of situations like this although she couldn't recall any specific examples. It was something about making them see you as a person with feelings and dreams. She had plenty of those.

"Why are you doing this? I thought we were friends."

The words came out choked but at least she'd managed to speak. Fear had taken up residence in her abdomen and she had to swallow hard to keep her stomach contents down.

"Women have never been my friends. You act like you are and then you laugh at me." Gordon's expression had gone blank, his eyes going to that cold dark place she'd seen earlier. Twisting the top off one of the gas cans, he poured the contents all over the bales and the wood structure. He tossed the empty away and reached for the second one.

"I've never laughed at you, Gordon. I wouldn't do that. Ever. I don't understand why you're doing this. Don't do this."

Her voice had gone up and sounded shrill to her own ears. She shuddered as he stopped to gaze down at her as if she were a bug to be studied and then stomped on.

"I can't let you talk to Tonya," he said flatly.

"You know Tonya? What will she tell me, Gordon? Did you hurt Casey?"

Jazz had to concentrate on her breathing so she wouldn't hyperventilate. In and out. In and out. Slowly, trying to control her racing heart.

"I would have made her a star but she laughed at me."

"I'm sure you didn't mean to hurt her."

Her fingers curled tightly around the rough rope as she tried to control her impulse to get up and just run. He'd catch her in seconds, overpowering her. Stay calm. Think.

"I didn't want to hurt her." He twisted the cap off the second can, the acrid smell of gasoline already assailing her nostrils. "I didn't want to hurt any of them but they shouldn't have laughed. Sandy laughed and pointed at me. She said she was going to tell Tony and the whole crew. I couldn't let her do that."

God, he killed Sandy too. And what was he saying about *any* of them? How many were there?

"I would never laugh at you. I'm your friend. You were sweet to me when I told you I wanted to be a star."

"You'll tell your sheriff boyfriend about me and I can't let that happen. I'm sorry, Jazz. I wish things could be different. You're just like all the young girls I've talked to over the years. Big dreams, a pretty face, but little talent. You never would have survived in Hollywood. I'm saving you years of heartache."

By murdering me? Fuck you.

Focus. She took another steadying breath and tried to make herself sound friendly but cowed. Let him think he was powerful.

"I won't tell Griffin. I won't tell anyone."

She might as well have said it to the door or the saddle propped against an old table. Gordon had tuned her out, splashing the gasoline all over the walls. He threw the second can on the stack of hay bales and pulled a box of matches from his pocket.

One and this place would surely go up like a tinder box, the hay and old, dry wood combining with the accelerant to create an inferno.

With her inside.

"Don't do this." Her hands twisted on the ropes and she pictured the shovel hanging on the wall behind her. Her back and arms were slicked with sweat and her ribs hurt where her heart pounded in her chest. She was running out of time.

Gordon didn't answer, instead pulling a match from the book and striking it along the side before tossing it into the stack of hay. Instantly the tower of bales went up, the orange and yellow flames licking as high as the roof. Turning his back to her, he walked toward the far end of the barn where he'd soaked a stack of wood with gasoline.

This was her only chance.

Pushing to her feet as quickly as she could, she grabbed the shovel from the wall even as sparks from the rapidly growing fire shot around her like fireworks. Running up behind him, she wound up and swung the heavy implement as hard as she could at the back of his head. He seemed to freeze for a moment, and the lit match dropped from his still fingers.

At first she thought she hadn't hit him hard enough but then his legs seemed to crumple under him and he went down to the floor. The heat from the flames seemed to sear her skin and she had to bat at her hair as white-hot sparks fell on her head. The smell of burnt hair and smoke made her cough and retch and she stumbled out of the barn.

Scrambling on shaky legs to get away from the fiery structure, she slammed to her knees into the dirt still trembling with half fear and half relief. A part of her hated leaving Gordon to perish in that fire, but he'd left her few options.

It was either him or me.

Levering to her feet, she had to grab onto a tree for support as she sucked in the clean, fresh air. She looked all around her and almost fainted with gratitude when she saw a house at the top of the hill. She could call Griffin from there. He wouldn't have any idea that she was in trouble or that Gordon was the killer.

Using her shirt to wipe the sweat from her face, she watched in horror as Gordon stumbled from the blaze, staggering but clearly still alive. Soot and blood stained his clothes and he was unsteady on his feet. He wasn't giving up and neither could she.

Turning towards the house, she sprinted as fast as she could up the hill hoping against hope he hadn't seen her. Her breath laboring and her heart racing faster than her feet, she pressed a hand to her rib where a stitch was slowing her down. She slipped on the loose gravel but managed to find her footing again, using her fingers to dig at the ground. One look over her shoulder told her Gordon wasn't giving up. Slowed down but determined, he was making his way up the hill, never taking his eyes from her.

He was coming.

Chapter Twenty-Three

Griffin pushed the accelerator of the SUV all the way to the floor. He'd punch his foot through the fucking floorboard if he thought it would make this thing go any damn faster. The needle on the speedometer read a hundred and twenty but it wasn't nearly quick enough.

Deep in his gut he knew something bad had happened to Jazz. The fact that Adam and Levi had seen his truck abandoned on the side of the road with the keys still in the ignition, her purse on the seat, and no sign of Jazz was deeply disturbing. If she wasn't walking to the next town, where was she? She was a city girl and he doubted she would take a ride from a stranger.

"We'll find her."

Reed's softly spoken words from the passenger seat did nothing to calm Griffin in the least. His pulse was racing and a band was tightening around his chest as one nightmare scenario after another raced through his mind.

"She's disappeared. Gordon's on the loose and was seen driving this direction. I have a bad feeling, man."

"We don't even know why he killed those other women. What is his MO? Do they all remind him of his mother or something? You don't know he's taken Jazz."

But Griffin did know. Deep down inside, fear was gnawing away at his gut. Reed was trying to make Griffin feel better but there was only one thing that would do that. He needed to see Jazz safe and sound with that beautiful smile on her face.

"It's too much of a coincidence, don't you think?"

Reed's lips twisted and he scraped his fingers through his hair. "It is a bit of a coincidence. One I wouldn't like, I admit."

Griffin slowed down as his truck came into view. Pulling his own vehicle directly behind it, he jumped out of the SUV so he could examine the truck and the area. Levi was standing next to it and walked up to meet him.

"Tell me what you've seen."

Griffin didn't bother with greetings or social niceties and Levi appeared to understand. He nodded and pointed to the cab of the truck.

"The keys are still in the ignition and her purse is on the seat. I tried to start the truck but no luck. I checked under the hood but there's nothing loose. Before Adam left to find Jazz, we tried jumper cables but that didn't work. Then I checked the gas tank. Empty with a big hole in it."

"I know for a fact that tank was filled three-quarters full," Griffin growled. "I don't have a fucking gas leak. It just came out of the shop."

"You do." Levi knelt by the rear tire of the truck. "I crawled underneath while I was waiting for you guys. You can feel the gouge in the tank. It's not something that just spontaneously happens. Someone or something put that hole there."

"Still think it's all a coincidence?" Griffin asked Reed, who was watching the proceedings with a grim expression. "My truck was parked behind the station this morning. Gordon could have got to it. He knew she would run out of gas and followed her. Hell, she'd never think Gordon could hurt her. She might even have got in his car of her own free will. Son of a fucking bitch. This is all my fault."

He'd failed Jazz. The one woman who had made him feel like there might be a future and he'd fucked it all up. He was a sorry excuse for a lawman and she was paying the price.

"It is not your goddamn fault." Tanner stepped forward, his brows pulled down and his lips pressed together. "This is no one's fault. Got it?"

"No." Griffin shook his head. "I was focused on Tony because he was sleeping with Sandy. If I'd loo–"

"Just fucking stop this shit. Stop second guessing yourself." Reed cut him off. "Gordon didn't have a motive that you knew of. We follow the evidence. That's what we do. If there wasn't anything against this guy there was nothing for you to do."

"Now what do we do?" Seth asked, his arms crossed over his chest. "Assuming this guy has Jazz, where would he take her?"

"We need to check the Rinehart place." All Griffin had was his intuition at this point, but it speaking loud and clear. With Jazz's life possibly on the line, waiting for a warrant was not going to happen.

"I think that's a very good idea. And fuck." Jared pointed into the distance. "I see smoke on the horizon. Isn't that the same direction we're headed?"

With a growing sense of horror, Griffin saw the tendrils of dark smoke begin to fill the clear blue sky. Something on the Rinehart spread was on fire, and Jazz might be caught up in it.

Finally at the top of the hill, Jazz didn't take the time to look over her shoulder. She could hear Gordon's footsteps in the thick grass. That was enough. Running straight to the house, she pulled on the doorknob, rattling the hinges, but it wouldn't budge. Banging on the door, she peered anxiously into the home through the dirty and smudged windows. Her heart fell as she took in the rooms devoid of any furniture or humans.

This house had been empty for a long time.

Even if she could get into the home, the chances of a working telephone were nil. Once inside, could Gordon trap her there? Possibly even setting fire to the house as well? She couldn't take the chance of being cornered.

One glance over her shoulder told her that Gordon was gaining on her. She had to make a decision and make it now. There was no time to waste. Running to the far side of the structure, she was hidden from Gordon's gaze. For mere moments. She frantically looked around for a weapon but there was nothing but a grove of shade trees the hung over the large yard.

Trees.

Not hesitating for a second, she braced her leg on the trunk of an old oak and grabbed one of the lower branches. She hadn't climbed a tree since she was a child but some things you never forget. Especially when your life just might depend on you remembering.

Grunting with the effort, Jazz managed to pull herself up into the top part of the branches, skinning both her knees and shins along the way. The thick foliage of July gave her decent camouflage despite the pink of her blouse. Its bright color had dulled considerably between the dirt, sweat, soot, and blood that now covered it.

Balling herself up as small as possible, she balanced on the upper branch, her entire body trembling with fear. She had to press her hand over her mouth to keep the scream that was building inside of her from escaping and announcing her location.

She couldn't lose control now. She had to keep herself together if she had any hope of coming out of this alive. If Gordon found her, she didn't stand a chance in hand to hand combat with him. He was taller, heavier, and stronger and could easily overpower her small frame.

Time seemed to stand still as she waited in the silence. It could have been seconds or minutes, the only measure the frantic beating of her heart. Teeth chattering together from the chill of terror that swept through her body, she sat perched in the tree shaking like one of its leaves in the cruel Montana wind. It was almost a relief when Gordon came striding into sight. Whatever daze he'd been in after she'd hit him was long gone, although the back of his head was matted with blood.

He paused under the shade trees, looking from side to side as if she might be hiding behind one of the thick trunks. Maybe he'd think she ran in another direction. Or perhaps found a way into the house. Even from where she sat, she could hear his labored breathing and see the angry set of his shoulders and features. Far from the calm, almost robotic man he'd been earlier, now he was clearly enraged.

Jazz relaxed slightly as he stalked off to the front side of the house. Pressing her hands to her face, hot, salty tears leaked down her dirty cheeks even as the smoke from the barn made her throat ache. She had to swallow hard several times to keep from coughing and giving herself away. Gordon wasn't far and he could come back at any minute. She tried to scrub away the wetness from her face as she silently screamed in her head.

Wrapping her arms around her torso to stop the shaking, she closed her eyes and imagined Griffin's handsome face. So strong and good, he'd captured her interest, then her respect, and now her heart.

Yes, her heart.

No more denying or pretending it hadn't happened. She loved Griffin Sawyer. Every part of him. The passionate lover. The considerate boyfriend. Heck, even the control-freak room-mate who didn't want to share the remote. She loved him. She was only sorry she might not get a chance to see him again. To tell him he was loved.

She'd spent her whole life trying to get love and approval. First from her parents and then from an audience. Twisting and molding herself into something new with each role. Something she wasn't and never would be. With Griffin she was simply herself. All the struggling to become a star suddenly seemed silly and stupid. She wanted to be loved for who she really was. End of story.

When Gordon came back into her sight, she bit down onto her knuckles to keep from whimpering. His head was whipping from side to side and his breathing was even heavier now, whether from fury or the smoke she couldn't tell.

Her breath caught as he stood still under the tree and leaned his head back so he was looking up into the branches. She froze in place, every muscle in her body paralyzed with fear as he circled the tree gazing up. Directly at her.

"You fucking cunt. Get down here right now."

✧ ✧ ✧ ✧

The three vehicles pulled up to the burning building, tires screeching. Griffin barely had the SUV in park before he jumped out, running toward the now destroyed stable. The roof had caved in and flames leaped from the rubble as thick, black smoke filled the air. If anyone was in that building there was no way they could have survived.

The bile in his stomach rose to his throat, choking him along with the dust and smoke. He stared at the destruction for a long moment before praying to the God he hadn't spoken to in quite awhile that Jazz wasn't in there. That she was somewhere safe.

"That's Gordon's rental car." Levi was pointing to the sedan sitting about ten feet away. Griffin ran over to the vehicle and circled it, coming to a horrified halt near the trunk.

"Blood."

A smear of blood was on the bumper easily seen on the shiny surface. He didn't know for sure it was Jazz's blood but his the gut instinct he'd come to rely on so heavily when he was overseas was screaming at him now. His woman was in danger.

Casting his gaze around the property, his eyes went to the abandoned home on the top of the hill. Was that the kill site? Or the stable that was now in ashes, any evidence destroyed?

"Let's spread out and search. Reed, Jared, and I will search the house. You guys head for the outbuildings."

There were still several smaller buildings on the property where Gordon might take Jazz. But Griffin's money was on the house. Running up the hill with Jared and Reed at his heels, he froze when he heard a man's shouting.

"Listen," he hissed, holding his arm out so his friends would halt. The yelling was coming from the back of the house. Pulling his firearm, he nodded to Jared and Reed who both fanned out, circling around the far side of the structure. Griffin could clearly hear Gordon screaming curses but had yet to lay eyes on him.

Flattening his back against the side of the house, Griffin slid slowly to the corner and peered around to the backyard. Gordon was shouting up into a tree and struggling to climb the slippery bark, coughing as he breathed in the smoky air.

"Freeze, Gordon. This is Sheriff Griffin Sawyer with the Hope Lake Police Department." Griffin's voice cut through the heavy air. "Drop whatever weapon you may have and get on your knees on the ground."

"You fucking bitch! You goddamn cunt!" Gordon ranted and raved in a raspy voice even as he slid down the trunk once again and onto the ground. From Griffin's vantage point, the man didn't appear to have a weapon but one could never tell. Far too experienced to assume anything, Griffin kept his own firearm drawn and ready.

"Kneel on the ground," he commanded but Gordon wasn't listening. Screaming at the top of his smoke-filled lungs, he looked past furious and bordering on crazed.

Griffin moved out into the backyard and Reed and Jared followed. Gordon seemed oblivious to the fact that he had three loaded guns pointed right at him, instead ranting about some cosmic unfairness.

Stopping about three feet from Gordon, Griffin lifted the gun higher and inspected the scene. Gordon's hands were empty but he still might have a weapon in his pockets or pants.

"Shut up." Griffin normally had copious amounts of patience, but when it came to Jazz…

"Where is Jazz?"

Gordon began yelling again but this time he pointed to the top of the tree. Taking a few deep breaths, Griffin braced himself for the question he was afraid to ask.

"Jazz? Is that you? Are you okay?"

Miraculously, his voice sounded even and in control despite him feeling anything but. If this guy had hurt Griffin's woman, he was going to wish he'd never been born at all.

"Jazz?" he repeated when there was no answer. Was Gordon just one crazy bastard and shouting at trees? If so, where was Jazz?

"Yes. Yes, I'm okay."

The voice was small and the coughing and hacking that followed sounded terrible but Griffin had never heard such sweet music. Almost dizzy with relief, he had to discipline himself to keep from taking his eyes from Gordon and looking up into the tree. Until he could see for himself that she was alright, he wouldn't truly believe it.

The sound of sirens in the distance but growing closer alerted him to the fact that firemen would soon be swarming the scene. He had to do everything he could to shut down this situation now so they wouldn't be heading into a dangerous stand-off.

"Get down on the ground, Gordon."

Griffin's teeth were gritted together and he could see Jared and Reed moving closer and surrounding their suspect. Gordon finally appeared to be cognizant of the fact that he had three cops with drawn guns on him. His eyes were darting back and forth as if looking for somewhere to escape.

"There's nowhere to go. It's all over. Get down on the ground."

There was no sound but the rustle of a few leaves as Gordon weighed his options, none of them good. For a moment it looked like the man might run, and Griffin tightened his hold of the firearm. Instead Gordon fell to his knees, his shoulders shaking with heavy sobs.

Jared and Reed kept their guns on Gordon as Griffin holstered his weapon and then pressed the man to his stomach. Cuffing his hands behind his back. Heaving a sigh of relief, he exhaled the breath he'd been holding as he'd waited for Gordon to decide what he was going to do.

Wiping the sweat from his brow, he let Jared and Reed deal with the prisoner while Griffin stood to coax Jazz down from her perch in the tree.

"C'mon, Hollywood," he crooned. She was barely visible through the thick cover of greenery, but he could see her pink blouse and part of a bare leg. "We've got him. It's safe, honey."

A small movement in the branches, then her pink tennis shoes, and then the bottom half of her tiny frame. So slowly he almost went up after her, she climbed down from the tree. Once on a lower branch, he held his arms out to her.

"I've got you, honey. Just jump. I've got you."

The trust on her face as she did as he asked almost did him in. He didn't deserve that trust. Hadn't earned it with how he'd handled this case but she'd given it to him anyway. His chest didn't feel big enough for his heart as he cradled her trembling body to his own.

His throat tightened painfully and he carried her down the hill to where fire trucks and an ambulance had arrived. If he stayed anywhere near Gordon Schofield, Griffin was going to do something that would definitely get him fired. And maybe some jail time. He knew his friends would handle Gordon.

"Griffin, I–" Jazz broke out into a coughing fit, her shoulders shaking.

"Easy, honey. Let these guys help you and then you can tell me all about it. I know Gordon killed Casey and Sandy."

He kept his tone low and soothing and her head dropped onto his shoulder. By the time the EMTs ran to him with a stretcher, he didn't want to hand her over.

He never wanted to let her go.

Chapter Twenty-Four

Jazz luxuriated in the steamy water of Griffin's bathtub, sinking down to her chin. She had three butterfly bandages on a nasty gash on her forehead, a black eye, minor scrapes and cuts on her legs and arms, and a myriad of bruises. But she was alive.

She'd been kept overnight at the county hospital for observation as she'd sucked down quite a bit of smoke. They'd given her a pain pill and she'd slept for hours, only waking this morning when the nurse had bustled in to help her dress.

She'd been horrified at her reflection in the bathroom mirror. They'd tried to clean her up last night but she was still dirty and sweaty. Her hair had burned where sparks had fallen on her head and at least six inches would need to be lopped off. The purplish shiner on her eye was puffy and sore but it could have been much worse. She was grateful Griffin and his friends had saved her. Some bruises and a haircut seemed minor, really.

Even now as she ran the events of yesterday through her mind, it seemed like a really terrible dream that suddenly turned out okay. When Griffin had shown up, Jazz hadn't believed it was real. Perhaps she'd dreamed him up out of her subconscious? That her fear had conjured up the man she loved just when she needed him most? It had been too good to be true.

Then as it had dawned on her that she wasn't hearing things, that it was real and Griffin was truly there to save her, she'd been afraid to make a sound in case she distracted him. The thought seemed silly now as Gordon would never win over Griffin, but at the time she hadn't wanted to take the chance.

"I have to go back to the office, honey. Just for a little while." Griffin was standing in the doorway of the bathroom. He'd been great about picking her up from the hospital and making her comfortable today but she knew he'd rather be anywhere else. He'd made it very clear when they'd first met that he didn't do the caring and nursing thing. "Ava and Presley are here to keep you company. Madison is going to check in later today. She's a doctor."

"I'm fine. Where is Gordon?"

For some reason, she still needed to hear that he was behind bars. Logically she knew he wasn't going to break out of jail, but emotionally she needed the reassurance.

"He's in jail," Griffin said, his tone gentle. "That's where he's staying until the county authorities come get him. Hope Lake doesn't have the facilities to keep a prisoner more than overnight. He won't come near you again, I promise."

"I know," she said in a small voice. She hated being like this, being scared. Griffin probably felt as though he was obligated to care for her. She needed to get over this and start standing on her own two feet.

When he'd pulled her from that tree yesterday, she'd almost told him how much she loved him and that she didn't want to be a star anymore. Today she was glad she hadn't. In the emotion of the moment, he might have said it back whether he really felt it or not. She didn't want to have to wonder if he'd said it out of duress. There had to be a better time to tell him.

"You've been in the tub awhile, are you ready to get out? I can help you get dressed. You won't want anything rough on your scratched skin so I was thinking you could wear one of my t-shirts."

Griffin didn't wait for her to answer. He reached down, his strong hands under her arms, and lifted her from the water until she stood on the bathmat. Wrapping a thick towel around her, he pressed a chaste kiss to the undamaged side of her face, and then proceeded to gently dry her skin. His touch was so tender she almost cried and had to swallow back a sob.

"Wait here and I'll get you something to wear."

Griffin disappeared out of the bathroom so she tucked the towel around her and reached for her toothbrush. She wasn't so helpless that she couldn't clean her own teeth.

She was done by the time he returned and he very carefully, avoiding her scraped skin, slid the panties up her legs and pulled the soft cotton shirt over her head. Several sizes too big, it hung to her knees. She couldn't hold back a giggle at the irony of the situation.

"What's so funny, Hollywood?" His lips had curved into a smile.

"You," she admitted. "Normally you're taking those panties off, not putting them on."

"That's true, but I don't think you're in any shape to be playing bedroom games. But I promise when you get better I'll take them off." His fingers brushed her cheek. "It's good to see you smile, honey."

"It's good to be smiling." It did feel good. She didn't want to wallow in the events of yesterday. Something bad had happened to her but she was standing here alive and well with the man she loved. "I'm okay, Griffin."

"I know you are." He nodded in a somber manner. "But you had a traumatic experience yesterday and you're all banged up. Maybe taking a day or two to heal wouldn't be a bad idea."

"Are you asking me or telling me?"

Griffin barked with laughter. "Since you asked, telling you. Remember what the doctor said. Take it easy."

Looking down, her hands were wrung together tightly. She slowly pulled them apart and took a deep breath. "I will. I promise. Now tell me about Ava and Presley. I met Ava that one day, but I've never met Presley. What is she like? What are they both like?"

"Ava is now completely normal since she's finished her book. You'll really like her—she's a real sweetheart. Presley is too, although much livelier. She really keeps Seth on his toes."

"It's nice of them to keep me company today."

It was an understatement to say that Jazz didn't want to be left alone.

"I'm sorry I have to go in to the station." Griffin's expression was troubled and she tried to wave away his concerns but he stubbornly shook his head. "No, I mean it. I'm sorry I have to go but there's paperwork that need to be filed and formal statements. Gordon is talking and I need to be there for that."

"I know you have to work. I can take care of myself."

"After what you've been through you should let yourself be spoiled a little. In fact, Ava brought some fresh fruit and yogurt. She thought it might be easy on your stomach."

They'd tried to feed her at the hospital last night and again this morning, but Jazz's system had rebelled at the mere thought. Her insides were still twisted into knots of fear.

"That was thoughtful," Jazz said instead as he shoved his hat on his head. She had to squelch her desire to beg him to stay and hold her all day long. "What time will you be home?"

She shouldn't have asked but she couldn't help herself. She wanted him close by.

"As soon as I can. I'll call and check on you later."

Griffin pulled her into his strong arms, his warmth and scent enfolding her protectively. She sighed and rested her head on his broad chest. For the first time this morning she felt completely safe. He stroked her back and hair but then reluctantly pulled away with a sigh.

"Go to work. I'll be okay," she assured him, feeling crappy about his conflicted expression. He wanted to go and she was making this difficult. "Why don't you introduce me to our guests?"

Wrapping his arm around her shoulders, they walked toward the living room. She'd be fine today. She'd talk girl talk with her guests and pretend that everything was exactly the same as it was before yesterday. Before she was afraid. Afraid that Gordon would kill her.

And terrified that Griffin didn't love her.

"Jazz can stay with us," Griffin's mother insisted, her voice loud enough the whole damn station could probably hear. "Since you have to work, it's the perfect solution."

Griffin intended to get through work and get back to Jazz as quickly as humanly possible. He wasn't hanging out here at the station house for fun. As for Jazz going to stay with his parents, that was far from a perfect solution. He needed her to be in his home.

"Once I get done with these statements I'm heading home. I'm perfectly capable of taking care of Jazz, Mom. Ava and Presley are staying with her today and I'll try and stay home with her tomorrow if I can. We're fine."

His mother crossed her arms over her chest and lifted an eyebrow. He knew that look and he was about to get cross-examined like a suspect. He'd learned at the feet of a master.

"Pardon me for pointing this out, my son, but since when do you *take care* of people? I've seen you shun your siblings for daring to cough in your presence. You've shuttled girlfriends out of your life for having the nerve to sneeze or perhaps cry and need comfort. Are you sure you're equipped to handle a needy young woman who has been terrorized by a serial killer and physically hurt? Are you prepared to comfort her, son? She's going to need that after what she's been through."

The bustling station house had gone dead silent in the wake of his mother's sharply worded questions, but Griffin wasn't intimidated. He knew exactly where his mother was coming from. Everybody in the station could go pound sand. He wouldn't fuck this up.

Calling on all the patience he might still have inside after everything that had happened in the last twenty-four hours, he stood up straight and tall. He wanted his mother to know he was damn serious about this. About Jazz.

"I'm ready and willing to give Jazz whatever she needs to get through this. She's my woman and my responsibility. I'm working here as hard and as fast as possible so I can get home to her. If she needs to cry, I'll be there with a shoulder. If she needs someone to fix her soup, I'll do it. If she needs someone to scare away monsters under the fucking bed, I'll do that too."

His mother's shoulders relaxed and a smile spread across her face. "No need to use that kind of language, young man. I'm just glad you've learned it at last."

"Learned what?" he asked, anxious to get back to work. His mother was smiling like a Cheshire cat and he had a sneaking suspicion why.

"That taking care of someone you love isn't a burden," she answered simply. "It's a privilege."

Hanging his head, he stared at his boots trying to think of something to say that didn't make him sound like a selfish jerk. Except that he had been a tad too self-involved in the past.

"I've figured that out." He lifted his head and gazed into his mother's kind eyes. She was looking at him not with disgust but with pride.

"It's all I could hope for. You're already a good, honorable man. You just needed to learn to open your heart a little and let someone in. I like Jazz, by the way. Not that it's important. It's only important how you feel, but she seems like a fine young woman. She'll be good for you."

"I love her." The words came out slightly strangled and he could feel the heat rise in his cheeks but his mother seemed to understand.

"I'm guessing she loves you too."

She couldn't know that, not for sure. She only thought it because she was his mother.

"She wants to be a star, Mom. What can I offer her that would make her stay?"

Saying his worst fear out loud was harder than he'd imagined.

"You." His mother patted his hand and smiled. "In the end, things don't matter anyway. You're either enough or you aren't. Your father and I didn't have two nickels to rub together when we got married, and we don't have much more now. But we have each other and you kids. That's all I've ever needed."

"I won't stand in the way of her dreams."

Turning toward the door, she nodded in agreement. "I know you won't. Just be sure you know what those dreams really are. You might be surprised. And don't forget your own dreams along the way. They're just as important."

If all he had was himself to counter glamour, fame and fortune, he was up shit creek without a paddle. As soon as she was healed, Jazz would probably want to leave this place and everyone associated with it. He couldn't think of one logical reason she should stay.

"Hold still," Presley warned as she ran the sharp scissors along the ends of Jazz's hair. "I'm almost done."

Jazz's day with Ava Wright and Presley Reilly had actually been good. Both women were warm and friendly, clucking over Jazz like mother hens. They'd made sure she was comfortable and fed all the while trying to draw her out about the ordeal from yesterday. Eventually she'd given in and recounted the story to the two women as unemotionally as she could. They'd listened without interrupting and then at the end each given her a huge hug. Presley had even muttered something about kicking Gordon in the balls which had only served to make Jazz laugh.

Presley had then offered to trim Jazz's hair and now here she was, her locks in the hands of someone she'd just met.

"I'm holding still but I want to see."

"Just one minute." There were a few more snips and then Presley stood back with a huge grin on her face. "Ta da! All done. You look gorgeous, if I do say so myself."

Ava helped Jazz pull off the towel they'd wrapped around her shoulders. "It does look good, Jazz. I wasn't sure if Presley knew what she was doing but damn, she does."

It was a little late to be hearing that Ava hadn't had any confidence in Presley. Standing, Jazz padded into the bathroom and checked her new hairdo in the mirror.

Presley had done well. Jazz's hair had once been down to the middle of her back but now bounced in waves around her shoulders. Shiny and healthy, it glowed with life even as her skin looked pale and drawn in contrast to the purple-blue bruise on her cheek and eye.

Still staring at her reflection, she was shocked to see tears sliding down her face. It all seemed like too much. She'd been trying to hold everything in so she wouldn't scare the shit out of Griffin but she simply couldn't stem the tide any longer. Her breath caught in a sob and she sat down on the side of the bathtub as her knees turned to water.

"Oh shit! You don't like it? I'm so sorry! Fuck." Presley was kneeling down next to Jazz, Ava on the other side. They were patting her back and apologizing as Jazz tried to get out the words that the haircut was fine. It was everything else that had gone in the crapper.

More tears and hiccups until Jazz finally caught her breath. "It's not my hair. You did a good job."

Ava and Presley exchanged a glance and Ava put her arm around Jazz. "Let me guess. You just need a good cry to get everything out, huh? Men just don't understand. You go for it."

Jazz nodded, more tears making words impossible. The two women let her cry until she was drained, not one tear left in her body. Ava pulled some toilet paper from the roll and handed it to Jazz who dried her eyes. Amazingly she did feel better. The stress she'd had dammed up inside of her had burst wide open but was now free to leave. She wasn't sorry to see it go.

"Thank you." Jazz dabbed carefully at her injured cheek. "I think I did really need that."

Presley sat back on her heels and smiled. "Do you really feel better? You can cry more if you need to. After Bennett was born I'd burst into tears at the drop of a hat. I once cried because he'd grown out of a pair of footie pajamas. They were my favorite pair and he looked so cute in them. When Seth got home I was blubbering that Ben was all grown up and going to leave us. I think he was two months old at the time."

Ava burst into laughter at Presley's confession. "Oh man, I can just see poor Seth's expression too. I wish I'd been there."

"I'm sure he wished that too. He would have let you take care of me. As it was, he just patted me on the back and took Bennett to his parents' house for a few hours. I had a nap and felt a hundred percent better when I woke up. Sleep deprivation is hell, don't you know."

"I'll remind Logan how lucky he is," giggled Ava. "He's got it easy with me."

"Are you kidding?" Jazz couldn't resist reminding the woman of how they'd met. "When we were there a week ago he had to promise you cheesecake and pizza to get you to sleep."

Slapping a hand over her mouth, Ava's eyes went wide. "Shit, I forgot you saw that. I guess my terrible secret is out. I torture the poor man when I'm near the end of a book. Good thing he loves me."

"Good thing all our men love us," Presley agreed with a twinkle in her eye. "I doubt any of the three of us is a day at the beach to live with, but then neither are the boys."

A shooting pain pierced Jazz's heart. She shook her head in denial.

"He doesn't love me."

"What makes you say that?" Ava's brows shot up. "I've never seen Griffin look at anyone like he looks at you."

"He's never said it," she said, misery in her voice.

"Have you?" Presley shot back. "Don't bother answering. I can see it's no. Is it so out of the realm of possibility that he might love you and just not said it yet? Men can be slow that way. I had to say it to Seth first."

Ava rolled her eyes. "Don't even get me started on Logan. I didn't think he'd ever say it. He was the original *baby don't get hooked on me* kind of guy. I think the town was taking bets as to whether he would actually show up at the altar."

It was way too soon to be thinking matrimonial. She only wanted a future. Rings and weddings weren't important.

"Griffin likes things a certain way. No one messing with his privacy or his life. Even if he does love me, maybe he won't want things to change."

"Doubt he can stop things from changing." Presley shrugged and shook her head. "Life has a way of moving along whether you like it or not. He'll just have to suck it up and deal with it."

"Do you want to tell him that?" Jazz had to smile at Presley's pitiless expression. She probably did keep Seth on his toes.

"I would but I think it's going to have to come from you. Now let's go find the ice cream in this joint. After a good cry a woman needs ice cream."

Jazz couldn't argue with the logic. A big bowl – with hot fudge sauce – sounded like exactly what she needed right now.

There would be a time to discuss the future with Griffin but today wasn't it. Tomorrow wasn't looking too good either.

Chapter Twenty-Five

"For the love of all that's good and holy, I'm fine." Jazz groaned and snapped her book shut. She'd been reading out on the deck when Griffin had urged her to come inside because it might be too hot. This coming from the man who had worried yesterday that the house was too cold. The day before he'd been concerned she wasn't eating enough protein and getting enough sunshine. "Right as rain. All better."

She wasn't lying. The fear that had wrapped itself around her that first day had dissipated along with the moments of panic. Her crying jag had done her good and each day since she'd grown stronger as her bruises and cuts healed. Even her face was starting to look more normal, the swelling gone. The bruise had turned a nasty shade of yellow-green but some crafty makeup would cover it if she needed to leave the house.

"It's been less than a week," he argued. "You went through something really traumatic."

"I did and now I'm fine. You've taken really good care of me."

He had actually. Although he'd had to work, he'd made sure she had everything she could ever possibly need. Except his love, of course. He didn't appear to be offering that up on a platter. If anything, he'd pulled away from her, hardly touching except at night. Then he'd cuddle her close and they'd fall asleep wrapped around each other.

"I just want you to be okay."

She sighed and set the book down on the table. "I know you do. That's why you won't let me read the paper or watch the news. You've protected me from everything involved with Gordon including the press. I haven't seen any reporters. How are you keeping them away?"

Red stained his cheekbones and his lips pulled back in a snarl. "I threatened to throw their ass in jail if they came within a mile of you."

"I'm surprised they listened."

"Let's just say I left them in no doubt about being serious."

His expression convinced her. She would have hated to have been one of the reporters who had defied his edict.

"I'm going to have to talk to them eventually," she replied, keeping her tone reasonable. The press would hound her until she told her story.

"You don't have to say shit to them." His silver-gray eyes were hard and flat. "I won't let them near you, Jazz."

"I can't stay locked in this house forever, although the view is nice. I have to leave sometime."

His body seemed to stiffen and he looked out over the lake. "You mean back to Hollywood?"

Is that where he wanted her? Was he tired of ministering to the invalid?

"I was only thinking about a trip to the diner, but yeah, I guess Los Angeles. I mean, I can't stay here forever, can I?" Jazz held her breath and hoped, her heart squeezing in her chest.

Say yes. Say yes.

"I guess not. You'll be wanting to get back." Griffin nodded toward the doors leading to the house. "Are you hungry for dinner? I can make something."

She wasn't hungry. She was tired of the distance he'd placed between them. They hadn't made love since before. Before Gordon. They needed to eradicate the specter of what had happened from between them.

"Tell me."

Griffin shook his head, not looking into her eyes. "It's best if—"

"Tell me," she pleaded. "I know you're trying to protect me, but I'm fine. Tell me everything. What he said. What he's done. Then we can just bless and release this whole thing."

Griffin sank into the other chair at the table, his expression bleak. "I don't know where to start."

"Start anywhere you like. You'll figure it out. Just talk."

Pulling her knees up so her heels were balanced on the edge of the chair, she wrapped her arms around her legs. Listening to this was not going to be pleasant but it needed to be done. She'd been floating in a land of make believe for days. Time for a reality check.

"He admits to murdering six women," Griffin began, sitting back in the chair, his features like stone. "I don't know if he's telling the truth. Maybe he's killed more or less. The only thing we know for sure right now is his DNA links to both Casey and Sandy."

"Why? What did they do to him?" She already knew why he'd gone after her, but what had set him off to attack the others?

"Apparently he has...um...issues saluting the captain, so to speak." Griffin was rubbing his forehead and his eyes were down. For a moment, she had no idea what he was talking about and then her brain worked out his cryptic words.

"Oh."

"Yeah, *oh*. He also, from what we can tell, has an anger management problem. When he can't…perform, well, according to him females are sometimes less than understanding. He got very upset when women supposedly laughed at him. That was his trigger."

"He said that Sandy threatened to tell the whole crew." Jazz marveled at how troubled someone could be and everyone around them had no idea. He'd seemed like a perfectly normal person when deep down he'd been something akin to a monster.

"I'm sure some psychiatrist will make a career of studying him and his motivations. Personally I don't give a shit. He's a murderer and my job is to find him and catch him. Mission accomplished."

"Did he say how he met Casey? That's the one thing I don't understand. And how did you not know he was in town all those months ago?" Jazz smiled and reached out to place her hand over his. "You know everything that goes on around here."

"You'd think but that's not the case. Old Otis and the rest of the town council had been working on this reality show deal for almost a year. They knew I'd blow a blood vessel if I found out so they told him to lie low and stay at a motel out of town. As for how he met Casey, he ate at the restaurant where she was a waitress. He was going to make her a star until everything went south."

"And now what happens?" Griffin laced their fingers together and she felt the now familiar pull towards him. She needed his arms around her and the passion they created together. It had been way too long since she'd felt close to him.

"The state and county prosecutors take it from here. Any other state that wants to go after him will have to stand in line. He won't be getting out of prison. Ever. That's a good thing."

"Thank you for saving me," she said softly as she rose from her chair and walked around the table to stand next to him.

"I'd do anything for you." His voice was like a soft caress on her skin. This man could do magic without even a touch.

"I hope that's true." She leaned forward so her hands were on each arm of the chair. "Will you take me fishing?"

His eyes opened in surprise and a smile appeared on his face. "Fishing? You want to go fishing? The sun will be going down soon."

"We can't fish in the dark?" Jazz gave him a playful smile. It was time to put all the bad stuff behind them. She wanted to enjoy and savor every moment they had left together.

"I reckon we could. Who knows what we might catch."

From the smug look on her face it was clear he knew she wasn't thinking about fishing poles and drowning worms. She could only hope she had a whopper of a fish tale by tomorrow morning.

◊　◊　◊　◊

Jazz was right.

It was good to talk about Gordon and then move on. Griffin had wondered how traumatized Jazz had really been and whether she would be able to leave it all behind quickly. Tonight had allayed those fears. His woman was strong and resilient. He'd seen grown ass men that couldn't have handled what she'd been through.

Steering the boat into the center of the lake, he killed the engine, content to let it drift over the sedate water. There wasn't a ripple in the glasslike surface and the sun was beginning to sink down below the horizon. After everything that had happened in the last weeks, there was nothing but peace and serenity. He drank it up, inhaling it greedily. It was this chance to let the cares of the world go and recharge that kept him sane. He wanted to share this with Jazz, not only tonight but forever.

"It's so quiet here." Jazz's voice was hushed but her expression was radiant. She was luxuriating in this other world as much as he was. "Do you ever get used to it? I mean, take it for granted?"

Griffin shook his head as he gazed not at the scenery but at the most beautiful woman he'd ever known. He'd never get used to the way she made his heart feel. He'd never believed he would ever feel this way about anyone, but here she was.

"I come out here a lot. Sometimes to think, but sometimes to clear my head. It's a good place to center yourself. Remember the important things."

"Yes," she nodded. "It would be ideal for that."

She turned so her chair was facing him and then crooked her finger at him, her smile tempting and promising at the same time. His cock was quick to respond to the blatant seduction and he stood and took the few steps to where she was seated.

Kneeling on the floor of the boat in front of her, he cupped her face in his hands and fused their lips together. So good. He let his tongue explore her mouth, no hurry, taking his time. Eventually she would be gone and all he would have were the memories they'd created together. They'd have to be enough to carry him through the next sixty or seventy years.

When they broke apart she sighed, her breath warm and sweet on his face. Her hands slid up his arms and over his shoulders, her blue eyes growing dark with passion. She laced her fingers at the base of his neck and pulled him down to her again. Letting his lips blaze a path across her jaw and to her ear, he busied his hands by slipping them under her oversized t-shirt and caressing the satin skin he found. Her sweet scent tantalized him and he buried his face deeper into the softness of her neck. His cock pressed against the button-fly of his jeans and he had to recite baseball stats to keep from blowing his cool.

Nipping at the sensitive flesh of her earlobe, Jazz moaned and her legs wrapped around his waist. Chuckling at her eagerness, he pressed his jean covered cock against the heat of her pussy. She responded by enthusiastically mimicking his movements until they were both breathless and his dick ached in frustration.

"I won't let you hurry this, Hollywood."

Scraping her nails down his shirt-covered back, she groaned and kicked her legs. "Your legendary patience isn't required at the moment. Fuck me now, Griffin."

"I promise you won't have any complaints when we're done. Just relax and let's get these clothes out of the way."

Jazz wriggled with excitement, her face lighting up as together they stripped her shorts, shirt, bra, and panties. She immediately reached for the hem of his shirt, tugging impatiently. If he hadn't intervened to help, she might have ripped the shirt right off his back.

"Easy, Hollywood. We'll get there. I need a taste first."

But her nimble fingers were already plucking at his fly, and he groaned in relief as his cock received some much needed breathing room. Pushing at his jeans, he allowed her to assist in their removal but stayed her hands when she went for his boxers.

She stuck out her lip in the prettiest pout he'd ever seen. But he still wasn't going to give in.

"You are no fun." Jazz stuck her tongue out and Griffin's filthy mind thought of several things that she could do with it. A couple that might shock the hell out of her.

"I'm plenty of fun. But if we let the monster loose, this will be all over in minutes."

He leaned forward and captured a pink nipple into his mouth and worried the turgid flesh with his teeth until she was writhing and laughing underneath him.

"The monster? That is too funny. Can I call it the monster too?" Her giggling made his heart swell in his chest and he wondered how in the world he would ever get over her when she was gone. He was a slave to making her happy, wanting everything in the world for her.

"You can name him anything you want, honey. He's all yours."

Her small hands caressed his cock through the cotton fabric making him choke and cough as he fought for control. Capturing her wrists, he pinned them behind her neck on the back of the chair while using his tongue and teeth to play with her gorgeous breasts. He ran his tongue around a hard nub before leaving a wet trail down and around, tickling the sensitive underside.

"Griffin." His name was a soft but urgent plea falling from her swollen lips. Shifting his hands, he scooped up her legs and draped them over his shoulders before capturing her wrists again, one in each hand. Jazz was for all intents and purposes pinned to the chair and spread wide for his pleasure.

And pleasure it was indeed. Even in the waning light, he could see her pink pussy, puffy and shiny with her honey, just waiting to be licked. Pushing her legs wider with his shoulders, he drew his tongue through the folds of her slit, up and down, side to side, everywhere but her clit until she was moaning with pleasure and mewling in frustration.

Griffin set a leisurely pace exploring every nook and cranny even as she tried to buck under him, to get his mouth where she needed it most. Her pussy was pouring honey now and the seat, along with her thighs, were glistening with juices.

"I think you like being restrained like this, Hollywood. I think you like being helpless."

"Asshole," she hissed but it turned into a strangled moan as he flicked his tongue lightly on her swollen button.

"Naughty girl with language like that. I can keep this up all night long if you're going to have an attitude," he chided playfully before running his tongue around her clit. Her hips jerked but he had her firmly held still. Her legs trembling, he knew she was just about to the pinnacle.

"Please, Griffin. Please."

He couldn't ignore her begging. Closing his mouth over her clit, he sucked gently even as his tongue fluttered along the side. Her reaction was instantaneous, her body arching, her muscles tightening. When she cried out his name, his cock almost exploded at the hoarse sounds of ecstasy and need.

Not sure he could hold back much longer, he slid an arm under her bottom and lifted her off the chair so he could switch places with her, shucking his briefs on the way. He settled her on his lap with her legs straddling him as he fished in his jeans pocket for protection.

After he rolled it on, he placed his hands on her hips while she braced her feet on the floor of the boat. He helped her rise up and then slowly lower herself down on his painfully aroused cock. Each inch that he gave her pushed him further to the edge of madness until finally he was in to the hilt, her tight hot pussy wrapped snugly around him.

Not ready to move yet, he instead let his hands run up and down her torso, stopping to caress a nipple or brush her already swollen clit. Her hands clung to his shoulders and her fingers dug into the muscles as she thrust her breasts forward and let her head fall back.

There was never a more beautiful sight to behold than this woman at this very moment. The sun had fully set and her body was now bathed in moonlight, the curves and shadows playing a game of hide and seek as they began to move.

Slowly he lifted her up until only the head of his cock was inside of her, and then down until her clit rubbed his groin. Each time she undulated her hips for the maximum contact, driving them both straight to heaven and hell, the rocking of the boat only intensifying the effects.

Sweat broke out on his skin as his thrusting sped up, faster and harder. His breathing grew ragged and the pressure built at the base of his spine. He simply couldn't hold on much longer.

"C'mon, honey. Let yourself go," he urged, his words barely audible. Jazz responded by slamming her hips down even harder until her entire frame went rigid and her pussy clamped down on his cock. Jazz's eyes were closed, her lips parted, her breath coming in pants, and her toes curled.

His dick swelled and jerked as his own orgasm roared through him, the waves relentless. He tried to keep his gaze on her but he couldn't stop his eyes from squeezing shut and the groan that seemed to come from deep within. Nothing in his life had prepared him for how he felt with Jazz.

His heart pounding against his ribs, he held her close until the cool lake air dried the moisture on their skin. He helped her re-dress without a word and then pulled on his own clothes. There wasn't much to be said. The only appropriate words at a time like this were *I love you*.

Did he have the guts to tell her now? He'd sworn when he'd found her that day that he would but the right moment had never presented itself. Maybe there wasn't a right moment for something like this. Maybe he would have to create the moment.

All the way back to the dock, he worked up his courage, going over and over the words in his head until they sounded just right. He wanted her to know he loved her but that he didn't expect her to change her life for him. He respected her dreams but he didn't know how to say it.

He helped her out of the boat and they walked into the kitchen. A chirping sound made him look around the room in question. It sounded like a cricket.

"That's my cell." Jazz reached into her purse that was sitting on the island, the zipper open. The crime lab had released her phone and several others since they'd found no evidence pertaining to Gordon's case. "It's my agent. I better call her back."

Pressing a few buttons, Jazz sat at one of the barstools while Griffin pulled a couple of steaks from the refrigerator for dinner. If things went well, they could eat and still have time for more fun in the bathtub. Or the shower. Or even the bed. He wasn't a fussy man.

"Hi, Eleanor. It's Jazz. What's up?"

Griffon could only hear Jazz's side of the conversation which was a few "ohs", "ums", and "wows." A sinking feeling started growing in the pit of his stomach and he stopped what he was doing, unashamedly listening in.

"That's certainly something I should think about. I'll call you in the morning, okay?"

Jazz hung up her phone and slid it back into her purse. Her eyes wouldn't meet his as her gaze seemed to dart around the room, landing here and there but never looking directly at him.

"So is everything okay?" Griffin had to say something to break the wall of tension that had quickly sprung up between them. It was accompanied by the tightening of his chest that was making it hard to catch his breath.

"That was my agent." Jazz traced patterns on the counter with her fingernail, her head down. "I've got an offer for a part in a movie."

The growing knot in his throat made it difficult to speak but he swallowed hard, determined to get the words out. "That's wonderful. What kind of movie?"

"A romantic comedy. It's a supporting role. I'd play the lead actress's best friend. The original actress signed had to pull out due to emergency surgery. They need me on the set Monday."

That was only three days away. His fingers tightened on the pan he was holding but he somehow managed to smile.

"That's great news, honey. I guess this was the break you've been waiting for. This was why you signed up to do the show."

He had to congratulate himself on sounding near normal. He didn't want Jazz to know how much this was killing him inside.

Her happiness came first. He wouldn't be selfish.

She looked up, conflict clear in her eyes. It was some consolation that she wasn't doing a dance in his kitchen about the movie offer. She did care for him, he knew that much. But caring and wanting to spend the rest of your life in a small town in Montana were two very different things.

"I told her I would call her in the morning with my decision."

"Is there a downside to the offer?" he asked carefully as he placed the steaks on the broiler and sprinkled seasoning on the raw meat. "Money? Location?"

"The money's fine and the location is New York. I've never been there before." Jazz was back to tracing patterns again and not looking at him.

"I've never been there either. Like to go someday."

Griffin slid the broiler pan into the oven and went around to the other side of the island sitting in the barstool next to her, making it difficult for her not to look at him.

"I'm proud of you, Hollywood. I think you'll do a great job."

"Gordon said I was just like all the other girls he'd dealt with. Pretty face but little talent."

"Fuck Gordon Schofield. He's a fucking murderer who has anger issues with women. I wouldn't take his word for it, honey. I bet you have talent. I'd wager cash money on it."

She finally gave him a smile and sat up in her chair. "I think you're full of shit. What if I screw this up?"

"You won't. You'll be amazing. I can't wait to see you on the big screen."

She took a deep breath and finally met his gaze. "I'd have to leave on Saturday."

He refused to make her feel guilty for grabbing this opportunity. "I'll take the day and drive you to the airport in Billings. You won't need to worry about renting a car or anything."

"I guess it's settled then. I'll call my agent in the morning and then get a plane ticket." She hopped up from her seat and peeked into the oven. "I'm starving. I'll microwave a couple of baked potatoes to go with them."

He nodded but didn't answer out loud as she bustled around the kitchen. Watching her every move and trying to imprint it in his memory, he struggled to control the feelings of desolation that swamped him. He'd finally fallen in love but with a woman who couldn't stay. He needed to step back and give her wings to fly.

He could have asked her to stay but what then? He never wanted her to look at him someday in the future and curse him for ruining her dream.

He'd let her go but make sure she knew he would be waiting right here in case she ever wanted to come back.

Chapter Twenty-Six

J azz folded her last pair of jeans and placed it in the suitcase open on the bed. Pants were done and now she needed to move on to shirts. She'd been moving in slow motion this morning, dragging her feet.

She should be jumping up and down excited. This opportunity was what she'd worked for, dreamed of. This was her moment. The brass ring was right there all shiny and waiting for her to grab it.

Then why was she so fucking miserable? The thought of leaving Griffin and Hope Lake was tearing at her gut and making her heart ache. Just a few weeks of being here with him and she couldn't imagine her life any other way. Los Angeles, the smog, the traffic, the empty show business life she'd led held no appeal. The fact was she really didn't give a shit about this role. Or any other role. Her dream as a child wasn't her dream as an adult.

Wasn't that how it was supposed to be? There were sayings about putting away childish things. Her dream of fame and fortune had been the hope of a little girl whose parents didn't give her any attention or approval. Funny how she didn't need it anymore. She approved of herself, and that's what was important.

The singsong ring of her cell phone interrupted her jumbled thoughts, and she smiled when she saw who was calling.

Caitlin.

"Hey, girl. I was going to call you later. What's going on?"

"I just got your text. Holy shit, you're going to do a movie with Howard Deals? He's a great director." There was excitement in Caitlin's voice and Jazz wished she could share it.

"Yes, I'm packing now." Jazz tried to inject some enthusiasm into her tone. "Griffin is taking me to the airport soon."

"You know it might be the phone connection but you sound like Griffin's driving you to your own execution. Is something wrong? Don't you want the part?"

It was honesty time. Caitlin had a world-class bullshit detector so lying wasn't an option.

"No. No, I don't. But if I don't take it, what will I do?"

Jazz fell back on the bed staring at the ceiling and feeling like hell. Her brain was all muddled and she couldn't seem to think straight in the least.

"Wow, I didn't expect this. I mean, I knew you were falling for that sheriff guy but this is way out there."

Jazz could hear the incredulity in Caitlin's voice. "You could tell? Am I that obvious?"

"Kind of. It was the way you talked about him, I guess. Even before he saved you from Gordon." There was a long pause. "Do you love him?"

"Yes." Jazz expelled the breath she'd been holding. "I do. But I don't know if he loves me."

"Have you asked him?"

"It's never really come up in conversation." Jazz rubbed her forehead and pushed the hair off her face. "But here's the thing. If I'm not an actress, well, then what am I? A waitress? I don't mind waiting tables, sometimes I really enjoy it, but I always imagined my life doing something creative."

"That's not surprising—you're a creative person, Jazz. But you have other options. You take amazing photos, for example. You also paint and write. I love that script you were working on. I kept saying you should show it to Tony."

Jazz was surprised Caitlin brought up her now ex-boyfriend. During their last conversation, she'd said she never wanted to hear his name in her presence ever again. Jazz didn't blame her.

To cover up his own dalliance with another woman, this time one of the crew, he'd provided Gordon with an alibi for Sandy's murder in exchange for Gordon providing one for him. The fact that Tony hadn't thought for one minute that Gordon was a killer and that he was simply covering up his own philandering wasn't the point. Tony was a lying cheating snake. He'd had his dick in no less than two—and who knew, maybe more—women in the last two weeks. Caitlin was well rid of him.

"I wouldn't tell Tony what time it is," Jazz said sharply. She hoped Caitlin wasn't softening her attitude about the jerk.

"Neither would I," Caitlin assured her. "Although I did talk to him last night. Again. He gave me the usual song and dance about how those women didn't mean a thing to him but I did. Wow, lucky me. Then I asked him about how he provided an alibi for a serial killer and he blubbered something about needing to keep that woman he was porking a secret and he never in a million years thought Gordon was capable of something like that."

"I don't think any of us thought that but we didn't lie."

"Exactly. I told him I didn't want to be with someone who thought not telling the truth was a valid excuse."

"What did he say to that?" Jazz set the phone on the mattress and grabbed a shirt to fold from the pile of clothes on the bed.

"He mumbled something and then hung up. But here's the kicker, I got fired this morning so I guess he got his revenge."

Jazz dropped the shirt and grabbed the phone pressing it to her ear. "Are you fucking kidding me? That slimeball. I can't believe he called one of his buddies and got you fired. What a dickhead."

"Those were just a few names I called him today. The show's producer called me this morning. Told me they wanted to take the show in a different direction. In other words, my character is getting killed off. I've got about two weeks left."

"I'm so sorry you got dragged into this, Cait. So very sorry." Caitlin was too nice a person to have this happen to her. She was a good actress too. "Screw that soap. You'll get a better job."

"Maybe. I'm kind of with you on this whole acting thing, Jazz. I'm thinking about hanging it up. Doing something else. Anything else. I'm tired of obsessing about my looks and my weight. It's not healthy and it sucks. I've saved some money. I'll be okay for awhile."

Completely taken aback, Jazz didn't know what to say. She'd thought Caitlin was happy so this news had come out of left field.

"I'm shocked to hear you say it but if that's what you want, you know I'm rooting for you."

"And I'm rooting for you too, Jazz. Don't get trapped in something you think you ought to do. Do whatever you want. I'm listening to my gut from now on. What does yours tell you?"

"To stay." The words were out of Jazz's mouth before she could stop them. But once she said it, a great weight was lifted from her shoulders. She didn't want to go back to her life in Los

Angeles. She didn't want to be a star and have reporters and the press following her around. She wanted to live a quiet life with the man she loved.

And maybe learn to fish.

The question of what she wanted to be when she grew up was still unanswered but she now had the money and the time to think it over.

"Should I start packing your things up and send them to Montana?" The amused tone in Caitlin's voice made Jazz laugh.

"I'd hardly be called a friend if I did that to you. If I stay here, I'll come home and pack up my stuff. But I don't like leaving you with all that rent, especially if you just lost your job."

"Maybe I should come to Montana," Caitlin joked. "Are the prices reasonable?"

"I'd love it if you came here," Jazz exclaimed. "I'd have a built in friend."

"I was only kidding," Caitlin protested with a nervous laugh. "I'm a West Coast girl, remember?"

"Fine, but promise me you'll visit. It's very pretty here. Griffin can take us fishing."

"I promise. Listen, I need to go. I'm meeting a couple of people for spin class. Call me tomorrow and tell me the latest. What are you going to say to Griffin about staying?"

A few thoughts had started ruminating in Jazz's mind. "I'm not planning to tell him anything. I'm going to show him. Wish me luck because I'm going out on a limb here. Way out."

"Then good luck. Things will work out for you. I think this Griffin guy is very lucky."

"I completely agree. I'll call you tomorrow."

Jazz hung up and tossed her phone down on the bed. Staring at the suitcase, she made a few risky decisions. She was either going to be the happiest woman in the world or the most miserable.

No time like the present to find out which it would be. Grabbing up a stack of clothes, she began unpacking her suitcase. She wasn't going anywhere.

She was staying to be with Griffin.

Griffin's dad climbed out of the boat with a bucket of fish in one hand and his fishing pole in the other. He'd come over early this morning, much to Griffin's chagrin, "to catch a few and get some peace and quiet." Griffin had been cuddled up close to Jazz sleeping when he'd heard the bang of his dad's equipment and the stomp of his boots. So much for sleeping in and making love to Jazz one last time.

Now it was mere minutes before he needed to load the woman he loved and her luggage into his truck, driving her to the airport and out of his life. He wanted to scream that life wasn't fair and rail against the pain that was twisting his heart but it wouldn't do a damn bit of good. If his father had taught Griffin anything, it was to stand up and be a man. That's what he would do.

"Looks like you had a good day." Griffin pointed to the fish in the bucket trying to get his mind off the woman in his bedroom who was currently packing her belongings.

"More than we can eat. Why don't you and Jazz come over tonight and help us? I'll get out the fish fryer and we'll even have a bonfire. Make s'mores. You loved those when you were a kid."

Liam Sawyer still thought all of his children were about ten years old. That was probably going to never change.

"I'm afraid we can't come. I have to take Jazz to the airport in Billings. She got a big part in a movie."

"Good for her. How long will she be gone? We'll have to have a celebration when she gets back. Your mother will bake a cake or something."

His dad's face was lit up even as Griffin was feeling miserable. He hated to wipe that grin off his father's face but his dad would find out sooner or later.

"Actually that's the thing, Dad. She's leaving."

His dad frowned and looked confused. "You mean she's not coming back? Why not?"

Griffin blew out a breath and tried to control his frustration. "Because her dream is to be a famous actress. You can't do that from a dinky town in Montana. She has to go."

"So that's that?" his father asked flatly. "She leaves and breaks your heart, and you sit back and take it."

"I'm not sitting back and taking anything. I'm being supportive," Griffin argued. "Do you honestly believe I should ask her to stay and give it all up?"

"Don't ask. Offer. Tell her how things could be if she stayed, and then let her make an informed decision."

Rubbing the back of his neck, Griffin shook his head. He wouldn't guilt her into staying.

"She's wanted this since she was a kid, Dad."

His father snorted and turned toward the deck stairs. "You wanted to drive an ice cream truck when you were a kid but the lure of all you can eat sweets didn't last. All I can say is that it's going to be hard for you to drive to Billings with your head up your ass. March in there and tell her to come back when she's done making the movie. You two can compromise on this. Make it work. It won't be easy but it might be worth it."

His father clomped down the steps and headed for his truck parked at the side of the house while Griffin contemplated their exchange. He could tell Jazz that he loved her more than anything in this world and that he would wait here for her in between movies. The more he thought about it the more it just might work.

She'd have a quiet place to come and get away, and he'd get at least a small part of Jazz. A little bit would have to be enough.

Chapter Twenty-Seven

The time to take Jazz to the airport had arrived.

Griffin had practiced what he would say on the drive there while he'd cleaned up the boat. Nothing grounded him like this lake and simply being near it seemed to clear his head. He felt more at peace now than he had since she'd received that call last night.

He would tell her how much he loved her and that he would always be here for her. That he wanted her to chase her dreams and just hoped he could still be a part of her life going forward.

It sounded good in his head. He hoped it went over just as well. He washed his hands in the kitchen sink and dried them on a towel. The house seemed overly warm but it was probably just his nerves setting in. It was only his entire happiness that was on the line.

Jazz was lounged in the living room flipping channels on the television. Dressed in cut off sweat pants and one of his big t-shirts she didn't look like a woman about to leave for the airport.

"Honey? We need to leave if you're going to make your flight. Are you ready?"

"I'm not going," she replied, barely glancing at him as she continued to channel surf.

"You're not going?" he repeated. "I don't understand."

"I'm not going. I hope you're okay with it. I've taken over three-quarters of your closet, several drawers and pretty much all of the bathroom vanity. The remote is mine now too." She held up the control. "Oh, and I changed the thermostat. I was cold."

That explained why the house was ungodly warm.

Something inside of him grabbed onto her words and he felt hope bloom. His Hollywood didn't want to leave any more than he wanted her to. But he needed confirmation. He walked back to the bedroom and sure enough she'd taken over. Clothes were stuffed in the closet and drawers while her makeup and toiletries were strewn haphazardly across the countertops.

Damn if it wasn't a beautiful sight. Uncluttered vanities and ample closet space were overrated. He walked back into the living room.

"Did the part fall through?"

"No. I just decided not to go." Finally she twisted around so she was looking up at him. He saw the same hope he was feeling in those gorgeous blue eyes. The same fear as well, but she'd been more brave. His woman had taken the bull by the horns and he would be forever grateful. "Any problems with that, Sheriff?"

Fighting the first smile he'd had all day, he shook his head. "Can't think of one. I was getting tired of controlling the remote and the thermostat anyway. You'll probably do a better job at selecting the shows or the temperature."

Jazz blinked several times and he could swear her eyes glistened with tears. Happy ones. Her lips had curved into that beautiful smile that never ceased to make his heart tight in his chest.

"I'll share."

"Are you sure?" His heart pounding, he wasn't asking about the remote. He needed to know she was really and truly sure about this.

"I'm sure." She set the remote on the table and laughed. "A funny thing happened on the way to super-stardom. I found out it wasn't all it was cracked up to be. I've got a few new dreams now."

"Care to tell me about them?" He sat down next to her on the couch and reached out to tuck an errant strand of hair behind her ear.

Giggling, she stood and took a few steps back. "I might but later. How about we play a game? I'll ask a question and if you get it right, I'll take off a piece of clothing."

He was game alright. All in. This day had started out being the worst of his life but things had definitely taken a positive—and playful—turn.

"I'm ready." Griffin lounged back on the couch with a smile on his face. This woman was damn near perfect, and he would make sure she knew she was loved every day for the rest of her life. "Ask away."

He intended for Jazz to lose every bit of clothing on her delectable body.

Griffin Sawyer had a smirk on his handsome face, lying back on the sofa like a sultan waiting for his slave girl to strip. Which was basically what she was about to do. But on her terms.

She fingered the hem of the oversized shirt she'd stolen from Griffin and smiled in what she hoped was a teasing manner. "First question. Are you really okay with me changing the thermostat?"

The man she loved smiled tenderly and her heart did a little dance. "It's a tad warm for me but I guess I could just take my clothes off."

Now there was an idea. A good one. He could be naked all the time.

"Good answer." Jazz pulled the shirt over her head and tossed it away. The next question was much harder to ask. "Second question. Would you have just let me leave?"

Griffin sat up, his silver-gray eyes intense as he looked into her own. "No. I'd already decided to ask you to come back when you finished the movie. I was going to tell you that this could be your home when you weren't working. That I'd wait for you."

Another excellent answer. She tugged at the strings holding up her sweats and slid them down her legs. Taking a deep breath, she stepped farther out on a limb. Hopefully he would be there to catch her if she fell, just like before.

Her fingers went to the back catch of her bra but paused. "Third question. Do you think I love you?"

"Yes," Griffin nodded, leaning forward so his elbows were on his knees, his gaze intent. "I think you love me, Hollywood. I—"

"Last question," she trilled, slipping her bra off and standing in front of him in nothing but a flimsy pair of panties. His heated gaze told her he liked what he was seeing. She swallowed hard, trying to dislodge her heart which had crawled up into her throat. This was the most important question she might ever ask in her life. "Do you love me?"

This time he stood and pulled her into his arms. "Dear God, yes. More than you know. Hell, more than I thought was even possible. I'm sorry I didn't say it before."

They kissed then and Jazz could swear she saw and heard fireworks go off between them. This was more. Love made it mean so much.

He pulled back and smiled, his fingers wrapping around the edge of her panties. "I think I won these, Hollywood. Best be stripping these off."

But he didn't give her a chance. Instead he slid them down her legs and then twirled them in the air on his finger before tossing them over his shoulder. He had a wicked grin on his face and she couldn't wait to see what he had planned.

Her heart felt so full at this moment. She would have given him anything because he'd given her everything that mattered. Himself.

"I'm going to make you very happy, Hollywood. I promise."

Griffin scooped her up and carried her into the bedroom, laying her gently on the mattress. Running her hands up his chest, her fingers sliding under his shirt, she explored the dips and planes of his torso, loving the way the muscles bunched and moved under her palms. He got the hint and immediately pulled it over his head then stood to strip off the rest of his clothes.

Standing before her looking more beautiful than any marble statue, he gently eased himself on top of her, his large body covering hers. She felt tiny and protected cradled in his arms as his lips tempted and teased her own before traveling down her neck to her already aching breasts.

Heat swept through her and arousal tightened in her belly as his tongue flicked over her tight nipples and then down to her bellybutton. She giggled as he nibbled on her ribs then sucked in a breath as a thick finger pressed inside her already drenched pussy.

The room tilted as he added a second finger, rubbing the sweet spot deep inside and making her legs shake as she built toward her orgasm.

So good.

"That's it, honey. Let it take you."

As if she had any choice. She was powerless to the ecstasy that had taken hold, its willing supplicant.

He slid down further, his head bent over her pussy. Her legs were splayed wide, nothing hidden from his heated gaze. She could feel his warm breath on her clit as his lips and tongue fluttered around the button. Her cunt clenched in need and she panted and moaned as he took his own sweet time. She was always in awe of his patience.

But this time she wanted to give as well as receive. Twisting from his grip, she slid to the floor while pushing his legs apart. Insinuating herself between his knees, she swiped her tongue along his impressive cock from base to tip before swirling it around the head. A groan tore from his throat and she swallowed him down until he bumped the back of her throat. She moved her head, tightening her lips and flicking her tongue back and forth.

His cock seemed to swell in her mouth, but before she could bring him to completion he jerked back with a curse.

"No, Hollywood. I'm going to come inside of you." His voice sounded hoarse, almost pained.

"My mouth is inside of me," she pouted. "You never let me have any fun."

"Fun? That's exactly what we're going to have," he promised, lifting her so she was lying next to him on the bed. He rolled her under him even as he reached into the bedside table drawer for protection. It was only moments later and he was inside, his large cock filling her until she almost cried out with the pleasure.

Their gazes locked as he moved in and out, rubbing all the sensitive spots he'd found since they'd been together and taking them to the next level. She wrapped her legs around his waist, but he pulled back slightly and lifted her ankles so they draped over his shoulders. It served to drive his cock even deeper and sent even more arrows of pleasure to every part of her body.

The angle was perfect for rubbing her clit and sending her even closer to the precipice, teetering on the edge and ready to fall. His mouth captured hers, the kiss long, wet, deep, and full of promises.

Her climax took her by surprise. Catching her breath, it rolled through her as colored lights danced in front of her eyes and the room spun. Dizzy with arousal, she clung to Griffin's strong shoulders as he too reached the peak.

"Jazz. Love you." His tone was gritty and harsh but the words were sweet. She whispered words of love back to him, her lips near his ear as they cuddled together afterward. Laying her head on his chest, she could feel the rise and fall of his breathing and the steady thump of his heart.

She hadn't given up anything to be with Griffin. If anything, he'd opened a new world for her. There were so many things she could do or be.

"I think I'm going to write a book," she said. "Or maybe do some painting. I have money until I figure things out. I won't be a financial burden."

His chuckle vibrated under her cheek. "I wasn't worried about that, honey. I think writing sounds good. Painting too. You'll find your path. I'll help in any way I can."

Everything would be fine, as long as that path was shared with Griffin. Being together was the most important thing.

"I love you, Sheriff."

"I love you, Hollywood. I don't suppose we can negotiate on the thermostat? It's awfully warm in here, honey."

Shaking with laughter, she nodded and kissed his lips. "It's about to get hotter. Hold on to your cowboy hat."

It was a long time before they got out of bed but Griffin did eventually get to lower the temperature. Jazz simply cuddled close and draped herself over his body, her head pillowed on his shoulder.

Just the way they liked to sleep.

Epilogue

Griffin entered the roadhouse, the smell of beer and cigarettes hanging in the air. It must have been quite a party crowd in the bar last night from the odors left behind this morning. Too bad he rarely went out these days. These last weeks with Jazz he'd found he had no reason to leave the house except to work. They spent a great deal of time in bed.

"Where's Logan? I thought I'd be the last to get here."

Griffin slid into a chair at the table and grabbed a soda, popping it open. Every spot at the table was filled except for one.

"Trouble leaving paradise?" Reed taunted. "Do you and Jazz ever get out of bed and leave the damn house? Last time I stopped by it took you ten minutes to answer the door."

It had taken that long to find their clothes.

"You're just jealous."

Tanner almost spit out a mouthful of root beer. "Stop that shit. Don't make me laugh. Reed is never happier than when he's alone. Having only one woman might actually make him crazy."

"He's crazier than shit now," Dare said gruffly, his brows pulled together in a frown as usual. "Can't get much worse."

"Famous last words." Evan chuckled and took a big drink of ginger ale.

"You guys getting settled in your new jobs?" Griffin asked the two men. "Anything we can do to help?"

Evan shook his head. "It's okay. Still figuring out some things but it's nice to be in charge for a damn change. I'd forgotten what it was like not to be a cog in the wheel of the Federal government."

"I don't have any complaints." Dare shrugged but didn't elaborate. Griffin wondered if the man's family situation was any better but didn't want to ask in front of everyone.

"There's Logan." Seth nodded towards the door where Logan Wright was striding in. He sat down at the table with a sort of dazed expression.

Jared looked at Logan and frowned. "Are you okay? Did you get in a car accident and the airbag hit you in the face or something?"

Logan's eyes had a faraway look to them. "I'm having a baby. I mean Ava's having a baby." He shook his head. "What I'm trying to say is we're having a baby."

Seth and Tanner slapped Logan on the back and everyone gave their congratulations, although Logan simply nodded at the well wishes.

"You look a little shell-shocked. Was the baby an accident?" Seth asked, his gaze darting from one sheriff to another.

Logan sat back in his chair and accepted a soda from Tanner. He popped the lid and drank down about half in a few gulps.

"Sex works," he finally said, his voice sounding choked.

Tanner looked like he wanted to bust out laughing but instead he patted Logan on the back again.

"It does indeed, but I'm not sure what you mean by that specifically."

Logan scraped his hand down his face. "It wasn't an accident. We were trying."

"Then why are you acting so shocked?" Reed asked, a puzzled look on his face. "Are you having buyer's remorse? Too late now, man."

"It's just—how do I say this? Sex makes a baby," he said awkwardly. "You know in health class they say that an egg and a sperm make a baby but it's not something you really think about. I mean, it's not something you can see so it seems sort of, I don't know, abstract. But then you have unprotected sex on purpose." Logan took a deep breath. "And it happens."

"Luckily for mankind, not every damn time," Jared laughed. "There's just one question. Are you happy about it or not?"

Logan didn't answer for a moment and then his face split into that patented grin of his. "I'm happy. Hell, I'm going to be a dad."

This time Logan actually heard their congratulations and thanked them. The meeting continued quickly, their towns fairly quiet since the press had left. Jazz had given an interview and then one by one the reporters had left town. Now Hope Lake was as boring as it had been before the reality show.

Thank the Lord.

The meeting broke up and they all wandered out to their trucks. Reed was parked next to Griffin and they walked together.

"In the mood to split a pizza?" Reed asked, patting his stomach. "I didn't have breakfast."

"Wish I could but Jazz and I are headed to Billings today to pick up her friend Caitlin at the airport. She's coming for a visit since she got fired from that soap she was on. She's going to stay for a few weeks and then Jazz is traveling back with her to pack up her things."

"For good? She's done with Hollywood?"

Thinking about what had happened last night, Griffin smiled. "Forever. At least that's what she promised me when I offered her a diamond ring and my last name."

A smile broke out on Reed's face. "Shit, man, why didn't you say anything? That's great. Congratulations."

"Thanks. I know it seems fast to some people but we're sure of what we want." Griffin nodded toward Logan who was backing out of the parking lot. "I was going to say something today but then it seemed wrong to steal Logan's thunder. I'll tell them next time."

"And you don't like being the center of attention anyway." Reed said what Griffin had been thinking.

"That's what got me into this mess."

"You don't look too miserable to me. Makes a man almost wish for true love in his life." Reed snorted with laughter. "Almost."

"Be careful. I thought I was immune to all this love and happiness. Bam. It comes out of nowhere."

Reed opened the door of his truck and swung into the driver's seat. "The secret is to duck and weave. After all these years, I think I'm safe. Who'd want me anyway?"

Reed started up the engine and waved as he pulled out of the parking lot. Griffin wondered if his friend had said the last part in jest or if perhaps he really believed it. It didn't matter as Griffin would never know the truth. Reed played his cards much too close to his chest for anyone to see any deeper than he allowed.

The vibration of Griffin's phone had him reaching into his pocket. Jazz.

"Hey, beautiful."

"Hey, handsome. Caitlin's flight has been delayed for a couple of hours. Smog or something. We'll have some time to kill before we leave for the airport. We could go visit your family if you want."

Jazz's parents may not have loved her but Griffin's mom and dad had practically adopted her, showering her with all the parental love she'd been missing. But Griffin didn't want to share her with them today.

"I have something else in mind."

"Does that something else include clothes?" she asked, a playful tone in her voice. Griffin could picture her flirty smile.

"Nope. Not a stitch."

"How about we play a game? I'll ask a question and if you answer it right, I'll take off a piece of clothing. First question. Do you love me, Sheriff?"

"I love you," he growled, frustrated that he wasn't with her right now, this very minute.

"You win." Her voice was soft, almost a whisper and his heart contracted in his chest. He had won. Not a reality show or money. He'd won at love, and that was worth more than fame or fortune. Stardom was fleeting, but love was for a lifetime.

The End

Cowboy Command
Cowboy Justice Association
Book One

Sometimes you have to die to be born.

One minute Katie is eating lunch with her sister, the next she barely escapes a car bomb meant to kill her. If that wasn't enough, someone sets fire to her home and burns it to the ground. Luckily, Federal agents are going to give her a new identity until she can testify against the man who wants her dead. They change her name to Presley, her hair color to brown, and her shorts and sandals to jeans and cowboy boots. She's not thrilled about being sent to a small town in Montana to hide, but she wants to stay alive.

Sheriff Seth Reilly is doing a favor for an old Army buddy. He's promised to watch over a woman whose life is in danger, but he didn't plan on her being so young and beautiful. He's tempted, but she's a bundle of trouble. Seth likes his women calm and sedate. Presley is the kind of woman who would keep him up at night and make him crazy. Too bad he's starting to enjoy it.

Passion flares between Seth and Presley, heating up the cold Montana nights. Knowing they only have a short time together, they vow not to fall in love. But when danger finds Presley, Seth will risk everything to keep her safe until she can testify. Will Presley get her old life back or start a new life with Seth instead?

Justice Healed
Cowboy Justice Association
Book Two

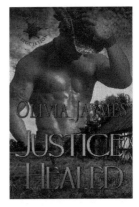

You can't go home again, but if you do, pretend you want to be there.

Dr. Madison Shay has left Chicago and moved back to her small town roots to take over her father's medical practice. She's not the skinny, gawky red haired, four-eyed girl any longer but it sure feels that way. She still remembers the painful teasing from her classmates and always feeling like she didn't belong. She wants this time to be different but deep down she knows she'll never be part of the cool crowd.

Sheriff Tanner Marks might have been the captain of the football team years ago but things aren't as rosy now. He has a son who hates him, and an ex-wife who is about to marry a man Tanner thinks might be a criminal. He doesn't really have time in his life for a woman. Considering the things he's done in his past, he's not sure he deserves one either. He can't help but feel envious of his friend, Seth Reilly, though. He found the love of a good woman. Is it too much to ask that fate send him someone as well?

Madison and Tanner aren't looking for love but it feels like the town has other plans. They keep finding themselves thrown together and it's not unpleasant in the least. In fact, they're starting to enjoy themselves. There just might be a future for them after all.

When a drug war between two cartels breaks out, their little town is caught in the crossfire. Tanner will call in every favor he can, from the five cowboy cops he trusts most in the world, to keep his town and the woman he loves safe. He's going to show the bad guys what cowboy justice really means.

Cowboy Truth
Cowboy Justice Association
Book Three

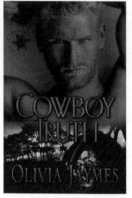

People will do desperate things to keep the truth dead and buried.

Sheriff Logan Wright might be the sexiest bad boy Ava Hayworth has ever seen but she's not interested in the least. He can have every other woman in town and probably already has. All she wants is to help him solve the murder of a prominent local citizen by a mysterious vigilante serial killer. A fling with a smokin' hot cowboy cop isn't in her plans.

Logan doesn't need a mystery writer who thinks she's a detective, trailing after him while he tries to do his job. She's smart and cute, but he doesn't want her to get hurt. By him or the investigation. He enjoys the pleasures of women – many women – and that's not going to change.

But as painful secrets are revealed, Logan begins to depend on Ava for more than just friendship. She's the first woman he's known who has kept her promises. It shakes him to his very core, challenging long held beliefs.

Everything Logan wants, but never thought he could have, is within his grasp. With the help of Ava and his friends, he's going to have to fight the past if he wants any kind of a future.

Cowboy Famous
Cowboy Justice Association
Book Four

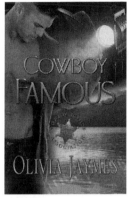

Sheriff Griffin Sawyer likes his town quiet and his life uncomplicated. Fishing – alone – on a serene and sunny afternoon is one of his favorite things to do. So is coming home to a place that isn't littered with cosmetics, clothes, and panties. After growing up one of ten children, sharing his bathroom, his closet, or his thermostat is not high on his to-do list. Women have their place. Just not his place.

Jazz Oliver wants to be a star. Unfortunately, Hollywood hasn't been kind. The day she loses out on the part of a lifetime is also the day she gets fired from her crappy waitress job. Down and out and deep in debt, she's desperate for money and a big break. It's the only reason she's allowed herself to be signed up as a contestant on a reality show in some backwater town in Montana.

From their first meeting, the attraction simmers between the sheriff and the Hollywood starlet. Jazz knows Griffin needs his space, and he knows she will only be in town a short while. The one thing they both want? More of the hot, sultry nights they've been sharing. When they're together their differences don't seem to be any problem at all.

But when casual, naughty fun turns into something more, Griffin is stumped as to what to do. Having spent most of his adult life keeping women at arm's length, he doesn't know how to get one to stay. He needs to find a way to convince her – and himself – that he's finally ready to share everything. Even the remote control.

The Deputies
Cowboy Justice Association

Second chances. Unrequited crushes. Brand new love.

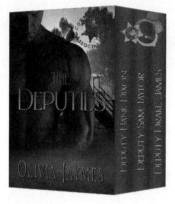

Deputy Hank Dixon:

When Hank's estranged wife shows up ready to mend their broken marriage, he has a hard time believing she's sincere. She's hurt him badly in the past and he's not sure he's ready to let her stomp on his heart all over again.

Alyssa has learned from her mistakes and is ready to do whatever it takes to get her husband back. She wants to spend the rest of her life showing Hank that he'll always come first for her.

But this stubborn cowboy cop isn't going to trust so easily. He wants more time but fate has other plans. When tragedy strikes, can Hank put the past behind him and embrace a future with the woman he loves?

Deputy Sam Taylor:

Sam's been alone a long time and that suits him just fine. On a night he plucks a scared woman from a car accident during a snowstorm, he finally realizes he's been missing out. Tabby is everything he's ever wanted in a woman. Too bad she's just passing through town.

Tabby's life is busy and complicated. The last thing she has time for is a sexier than hell cop that makes her weak at the knees just by smiling. She shouldn't get involved with him but she can't help herself. He's just so damn perfect.

When it comes time for Tabby to leave, Sam knows she's changed his life forever. And forever is a long time. Can this handsome deputy convince Tabby that he's worth changing her life for?

Deputy Drake James:

Tori Saunders has been in love with Drake forever. At least it feels that way. Now she's back in her hometown and she's determined to make the hotter than sin deputy her man. She's got it all planned. All she needs is a little cooperation from Drake.

Drake takes one look at Tori and decides some steamy nights between the sheets sound like just what the doctor ordered. The sexy pastry chef seduces him with her sweet desserts and sweeter curves. Together they really cook in the kitchen.

But when Drake finds out that Tori's planned out their entire lives together right down to the names of their kids, he ends the relationship then and there. It's not like he'd fallen for Tori. Or thought she was wonderful, and smart, and sexy. Nope, this cop is just fine without Tori Saunders. Except he's not. Looks like Drake has some work to do to win back the love of his life.

Publisher's warning: This book contains sexy scenes including some hot lovin' on the kitchen counter, up against a tree, and in front of a roaring fire.

Note – While these novellas are part of the Cowboy Justice Association series, the stories stand alone and may be read out of order.

About the Author

Olivia Jaymes is a wife, mother, lover of sexy romance, and caffeine addict. She lives with her husband and son in central Florida and spends her days with handsome alpha males and spunky heroines.

She is currently working on a series of full length novels called The Cowboy Justice Association. It's a contemporary erotic romance series about six lawmen in southern Montana who work to keep the peace but can't seem to find it in their own lives.

Visit Olivia Jaymes at: www.OliviaJaymes.com

7279119R00187

Printed in Great Britain
by Amazon.co.uk, Ltd.,
Marston Gate.